D0880777

YALE STUDIES IN ENGLISH, 187

821.309
B72

7.00

THE CLASSICS AND ENGLISH RENAISSANCE POETRY

THREE CASE STUDIES

Gordon Braden

NEW HAVEN AND LONDON, YALE UNIVERSITY PRESS, 1978

72921

Published with assistance from the
Kingsley Trust Association Publication Fund
established by the Scroll and Key Society of Yale College.

Copyright © 1978 by Yale University.
All rights reserved. This book may not be
reproduced, in whole or in part, in any form
(except by reviewers for the public press),
without written permission from the publishers.

Designed by Sally Sullivan
and set in Monophoto Bembo type
by Asco Trade Typesetting Ltd., Hong Kong.
Printed in the United States of America by
The Murray Printing Company, Westford, Massachusetts.

Published in Great Britain, Europe, Africa, and
Asia (except Japan) by Yale University Press,
Ltd., London. Distributed in Latin America by
Kaiman & Polon, Inc., New York City; in
Australia and New Zealand by Book & Film
Services, Artarmon, N.S.W., Australia; and in
Japan by Harper & Row, Publishers, Tokyo Office.

Library of Congress Cataloging in Publication Data

Braden, Gordon, 1947–
    The classics and English Renaissance poetry.

    (Yale studies in English; 187)
    "An earlier version of the whole book was submitted as a
doctoral dissertation to the Yale Graduate School."
    Bibliography: p.
    Includes index.
    1. English poetry—Early modern, 1500–1700—History and
criticism. 2. Classical literature—History and criticism.
3. Golding, Arthur, 1536–1606—Style. 4. Musaeus. Hero et
Leander. 5. Herrick, Robert, 1591–1674—Criticism and
interpretation. I. Title. II. Series.
PR508.C68B7   821'.3'09   77-10888
ISBN 0-300-02154-2

Douglass Parker
His Book

CONTENTS

Acknowledgments		ix
Introduction		xi
Editorial Note		xv
1.	GOLDING'S OVID	1
2.	"THE DIVINE POEM OF MUSAEUS"	55
3.	ROBERT HERRICK AND CLASSICAL LYRIC POETRY	154
	Appendix: Herrick's Edition of "Anacreon"	255
	Notes	259
	Bibliography	276
	Index of Principal Authors and Works	293
	General Index	299

ACKNOWLEDGMENTS

My dedicatee introduced me to Nonnos, though that is not even the main reason for remembering him here; to him and to William Arrowsmith I owe most of my original interest in classical literature, and my sense of what is at stake in the study of it. I hope these somewhat belated results of their inspiration and example will please them. More immediate debts accrued during four years spent in New Haven, especially to Eileen Blumenthal, Robert Byer, A. Bartlett Giamatti, Bari Watkins (who makes a cameo appearance infra in an unattributed quotation), Helen Whall-Seligman, and Jack Winkler. And to Prentiss Moore and Eve Sedgwick in particular I owe more of a sense of shared enterprise than they are likely to know. For specific encouragement and advice, however, I owe most of all to Richard S. Sylvester, who supplied the original commissions for two of the following essays and guided the writing of all of them with patience and a certain amount of firmness, as well as a helpful and sometimes uncanny sense of what I was up to; he should at least be identified as, among other things, the author of the "fully Marlovian" pentameter on p. 39.

My thanks to Eileen Zimmer, Peggy Dorrier, Darnell McGehee, and Doris Roach for typing a very difficult manuscript, and to Ellen Graham and Barbara Folsom of the Yale University Press for doing their best to make it presentable. An earlier version of the whole book was submitted as a doctoral dissertation to the Yale Graduate School. A highly abbreviated version of chapter 3 has appeared in *Trust to Good Verses: Herrick Tercentenary Essays*, for which it received vigorous editorial scrubbing by Roger Rollin and especially J. Max Patrick; this material is used here courtesy of the University of Pittsburgh Press.

INTRODUCTION

Chi. O'tis a verse in *Horace*, I know it well.
I read it in the Grammer long agoe.
　Moore. I just, a verse in *Horace*: right, you have it.

Titus Andronicus 4.2.22–24

That the spectacular achievements of Renaissance literature were some-how intricately involved with the "rediscovery" of classical antiquity is one of the best documented commonplaces of literary history. The three essays which follow are case studies in that commonplace. The subjects were chosen to span the English Renaissance and also to represent distinct kinds of use to which classical literature was put—translation, imitation, quotation—but, a few factitious links aside (the first essay ends and the second begins, for example, with remarks about storytelling), they are not intended to offer any inclusive panorama of the field or to yield any synoptic thesis about that field. I have made a conscious effort to let each essay grow according to its own logic and pursue its own conclusions. They are, nevertheless, bound together, if not by any particular argument, at least by a fairly clear sense of enterprise, a conviction as to why this venerable topic might be worth taking up again.

In a few cases my purpose has been simply to explore neglected evidence, particularly as regards Greek texts. If the sections on Mousaios and the Anacreontea are awkwardly long, that is because I felt those authors needed more careful and detailed attention than they have usually received, even from critics who acknowledge their importance. One can defer (as I do in my first essay) to a well-established sense, or at least an ongoing controversy, as to what "Ovidian" means, but not to any comparably informed sense of the "Anacreontic"; and I have tried here to supply that lack, and a few others like it. But my more inclusive concern has been to reassess all the evidence, familiar and unfamiliar, and especially to take seriously, in a somewhat new way, the literal, obvious, and even superficial character of much of the classical "influence" on Renaissance literature.

The very reason we can be so sure of the importance of the classics to Renaissance writers is their own disinclination to hide it. Indeed, since the use of classical materials conferred a powerful cachet on the new work, much of that use is in the form of blatant Graeco-Latin décor, aggressively displayed, up front, to attract and impress an audience. Modern criticism tends to be somewhat embarrassed by this dimension and to search particular instances quickly for more edifying implications; but to lose contact with the sheer urge to flaunt, as surely present in Shakespeare as in Nicholas Grimald, is to lose contact with one of the animating drives of the age and to render its achievements that much more unaccountable. The impulse to display is something more openly acknowledged in literature of the Renaissance than in perhaps any other period, and for this impulse the classics provided an imposing body of material over which one might hope to demonstrate mastery. For later times responsible writing would involve, with some deviousness, the suppressing or effacing of this impulse; but part of the central appeal of Renaissance culture is that the desire to show off did not seem condemned to blunt itself in its own stupidity, but could ramify with great intelligence and complexity. And to see the Renaissance encounter with the classics in this light is to gain at least some idea of why that encounter was so energizing and productive.

Indeed, probably the most compelling question about this subject is, what does it have to tell us about just how Renaissance literature was able to happen? Showing-off décor, in this regard, is a relatively minor matter in comparison to the more perplexing habit that is perhaps the dominant subject of the pages which follow: the pervasive fondness of Renaissance writers for tracing the very wording of classical texts more or less directly into their own works. These borrowings are sometimes identified as such and sometimes not; and the degree to which a recognition is presumed on the part of the reader seems to vary. What is fairly constant and to me most fascinating is the relative literalness of these quotations; when the original text is adduced, the connection is

usually unmistakable. Such evidence offers us an extraordinarily concrete look at exactly what had to have been on the author's mind at
exactly this moment. Whatever else may have been going on, he was
on the most immediate level occupied with translating and transcribing,
from memory or from a book at hand, just these words. That does not,
of course, allow us to say anything else about the new work with comparable certainty, but we have at least been granted an unusual glimpse
of how the writing of that work took place, of how the attention was
anchored in producing what we now have.

We no longer teach or encourage people to write that way, and the
Renaissance practice in general is likely to strike us as restrictive and
superficial. It was nevertheless prominently involved in the creation
of much of our greatest and most original literature, and we cannot
accurately praise those accomplishments without understanding something of the nature and significance and value of such a method of
composition: specific foreign bodies continually and consciously received into the intimate occasion of writing.

What follows is, accordingly, an attempt to look very closely at the
specific verbal interface between classical and Renaissance texts, at what,
concretely, the later authors made of the words of their predecessors,
and to talk about the larger and seemingly more important features of
the Renaissance work in ways that are continuous with an account of
this molecular activity—on the assumption that that activity is where
much of the poetic energy of the Renaissance was located and shaped
and perhaps even produced. To put a Greek or Latin phrase or passage
into an English poem involves immediate problems of translation—how
to make English words do, often, something new—and also larger
problems of accommodation, of making the importation an integral
and satisfying part of the English work. The result is, at best, an intricate
process of negotiation in which certain new kinds of English poetry
are brought into existence.

I have hoped by this approach both to decipher some of the author's
literal intentions—copying out just these words—and to relate the
literalness of his intention to the whole of his accomplishment: indeed,
perhaps to see the function of a certain literalmindedness as a strategy
in the deployment of creative energies. It is certainly for its strategic
usefulness to the working literary mind that the whole phenomenon
of Renaissance classicism has its greatest claim on our attention; when
judged by other standards, it tends to show only its failings. In its

comparative superficiality, the Renaissance encounter with the classics produced little that could be called genuinely "classical" in form or spirit—nothing, for example, to set beside Pope's Horatian imitations—and indeed often entailed, through faulty scholarship, some radical misconceptions about the material under study. But this very naïveté about concepts and "spirits" may have been one of the major Renaissance strengths in dealing with the classics. The Augustan attempt to define the truly classical spirit resulted in a sharp reduction and simplification of the range of extant Greek and Latin literature; we have ourselves as a consequence lost touch with much that is playful and unruly (and corrupt) in the classics, whereas Renaissance readers could be much more open to what that literature actually has to offer.

More generally, the oblique and opportunistic way of the Renaissance with the classical tradition helped to dissipate any sense of the completeness of that tradition; rather, the tradition provided an array of immediate possibilities for further writing: How can I work in these words? The obvious humbug here is typical enough of the age, but to find this approach simply meretricious is to overglamorize the classics and in a certain way not to take them seriously. Certainly, for any full engagement with literature, the question "What did the author mean by this?" is intricately symbiotic with "Why might I want to say it?" And my argument is not that the Renaissance encounter with the classics lacked depths, but that in reaching its depths it was ballasted by a great sense of the literal. What possibly steadied the whole enterprise was this continuing reminder, both astringent and liberating, that even the most prestigious literature is, whatever else it may be, a bunch of words.

EDITORIAL NOTE

For all quoted texts I have normalized "i" / "j" and "u" / "v," though "normalization" means different things for Latin and for the vernaculars. Abbreviations have been expanded, and a few obvious mistakes, mostly of punctuation, silently corrected.

For the sake of the old spelling, quotations from Shakespeare's plays are taken, with some caution, from *The First Folio*, edited by Charlton Hinman (New York, 1968); reference is given to act, scene, and line as I find them in *The Riverside Shakespeare*, edited by G. Blakemore Evans et al. (Boston, 1974). Quotations from Jonson are from *Ben Jonson*, edited by C. H. Herford and Percy and Evelyn Simpson (Oxford, 1925–52); reference is given, where practicable, to individual work and line number, but always to volume and page in this edition. Quotations from Marlowe are from *The Complete Works*, edited by Fredson Bowers (Cambridge, 1973). Other textual matters, including some occasionally complex systems of reference, are dealt with in the opening notes to the chapters.

Unidentified translations of Greek and Latin texts are my own and are meant solely to serve the immediate needs of my argument. Some, such as those of Martial, are fairly casual, while others—especially those of Mousaios—are meant to be painfully literal in reproducing certain lineaments of the original.

Abbreviations of periodicals in the notes and the bibliography are those of the *MLA Bibliography* (1974 ed.).

1 GOLDING'S OVID

Arthur Golding's translation of Ovid's *Metamorphosis* (as Golding spelled it) was the first complete English version of that poem to be published, and its appearance—four books in 1565, the complete work in 1567—was an important event, a major contribution to what was becoming a systematic, cooperative effort to make the Greek and Roman classics available to a new and wider audience. Golding was immediately hailed as the man

> whych *Ovid* did translate:
> And by the thondryng of hys verse hath set in chayre of state.[1]

And if Ovid became firmly established for another half-century as one of the most vital classical influences on English literature, Golding seems to have been in great part responsible. Thomas Peend, perhaps a bit deviously, claimed that Golding's decisive accomplishment forestalled a similar project of his own;[2] as far as we know, no other complete translation was even attempted until that of George Sandys (1626), by which time the *Metamorphoses* had already played its large if still somewhat mysterious role in the transformation of English literature. The ability to read Ovid in the original was of course widespread, but that does not seem to have inhibited the circulation of Golding's book. It went through eight editions by 1612,[3] and its wording keeps turning up in the literature of the time,[4] as do expressions of praise, gratitude, and even affection for the translator:

Equally ... may I well adjoyne Master *Arthur Golding*, for hys
labour in englishing *Ovids Metamorphosis*, for which Gentleman
surely our Country hath for many respects greatly to gyve God
thankes: as for him which hath taken infinite paynes without
ceasing, travelleth as yet indefatigably, and is addicted without
society by his continuall laboure to profit this nation and speeche
in all kind of good learning.[5]

Especially for those with small Latin, Golding would have been in-
dispensable as an aid to reading the *Metamorphoses* during the crucial
years of the Shakespearean moment; and since we can scarcely imagine
that moment without that book, the simple historical importance of
Golding's translation is not to be doubted.

More serious, intrinsic literary values, however, have in our time
been claimed for the translation, and the resulting controversy has done
curious things to our scrutiny of Golding's work. One of Ezra Pound's
more effective bits of literary propaganda was to call the translation
unambiguously "the most beautiful book in the language,"[6] and to
lament the lack of an easily obtainable text. That startling catch-phrase
circulated widely, and the 1960s saw two complete and independent
paperback editions, while Keats's still famous recommendation has
failed to produce even one of Chapman's Homer. Yet if Golding's
translation is once more, after four centuries, easily available, even
his editors are not sure why; and Pound's recommendation is almost
invariably cited at least with puzzlement and often with irritation.

Thus, though Macmillan quotes Pound in a blurb on the cover—to
get people to buy the book—Nims in the introduction fusses about
Pound's actual familiarity with the text, catches him on some glossarial
gaffes, and goes on to explain how Golding, if anything, systematically
misses most of the distinctive beauties of the original. What Golding
offers in return, according to Nims, is a certain beefeating quaintness:
"turning the sophisticated Roman into a ruddy country gentleman
with tremendous gusto, a sharp eye on the life around him, an ear for
racy speech, and a gift for energetic doggerel."[7] Such an ethos may
be, to use Nims's word, "engaging," but it is in itself hardly strong
enough to sustain a poem longer than *Paradise Lost* or the *Divine Comedy*.
Pound thought that Golding did have such staying power; the remark
about beauty is just an attention-getting device for more sober claims,
in which Golding's literary value is seen as inextricably involved with
his historical significance:

I do not honestly think that anyone can know anything about the art of lucid narrative in English, or let us say about the history of the development of English narrative-writing (verse or prose) without seeing the whole of the volume . . . . Though it is the most beautiful book in the language, I am not here citing it for decorative purpose but for the narrative quality.[8]

That is the level on which Golding's translation still asks to be examined: did it contribute anything on its own, aside from its role as a source-book of stories, to the development of English poetry in the later sixteenth century? It was, after all, one of the longest and, apparently, most widely read poems in English during a seminal period of our literary history, and at least one contemporary claimed it had proved "that the English tongue lacketh neyther variety nor currantnesse of phrase for any matter."[9] How important was it that the *Metamorphoses* was represented in just this translation rather than in some other? Pound's rhetorical strategy has evidently misfired; Nims, busy swatting at the gadfly phrase about beauty, does not raise such questions, and by and large Pound's enthusiasm for Golding has had considerable influence without really being taken seriously and probed for its justifications.

The sole document in that line is a brief review by Robert Lowell of a modern translation of the *Metamorphoses*.[10] Pound's mere presence in the field is enough to make some scholars twitch uncontrollably: "Ezra Pound the American poet, we are told, admires Golding's verse: I am very sure Shakespeare, a different kind of poet, did not."[11] But the general result has been enough smoke to convince the author of a book on Elizabethan narrative poetry that "Enough has been written of Golding's translation to warrant foregoing a discussion of it."[12] That is simply not true; the only treatments of any length are two unpublished dissertations. Otherwise, Golding figures unexceptionally as a paragraph or a few pages in surveys of the Ovidian tradition or the Elizabethan translation movement. The only professional treatment with any aroused intelligence is Wortham's discussion of Golding's prose.[13]

As a result, even Golding's historical importance has been studied, for the most part, only in fairly narrow terms: "Those I know best," writes Baldwin, "merely find Golding a necessary evil in the background of Shakspere."[14] Shakespeare's use of the *Metamorphoses* is indisputable; the question usually posed has been whether he read it in Latin or

English, and Golding has been combed for evidence in support of the
latter possibility.[15] The question is, we are now aware, a false one:
the use of a translation by a Renaissance reader would not necessarily
preclude intelligent recourse to the original text, nor—more importantly—would knowledge or even mastery of Latin preclude interest
in a translation. Yet the attempt to answer the question as posed has
at least occasioned most of what detailed attention Golding's poetry
has received.[16]

Much of the evidence of Golding's influence on Shakespeare is
relatively circumstantial; it proves little bit by bit but makes a strong
case as a mass of probabilities, in view of the considerable likelihood
of it all. For example, of Jupiter as he prepares to carry off Europa,
Ovid says just that he "moos," "mugit" (ii.851). Golding interprets
this a bit more; the bull "Goes lowing gently up and downe" (II.
1063). "Bull *Jove* sir," we hear in *Much Ado about Nothing*, "had an
amiable low" (5.4.48). Elyot and Cooper both translate *mugio* with
the somewhat noisier "bellow," but it would be no great imaginative
feat on Shakespeare's part to render the verb instead as "low," or even
to imagine, without reading Ovid, that that is what Jupiter would be
doing in such a situation. Still, "amiable" suggests a condensation and
psychologizing of "gently up and downe," and Golding's adverbs and
Shakespeare's adjective do describe roughly the same *kind* of mooing.

The Cimmerians appear unmodified in the *Metamorphoses* (xi.592);
Golding calls them "darke" (XI.687), possibly because of a note in
his edition telling him that they come from a land without sunlight,
and he thereby makes possible a confusion with the Ethiopians. Sure
enough, in *Titus Andronicus* a Moor is called a "swarth Cymerion"
(2.3.72). In *A Midsummer Night's Dream* Shakespeare apparently quotes
about half of one of Golding's lines almost verbatim:

> Verque nouum stabat cinctum florente corona
>
> [ii.27]

> There stoode the springtime with a crowne of fresh and fragrant
> floures
>
> [II.33]

> For she his hairy temples then had rounded,
> With coronet of fresh and fragrant flowers.
>
> [4.1.51–52]

Also, a few lines later Golding expands the Latin considerably in a
way that Shakespeare may have picked up on earlier in the same play:

> et glacialis Hiems canos hirsuta capillos.
>
> [ii.30]

> And lastly quaking for the colde, stood Winter all forlorne,
> With rugged heade as white as Dove, and garments all to torne,
> Forladen with the Isycles that dangled up and downe
> Uppon his gray and hoarie bearde and snowie frozen crowne.
>
> [II.36–39]

It looks very much as though Shakespeare, while keeping the Latin
name, adopted and sharpened Golding's image and conflated it in a
memorable way with the line about the spring:

> And on old *Hyems* chinne and Icie crowne,
> An odorous Chaplet of sweet Sommer buds
> Is as in mockry set.
>
> [2.1.109–11]

Sometimes individual words seem to have caught in Shakespeare's
ear. Ovid describes the house of Baucis and Philemon as "stipulis et
canna tecta palustri" (viii.630); Golding reports that "The roofe therof
was thatched all with straw and fennish reede" (VIII.806), and two
references to the same story in Shakespeare mention "thatch" (*Much
Ado* 2.1.96–98; *As You Like It* 3.3.10–11). "Roping," an odd term
used twice in one play (*Henry V* 3.5.23, 4.2.48—the former instance
involving mention of icicles and thatch) and nowhere else in Shakespeare, has been traced to Golding (I.136, XII.478). A crux in *King
Lear*, "Hornes wealk'd" (4.6.71), can be glossed from Golding, "crooked
welked hornes" (V.417), where from the evidence of the Latin ("recuruis
... cornibus," v.327–28) it appears that Golding is practicing his
habit of translating by multiple synonyms.

Some of the really hard evidence of direct borrowing, however,
softens a bit under scrutiny. "Ringwood" (III.270) is Golding's translation of the name of one of Actaeon's hounds, Hylactor (iii.224); in
The Merry Wives of Windsor Pistol counsels, "prevent: Or goe thou
like Sir *Acteon* he, with Ring-wood at thy heeles" (2.1.117–18). Anders,
however, cites a popular ballad containing the same name;[17] and
Baldwin, in considering the matter, thinks it just as likely that Shake-

speare got the name from Jonson (*Entertainment at Althorp* 217–19; 7:128), who himself may have fetched it from Golding.[18] The *locus classicissimus* of Shakespeare-Golding studies—and, indeed, the site of the earliest recorded act of Shakespearean *Quellenforschung* to be committed in the Western hemisphere[19]—is, symbolically enough, Prospero's renunciation of his own semi-Ovidian magic:

> Ye Elves of hils, brooks, standing lakes and groves
> [*Tempest* 5.1.33]

Golding's version of an incantation by Medea begins quite similarly:

> auraeque et uenti montesque amnesque lacusque,
> dique omnes nemorum
> [vii.197–98]

> Ye Ayres and windes: ye Elves of Hilles, of Brookes, of Woods
>   alone,
> Of standing Lakes
> [VII.265–66]

Verbal parallels continue, less densely, for another dozen lines or so. However, there is at least one phrase in the Latin—"conuulsaque robora terra" (vii.204)—that Golding obscures—"trees doe drawe" (VII.272)—but Shakespeare translates: "rifted *Joves* stowt Oke" (5.1.45). At the very least, Shakespeare used the Latin along with Golding; and Baldwin gives plausible alternative sources for the other similarities, including the translation of *di* as "elves." "I see nothing to indicate certainly that for this particular line Shakspere had even his worse eye on Golding."[20]

The tone of Baldwin's remark should remind us that much of this work has been polemical, an attempt to save or discredit Shakespeare's classical scholarship by seeing whether or not he used a trot: hence Baldwin's glee in being able to pin a Golding on Jonson, who started the whole argument. The unsurprising conclusion of all this labor is that Shakespeare could and did read Ovid in the original but consulted Golding too. The information thus gathered, however, can perhaps lead to more cogent insights into the talents of both men: i.e., what sort of thing was it in Golding that attracted Shakespeare's attention? Certain aspects of Golding's mildly eccentric diction did, for one thing. But Shakespeare also seems interested precisely in Golding's "padding" of the Latin. Since Golding's translation is by and large fairly close, these additions are in themselves relatively trivial in content; but at several points Shakespeare may be observed condensing them into an only slightly more trenchant form. To a comparatively straight-forward Latin term, "mugit," Golding will give a somewhat decorative obliquity, "lowing gently up and downe," and Shakespeare will sharpen the focus: "an amiable low." Ovid's bull is more directly occupied in being a bull:

> mixtusque iuuencis
> mugit et in teneris formosus obambulat herbis.

> [ii.850–51]

[Mixing with the heifers, he moos, and, handsome, walks around in the tender grass.]

Golding and Shakespeare give the animal a much more human kind of craftiness, a deceptively bland pleasantness, a kind of false, indolent innocence. In English Jupiter seems rather more detached from his role than he is in Latin, as the English poets themselves seem more bemused by the event than Ovid is. What for Golding is a casual addition to the text at hand can be for Shakespeare a desirable thing in itself, perhaps because of its very casualness: "the Isycles that dangled up and downe." Decoration lightly borne is an important part of Shakespeare's poetics, and in Golding's off-handed expansions he may have found a useful source of examples. To be sure, the triangular search pattern that is used on Ovid, Golding, and Shakespeare is such as would detect mainly examples that support such an analysis: in the absence of really solid verbal parallels, all that can effectively be noted is what Golding added. But the fact that a fair number of examples can be assembled in this way suggests that we are on the right track.

I will be returning to these matters later, but from a slightly dif-ferent direction. For my main purpose here is not to come at Golding through Shakespeare, but, as much as possible, to come at Golding through Golding himself, who was, after all, a man closer to being Shakespeare's social and cultural opposite than his fellow. Born (1536) of moderately wealthy gentry in Essex, and educated at Jesus College, Cambridge, Golding moved through the Elizabethan world on a fairly high plane. His half-sister married the sixteenth Earl of Oxford, and two of Golding's translations are dedicated to their son, Edward

de Vere, for whose education Golding may have had some responsibility (and who of course was long considered, by those embarrassed
by Shakespeare's low origins, to have had a hand in the Shakespearean
corpus). Golding was associated with Burghley and Leicester, to both
of whom he dedicated several of his translations; the 1565 edition of
the first four books of the *Metamorphosis* bears a dedication to Leicester
dated from Cecil House. Philip Sidney, leaving for Holland in 1586,
chose Golding to complete his translation of Mornay's *De la verité de
la religion chrestienne*. The Inner Temple admitted Golding in 1574
"without payment"—the equivalent, according to his biographer, of
being awarded an L.L.D.—and he was a member of Archbishop
Parker's College of Antiquaries, along with the likes of William
Camden, Robert Cotton, and John Stow.[21] Golding was well established, even more so than Spenser, and far more than Shakespeare, in
the respectable and even aristocratic circles of Elizabethan literary life.

And insofar as Elizabethan society forced one to take sides, Golding
was Shakespeare's opposite, even his enemy, in a more serious way as
well. For Golding was a Puritan, the declared enemy of

> taverning, tipling, gaming, playing, and beholding of Beare-
> baytings and Stageplayes, to the utter dishonor of GOD, impeach-
> ment of all godlynesse, and unnecessarie consuming of mennes
> substances which ought to be better employed.[22]

Golding's favorite author to translate was Calvin (seven separate works
between 1567 and 1578, the first exactly contemporary with the Ovid).
Moral didacticism, mixed with anti-Papist rhetoric, fills most of his
prefaces—especially, with good reason, the dedications to the young
Earl of Oxford—and there is nothing in their tone or in what we know
of Golding's life to suggest that he might not be serious. And, of course,
in spite of the fact that Nims sticks this material at the back of his edition,
on the reasonable assumption that the modern reader does not want
to see it, Golding printed his *Metamorphosis* with a 600–line versified
moral and partly theological allegorization addressed to Leicester, and
a 200-line reassurance to the possibly alarmed reader in much the same
vein, though with a recognition that this sort of thing is not for everyone:

> If any stomacke be so weake as that it cannot brooke,
> The lively setting forth of things described in this booke,
> I give him counsell too absteine untill he bee more strong
>
> [215–17]

It is for these reasons that Golding's connection with Ovid is often considered a matter for surprise and something of a puzzle; but it is more useful to take the situation as a way of defining a certain historical moment, both in Golding's own life and in the course of English culture. "Only an Elizabethan," as Bush says, "could pass from the mood of Calvin to that of Giulio Romano."[23] Certainly ca. 1567 Elizabethan society showed only early signs of its later cleavage, and one could hold together honorably possibilities that in time would insist on a choice. Protestant England seemed less threatened than it did later, or rather threatened much more by external than by internal forces. The appearance of Golding's first four books of Ovid (1565) coincides with only the first-known appearance of the word "Puritan" in print, and then as a term of abuse applied by Catholics to Protestants.[24] The first major public dispute within the Protestant establishment, the vestimentary controversy, was still incubating.

The historical consciousness here involved can be found to an extent in Golding's writings; in a pamphlet on the 1580 earthquake ("Let us enter into ourselves, and examine our time paste") he recalls the euphoria at Elizabeth's accession:

> Since the sharpe tryall which GOD made of us in the raigne of Queene Marie, (at which time we vowed all obedience to GOD, if he woulde voutchsafe to deliver us againe from the bondage of the Romishe Anti-chryst, into the libertie of the Gospell of his sonne Jesus Chryste) he hearkening effectually to our requestes, hath given us a long resting and refreshing-time, blessed with innumerable benefites both of body and soule: For peace, health, and plentie of al things necessarie for the life of man, we have had a golden worlde above all the rest of oure neyghbours rounde about us.[25]

But from the perspective of 1580 he sees with bitterness a country that had not lived up to its own blessings:

> we have growen in godliness as the Moone doth in light when she is past the full. For who sees not the emulation that remaynes stil among us for excesse of apparell, fare, and building? Who perceiveth not the disdaine of superiors to their inferiors, the grudge and heartburning of inferiors towardes their superiors, and the want of love in al states one towardes another?[26]

That last phrase is perhaps the one to underline: Elizabethan society no longer seems unproblematically cohesive, and stern measures are called for.

The rhetoric may be partly discounted, but there is clearly personal experience behind Golding's despair. In 1564 he dedicated to the young Oxford, then fourteen, a translation of Justinus, "a worke conteynyng brieflie great plentie of moste delectable Hystories, and notable examples, worthie not onelie to be read, but also to be embraced and followed of all menne."[27] Like, presumably, Ovid, the first installment of whom appeared the following year, Justinus will instruct as he delights. In particular, Oxford's own fondness for such literature offers great promise for the future of the realm:

> For ... it is not unknowen to others, and I have had experience therof myself, howe earnest a desire your honor hath naturally graffed in you, to read, peruse, and communicate with others, as well the Histories of auncient tyme, and thynges done long ago, as also of the present estate of thinges in oure dayes, and that not withoute a certayn pregnancie of witte and rypenesse of under-standyng: The which do not only now rejoyse the hartes of all such as beare faithfull affection to thonorable house of your ances-tours, but also stirre up a greate hope and expectacion of such wysedom and experience in you in time to come, as is mete and besemyng for so noble a race.[28]

By 1571, however, Edward's flamboyant and erratic life had led Golding to see in him a more ominous potential. Putting by the young man's preference for "some Historie of the Conquestes and affaires of mightie Princes"[29] such as had been presented to him seven years before, Golding dedicates to him a translation of Calvin's commentaries on the Psalms, and adds some strong warnings:

> if you should become eyther a counterfayt Protestant, or a perverse Papist, or a colde and carelesse newter (which God forbid) the harme could not be expressed which you should do to your native Cuntrie. . . . I assure your Lordshippe I write not these things as though I suspected you to be digressed from that soundness and sinceritie, wherein you were continually trayned and traded . . . or as though I mistrusted your Lordship to be degenerated from the excellent towardnes, which by foreward proof hath given

glad foretokens and (I trust also) luckye hansels of an honorable age too ensue: but bycause the love that I owe to God and his religion, the care that I have of the church and my native cuntrie, the dutie wherin Nature hath bound mee to your Lordship, and (which is an occasion too make all good and honest men look about them) the perilousnes of this present time wher in all meanes possible are practized to overthrowe Christes kingdome, and to abolishe all faithfulnes from among men, make mee to feare and forecast, not so much what is true, as what may bee noysome and hurtful: and therfore I seek rather too profite by wholesome admonition, than to delight by pleasant speeches. These be no dayes of daliance. . . . [30]

The sneer in "the colde and carelesse newter" implies an insistence on taking sides. More importantly, there is a slight shift in literary theory: instruction is now opposed to pleasure. For nowadays the enemies of God, "after the maner of *Panthers* and *Mermaides*, astonne the senses with a deadly sweetnes, and work destruction by delighting."[31] As the panther and mermaids (sirens) show,[32] Golding has not purged the Ovidian world from his writings—Ceyx and Alcyone turn up at the conclusion of the dedication—but he is much more on his guard. Golding's specific fears were partly borne out: Oxford did become a Catholic, secretly, in 1576, though he recanted publicly five years later. But more than that, his general style of reckless frivolity and extravagance would represent to a Puritan the decadent nobility at its godless worst. Golding and Oxford face off a bit like Roundhead and Cavalier, and the failure of the young earl to honor his uncle's instructions anticipates a wider cultural split.

Other failures plagued Golding's life. He was, when he wrote the earthquake pamphlet, involved in seemingly endless litigation (1575–89) to gain possession of the estate left him by his elder brother; that one of his chief opponents was his brother's notoriously polyandrous stepdaughter (i.e. Golding's niece, to make a pair with his nephew) may have seemed to him a perfect sign of the times. Other legal troubles are alluded to in the 1571 dedication to Oxford and a 1574 dedication to Cecil. When Golding finally did obtain his patrimony, he was so badly in debt that he lost it for good in 1596; sometime between 1591 and 1593 he even served time in the Fleet. His social contacts did him, eventually, little good. Toward the end of his life, in need of money,

he applied for a royal copyright on several of his books and thus officially labeled himself a professional writer. His and Shakespeare's lives,
in fact, end on about the same social level, with Golding if anything
a bit lower; he retired to his birthplace in Essex and "lived the quiet
life of a country gentleman in embarrassed circumstances."[33]

The desire that the *Metamorphosis* be read moralistically is thus one
of several interrelated failures of intention. After Ovid, Golding never
published another translation of pagan imaginative literature. He did
have some work in manuscript on "Aesop," who was in fact more or
less what Golding wanted Ovid to be, but it was never printed.[34]
Certain balances shifted. Wortham, studying the progress of Golding's
prose, finds an alteration in the very concept of translation, a cutting
back of expansion and elaboration (those things that attracted Shakespeare) in the direction of exact verbal correspondence—"what might
almost be called 'the Calvinist principle of translation,'"[35] since the
underlying purpose is the transmission of exact doctrine by fidelity
to the letter. But that principle applies to religious works; it seems,
on the other hand, likely that if Golding had done the *Metamorphosis*
later in his career, he would not have kept the text itself so free of his
Puritan concerns. As it is, the moralization is almost all in the two
prefaces, and Ovid himself is remarkably unaltered. Golding's theory
of translation there, for example, is nothing like the contemporary one
of Bishop Drant on translating Horace:

> I have done as the people of god wer commanded to do with their
> captive women that were hansome and beautifull: I have shaved
> of his heare, and pared of his nayles (that is) I have wyped awaye
> all his vanitie and superfluitie of matter.[36]

Golding does do some small-time Christianizing: "sacerdotes" (viii.
707) are "Chapleynes" (VIII.889); *inpietas* (iv.4) equals "heresie" (IV.4);
"Sainct *Minerva*" ("Pallas ... dea," iv.38) appears at IV.47; and Envy's
"murmura parua" (ii.788) become the "Divels Paternoster" (II.984).
Of potentially more doctrinal import is the decision, in accord with
the epistle to Leicester (306 ff.), to render *deus* and sometimes even *di*
as "God." But Golding is not consistent or even particularly careful:
"cura deum di sunt" (viii.724) becomes, awkwardly, "let them whom
God dooth love be Gods" (VIII.908). And very often, when the Latin
does not mention any deities at all, but merely includes some indication
of general excitement, Golding will get into the spirit of things by
breaking the third commandment: "utinam uelocior esses" (x.630),

"I would too God a litle more thy feete of swiftnesse had" (X.741). This is fairly casual theology, and serves mainly as part of a general shifting of ethnic coloration. The *fata* (vi.5) that Athena intends for Arachne turn out to be the testing of a claim to benefit of clergy:

> And therewithall she purposed to put the Lydian Maide
> *Arachne* to hir neckeverse
>
> [VI.7–8]

Similarly, Jove's "concilium" of the gods (i.167) becomes a "Court of Parliament" (I.191), and the "deorum / atria nobilium" (i.171–72) show up as "The sumptuous houses of the Pieres" (I.198). More mundanely, Midas's *tiara* (xi.181) is a "nyghtcappe" (XI.204), Atalanta's "ablata citis talaria plantis" (x.591) are "the labells of her socks" (X.690), etc. The poem is not being recast in any detail or rigor as a Christian allegory, but simply being moved to England; Ovid was conscious of performing a similar activity himself:

> hic locus est, quem, si uerbis audacia detur,
> haud timeam magni dixisse Palatia caeli.
>
> [i.175–76]

[This is the place that—if I may be so bold—I would not hesitate to call heaven's Palatine Hill.]

At times Golding does intrude a moral comment on some of the characters' actions in the story—which is not the same thing as turning the story into a moral allegory. Ovid describes the infant Adonis as "ille sorore / natus auoque suo" (x.520–21), "that child of his own sister and grandfather." In Golding this becomes:

> That wretched imp whom wickedly his graundfather begate,
> And whom his cursed suster bare
>
> [X.598–99]

A few lines later Myrrha's "ignes" (524) become her "villanye" (605). But Ovid himself makes similar evaluations in telling Myrrha's story— "dira canam" (300), "I sing of fearful things":

> scelus est odisse parentem,
> hic amor est odio maius scelus.
>
> [314–15]

[It is a crime to hate one's parent, but this love is a crime greater than hate.]

Myrrha's act is "nefas" (307), "an abomination," and her love is *foedus* (319), "foul"; the *semina* in her womb are *concepta crimina* (470), etc. Golding is taking his cues from Ovid. Again to compare him with his contemporaries, there is nothing in Golding like Stanyhurst's crude disregard for context in his rendering of Vergil's lines on Dido:

> nec iam furtiuum Dido meditatur amorem:
> coniugium uocat, hoc praetexit nomine culpam.
>
> [*Aen.* 4.171–72]

> No more dooth she laboure too mask her Phansye with hudwinck,
> With thee name of wedlock her carnal lecherye cloaking
>
> [4.176–77][37]

Vergil's restraint and implicit sympathy are part of the emotional design of the whole episode. Even Phaer, a lesser talent than Golding but whose affinities with him will be discussed later, keeps more faith with the Latin:

> Nor longer now for love in stelth quene Dido her provides,
> But wedlock this she calls, with wedlocks name her faut she hides.[38]

Golding's most memorable intrusions of authorial comment are not Puritan at all, but show a very secular combination of impatience and amusement; e.g. of Narcissus:

> spem sine corpore amat, corpus putat esse, quod umbra est
>
> [iii.417]

> He feedes a hope without cause why. For like a foolishe noddie
> He thinkes the shadow that he sees, to be a lively boddie.
>
> [III.521–22]

The spirit behind Golding's lines is closer to Nashe than to Calvin. Narcissus may still in some sense be, as Golding calls him in the epistle to Leicester, a cautionary example of "scornfulnesse and pryde" (105); but what has moved Golding to add his two-cents'-worth to the actual text of the translation is the much simpler spectacle of a nitwit who just doesn't know what he's looking at. One of Ovid's own overtly allegorical figures, Invidia, rises at Minerva's summons from a meal of snake-flesh and slouches horrifically forward like Yeats's rough beast, "passuque incedit inerti" (ii.772); but to Golding she is just a problem on a crowded sidewalk: "slouthfully she goes / With lumpish leysure like a Snayle" (II.962–63). Ovid's little aphorisms, seemingly ideal material for edifying formulations, are subject to similar diversion:

> Turpe quidem contendere erat, sed cedere uisum
> turpius
>
> [v.315–16]

Now in good sooth it was a shame to cope with suchie Drudges,
But yet more shame it was to yeeld.

> [V.400–01]

The Latin does not mention the contestants. Rather than presenting a categorical imperative, Golding shows us Athena rolling up her sleeves and preparing to fight the battle of the *Dunciad*. Golding's Puritan moral purpose fades into the psychology of urban journalism.

Golding's only really substantive additions to the content of the Ovidian text are secular as well, though of a different kind. These are the intruded glosses, never allegorizing but merely explanatory in an antiquarian way. For "Minturnaeque graues" (xv.716) we read "*Minturne* of infected ayre bycause it stands so lowe" (XV.801). The added information was clearly fetched from the large body of annotations that had gathered around the text of the *Metamorphoses* by Golding's time; in a note by Raffaele Regio we find the Ovidian phrase glossed thus: "of morbid, heavy (*grauis*), and noxious air. Minturnae is a Latin town surrounded by a swamp, and divided by the river Liri." [39] Such notes were the products specifically of Renaissance humanism, and represented a comparatively new approach to the reading of Ovid. Regio's edition (1492) was a significant event, since it offered the first major humanist alternative to the medieval tradition of the *Ovide moralisé*. [40] Regio's notes are all either of the sort just given, or else concern minutiae of grammar and text; supplemented in 1543 by Jacob Molsheyn (Micyllus), they were very widely reprinted in the sixteenth century. It is clear from numerous other examples that Golding used one of these supplemented editions, though it has not been determined precisely which one. [41] Despite the moralistic packaging, Golding's translation is solidly humanist in its content, and his scholarly and antiquarian interests, at least here, are far more important than his religious allegiances.

Where Golding's Puritan cast of mind does make itself felt in practical terms is on the level of style. His simple purpose in translating his authors was to make them available to as wide an audience as possible, and he

was accordingly, like many Puritans, strongly against borrowings from
Latin and other languages. In the linguistic polemics of the mid-sixteenth
century, Golding solidly defended the potential of the native language:

> And were wee given as well to like our owne,
> And for two clense it from the noisome weede
> Of affectation which hath overgrowne
> Ungraciously the good and native seede,
> As for to borrowe where wee have no neede:
>   It would pricke neere the learned tungs in strength,
>   Perchaunce and match mee some of them at length.[42]

Golding's own diction is fairly consistently nativist; an occasional
Miltonic exception proves the rule:

> nec non Peneos nec non Sphercheides undae
> contribuere aliquid
>
> [vii.230–31]
>
> *Peneus* and *Sperchius* streames contributarie were
> [VII.303]

The very line stands out on Golding's page as exceptionally short. For
the most part, he avoids intrusively Latinate terms. But he is also alert
to the problems involved in this stance, especially when translating a
foreign work; in the dedication of his translation of Mornay, he describes one partial solution to the lexical deficiencies of English:

> great care hath bene taken, by forming and deryving of fit names
> and termes, out of the fountaynes of our owne tongue, though
> not altogether most usuall, yet alwaies conceyvable and easie to be
> understood; rather than by usurping the Latin termes, or by bor-
> rowing the words of any forreine language. . . . [43]

The result of this plan is a number of compounded terms, some of them
striking and a bit perplexing: for example, "fleshstrings" for "muscles."
But the method is indigenously and sensibly English, and many of
Golding's "neologisms" now seem odd only in typography: "comedie-
writer," "bacemynded," etc.[44]

Some of this style of lexical compensation may be found in the
Metamorphosis: "watershotte," for example (XV.292), as a translation
for "decursus aquarum" (xv.266). But the principal oddities of diction

in the Ovid translation are of a different sort—the quirky, vigorous little terms that are what a casual reader of Golding is most likely to notice and remember: "queach," "gnorr," "snudge," "flacker," "chank," "frosh," "whewl," and so on. Some of these words sound eccentric only because they have passed out of general currency— Coverdale writes of "flackering" as something that the seraphim do with their wings—but many, on the evidence of the *OED*, appear to have begun (and ended) their literary careers with Golding. This diction gives an "archaic" flavor to the translation today, but Golding is not really archaizing in the sense that Spenser archaizes. Golding's words generally have no literary precedent, and would seem to be part of an attempt to augment the available *Kunstsprache* from colloquial rather than literary resources. C. S. Lewis classifies Golding's work as Drab Age verse, but if so it is Late Drab, or Transitional Drab between the unaroused Traditional Drab and a hyped-up nativism that never quite materialized. Golding is at least experimenting with one possible way out of the uneasy state of mid-century English verse. Traces of a comparable diction may be found in some other poets of the time, such as Turberville;[45] but eventually the literary culture opted for different modes of verbal heightening. The particular tradition of Golding's diction may be said to have ended with its *amplificatio ad absurdum* in Stanyhurst (1582): "Lowd dub a dub tabering with frapping rip rap of *Aetna*."[46]

The principal justification behind Latinate neologisms was the wish to provide exact equivalents for individual Latin words. Golding's compound formations do something of this sort; but his general run of amplified native diction has the rather different effect of supplying him with a large number of roughly synonymous ways of translating the same term. Golding tends to pursue not exact denotation but multiple nuance, and he often renders a single Latin word twice or more: "exsultauere" (i.134), "leape and daunce" (I.151); "placidum" (xv.116), "meeke and meeld" (XV.127); "hirtus" (viii.801), "harsh and shirle" (VIII.995); "pugnes" (iv.370), "Strive, struggle, wrest and writhe" (IV.459).

This habit is by no means peculiar to Golding, who in fact displays it less in his later work; as a technique for English translators it is at least as old as King Alfred, though Sørensen traces a more immediate line back to Erasmus's *De Copia* by way of Cooper's *Thesaurus*.[47] Golding's doublets should be distinguished from those used by, say,

Caxton to establish exact foreign cognates in English usage: "exult and leap," "placid and mild," etc.[48] In Golding's hands the method is almost wholly nativist, and the effect is to change the very texture of discourse: Golding's English becomes a wordy language of examples and variants where Ovid's Latin is a concise language of concepts. This contrast merely duplicates the larger contrast of the two languages themselves; mid-sixteenth-century English, for one thing, was relatively deficient in the generic terms that come readily to hand in either Latin or modern English. For "non ulla armenta" (iii.585) Golding has "nor horse, nor Asse, nor Cow nor Booll" (III.742), as though despairing of a sufficiently inclusive but exact categorical label. "Cattle" was still too general, and the more definitive "livestock" not available until the eighteenth century.

Still, he could have used the Old English "herds," which is what Sandys adopts without further elaboration (p.143); it is not hard to imagine that Golding actually preferred plenitude and detail over legalistic precision. Latin abstractions have a vigor derived from their literary and cultural context; lexical difficulties aside, it was often that context which refused to be translated into sixteenth-century English. Golding's eccentric diction and doublets are part of a general attempt to restore panache to what might otherwise be bland paraphrase, to fill out lost meaning with simple energy. If Ovid's dryads "festas duxere choreas" (viii.746), "led a festive chorus"—i.e., performed in an established tradition of vigorous but ordered public celebration—Golding's "Woodnymphes . . . did fetch theyr frisks aloft" (VIII.933)—kicked up their heels as the mood struck them. There was no English word that meant as much as *chorea* (which has the Greek behind it), and Golding wanted his characters to be doing something that his readers could understand their wanting to do.

Tudor translators of the classical epics all seem to face a choice between dignity and vigor. Surrey opted for the former, in the interests of preserving, if nothing else, the "classicism" of the original, i.e., the composure of its surface. He does not Latinize greatly in his diction, but he does not step up the native idiom either. It appears, in fact, that he was consciously stepping down the livelier translation of Douglas: not "dryvis on swyftly stokkis, treis and stanys," but "overwhelmes the grove."[49] But Surrey's sense of the "classical," like other aspects of his work, was ahead of its time, an anticipation of an Augustan concept of poetic decorum. In the context of the mid-sixteenth century,

Surrey's *Aeneid* has an aristocratic aloofness from popular literary culture. Although it enters the London scene early, in 1554, it does so with a sense of having been fetched from another world; William Owen recounts the sheer difficulty of finding a copy to publish:

> I coulde understand of no man that had a copye thereof, but he was more wyllyng the same should be kept as a private treasure in the handes of a fewe, then publyshed to the common profyt and delectacion of many.[50]

For an understanding of how, in mid-century London, a writer would translate if he expected to be read, we turn to Thomas Phaer, and discover a colloquial liveliness not wholly under control:

> quidue dolens regina deum tot uoluere casus
> insignem pietate uirum, tot adire labores
> impulerit. tantaene animis caelestibus irae?
>
> > [*Aen.* 1.9–11]

What ailyd so the quene of gods to dryve thus cruelly
This noble prince of vertue mylde from place to place to toile,
Such paines to take? may heavenly mynds so sore in rancour
  boile?

"Vertue mylde" is the merest filler for "insignem pietate"; Phaer has not been stirred by the making of moral definitions but by the sense of aroused forces: "What ailyd so the quene?" That way of phrasing the epic question, with hints of physical pain rather than emotional (*ira*), contributes to a general effect of, to use Phaer's own word, boiling; indeed, for "boile" there is no verb at all in the Latin, only an understood *sunt*. Juno's motives, her sense of a definite wrong to be avenged, fade into the background, and hence so does her dignity. Surrey certainly would not have placed "boile" in such dangerous proximity to "paines" and "sore" as to evoke such an "unclassical" overtone: the *OED* rewards the inquirer with a quotation from Bulleyn (1562) concerning "Painfull sores, Biles and pusshes." Taken together with "What ailyd," the words suggest that Juno's problem may actually be physiological—piles, perhaps (rhymes with "Biles").

From a later, more aristocratic perspective, Puttenham criticizes Stanyhurst for such embarrassments of diction as having Aeneas "trudge" to Italy: "which terme became better to be spoken of a beggar,

or of a rogue, or a lackey, for so wee use to say to such maner of people
'be trudging hence.'"[51] Elsewhere Puttenham warmly praises Phaer
implicitly by comparison; but Phaer's idiom contains an only slightly
more subdued potential for similar insults to his characters. "At the
very least," writes Lewis with regard to the diction of the Drab Age
translators, "we are probably safe in inferring... that none of them
was being strongly affected by a humanistic feeling for dignity."[52]

If Golding fares better in this regard, it is because he is alert enough
to work with this potential rather than against it. Frequently he will raise
indignity into absurdity; here, for instance, are the rites of Dionysos,
in the midst of one of Ovid's most harrowing stories:

> Tempus erat, quo sacra solent trieterica Bacchi
> Sithoniae celebrare nurus: (nox conscia sacris,
> nocte sonat Rhodope tinnitibus aeris acuti)
> nocte sua est egressa domo regina deique
> ritibus instruitur furialiaque accipit arma
>
> [vi.587–91]

> It was the time that wives of *Thrace* were wont to celebrate
> The three yeare rites of *Bacchus* which were done a nighttimes
>   late.
> A nighttimes soundeth *Rhodope* of tincling pannes and pots:
> A nighttimes giving up hir house, abrode Queene *Progne* trots,
> Disguisde like *Bacchus* other froes, and armed to the proofe
> With all the frenticke furniture that serves for that behoofe.
>
> [VI.748–53]

The tone of Golding's fourth line might be a momentary gaffe if it
were not for "pannes and pots," indeed, "tincling pannes and pots"
—which in turn makes us suspicious of "wives" and maybe even the
choice of the word "furniture" (for "arma"). Should any doubt remain,
see IV.35 ff. Golding gives us not Ovid's "nurus," young women
gripped in religious ecstasy, but a gaggle of middle-aged housewives
fetching their frisks while no one is watching (the effect, I think, of
adding "late" to "nighttimes"). Furthermore, they do not really give
up their houses but take them along: pans and pots, maybe even furniture. The action of "trots" fits right in; it suggests an energetically
animated cartoon. Golding's lines, perhaps drawing on the heritage
of Skelton, have an efficient life of their own, and at least answer vision
with vision; they may also reflect an awareness that a genuine Greek

Dionysiac ecstasy stood not much more chance of making it in English at Golding's moment in history than did those *festae choreae*. Nor can it really be said that the energy that grips the mad housewife is not Dionysiac; it just takes in her a more civilized and hence sillier form.[53]

There is something to be said for being able to do this sort of thing swiftly and mercilessly, to organize rather than attempt to ignore the hints of the ridiculous arising from sounds and diction of the "pots"/ "trots" variety. Spenser occasionally finds himself snarled in just such hints:

> then gan softly feele
> Her feeble pulse, to prove if any drop
> Of living bloud yet in her veynes did hop;
> Which when he felt to move, he hoped faire
> To call backe life to her forsaken shop
>
> [*FQ* 2.1.43]

The effects at which Spenser aims are more seductive and alluring, and hence more vulnerable than Golding's. Spenser's Bacchus, derived from an Ovidian text, is good enough to allow comparison of the two poets on a common ground:

> So proov'd it eke that gracious God of wine,
> When for to compasse *Philliras* hard love,
> He turnd himselfe into a fruitfull vine,
> And into her faire bosome made his grapes decline.
>
> [3.11.43]

The context is Britomart's uneasy survey of the erotic tapestries in the House of Busirane; Spenser's procedure is to conjure up an exotic sensuality as an attraction to be resisted by moral determination. Golding, in translating the text from which this is expanded, exploits a rhyme that Spenser had to avoid at all costs:

> Liber ut Erigonen falsa deceperit uua
>
> [vi.125]

> And how the faire *Erygone* by chaunce did suffer rape
> By *Bacchus* who deceyved hir in likenesse of a grape.
>
> [VI.156–57]

That "by chaunce" is good. Instead of presenting the erotic heritage of classical literature as a seductive allurement, Golding displays it

as a bright curiosity, inviting giggles rather than participation. In a
way, Golding might lay claim to being a much more practical moralist
than Spenser.

The effect of Golding's lines here is greatly enhanced by his meter.
The fourteener, to modern ears, seems particularly suited for comic
effects; it is similar in many ways to some of the long lines of Greek
and Roman comedy, and is always turning up in translations of Aristophanes. The early Elizabethan poets, however, did not see it that
way. To them the meter looked like the logical English equivalent of
the august dactylic hexameter. The example of Phaer's translation
seems to have set a strong precedent; as late as 1611, when the fourteener
itself had long passed out of general poetic currency, Chapman was
still using it to translate Homer. He strongly defended the tradition
in some introductory verses to his *Iliads*:

> The long verse hath by proofe receiv'd applause
>   Beyond each other number, and the foile
> That squint-ey'd Envie takes is censur'd plaine:
>   For this long Poeme askes this length of verse . . .
>   ["To the Reader" 157–60][54]

But the fact that Chapman felt constrained to defend his choice is
telling; by his time it was widely recognized that the meter has serious
problems. Its length seems to require that the line be read relatively
quickly, end to end, in order to make sense to the ear as a rhythmic
unit; and the result tends to be a kind of lickety-split lightness that will
not support any very grave style of utterance. Chapman's own use of
the meter has to be persistently and sometimes violently subversive of
this tendency. He relies heavily on enjambment, variable caesurae,
and especially on a highly spondaic movement to slow and twist
things:

> The other Gods and knights at armes all night slept. Onely Jove
> Sweet slumber seisd not: he discourst how best he might
>   approve
> His vow made for Achilles' grace and make the Grecians find
> His misse in much death. Al waies cast, this counsel serv'd his
>   mind
> With most allowance—to dispatch a harmefull dreame to greet
> The king of men . . .
>   [*Il.* 2.1–6]

Possibly just tired of the struggle, Chapman switched without comment
to pentameter couplets for his *Odysses*.

When Golding breaks up the rhythm of the fourteener, however,
it is with a sense of mere clumsiness rather than purposeful sabotage:
"That under all one roofe well nie both twaine conveyed were" (IV.70).
The trouble with lines like these, as any reader of *Cambises* will recognize, is endemic to the early fourteeners, and indeed to almost all
English verse before the 1580s. Historically, Golding's dilemma was
exactly the inverse of Chapman's: not to escape from the cadence of
the fourteener but to establish it. Consequently, Golding generally
seems to be moving toward the "comic" fourteener rather than away
from it:

> Theyr first encounter was with cuppes and Cannes throwen
>   overthwart,
> And brittle tankerds, and with boawles, pannes, dishes, potts,
>   and trayes
>
> [XII.271–72]

There are several spondees in that second line, but their effect is not,
like that of Chapman's spondees, to retard the movement. Rather, the
very point of the accentual clotting is that it does not clot; as in Gilbert
and Sullivan, a seemingly unmanageable mass of verbal objects is being
handled with pell-mell efficiency. This mode of rapid listing is one of
Golding's favorites, and he will go out of his way to obtain it. The
Latin for the lines above (xii.242–43) only names three types of things
thrown; elsewhere, Golding will, against all habit, actually condense
in order to create a doggerel catalogue:

> perque hiemes aestusque et inaequalis autumnos
> et breue uer spatiis exegit quattuor annum.
>
> [i.117–18]

> Foure seasons: Winter, Sommer, Spring, and Autumne of and on.
>
> [I.134]

Golding frequently exploits the underlying four-four-six jingle structure of the line to only slightly more subtle effect:

> The moyst with drie, the soft with hard, the light with things
>   of weight.
>
> [I.19]

No drenching Sea, no Mountaine hie, no wall, no locke,
   no barre

[III.563]

Shee notes, shee blurres, dislikes, and likes: and chaungeth this
   for that.

[IX.625]

   The poet whose sense of epic decorum encompasses lines like these
has no real quarrel with the basic nature of the fourteener, and most
of Golding's lines are engineered to move from start to finish with a
minimal amount of trouble:

   As with his Viall in his hand he stoode a good way off,
   There commeth to him *Petalus* and sayes in way of scoffe:
   Go sing the resdue to the ghostes about the Stygian Lake,
   And in the left side of his heade his dagger poynt he strake.
   He sanke downe deade with fingers still yet warbling on the
      string,
   And so mischaunce knit up with wo the song that he did sing.

[V.139–44]

The odd-numbered syllables are being fairly consistently kept light,
and even among the even-numbered syllables there are often only
four or five notable stresses to a line. A similar principle underlies much
of the later development of the pentameter, in stretching only three
or four stresses across ten syllables: one becomes aware of a rhetorical
cadence, for which the unit is the line, taking precedence over the
metrical grid, where the unit is the foot. Or to put it another way,
a speaking voice is adapting itself to the line as a basic underlying
unit of pace and breathing.

   The distribution of accents counts for more here than the mere
fact that the particular lines just quoted are end-stopped. In fact, Golding,
unlike Phaer, runs his lines over quite often, especially in the later
books; yet the basic sound of the meter, for better or worse, usually
remains quite audible:

   In fayth he is unmyndfull and unwoorthy of increace
   Of corne, that in his hart can fynd his tilman too releace
   From plowgh, too cut his throte: that in his hart can fynde
      (I say)

Those neckes with hatchets of too strike, whoose skinne is
    worne away
With labring ay for him: whoo turnd so oft his land most tough,
Whoo brought so many harvestes home. Yit is it not ynough
That such a great outrageousenesse committed is. They father
Theyr wickednesse uppon the Goddes. And falsly they doo
    gather
That in the death of peynfull Ox the hyghest dooth delyght.
[XV.133–41]

Compared with the example quoted earlier from Chapman, these
lines are simply variations on the basic cadence represented in the
first and last lines. The most fragmented of Golding's fourteeners do
not bring the movement to a standstill in the way that Chapman's
frequently do:

From plowgh, too cut his throte: that in his hart can fynde (I say)

His misse in much death. Al waies cast, this counsel serv'd his mind

Chapman is wrestling with his own well-developed sense of the iambic
pentameter as the natural English line ("Al waies cast, this counsel
serv'd his mind"). Golding is attempting to establish the fourteener
in such a position, and his run-ons—too loose, really, to be called
enjambments—do not fracture but highlight the underlying persistence of his metrical unit.

Golding's experiments here, similar to those made twenty years later
with the pentameter, are an almost inevitable consequence of the
ambitions claimed for the fourteener in his times. Lewis, who takes
the contrary modern view of the meter as the vehicle of a few very
limited kinds of effects, objects to the whole enterprise of the run-
ons: "the fourteener will not stand it."[55] But Lewis, I think, is simply
not listening; the lines quoted above show that the fourteener will
stand it, though not as well as the pentameter and certainly not, at
least in that example, to particularly memorable effect. Lewis singles
out as his horrible example one of Golding's more daring and demonstrably successful tricks:

My God *Apollos* temple I will set you open, and
Disclose the woondrous heavens themselves, and make you
    understand
The Oracles and secrets of the Godly majestye.
[XV.159–61]

That placement of "and" is a favorite of Golding's (e.g., a few lines earlier at XV.143); it is also a conspicuous feature of some of the subtlest pentameter music ever written:

> Our Revels now are ended: These our actors,
> (As I foretold you) were all Spirits, and
> Are melted into Ayre, into thin Ayre . . .
>
> [*Tempest* 4.1.148–50]

The juxtaposition is not wholly gratuitous; the contexts are similar enough to benefit in comparable ways from the slight, metrically induced pause after the conjunction: a flicker of unexpected anticipation and a resulting lilt of surprise to the next line. The Shakespearean effect, unassisted by rhyme, is a fairly advanced one in the history of the pentameter, whereas the rapidity of the fourteener makes this kind of quick hiatus much more immediately accessible to Golding. Still, Golding is doing the same sort of thing as Shakespeare, using an established metrical unit to shape utterance through our expectation of the cadence.

Of course, Golding did not "master" the fourteener. Nobody ever did, and it is purely a speculative issue whether anyone could. Often enough, Golding seems actively victimized by his meter, particularly in the matter of "padding." Despite the great length of the fourteener, Golding's translation is far from being line-for-line; it ends up about 2,500 lines longer than the original. Some of this wordiness involves restating particularly compact and difficult Latin locutions, but much is simply a matter of extra phrases of no great consequence except for filling out the line:

> Vnde sit infamis, quare male fortibus undis
> Salmacis eneruet tactosque remolliat artus,
> discite. causa latet, uis est notissima fontis.
>
> [iv.285–87]

Learne why the fountaine *Salmacis* diffamed is of yore,
Why with his waters overstrong it weakneth men so sore
That whoso bathes him there, commes thence a perfect man no
     more.
The operation of this Well is knowne to every wight:
But few can tell the cause thereof, the which I will recite.

> [IV.347–51]

I underscore Golding's additions with dashes, except for the third line, where the padding is too diffuse to localize. We might grant "to every wight" as a legitimate way of handling the superlative "notissima," but the other phrases, especially in the last line, are obviously just ways of meeting formal requirements in as slack a manner as possible. Any rhymed meter will encourage a writer to pad toward his rhyme; but a fourteener will, for starters, force him to make up four more syllables than a pentameter would. Often Golding will simply repeat himself to complete a line or even a couplet:

>   quo copia maior
> est data, plura petit turbaque uoracior ipsa est:
> sic epulas omnes Erysichthonis ora profani
> accipiunt poscuntque simul.
>
>   [viii.838–41]

>   with a furious mood
> The more it hath, the more it still desyreth evermore,
> Encreacing in devouring through encreasement of the store:
> So wicked *Erisicthons* mouth in swallowing of his meate
> Was ever hungry more and more, and longed ay to eate.
>   [VIII.1040–44]

Golding also pads his lines from within out of his collection of all-purpose *Flickwörter* (Swan's term). These words have almost no meaning of their own but are useful as a kind of metrical creosote, applicable ad lib where there is space to be filled: "do" and "did," "right" and "full" in their adverbial senses, "so," "thereat," "thereon," "whereby," "for" (as in "for why" or "for to"), and the omnipresent, irrelevant "me" (the "'ethical dative,' which indicates that although he is not personally involved in the events he is describing, he is taking a keen personal interest in them").[56] There are also numerous extra adjectives. Golding's conscience as a translator generally requires that they be adjectives that could reasonably be implied from the Latin, and so the results are usually bland. For "aetas/nec facies" (x.547–48), "Thy tender youth, thy beawty bryght, thy countnance fayre and brave" (X.634). Or:

>   nat lupus inter oues
>
>   [i.304]

> The grim and greedy Wolfe did swim among the siely sheepe
>   [I.355]

multi illum iuuenes, multae cupiere puellae

[iii.353]

The hearts of divers <u>trim</u> yong men his beautie gan to move,
And many a Ladie <u>fresh and faire</u> was taken in his love.

[III.439–40]

Curiously, removal of the otiose adjectives in this last example, along with some simple tightening of the locutions, can turn Golding's lines into a tight pentameter couplet:

Divers yong men his beautie gan to move,
And many a Ladie taken in his love.

It looks suspiciously as though Golding's lines have the content of pentameters spread across fourteen syllables. But the problem here is greater than simple verbosity, as is made clear by the useful counter-example of Sandys, who sixty years later did put the *Metamorphoses* into pentameter couplets:[57]

Many a love-sick Youth did him desire;
And many a Maid his beauty set on fire

[p. 136]

Although shorter than Golding's version, this particular example is wordier than Sandys himself generally is; he usually manages a line-for-line correspondence to the Latin, and actually begins by translating the first nine lines of the poem into eight of English. Ovid's hexameters average about fifteen syllables a line—rather high—and Sandys's feat of compression is quite remarkable.

But it is also not a fluke; historically, Sandys is best remembered for his part in the early development of the neoclassical closed couplet, with its sophisticated rhetoric of balanced concision, and he looks forward to Augustan poetry in a very direct way (Pope reports a visitation from his ghost).[58] In that poetry, much of the discursive load is shifted from the words themselves onto the patterns into which the words are fitted: meaning is implied by clear parallel and antithesis rather than strung out in chattier and more explanatory form. The peculiar aptness of Sandys's translation comes, of course, from the fact that Ovid himself is famous, among other things, for having established a similar rhetoric in Latin poetry—indeed, in historical lineage, it is the same rhetoric. This particular lineage is one that circumvents Golding, however; in the last

example given above, he shows no interest in the Latin "multi"/
"multae" parallel, which Sandys partially captures as "Many"/"many."
It is not hard to find more telling examples, especially among what
Nims calls Ovid's "showcase lines":

> sors tua mortalis, non est mortale, quod optas.
>
> [ii.56]

> Thy state is mortall, weake and frayle, the thing thou doest desire
> Is such, whereto no mortall man is able to aspire.
>
> [II.74–75]

> Thou, mortall, do'st no mortall thing desire
>
> [p. 81]

Neither translation is particularly resonant English poetry; but Sandys
does at least transmit something of the design of the Latin, and allows
Ovid's sentiment to stand out as a small verbal coup.

Sandys mimics the shape of Ovid's lines rather than just paraphrasing
their content:

> laudato pauone superbior, acrior igni,
> asperior tribulis, feta truculentior ursa
>
> [xiii.802–03]

> Prowder then peacocks prais'd, more rash then fire,
> Then Beares more cruell, sharper then the brier
>
> [p. 596]

Sandys's manipulation of "more" against the alternative form of the
comparative ("Prowder"/"sharper"//"more rash"/"more cruell")
utilizes a grammatical resource to supply the chiastic pattern maintained
in the Latin by the second adjectives ("laudato," "feta"); Sandys is more
concerned with translating that chiasmus than with a mere word such as
"feta," which does not make it into English at all. Beside Sandys's
elegant variations, Golding is numbingly straightforward:

> More prowd than Peacocke praysd, more feerce than fyre and
>   more extreeme:
> More rough than Breers, more cruell than the new delivered
>   Beare
>
> [XIII.945–46]

Even when Sandys cannot possibly imitate Ovid's rhetorical tricks
directly, he is ingenious at finding compensatory equivalents:[59]

> nec noua crescendo reparabat cornua Phoebe,
> nec circumfuso pendebat in aere tellus
>
> [i.11–12]

> Nor waxing *Phoebe* fill'd her wained hornes:
> Nor hung the selfe-poiz'd Earth in thin Ayre plac'd
>
> [p. 25]

For the Latinate separation of adjective and noun ("noua . . . cornua,"
"circumfuso . . . aere"), Sandys substitutes rhetorically paired phrases
("waxing . . . wained," "hung . . . plac'd," "Earth . . . Ayre"). Golding
transmits almost none of this:

> No Moone in growing did repayre hir hornes with borowed
>   light.
> Nor yet the earth amiddes the ayre did hang by wondrous slight
> Just peysed by hir proper weight.
>
> [I.11–13]

Sandys is able to map an important dimension of Ovid's style directly
onto a genuine, if as yet unexciting, English literary mode—a dimension
that Golding, with his talkative fourteener, consistently misses.

Sandys's "fidelity" to the original here is in a way just a lucky accident:
he happened to have access to a medium that was taking on a special
coherence and beginning to stand for something reasonably close to
what Ovid's medium stood for. The real question about Golding's
fourteeners is whether they manage to stand for something of their own,
as a coherent medium: can it mean something to write fourteeners in
the same way that it means something to write Augustan closed couplets?

As we have seen, Golding's meter is particularly appropriate to a kind
of comic vigorousness; but it can be conducive to subtler though related
effects, precisely through its more verbose tendencies. Occasionally the
adding of adjectives, for example, leads to a curious sort of alert dialogue
among them as a descant on the main sense of the sentence:

> And flowing streames of crooked brookes in winding bankes
>   he pent.
>
> [I.42]

> A swimming Bull, a swelling Sea, so lively had she wrought
>
> [VI.128]

> Round about the utmost Verdge was set
> A narrow Traile of pretie floures with leaves of Ivie fret.
>
> [VI.159–60]

> The specled serpent straight
> Comes trailing out in waving linkes, and knottie rolles of scales
>
> [III.46–47]

> The suttle ayre to flickring fowles
>
> [I.85]

No such events occur in Sandys:

> And Rivers, whom their winding borders fence
>
> [p. 26]

> The Bull appeares to live, the Sea to move.
>
> [p. 268]

> About her web a curious traile designes:
> Flowres intermixt with clasping ivy twines.
>
> [p. 269]

> He wreaths his scaly foldes into a heape
>
> [p. 128]

> ... the Birds resort to Ayre.
>
> [p. 27]

The bond among Golding's adjectives is not argumentative (parallel or antithesis) but tactile; almost superfluous to the business at hand, they, as it were, finger the sentence and pass it along. Shakespeare, who is known to have fancied certain of Golding's additions to the sense of the Latin, also on occasion fancied such writing as this:

> Thy Turphie-Mountaines, where live nibling Sheepe
> [*Tempest* 4.1.62]

Even less promising components of Golding's padding may be put to good use. Consider the final detail on Athena's tapestry:

> percussamque sua simulat de cuspide terram
> edere cum bacis fetum canentis oliuae;
> mirarique deos: operis Victoria finis.
>
> [vi.80–82]

> She makes the Earth (the which hir Speare doth seeme to strike)
>   to sende
> An Olyf tree with fruite thereon
>
> [VI.98–99]

Why "thereon"? Why not just "An Olyf tree with fruite"? But thus
trimmed, the phrase is a little too efficiently denotative for the occasion.
We are considering the surprising detail of Athena's *technē*, and under
such a spell understanding does not come all at once but unfolds as our
awareness of the details unfolds. We fondle the elements and pass them
on, one by one: an olive tree, oh yes, and look, with fruit. "Thereon"
both draws out the phrasing to keep "with fruite" from attaching too
smartly to "An Olyf tree," and also puts forward the basic movement in
question, a turning to look at things:

> An Olyf tree with fruite thereon: and that the Gods thereat
> Did wonder
>
> [99–100]

"Thereat" can take the stress because it holds in suspension, as the gods
turn to notice too, the rising awareness of amazement. And it does
something else as well, in supplying the sound with which this amazement is snapped up before we forget context:

> and with victorie she finisht up that plat.
>
> [100]

A brief psychic arc is deftly caught in Golding's extraneous words.
    Golding's translation is full of moments of quietly spreading astonish-
ment; it is an emotion that he seems to do particularly well, often
through just this exploitation of *Flickwörter*. A specific usage of "and"
has already been noted:

> A sacrifyse unblemished and fayrest untoo syght,
> (For beawtye woorketh them theyr bane) adornd with garlonds,
>   and
> With glittring gold, is cyted at the altar for too stand.
>
> [XV.142–44]

Despite the speaker's outrage at the scene that he is describing, the
"glittring gold" unexpectedly and briefly abstracts itself and dazzles
innocently, lifted up by the enjambment. The seemingly gratuitous

auxiliary verbs can take on a subdued glow, providing a continual kind
of shy emphasis:

> And in his visage which was stone a countnance did remaine
> Of wondring still.
>
> [V.256–57]

"Did" takes a metrical ictus but no rhetorical stress, as though the
speaker had half-conceived a notion that we might not believe him—it
did, you know—but had been distracted from even that gesture of self-
possession. Golding's automatic intensives—"right," "full," "so," etc.—
tend to come across in much the same way, not driving home an ascertainable point, but registering a general impression that this is all too
surprising to take in. The quality of astonishment is childlike and
generalizing, filling in its spaces with "every" and "all":

> To swell with every blast of winde, and every stormie flawe,
> And with their waves continually to beate upon the shore
> Of all the earth . . .
>
> [I.38–40]

Neither "every" nor the "all" is in the Latin (i.36–37), nor do those
words really have any narrative force in English. They attach freely to
the "real" words to report a sense of quickly widening horizons. If the
operative principle of Golding's fourteener is to spread the action out
and fill in the resulting gaps as lightly as possible, then the meter finds
its proper mood in passages such as these. The notorious cadence seems
to be enhancing, even controlling, the effect; it makes a difference
whether we print the lines as Golding does:

> My God *Apollos* temple I will set you open, and
> Disclose the woondrous heavens themselves, and make you
>   understand
> The Oracles and secrets of the Godly majestye.
>
> [XV.159–61]

> My God *Apollos* temple I will set you open,
> And disclose the woondrous heavens themselves,
> And make you understand the Oracles
> And secrets of the Godly majestye.

The latter is Old Testament aggression against the listener, the former
a tentative sharing of amazement. Golding's surprise has little in it of

awe or fear, but displays rather the freshness of unpredicated discovery.

There are some practical aspects to this emotion; on at least one occasion Golding's attunement to it gets him out of a tight spot. At the end of the story of Narcissus, his sisters come to bury his body, and find, of course, only a narcissus:

> nusquam corpus erat; croceum pro corpore florem
> inueniunt foliis medium cingentibus albis.

> [iii.509–10]

> [There was no corpse anywhere. Instead of a corpse they found a flower, yellow in the middle, with white petals surrounding it.]

And that is the last line of the story in Ovid: a spare botanical description that would send a small shiver of recognition through the Roman reader. But it would not necessarily do that for an English reader. Narcissus of the type described here are not native to England; they do not figure in the repertoire of flowers from which Shakespeare and Herrick, for example, draw so freely.[60] The specificity of Ovid's metamorphic plants, often involving etymological puns, posed several problems for Golding. At the end of Book 10, for example, he expanded the "poetic" image of wind shaking the flower while suppressing Ovid's reminder of the reason for the image: the flower sprung from Adonis's blood is the anemone, which is Greek for "wind-flower." In the case of the narcissus, Golding was luckier in finding a clincher that did not depend on the English reader's horticultural learning. An anonymous translation of *The Fable of Ovid treting of Narcissus* (1560) ends like this:

> Then body was ther none, but growing on the ground
> A yelowe flower wyth lylly leaves, in sted therof they founde.[61]

Unpromising stuff, but it does allow one to see how the poetic torsion might lie not so much in the flower itself but, "therof they founde" being at the position of stress, in the action of discovering it. We may be reasonably sure that Golding looked at this version because he uses the same rhyme-words and one phrase verbatim; but he rearranges things to mimic the movement of awareness better, and adds one crucial, small word to sound the right note:

> But as for bodie none remaind: In stead thereof they found
> A yellow floure with milke white leaves new sprong upon the
>   ground.

> [III.641–42]

The first line ends pointing to a discovery, and what resonance the flower itself might lack it picks up from being bracketed by "found" and "new." The poetry of Golding's second line pivots on that latter word. The Latin effect of sudden reawareness of the known is subtly changed into something closer to the original experience of Narcissus's sisters: a discovery of the unexpected and inexplicable. Ovid tells us what they found; Golding tells us that they found something new.

It is tempting to find in this note the translator's own relation to his material. What was Puritan Arthur Golding's reaction to Ovid? He was astonished. He was also, as noted earlier, often amused, but the reactions do not necessarily clash. They both make good use, after all, of the same meter:

> And men themselves contented well with plaine and simple
>   foode,
> That on the earth by natures gift without their travell stoode,
> Did live by Raspis, heppes and hawes, by cornelles, plummes
>   and cherries,
> By sloes and apples, nuttes and peares, and lothsome bramble
>   berries
>
>   [I.117–20]

That placing of "lothsome" is almost visionary: not repugnance but a minutely fastidious detachment that makes such alert and agile cataloguing possible. The great myth of the Golden Age dissolves into "the pert and nimble spirit of mirth" (*Midsummer Night's Dream* 1.1.13)—nimble because it is pert, with a smirk in fact very much like Puck's:

> And heere the maiden sleeping sound,
> On the danke and durty ground.
>
>   [2.2.74–75]

A Puckish smirk turns up often in Golding's translation, particularly when it is evaluating aberrant behavior ("like a foolishe noddie"), to which Golding's reaction seems to be something other than moral outrage.

And an analogy with Puck is further instructive because of the play that he inhabits. *A Midsummer Night's Dream* is one of Shakespeare's most Ovidian plays; and it is often said that the Pyramus and Thisbe episode, in slightly disguised fourteeners, is a "parody" of Golding's translation of the story, and an index of Shakespeare's attitude toward

Golding. But the question of parody is highly problematic in a play so
concerned with the interrelated absurdity of all our fictional structures:
"The best in this kind are but shadowes, and the worst are no worse . . ."
(5.1.211–12). And the play as a whole is remarkable for the way in
which smirkiness and wonder coexist in a single texture of prickly
delicacy:

> Fcede him with Apricocks, and Dewberries,
> With purple Grapes, greene Figs, and Mulberries,
> The honie-bags steale from the humble Bees,
> And for night-tapers crop their waxen thighes,
> And light them at the fierie-Glow-wormes eyes,
> To have my love to bed, and to arise:
> And plucke the wings from painted Butterflies,
> To fan the Moone-beames from his sleeping eies.
> Nod to him Elves, and doe him curtesies.
>
> [3.1.166–74]

Enchantment is saved from languor by its own absurdity; the minia-
turized fairy-world contains Puck's smirk, itself a miniature, as a kind
of catalyst. Reading Golding, we can trace the beginnings of a particular poetic world that Shakespeare twenty years later would bring to
its fullest development:

> Now from these trees flow gummy teares that Amber men doe
>   call.
> Which hardened with the heate of sunne as from the boughs they
>   fal,
> The trickling River doth receyve, and sendes as things of price
> To decke the daintie Dames of Rome and make them fine and
>   nice.
>
> [II.455–58]

Puck's example should disabuse us of the notion that beauty, at least of
a certain kind, is incompatible with the presence of a smart-ass.

> The deaw that fell upon a Monday night

Printed as pentameter, that line could slip into Shakespeare's play un-
noticed, or even admired; but it is actually from Golding (VII.349),
translating a Latin line (vii.268) that says nothing about the day of the
week.

A similar receptive but detached astonishment permeates much English writing of the time, even in more sober considerations: "For youth being let go forward upon hope, and chekt with dispaire while it rometh without purveyaunce, makes marveilous a doe before it will die." [62] That adjective is sympathetic and not, as it would be in a modern inflection, cynical; the marvelous is merely being subjected to the astringency of its proper context. That kind of balance is part of what we value in the sensibility we call "Elizabethan." To measure in a more practical way both Golding's occasional accomplishment and the popularity of the note that he caught, compare Abraham Fraunce trying to render a similar feeling in translating Heliodoros:

> But, good God, what a sight, what a strange sight, yea, what a
>   sweet sight,
> And yet a woeful sight . . . [63]

The Greek text behind this is much simpler: "a sight stranger than these struck them" (1.2). It was Fraunce's own concern to try to show how strangeness, sweetness, and woe coexist within the same sight. And to demonstrate the possibilities that lurk in Fraunce's gangly techniques, compare the real thing:

> A Foole, a foole: I met a foole i'th Forrest,
> A motley Foole (a miserable world:)
> As I do live by foode, I met a foole,
> Who laid him downe, and bask'd him in the Sun,
> And rail'd on Lady Fortune in good termes,
> In good set termes, and yet a motley foole.
>   [*As You Like It* 2.7.12–17]

That is Jaques, like Puck a joker in an enchanted world. If his relation to that world is more problematic than Puck's, that itself may be a sign of shifting balances in Shakespeare's imagination. We might say that when Oberon and Puck reappear as a team on the English stage, it is as Othello and Iago; the genuine partnership of spell and mockery is a thing of an earlier, though very real, moment. On one level Golding's translation helps to initiate that moment simply by injecting the pagan world of Ovidian mythology into the literary consciousness of Protestant England. The very fact that it was pagan, that in using it a sixteenth-century writer was using something that, to put it simply, he did not believe in, was a major part of its value in establishing the central *brio* of Renaissance style. The experience, if nothing else, can be a useful lesson in how to handle, with finesse and spirit, a substantial and obviously vital presence that one does not exactly trust. Our sense of Shakespeare's accomplishment is, perhaps, that in his work that presence becomes something very close to the human soul itself.

Golding's translation, as a piece of literature, is much more limited, but it has its relevance to that level of concern. Shakespeare, as we have seen, took some stylistic as well as mythological cues from Golding; and at their most effective Golding's general verbal habits, which in isolation are often mere clumsiness or opportunism, can sum up to a general way of simultaneously using and deflecting the rather aggressive presence both of Ovid and of the whole polished, rhetorical sheen of the classical tradition. Amusement and astonishment are merely the extreme products of Golding's stylistic approach; underlying both is a certain supple shyness felt from the very first lines:

> In noua fert animus mutatas dicere formas
> corpora; di, coeptis (nam uos mutastis et illas)
> adspirate meis primasque ab origine mundi
> ad mea perpetuum deducite tempora carmen!
>
> [i.1–4]

Of shapes transformde to bodies straunge, I purpose to entreate;
Ye gods vouchsafe (for you are they that wrought this wondrous
    feate)
To further this mine enterprise. And from the world begunne,
Graunt that my verse may to my time, his course directly runne.

[I.1–4]

Ovid, moved to speak by his spirit ("animus"), prays that it be augmented with the breath of divine inspiration ("adspirate"). Golding offers a modest prospectus ("I purpose to entreate") for aristocratic patronage ("To further this mine enterprise"). The contrast would be funny except for "straunge" and "wondrous"—the former a significant way to translate "noua" and the latter not in the Latin at all. Golding's diffidence is of a piece with his astonishment at his material; this awareness of dealing with a foreign object overshadows the epic invocation's traditional emphasis on the tuning of the bardic apparatus, that is, the speaker's own assertiveness.

This diffidence, both respecting and diffusing someone's attempt to

impress, is perhaps at the center of Golding's art as a translator. It is
tempting to see it also as the basic aesthetic of the fourteener, insomuch
as Golding's meter has a corporate identity that can be set against that
of the pentameter. Golding's opening for Book 2 is an unusually neat
case in point:

> The Princely Pallace of the Sunne stood gorgeous to beholde

A nicely rounded fourteener, not at all gangly, but it does, like so many
of Golding's lines, seem to fade toward the end. Indeed, excision of the
apparently otiose conclusion leaves an iambic pentameter: "The
Princely Pallace of the Sunne stood gorgeous." "Stood," effective as
a pivot in the longer line, merely bunches the accents awkwardly in
this one, so perhaps one more change is in order: "The Princely Pallace
of the Sunne was gorgeous." The cutting of Golding's line is particularly encouraged here by the specific rhetorical occasion, one that
would later engage the likes of Tamburlaine, whose spirit is so deeply
involved with the "strong line" of blank verse: "The wondrous Architecture of the world" (1 *Tamburlaine* 2.7.22). For Marlowe, it is often
felt, dramatic blank verse came less as an invention than as a discovery, a revelation of the basic assertive breathing unit inherent in the
language; consequently, we should not be surprised that Golding's
line about intimidating architecture should contain a semi-Marlovian
line within itself.

But it is only semi-Marlovian; there is something tantalizingly
inadequate about Golding's final adjective as it stands in the shortened
version of his line. "Gorgeous" has to take the stress, in a way that
Marlowe's "wondrous" does not, and Golding's word cannot quite
provide the needed resonant close. Gorgeousness is not an absolute
quality, but egregiously a matter of show; and to interact in any satisfactory way with "Princely," "gorgeous" requires at the very least
some registration of the power ("stood") with which this show is being
put forth.

Of course, we could also change the emphases in the line, for a fully
Marlovian result: "The Princely Pallace of the gorgeous Sunne." But
with that we would completely abandon Golding, who actually does
make good on the prominence that he gives to his tricky adjective. For
in his seemingly trivial last three syllables he refers us to the observer
on whom this Olympian structure is having its effect: "gorgeous to
beholde." Gorgeousness is precisely in the eye of the beholder; and the

reason Golding's line is not just a botched Marlovian pentameter is that the subject matter of the line is not the impressive object itself, standing alone, but the psychology of impressiveness, in which the observer is deeply implicated. The latter may be in part the subject of Marlowe's plays, but it is not the subject of his *lines*. The observer is, at least in this case, precisely what Golding adds to get from pentameter to fourteener. Even the fading close of Golding's line has its function: the visitor enters, as a visitor would, and as the builder had intended, shyly.

This example is admittedly something of a card trick, but another approach confirms that the issues raised are not peripheral. Golding's padding turns out to be exactly the phrase "gorgeous to beholde"; corresponding to his line in the Latin are only three words:

> Regia Solis erat. . . .

> [ii.1]

"Stood" instead of "was" turns out indeed to be an active choice. And attributing the impressiveness of the building to its being "gorgeous" was wholly Golding's idea; Ovid goes on to say only that the building was tall:

> sublimibus alta columnis

> [ii.1]

It is too early in English literature for *sublimis* to have suggested "gorgeous"; Golding quite knowingly shifts Ovid's height and dignity into decoration and display.

The passage as a whole is one of the most famous and imposing set pieces in Ovid's poem, and it is worth surveying as a whole in order to explore the various ramifications and possibilities of Golding's approach.[64] The pillars turn up in Golding's next line:

> On stately Pillars builded high of yellow burnisht golde

> [II.2]

In "builded" we catch a brief glimpse of the palace going up; again it is not a thing eternally there, but something engineered to particular effect. That effect, perhaps through mistranslation, is a bit more garish in Golding than in the original. In Ovid, the pillars themselves are not gold, but rather the whole palace is covered with gold decoration:

> clara micante auro

> [ii.2]

The indication of color is also Golding's contribution, although *fuluum aurum* is a common enough phrase elsewhere in Latin poetry. "Clara" is apparently the source of "burnisht": Ovid's metal shines because that is its nature, Golding's because someone has polished it. Golding applies "micante" forward to the next detail:

> flammasque imitante pyropo
>
> [ii.2]

> Beset with sparckling Carbuncles that like to fire did shine.
>
> [II.3]

Even with the appropriation of the extra word, Golding's expansion is remarkable, and again it is tempting to rewrite the line as pentameter: "Beset with Carbuncles sparckling like fire." But again a significant quality of Golding's line disappears in the condensation. The new line projects a Marlovian splendor of crowding, of sensory overload. The old line, in its thinning toward the end and the characteristically unstressed "did," renders a different style of astonishment: rarification of attention around the miraculous details of "fire" and "shine." Golding reports the gorgeous with a light scanning that keeps him from being overwhelmed. The next two lines sustain this sense of thinly observed brilliance:

> cuius ebur nitidum fastigia summa tegebat,
> argenti bifores radiabant lumine ualuae.
>
> [ii.3 4]

> The roofe was framed curiously of Yvorie pure and fine.
> The two doore leaves of silver cleare a radiant light did cast
>
> [II.4–5]

"Curiously," Golding's addition to the Latin in the first line, gives us the observer's response to the workmanship. "Pure and fine" is a doublet for "nitidum," though neither term quite specifies the physical reference of the adjective; both English words are terms of judgment. The placement of "did" in line 3 is repeated exactly in line 5, though to less effect. The whole line is rather awkward, and the overarching syntactic inversion creates an uncertainty as to whether "of silver cleare" goes with the doors or with the light. Our first guess would probably be the former; but "argenti" in the Latin surely goes with "lumine," and Golding's "cleare" further stresses silver as color rather than material.

Indeed, that is Golding's basic note; his line, a bit clumsily but unmistakably, dissolves into light, whereas Ovid's line is braced with the
bulk of those massive doors: "bifores . . . ualuae."

Ovid's emphasis is on the inhumanly monumental character of the
building, particularly on materials—gold, jewels, ivory, silver—with
the implication that the palace is as self-sufficient and permanent as they
are. Golding subtly rehumanizes and lightens the description by sur-
reptitiously restoring observer and builder, and focusing on the use of
these materials to increasingly refined aesthetic effect. The ensuing
transition is accordingly more awkward in English, and not merely
because Golding has problems with the semitechnical Latin terms:

> materiam superabat opus
>
> [ii.5]

> But yet the cunning workemanship of things therein farre past
> The stuffe wherof the doores were made.
>
> [II.6–7]

As Ovid shifts to describing the artwork on the doors, Golding continues to superimpose his own reaction of naïvely respectful amazement:

> For there a perfect plat,
> Had *Vulcane* drawne of all the worlde
>
> [II.7–8]

The Latin legitimates only "For there . . . Had *Vulcane* drawne," and
Ovid's craftsman does not "draw," he carves. The scenes described in
English are similarly more genial and off-handed:

> nam Mulciber illic
> aequora caelarat medias cingentia terras
> terrarumque orbem caelumque, quod imminet orbi.
>
> [ii.5–7]

> Both of the sourges that
> Embrace the earth with winding waves, and of the stedfast
> ground,
> And of the heaven it selfe also that both encloseth round.
>
> [II.8–10]

Ovid's tight cantilever series—"terras . . . terrarumque orbem . . . orbi"
(not to mention "caelarat . . . caelum")—which is an emblem of the
tense hierarchical organization of the physical universe, disappears

entirely. Instead we find a less diagrammatic play of qualities—"sourges" and "winding" against "stedfast"—under the semierotic sign of "embrace."

This casualness of Golding's becomes an operative principle for the whole ecphrasis; he begins to add purely incidental decoration—perhaps in some sense because it is less work to draw than to carve:

> caeruleos habet unda deos, Tritona canorum
> Proteaque ambiguum ballenarumque prementem
> Aegaeona suis inmania terga lacertis
> Doridaque et natas, quarum pars nare uidetur,
> pars in mole sedens uiridis siccare capillos,
> pisce uehi quaedam: facies non omnibus una,
> non diuersa tamen, qualem decet esse sororum.
>
> [ii.8–14]

> And first and formest in the Sea the Gods thereof did stande
> Loude sounding *Tryton* with his shirle and writhen Trumpe in
>   hande:
> Unstable *Protew* chaunging aye his figure and his hue,
> From shape to shape a thousande sithes as list him to renue:
> *Aëgeon* leaning boystrously on backes of mightie Whales
> And *Doris* with her daughters all: of which some cut the wales
> With splaied armes, some sate on rockes and dride their goodly
>   haire,
> And some did ryde uppon the backes of fishes here and theare.
> Not one in all poyntes fully lyke an other could ye see,
> Nor verie farre unlike, but such as sisters ought to bee.
>
> [II.11–20]

Again the vestigial observer, who turns out to be us: "could ye see." We have a bit more to look at in the English passage than in the Latin. The sea gods and the nymphs' hair have lost their color, but there is more than enough compensation. Triton has his horn, which we can apparently hear. Proteus is not just *ambiguus* but actually changing "a thousande sithes" as we watch. Doris's daughters do not simply "seem to swim," but "cut the wales / With splaied armes." The relatively frozen action of the Latin acquires more freedom, some of it psychological: Golding's Aegeon is "leaning boystrously," where Ovid's giant seems to be either fighting or clutching ("prementem"). And an incidental but consistent sense of openness is introduced in some of

Golding's padding: "as list him," "here and theare." That is the note on which Golding concludes this section of the description:

> terra uiros urbesque gerit siluasque ferasque
> fluminaque et nymphas et cetera numina ruris.
> haec super inposita est caeli fulgentis imago,
> signaque sex foribus dextris totidemque sinistris.
>
> [ii.15–18]

The Earth had townes, men, beasts, and Woods with sundrie
  trees and rods,
And running Ryvers with their Nymphes and other countrie
  Gods.
Directly over all these same the plat of heaven was pight,
Upon the two doore leaves, the signes of all the Zodiak bright,
Indifferently six on the left and six upon the right.

[II.21–25]

In his own subdued way, Golding builds toward a climax in that last line: the repetition of the phrase ("two doore leaves") from line 5, the wide-eyed summarizing quality of those two "all's," the introduction of the gloss about the zodiac to restate the celestial dimension of things, and, most of all, the use of the rhymed triplet. So, while the final line, when it comes, is not really bathetic, it is unexpectedly relaxed. "Indifferently" means "equally" here, but the Elizabethan overtones hover between justness and disinterest. Ovid's line, like his whole description, expresses the tense exactitude of the celestial order; Golding's adverb converts this into simple even-handedness. Curiously, it is just that adverb that fills the gap between pentameter and fourteener.

   The political aura here, predictably more Elizabethan than Roman, is of a rule distinguished less for its power and control than for its fairness. It is a rule that encompasses without strain a certain random "boisterousness" on the part of its subjects. In the next line the observer finally makes his appearance, and with slightly more self-assertion than in the Latin:

> Quo simul adcliui Clymeneia limite proles
> uenit et intrauit dubitati tecta parentis,
> protinus ad patrios sua fert uestigia uultus
> consistitque procul; neque enim propiora ferebat
> lumina
>
> [ii.19–23]

When *Clymens* sonne had climbed up at length with weerie pace,
And set his foote within his doubted fathers dwelling place,
Immediately he preaced forth to put him selfe in sight,
And stoode aloofe. For neere at hande he could not bide the
    light.

[II.26–29]

Golding's Phaethon enters less intimidated than worn out, and his
retreat from the divine presence seems generated as much by physical
discomfort and irritation ("could not bide") as awe. Nor does Golding
have any equivalent for the dramatic enjambment of "lumina"; Sandys
does, and while using some of Golding's phrasing restores the religious
overtones to the scene:

> Yet forc't to stand aloofe: for, mortall sight
> Could not indure t' approach so pure a light.

[p. 80]

Golding's character is not "forc't to stand aloofe"; he performs the
same action by his own volition. The intimidating light comes partly
from the jewels in Apollo's chair:

> purpurea uelatus ueste sedebat
> in solio Phoebus claris lucente smaragdis.

[ii.23–24]

But the very gems are quietly metamorphosed in Golding:

> In purple Robe and royall Throne of Emeraudes fresh and greene
> Did *Phoebus* sitte

[II.30–31]

Golding's jewels are not dazzling but pleasant, described as if they were
leaves in spring. A comparable change takes place in the court itself:

> a dextra laeuaque Dies et Mensis et Annus
> Saeculaque et positae spatiis aequalibus Horae

[ii.25–26]

Ovid's emphasis is on the exact disposition of the courtiers; but the
intimations of precision ("a dextra laeuaque," "positae spatiis aequali-
bus") wither in Golding, as the company swells to fill the fourteener
in a typically plentiful way:

and on eche hande stoode wayting well beseene,
Dayes, Monthes, yeares, ages, seasons, times, and eke the equall
    houres.

[II.31–32]

Again compare Sandys, whose phrasing produces an effect closer to
Ovid's:

With equall-raigning Houres, on either hand,
    The dayes, the Months, the Yeares, the Ages stand

[p. 80]

Golding sees the court as a human crowd rather than as a chess set, and
his incidental information ("well beseene") is not that it was orderly
but that it was nice to look at.

There follow the seasons, the first three of which Golding translates
in line-for-line equivalence with the Latin:

Verque nouum stabat cinctum florente corona,
    stabat nuda Aestas et spicea serta gerebat,
    stabat et Autumnus calcatis sordidus uuis

[ii.27–29]

There stoode the springtime with a crowne of fresh and fragrant
    floures:
There wayted Sommer naked starke all save a wheaten Hat:
And Autumne smerde with treading grapes late at the pressing
    Fat.

[II.33–35]

"Fresh," in the first line, makes explicit the vernal suggestions of
Apollo's emeralds. The wine vat and the Keatsian aura of "late" are
Golding's contributions, but in general the first three items in the
catalogue match the Latin closely. With the fourth item, however,
Golding opens up:

et glacialis Hiems canos hirsuta capillos.

[ii.30]

And lastly quaking for the colde, stood Winter all forlorne,
With rugged heade as white as Dove, and garments all to torne,
Forladen with the Isycles that dangled up and downe
Uppon his gray and hoarie bearde and snowie frozen crowne.

[II.36–39]

It is worth returning to Shakespeare's apparent use of the passage:

> And on old *Hyems* chinne and Icie crowne,
> An odorous chaplet of sweet Sommer buds
> Is as in mockry set.
>
> [*MND* 2.1.109–11]

The specific juxtaposition of spring and winter is Shakespeare's, but the mockery is subliminally present in Golding's Winter, on whose shivering head a dove has metaphorically perched. More overtly comic is the figure's own lugubrious isolation: "all forlorne," with Golding's familiar, childlike "all." That phrase should, by rule of symmetry, signal the end of Winter's description, but it seems rather to provoke three extra lines. Winter's misery is being given room to resonate; or, to put it another way, he is being picked on. In Apollo's court he is the entertainment. The joke against him, however, is neither particularly cruel nor particularly aggressive, and the expansion of his image testifies at least as much to the casualness of the general situation: "up and downe" again sounds the characteristic note, like that of Bull Jove gently lowing.

With this decreased formidability, we might expect Phaethon's behavior to be accordingly more self-possessed. The Latin, however, is explicit enough to keep this from being the case:

> Ipse loco medius rerum nouitate pauentem
> Sol oculis iuuenem, quibus adspicit omnia, uidit
>
> [ii.31–32]

> The Sunne thus sitting in the middes did cast his piercing eye,
> (With which full lightly when he list he all thinges doth espye)
> Upon his childe that stood aloofe agast and trembling sore
> At sight of such unwoonted thinges
>
> [II.40–43]

What happens is that Phaethon's reaction, although it stays the same in some external sense, becomes covertly funny. Again like Bull Jove, Phaethon seems to be acting out his programmed role with a certain detachment, even bemusement. In particular, his trembling resonates with the trembling of Winter, who in the Latin is apparently standing, like everyone else, at sharp attention; more generally, this gaping and shaking seem just a bit theatrical for the occasion. Of course, from a certain point of view most human passions are; and Golding gives this point of view Olympian embodiment in his version of Apollo's eye,

"With which full lightly when he list he all thinges doth espye." Again, it is Golding's off-handed filler—"full lightly" and "when he list" (cf. Proteus, l. 14)—that makes the difference. Like "indifferently," "lightly" has here a specific meaning ("easily") that is only marginal in modern English; but also as with "indifferently," the modern overtones of casual detachment are probably present as well. Golding's line is almost definitive; it indicates a way of looking at everything, with interest, but no compulsion to interfere: a style of omniscience that sees all, knows all, and does not mind. We are in various ways close to the sensibility of the early Shakespearean comedies, and the narrator's and to some extent the characters' ease in the presence of the patently stagey anticipates Theseus at a play: "The best in this kind are but shadowes, and the worst are no worse, if imagination amend them" (*MND* 5.1.211–12).

What does this all come to? In a way, obviously, Ovid's text is being trivialized, perhaps defensively trivialized; but in a more important way it is not. Theseus's famous remark, which has come up before, is worth sounding a bit more for its promulgation of a particular stance toward all fictional structures. On examination it can yield some unexpected conclusions; although Theseus seems to be saying that all this play-acting comes to nothing, he manages to imply that there is actually in the fictive enterprise itself a valuable core that mere incompetence or incomprehension in performance is hard put to spoil, and that the virtuo-so successes of certain individual performances are subject to the irony of this fact. In the case of narrative there is a fairly easy sense of what that core is: it is "the story." This is not a universal truth about narrative any more than Theseus's remark is a universal truth about art; rather, the assertion itself defines a zone within which one composes as if it were true. And I want to end by sketching a few ways in which much of Golding's poetry comes together around the function, simply enough, of storytelling.

Some of the reasons for saying this are blandly practical. Lewis, who has generally no use for Golding ("the indulgence which more than one writer has extended to his ugly fourteeners demands some explanation"), grants him his one irreducible virtue in just these terms: "we are . . . getting on with the story of Phaethon and Golding cannot kill it."[65] The compliment is backhanded, to say the least, but a compliment nevertheless; it *is* possible to kill Ovid's stories, as is proved by Golding's immediate predecessor in the field:

This man the fearefull hartes, inforcynge to hys nettes
The caulyng nimphe one daye, behelde that nether ever lettes

To talke to those that spake, nor yet hathe power of speche
Before by Ecco this I mene, the dobbeler of skreeche

[17–20]

The Fable of Ovid treting of Narcissus, dated just five years before Golding,
is almost literally unreadable, and not merely because of the misplaced
comma there in the second line. Golding's version of the same passage is
no particular prize, but it is in comparison instantly intelligible:

A babling Nymph that *Echo* hight: who hearing others talke,
By no meanes can restraine hir tongue but that it needes must
   walke,
Nor of hir selfe hath powre to ginne to speake to any wight,
Espyde him dryving into toyles the fearefull stagges of flight.

[III.443–46]

Part of the reason for the botch in the earlier version is that the translator
has, like Sandys, tried to mimic specific rhetorical effects of the word
order in the Latin, particularly the postponement of Echo's name until
the end:

adspicit hunc trepidos agitantem in retia ceruos
uocalis nymphe, quae nec reticere loquenti
nec prior ipsa loqui didicit, resonabilis Echo.

[iii.356–58]

Golding's eye is on the story rather than on the rhetoric, and his expansions are awkward not in being unintelligible but in being explanatory;
so also the example singled out for criticism by Lewis:

materiam superabat opus

But yet the cunning workemanship of things therein farre past
The stuffe wherof the doores were made.

In a simple and even naïve way Golding just wants to be easy to
follow; his silent insertion of glosses into his text serves the same purpose,
a smoothing out of puzzles before they get to us. There is a contrast in
Sandys's dense use of marginal notations, which both draw attention to
a problem in the text and refer us outside for an answer. (A marginalium
is used in the locus just discussed, to handle the business of Echo's post-
poned name.) Sandys's whole book, with its massive interstitial commentary testifying to a concern with "more than the story," is itself a
thing more to be studied than to be read. Golding's "commentary" is
vestigial in comparison, and conspicuously off to one side.

There are obvious reasons for these differences. Sandys would have
to assume that a half-century of general literary practice, as well as
Golding's own translation, had already made Ovid's material quite
widely known; it now needed, as it were, to be figured out. Golding,
like all of the Tudor translators, who are forever apologizing for or
even boasting about the speed with which they work, is simply in a
hurry to make the material available in the first place. The presuppositions involved here reach deeper than mere format or the handling of
specific *cruces*, and into the very feel of the two poets' media. The first
edition of Sandys's translation has no marginalia or commentary; but
the verse itself is already deliberative and analytic where Golding's is
thin and rapid. Paradoxically, it is Golding's very garrulity that makes
him seem to read faster; his additions do not arrest the attention but keep
out of its way, so that the reader covers a rather large number of syllables
between pauses. This diffuseness, like so much else in Golding's style,
suits the basic rapidity of the fourteener:

> This neighbrod bred acquaintance first, this neyghbrod first did
>   stirre
> The secret sparkes, this neighbrod first an entrance in did showe,
> For love to come to that to which it afterward did growe.
> And if that right had taken place, they had bene man and wife,
> But still their Parents went about to let which (for their life)
> They could not let. For both their hearts with equall flame did
>   burne.
> No man was privie to their thoughts. And for to serve their turne
> In steade of talke they used signes: the closelier they supprest
> The fire of love, the fiercer still it raged in their brest.
>
> > [IV.74–82]

Behind these nine lines are only six of Latin:

> notitiam primosque gradus uicinia fecit,
> tempore creuit amor; taedae quoque iure coissent,
> sed uetuere patres: quod non potuere uetare,
> ex aequo captis ardebant mentibus ambo.
> conscius omnis abest; nutu signisque loquuntur,
> quoque magis tegitur, tectus magis aestuat ignis.
>
> > [iv.59–64]

Some of Golding's expansions are explanatory: "In steade of talke," for
example, to clarify the meaning of "signes." But most of the extra

length seems due to simple wordiness; that it serves an important purpose nevertheless may be seen by comparing Sandys, who, while taking his opening phrase from Golding, translates the Latin into exactly six lines of English:

> This neighbourhood their first acquaintance bred;
> That, grew to love; Love sought a nuptiall bed;
> By Parents crost: yet equall flames their blood
> Alike incenst, which could not be withstood.
> Signes only utter their unwitnest loves:
> But hidden fire the violenter proves.

[p. 173]

The effort of compression shows, and the choppy movement is a bit like that of the versified "arguments" that Sandys appends to each book. Cryptic brevity and simple density of information play havoc with our sense of narrative continuity and flow. The result is staccato, impatient, and even a bit irritable. Sandys is the first of those translators who, as Robert Lowell puts it, "instead of the story, give us the buzz of their style."[66] Golding's unemphatically shambling medium is the more appropriate for sustaining the spacious "mood" of storytelling.

And in a more subtle way, so is his continuing sense of gingerly reaction to what he is saying. Part of what distinguishes the old art of storytelling from the relatively modern art of the novel is the latter's general air of objectivity and verisimilitude—which, of course, has to be intricately fabricated. With a storyteller, we are immediately aware of the story's coming to us through someone who does not necessarily "believe" the story, or believe that we will believe it, but who also knows, and knows that we know, that that is not really the point. The point is that he is telling us, and we are listening; toward the story itself it is possible to assume various stances of bravura and diffidence, whereas the novelist must usually pretend some much more rigorous and sober point of view. More pertinently, we may contrast what is evidently Sandys's greater anxiety about whether and just how Ovid's stories are "true"; hence his greater seriousness and sense of effort. But it is the storyteller's very silliness that defers to the satisfactory and external reality of "the story," which is not dependent on the teller's ability to be convincing or forceful. Astonishment, skepticism, amusement, et al., are simply the tools with which the story as object is held and presented.

And on this level—finally to put things in these terms—Golding keeps faith with his original and manages to give us the *Metamorphoses*

almost intact in one of its most significant dimensions. It is important for
his own sake that Golding is not translating Vergil or Homer but Ovid,
who is himself writing not an epic—the articulation of an encompassing
myth—but a compilation of stories. Indeed, if anything, the poem as a
whole is, like the *Canterbury Tales*, a poem about people telling stories
and how telling stories is one of the things that people do in order to get
through it all:

> "nos quoque, quas Pallas, melior dea, detinet" inquit,
> "utile opus manuum uario sermone leuemus . . ."
>
> [iv.38–39]

> Let us that serve a better Sainct *Minerva*, finde some talke
> To ease our labor while our handes about our profite walke.
>
> [IV.47–48]

That is one of the daughters of Minyas, as she prepares to tell, inter alia,
the story of Pyramus and Thisbe to her sisters while they do their weav-
ing. Such, according to Walter Benjamin, is one of the archetypical
scenes of storytelling;[67] and similar frame devices structure much of the
poem. The psychology of storytelling is everywhere evident in recogni-
tions of amazement and incredulity in the audience—"minus dubites"
(viii. 620), "pars fieri potuisse negant" (iv. 272)—and even in the teller:
"haut equidem credo" (xv. 359). One is continually listening to a teller
reacting to his own reportage: "Ovid is always there, cutting, dawdling,
hurrying, throwing in speeches; and gets carried away, wonderstruck
by his stories and wonderstruck at knowing that *he* is telling them."[68]

Ovid's is scarcely a vatic persona at all; and though I earlier treated the
poem's opening as a standard epic invocation in order to emphasize
Golding's diffidence, the contrast is not really that clear-cut: "In noua
fert animus mutatas dicere formas/corpora . . ." The diction, even for
Latin, is flat and abstract, and the phrase "fert animus" is particularly
curious. Essentially a prose locution, it is wholly unparalleled in epic
invocations, and, against the opening placement of "noua," seems to
record a shy emergence to some unpredictable occasion. Though
Golding obscures the particular effect, the bashfulness of his opening
lines is not wholly uncalled for. Certainly Sandys's conversion of the
tricky "fert animus" into the standard assertive epic *cano* is in its way
much more inaccurate: "Of bodies chang'd to other shapes I sing"
(p. 25).

Even when Sandys is being more literally "faithful," he misses certain general qualities of the original that Golding reproduces almost without trying. Sandys's imitation of Ovid's rhetorical conciseness and polish is, as we have already seen, an ambivalent blessing. The English either clots or simply becomes too arresting in the process; but Ovid's great accomplishment, as classical scholars have long recognized and admired in some detail, is precisely the systematic trimming of that apparatus to enhance the narrative flow.[69] The effect in reading Ovid is almost always that of great rapidity: "The essential thing was that the reader should glide easily on without pausing to reflect."[70] Statistically, in fact, Ovid's hexameters are notably more dactylic than Vergil's, so that the idea of translating him into fourteeners has more aptness than one might at first think.

Certain oddities of tone in Ovid similarly find equivalents in Golding that Sandys, with his greater assurance and seriousness, cannot render— including a sense of humor that sometimes seems to go completely haywire. With Golding's Dionysiac housewives compare Pyramus's suicide:

> cruor emicat alte,
> non aliter quam cum uitiato fistula plumbo
> scinditur et tenui stridente foramine longas
> eiaculatur aquas atque ictibus aera rumpit.
>
> [iv.121–24]

> The bloud did spin on hie
> As when a Conduite pipe is crackt, the water bursting out
> Doth shote itselfe a great way off and pierce the Ayre about.
>
> [IV.147–49]

Numberless generations of students have been stopped cold by this simile. Gower carefully omitted it from a generally close retelling in the *Confessio Amantis*. Shakespeare, while suppressing the details, heightened what seems to be the general effect:

> Now am I dead, now am I fled, my soule is in the sky,
> Tongue lose thy light, Moone take thy flight,
> Now dye, dye, dye, dye, dye.
>
> [*MND* 5.1.301–06]

Yet Ovid is not exactly writing a "parody"—as if that were the only alternative. Our perception of Ovid's poem is probably clouded by our

preconceptions of the "classical"; one recent critic even discusses the
Metamorphoses as a good example of an inclusive "counter-classical"
sensibility, for which the basis is not the harmonious but the antic.[71]
That would be the Latin poem that Golding's translation might enable
us to see.

Individual occasions, however, do not quite superimpose. Golding's
lines about the waterpipe, for example, are not a particularly good
example of his own brand of humor; nor, as we have seen several times,
do his more characteristic reactions to the stories usually map onto
specific details of the Latin text. The success of the translation is not, I
think, derived from Golding's hermeneutic powers per se, but from an
enveloping similarity of situation. Ovid, after all, an urbane Roman
collecting Greek myths, would not necessarily have "believed" them
any more than Golding would have, certainly not in the way that one
believes one's own tribal myths; rather, he was in a position, like
Golding, to appreciate their purely fictive vitality and potential.
Golding comes to the same situation by a different route. What Golding
was facing was of course Ovid, and it may be suspected that Golding's
diffuse obliquity before the text itself is not sophisticated detachment
but a deep, naïve intimidation before its content and prestige. Shuffling
embarrassment is merely reorganized as a kind of geniality, a defen-
sive diffidence about the impact of what is being said.

But if this is the source of Golding's "tone," the result, as though by
luck or accident, is a version of the storyteller's working assumption
that human experience can be lived with—as we work at our loom, for
example—and need not overwhelm. The key to that assumption is
precisely the objectification of experience into those units called stories:
experience is not to be confronted but to be handled, or, rather, handed
over. The faith and purpose of storytelling, as Benjamin puts it, is
the possibility of exchanging experiences;[72] they are not unfocusable
spirits or presences, but real objects, permitting an almost tactile encounter. Golding's situation and talent converge into a similar relation
to his classical heritage; and a final statement of his "aesthetic" might be
that things are being handed over quickly.

2 "THE DIVINE POEM OF MUSAEUS"

I   The story of the lovers on the Hellespont was, during the sixteenth century, one of the most popular stories in Western European literature: "*Leander* and *Heroes* love," wrote Abraham Fraunce in 1592, "is in every mans mouth."[1] Fraunce may not even have had in mind what has become the most famous telling of that story. Christopher Marlowe still had a year to live, and the composition of his *Hero and Leander* is often, though not definitively, assigned to that year. And in any case, Fraunce does not mention Marlowe, but quotes from the Spanish poem of Juan Boscan—a reminder that when Marlowe came to the writing of his poem, he faced an already large and international tradition. Between 1494, the probable date for the first publication of the Greek poem from which the Renaissance tradition primarily derives, and 1616, the date of the publication of Chapman's English translation of it, there are more than a dozen full-dress versions of the story: in Latin, Italian, Spanish, French, German, and English.

It was a crowded field, and the special character of Marlowe's poem, its "deliberate over-exuberance,"[2] may be in great part simply Marlowe's way of standing out in the crowd. Exaggeration and mockery, implying some preexistent thing being amplified and parodied, are two of the most transparent strategies for showing off with a story that is already in every man's mouth. And, besides, Marlowe, some twenty-five years after the publication of Golding's Ovid, was writing in a time when the simple telling of a classical story was no way to get attention. To put things in these terms, however, is not to trivialize Marlowe's poem, but to help define his accomplishment. The result should, perhaps,

have been ghastly, a line of lucid storytelling run down into a weary
game of one-upmanship; the qualified failure of Shakespeare's *Venus
and Adonis* is instructive. But in Marlowe's case there emerged instead
something very like a definitive version of the tale, and the only version
in its tradition to have survived as major literature. The purpose of this
essay is to consider how that was so.

Marlowe's poem has been much discussed; if I have something new
to add, it is to argue that his accomplishment is not as unprecedented
as it looks but is paralleled, and to some extent informed, by the accomplishment of the original Greek poem itself. Superficially, that parallel
was invisible to Renaissance eyes. A major reason for the general
veneration of the Greek poem, and, doubtless, a major stimulus to
Marlowe's hybris, was the opinion of Renaissance readers that they
were in the presence of an extraordinarily primal text. That is the note
on which Chapman ends his "completion" of Marlowe's poem:

> And this true honor from their love–deaths sprung,
> They were the first that ever Poet sung.
>
> [6.292–93]

Not only was the Greek poem the earliest version of the story, it was
the earliest versified tragedy of love. Renaissance scholars were simply
identifying the "Mousaios" whose name is attached to the poem in the
manuscripts with the legendary colleague of Orpheus. They had no
other Mousaios with whom to identify him, and the poem did make
a convenient companion to the poems that had come down as ascribed
to Orpheus.[3] They thought that they had access to a whole stratum
of pre-Homeric Greek poetry to which we no longer lay claim. We
now know that the Greek *Hero and Leander* can be no earlier than the
fifth century A.D. and is quite far from being the first telling. The
story itself is at least as old as Ovid, who uses it in the *Heroides* (18 and
19); and a line in Ovid is strangely paralleled by one in Mousaios:

> idem nauigium, nauita, uector ero!
>
> [18.148]

[I will be at once boat, sailor, and passenger!]

> αὐτὸς ἐὼν ἐρέτης, αὐτόστολος, αὐτομάτη νηῦς.
>
> [255]

[himself being the rower, the self-sent, self-moving boat.]

The traditional Greek disdain for Roman culture waned somewhat in the late Empire, and a direct connection is certainly possible. However, the similarity is often attributed to a common Hellenistic ancestor; and we do have, from probably about Ovid's time, a papyrus fragment of (maybe) another Greek telling of the story.[4] And that fragment, though it has only about two dozen legible words, supplies another piece of evidence of Mousaios's close attention to previous versions. In the papyrus, during the account of Leander's last swim, something, probably Hero's lantern, is described as either *tēléscopos*, "far-seen," or *tēlescópos*, "far-seeing." Mousaios, just prior to Leander's first swim, calls Hero's lantern the latter (237). It is a fairly rare word—not a neologism (it occurs in Hesiod), but definitely a fancy word, a heightened epithet of the sort appropriate to epic, on an order with *tēlecleitos*, "far-famed." The persistence of this little poeticism suggests that, not only was Mousaios not the first to tell the story, but also, like Marlowe, he was writing in a long line of fairly self-conscious retellings.

That is essentially all we know about the history of the story in classical antiquity. The suggestions there aroused, however, suit very well with what we do have access to, namely the verbal style of Mousaios's poem. Indeed, that style is really our only, but also quite reliable, evidence for dating the poem. Self-consciously elaborate, violent, and even bombastic, as though in determined aggression against most previous norms of Greek literature, Mousaios's writing poses an intriguing analogy to Marlowe's own stylistic response to his artistic situation. It is very interesting that Renaissance readers could accept such Greek as Mousaios's as pre-Homeric; that says something about their own presuppositions about literary style, and perhaps also about their conception of the very act of writing. The available historical and literary evidence for assessing the character and meaning of Mousaios's style, however, has never really been brought to bear on the discussion of Marlowe's poem; the prevalent, mostly secondhand impression is that Mousaios's work

> unites classic form with the warm autumnal tint of decadence. . . . The story is not told with classic bareness of style, yet, compared with Marlowe's version, it seems almost Sophoclean, and its relative simplicity and naturalness are its strength. It is highly pictorial, but the pictures have the plastic clarity of figures on a Grecian urn. . . . What one feels is the beauty and pathos of the story as story.[5]

Bush's influential view is that Marlowe's response to Mousaios is deformed by Ovidian influences, "a not always agreeable sophistication."[6] To contest this idea, it is necessary to go directly to the Greek poem and confront a style that, a millennium before the Renaissance, already has much more on its mind than "the story as story."

Oddities begin in the first line, with the question of genre. Mousaios announces his poem as an epic, but a bit overeagerly for the Great Tradition:

$$Εἰπέ, θεά \ldots$$

[Speak, goddess . . .]

The most prestigious models begin, not with their inspirational pedigree, but with their subject matter:

$$Μῆνιν ἄειδε, θεά \ldots$$

[Of the anger sing, goddess . . .]

$$Ἄνδρα μοι ἔννεπε, Μοῦσα \ldots$$

[Of the man tell me, Muse. . .]

It has long been noted how Homer's initial nouns in the *Iliad* and the *Odyssey* define by contrast, like "the" and "a," the thematic possibilities of the genre: focused intent and unpredicated exploration. Within this well-delineated tradition Vergil can propose, with great economy, to bring both possibilities into alignment: "Arma uirumque cano. . . ." But even when not making such points, the classical epic tradition depends heavily on those emphatic opening nouns:

> Bella per Emathios plus quam ciuilia campos
> iusque datum sceleri canimus
>
> [Lucan, *De Bello Ciuili*]

> Fraternas acies alternaque regna profanis
> decertata odiis sontesque euoluere Thebas,
> Pierius menti calor incidit
>
> [Statius, *Thebaid*]

Servius, collecting these three Latin examples, formulates the rule: "thus the ancients would begin a poem with its own subject matter (*a titulo carminis sui*)."[7] The habits of English largely obscure this principle in translation; we tend to remember the *Iliad* as beginning with some variation on "Sing, goddess, the anger...." But not until the time of Mousaios does any extant epic invocation actually begin in quite this way.[8]

It is as though the bardic *afflatus* in Mousaios must carry the poem with its own energy, rather than rouse itself to an already potent subject matter—a suspicion borne out as the poem proceeds:

Εἰπέ, θεά, κρυφίων ἐπιμάρτυρα λύχνον ἐρώτων ...

[Speak, goddess, of the lantern, witness of the secret loves ...]

The poem could have begun *Lychnon aeide, thea*; but that would have been to follow the rules of parody—like Cowper's "I sing the Sofa" —since *lychnos*, "lantern," is decidedly not an epic noun. On the contrary, its original associations seem to have been mostly comic. It occurs only once in Homer (*Od.* 19.34), but twice in the three hundred lines of the burlesque *Batrachomyomachia* (129, 180); unknown in tragedy, it shows up once in Euripides's satyr play *Cyclops* (514) and is very common in Aristophanes. Later, it became part of the stock erotic paraphernalia of Hellenistic literature[9] and gained somewhat in dignity, but not really in epic appropriateness. A comprehensive theory of heroic love awaited the Renaissance; there remains a definite paradox in trying to write a Greek epic about a *lychnos*.

But this paradox does not issue directly in burlesque. Rather, the epic prestige is evoked first, and then the potential bathos is deflected by a curious elaborateness of phrasing that keeps the very specific absurdity—*lychnos* as epic noun—from being quite clear. The intricate (and not very classical) double-noun construction obscures the status of *lychnon* as the direct object of *eipe*, and also provides us, before we get to that tricky word, with suggestions of inexplicable portent: *cryphiōn epimartyra*, "witness of the secrets." And something strange is happening in the aural texture, something beginning with *cryphiōn*, but not in full swing until the last two words: *lychnon erōtōn*. Certain sounds are beginning to recirculate busily, in patterns more complicated than those of simple assonance or consonance: for instance, *cryphiōn epimartyra*; but primarily the series *-ōn*, *-non*, *-ōn*, which spans the whole phrase and supplies, yes, the rhyme for the next line:

καὶ νύχιον πλωτῆρα θαλασσοπόρων ὑμεναίων ...

[and the nocturnal swimmer of the sea-going nuptials ...]

[2]

Runs like *lychnon erōtōn | cai nychion* are quite common in the poem, but they are merely local densities in a generally thick current of sonic repetitions. The quick recycling, not just of individual phonemes, but of syllables and even larger configurations, has something manic about it. It is reminiscent of the verbal texture in parts of Aristophanes, and has some of the characteristics of comic patter in general—including the fact that it is moving too fast to be, in itself, specifically funny. A sense of excess energy is keeping us from quite savoring the humor of an epic about a *lychnos*. Instead, a more volatile emotional field is being projected, one in which the forces of light and dark are tightly intertwined—

lychnon

nychion

—and where these forces surround and define a perilous habitation for love, *erōtōn*. This thematic point is not "subtly reinforced" by the sound of the words, but pounded in; and a very emphatic *Wiederholung* is an operative principle of the poem on all levels. *Nychion* reasserts the thematic suggestions as well as the aural structure of *cryphiōn*; *hymenaiōn* repeats *erōtōn*. The only wholly "new" element in line 2 is the swimming, and that is given twice in a row: *plotēra thalassoporōn*.

Indeed, emphasis is more important than sense; just exactly how are the nuptials themselves "sea-going"? Obviously the concern here is not to answer or even pose such questions but to fuse two of the major components of the narrative—sex and the sea—through the force that imposing compound, *thalassoporos*. Like *tēlescopos*, it is a poetic epithet in the Homeric style, though unlike *tēlescopos* it has no specific Homeric or Hesiodic precedent, just analogy (*pontoporos*). The earliest instances of the word itself are in the Palatine Anthology (6.27.7, 9.376.2), where it is applied, much more reasonably, to a fisherman and a boat. Mousaios's poem is full of such compounds, many of them relatively or even, as far as we can tell, completely new; here both the word itself and the somewhat metaphorical application of it index a self-conscious raising of "poetic" temperature. The next line returns to the connection between sex and darkness:

καὶ γάμον ἀχλυόεντα, τὸν οὐκ ἴδεν ἄφθιτος Ἠώς . . .

[3]

[and the dark marriage, which immortal dawn did not see . . .]

The concern with what the sun sees mortals doing is an old one in Greek literature; but, even as a stock locution, the phrase picks up curious echoes from the use of *epimartys* in the first line. The interest in who witnesses what joins a selection of thematic issues that are beginning to recycle themselves almost as quickly as the sounds.

What follows that initial *eipe, thea* is thus not a simple statement of subject matter, of *titulus*, but a swirl of motifs that in even three lines can take on something of the character of obsessions: three terms for marriage, four slightly differing modes of obscurity. Of the actual details of the story, for example of the narrative function of the *lychnos*, we still know very little; those details begin to appear in the next line, though mainly by being attached to already developed motifs:

> καὶ Σηστὸν καὶ Ἄβυδον, ὅπῃ γάμον ἔννυχον Ἡροῦς
> νηχόμενόν τε Λέανδρον ὁμοῦ καὶ λύχνον ἀκούω . . .
>
> [4–5]

[and Sestos and Abydos, whence I hear of the nocturnal marriage of Hero and swimming Leander and also the lantern . . .]

The two main characters enter as occasions for the more general issues of swimming and nighttime copulation. And the line endings continue to propagate themselves forward: *Ēōs* (3) expands into *Hērous*, and the concluding vowels in each are collocated in *acouō*. Also, that last word participates in another, more violent sort of collocation. *Acouō*, "I hear," is an acceptable verb for general reportage: "I hear of." But still: *lychnon acouō*, "I hear a light"! If this is a slip, the bard is much too excited to correct it; he even exploits it as he shifts into higher gear:

> λύχνον ἀπαγγέλλοντα διακτορίην Ἀφροδίτης,
> Ἡροῦς νυκτιγάμοιο γαμοστόλον ἀγγελιώτην . . .
>
> [6–7]

[the lantern, announcing the office of Aphrodite, the marriage-preparing announcer of night-marrying Hero . . .]

Two hexameters of four words each—the first samples of the poem's mouth-filling diction at the stretch. The sesquipedalian compounds here do not add much to the paraphrasable meaning of the lines; they function, rather, as a way of recycling certain verbal counters more quickly than has been possible so far: *nyctigamoio gamostolon*. With these lines, the undercurrents of thematic and aural repetition converge to become the systematic reiteration of specific words and root-words. With the third use of *lychnon* and the *nyct-* root, and the third and fourth uses of *gamo-*, it becomes impossible to take these repetitions as incidental rhetorical elegance. The point is underscored by the new obsession generated in the lines themselves; the *angel-* root, the concern with "announcing," further literalizes the paradox of *lychnon acouō*, and also extends the earlier description of the *lychnos* as *epimartys*, "witness." The lantern does not just see but also testifies; it is not only a thematic object but is itself an oracular point of reference, a medium. As cognized subject matter, it is implicitly absurd, at least in an epic context; but as *angelos*, it is a fixation to which one attends, in expectation of its announcement, as to a radio in a dark room.

The complicity of *lychnos* with the nocturnal (*nychios*) is restated in the next lines:

λύχνον, Ἔρωτος ἄγαλμα, τὸν ὤφελεν αἰθέριος Ζεὺς
ἐννύχιον μετ᾽ ἄεθλον ἄγειν ἐς ὁμήγυριν ἄστρων
καί μιν ἐπικλῆσαι γαμοστόλον ἄστρον ἐρώτων . . .

[8–10]

[the lantern, jewel of Love, which heavenly Zeus should, after the nocturnal struggle, have placed in the company of the stars and called the marriage-preparing star of loves . . .]

The texture of repetitions thickens: *astron* and *erōs* each twice (once plural, once singular) in these three lines, *gamostolos* repeated from line 7, and all three brought together in a single aural tumble, *gamostolon astron erōtōn*. The rhyme and near-rhyme at the line-ends also continue, in a leap-frog fashion. The sigma in line 8 links back to lines 3, 4, and 6; the nu in lines 9 and 10 goes back to line 7 and forward for quite a ways: lines 9–14 all end in nu, and lines 9–12 all end in -ōn. But in the midst of all this activity, the *lychnos* has, after the distraction of the first five lines, established itself as the central obsession. Lines 6–12 are a syntactic pendant to the *lychnon* in line 5; and the term itself is beginning to enact a kind of imitative form, with the role of the word in the paragraph gradually being articulated as the role of the object in the story. In the midst of this verbal storm, one holds oneself, like Leander, to that *lychnon*, and on that fact turns the opening paragraph's remarkable close:

ὅττι πέλεν συνέριθος ἐρωμανέων ὀδυνάων,
ἀγγελίην τ᾽ ἐφύλαξεν ἀκοιμήτων ὑμεναίων,

πρὶν χαλεπὸν πνοιῇσιν ἀήμεναι ἐχθρὸν ἀήτην.
ἀλλ᾽ ἄγε μοι μέλποντι μίαν συνάειδε τελευτὴν
λύχνου σβεννυμένοιο καὶ ὀλλυμένοιο Λεάνδρου.

[11–15]

[because it was fellow to love-mad suffering, and guarded the announcement of the sleepless nuptials, until the hateful wind blew hard with its breath. But come to me as I croon, sing of the single end of the lantern quenched and dead Leander.]

The full rhetorical balance of that last line itself obviously portends the end of something. But more specifically, as the lamp that Leander had been watching suddenly went out, the word that we have been hearing suddenly changes, not *lychnon* but *lychnou*, the first time that we have encountered it or Leander in anything but the accusative case; and that sound -*ou* makes the first clean break in the chain of aural associations at the line-ends. The narrative symbolism of the phrase brackets the poem; on the morning after the storm, Hero discovers, in the same position in the line, *lychnou sbennymenoio* (338), "the lantern quenched." In both cases the phrase precedes the revelation of Leander's death, as though that death were a mere consequence of the quenching of the *lychnos*. And in general, as a way of starting a narrative poem, this opening paragraph implies that the story itself is but an epiphenomenon to the inner logic of its own swirling motifs.

But everyone knows (at least now) that the story came first; and Mousaios does get down to fairly efficient narrative business in the next lines:

Σηστὸς ἔην καὶ Ἄβυδος ἐναντίον ἐγγύθι πόντου·
γείτονές εἰσι πόληες.

[16–17]

[There was Sestos, and Abydos opposite near the sea. They are neighboring cities . . .]

Sestos and Abydos were mentioned in line 4, but we were not told anything about them, for example, that they are cities. Except for the rhyme with line 15, it is almost as if Mousaios were starting from scratch; Marlowe was to take the hint and ignore the opening paragraph (and the *lychnos*) entirely. But the implications of that first paragraph are nevertheless operative elsewhere, since the first fifteen lines merely give in concentrated form stylistic habits typical of the poem at large, and the narrative is subject to continual interruption by a powerful and suggestive foregrounding of verbal technique. The mildest form of this interruption is the tendency toward the "witty" and sententious; Leander speaks a kind of proto-Petrarchanism:

> δεινὸς Ἔρως καὶ πόντος ἀμείλιχος· ἀλλὰ θαλάσσης
> ἔστιν ὕδωρ, τὸ δ' Ἔρωτος ἐμὲ φλέγει ἐνδόμυχον πῦρ.
> ἄζεο πῦρ, κραδίη, μὴ δείδιθι νήχυτον ὕδωρ.
> δεῦρό μοι εἰς φιλότητα· τί δὴ ῥοθίων ἀλεγίζεις;
> ἀγνώσσεις, ὅτι Κύπρις ἀπόσπορός ἐστι θαλάσσης;
> καὶ κρατέει πόντοιο καὶ ἡμετέρων ὀδυνάων.

[245-50]

[Love is terrible, and the ocean pitiless. But the water is the sea's, while the internal fire of love burns me. Be afraid of the fire, heart; do not fear the flowing water. Now to my love; why do you worry about the currents? Don't you know that Aphrodite is born from the sea? She rules the ocean and our suffering.]

No character in Homer or Sophocles talks this way; such speeches advance neither plot nor characterization, except perhaps to project a certain tranced hysteria, which is in itself an abstraction from the on-going business of the narrative. The "proper" place for such talk is in epigram or elegy, where the speaker sets up his own context. More universalized sententiae are similarly abstractions from the flow:

> πειθοῦς γὰρ τάδε πάντα προάγγελα, παρθενικῆς δὲ
> πειθομένης ποτὶ λέκτρον ὑπόσχεσίς ἐστι σιωπή.

[164-65]

[These are all announcements of persuasion, and silence is admission to the bed of a persuaded virgin.]

But moments like these are not in themselves significant, except perhaps statistically, since most narratives, even Homer's, have their share of them, and they are not even the main locus of this poet's digressive energy. In this last example we are distracted from even the intellectual cleverness by the jingle *parthenicēs de / peithomenēs*, which, climaxing a long run of pi's that begins with another use of the *peitho-* root, makes much more memorably than the sententia as a whole the point that virginity exists to be had and knows it. And there is also that intrusive use of the *angel-* root—intrusive because of its obsessive but unexplained use throughout the poem; as we shall see, the same is true for *siōpē*, "silence." The ability of Mousaios's epigrammatic wit to draw attention to itself is nothing compared to the insidious power of these sub-sententious features.

The lines that most powerfully isolate themselves in the course of the poem do so not through cleverness or "point," but through a crowded patterning of verbal excess, as in the habit already noted of filling six feet with four words:[10]

> μαρμαρυγὴν χαρίεσσαν ἀπαστράπτουσα προσώπου...
>
> [56]

[hurling a graceful dazzle from her face ...]

The next line is only slightly less full:

> οἷά τε λευκοπάρῃος ἐπαντέλλουσα σελήνη.
>
> [57]

[such as the white-cheeked moon gives off.]

The general run of diction is full of such billowy poeticisms, especially compound adjectives and elaborate periphrases; they are kept under control, if at all, by an aggressive local activity of sonic and rhetorical analogy: *apastraptousa prosōpou / epantellousa selēnē*. It takes another whole line for Hero to blush, in meticulous balance around the central verb—

> ἄκρα δὲ χιονέης φοινίσσετο κύκλα παρειῆς ...
>
> [58]

[The outside circle of her snowy cheek reddened ...]

—followed by an intricately jingling simile:

> ὡς ῥόδον ἐκ καλύκων διδυμόχροον.
>
> [59]

[like a two-colored rose in its cup.]

And all this is in the course of three-and-a-half lines. The thickness of these effects is perhaps their most striking quality, and the thickening can occasionally be examined historically—for example, in an adaptation of one of Homer's most famous onomatopoetic routines:

> ἀλλὰ πολυφλοίσβοιο παρ' ἠιόνεσσι θαλάσσης ...
>
> [234]

[But on the beach of the much-resounding sea ...]

The Homeric formula does not quite take up the whole six feet: *para thina polyphloisboio thalassēs*. There is room left for something else to happen in the line—say, for the characters themselves to appear on the scene:

> τὼ δὲ βάτην παρὰ θῖνα πολυφλοίσβοιο θαλάσσης.
>
> [*Il.* 9.182; cf. 1.34, *Od.* 13.220]

[The two of them went along the shore of the much-resounding sea.]

In Mousaios the effect crowds the plot out of the line entirely. By substituting *ēionessi* for *thina* he expands the formula to fill up the whole line and also intensifies the sonic effect by picking up the omicron and iota from *polyphloisboio*, anticipating the double sigma (and eta) in *thalassēs*, and forcing the adjective and preposition into a directly alliterative position. In the Homeric formula, the vowel texture is more varied, and the latent alliteration of pi and theta is diffused rather than concentrated. Even more paradigmatic is the modification of another Homeric effect: *cyma cylindetai* (*Il.* 11.307), "wave is tumbled over." The tag was adapted by subsequent imitators, such as Quintus of Smyrna, who, however, diffuses the effect by separating verb and noun in two different lines (11.228–29). Mousaios, working in exactly the opposite direction, concentrates and expands: *cymati cyma cylindeto* (314), "wave was tumbled over onto wave."

The mere verbal repetition of this last example is also a technique of the poem in general, first of all for structuring local effects in a way that does not bother to avoid a certain sing-song quality:

> μῶμον ἀλευομένη ζηλήμονα θηλυτεράων—
> καὶ γὰρ ἐπ᾽ ἀγλαΐη ζηλήμονές εἰσι γυναῖκες . . .
>
> [36–37]

[avoiding the envious censure of females—for women are envious of beauty . . .]

> παρθενικῆς δ᾽ εὔοδμον εὔχροον αὐχένα κύσσας . . .
>
> [133]

[kissing the nicely smelling, nicely complexioned neck of the virgin . . .]

πάντοθι δ᾽ ἀγρομένοιο δυσάντεϊ κύματος ὁρμῇ
τυπτόμενος πεφόρητο, ποδῶν δέ οἱ ὤκλασεν ὁρμή.

[324–25]

[He was carried along, battered on all sides by the irresistible force
of the gathered waves, and the force of his feet slackened.]

A technique of minimal variation: each case plays the rhythmic function of a word against its meaning, with one shifting just slightly, the
other staying hypnotically the same. In the first and last examples syntactic function changes while metrical placement remains constant; in
the second, the *eu-* root functions as both mono- and disyllabic while
remaining semantically repetitious. This particular sort of repetition is
typical of the poem as a whole, which is thick with compounds of *eu-*,
peri-, and especially *poly-*. Hero's dress is *polydaidalos* (118), "very
elaborate"; her parents *polycteanoi* (125), "very rich"; Leander's words
polyplaneis (175), "very circuitous"; he himself *polyphoitos* (181), "very
well-traveled." Once more, the stylistic habit here may be observed
filling out a received poetic flourish. Callimachos describes two lovers
in modest elegiac pentameter:

καλοὶ νησάων ἀστέρες ἀμφότεροι.

[frag. 67.8]

[both beautiful stars of the islands.]

In Mousaios this becomes a typical hexameter, intricately but heavily
balanced around a central declaration of exorbitance:

ἀμφοτέρων πολίων περικαλλέες ἀστέρες ἄμφω...

[22]

[both the very beautiful stars of both cities ...]

The intensive particles place the action in a general context of excess;
but in so doing they only give thematic expression to a habit of verbal
iteration throughout the poem. Even for a story about mating and
swimming we seem to be hearing the words *gamos, hymenaios, parthenos, thalassa, pontos,* and their compounds a great deal—a sense which
can be partially quantified. In the 6,212 lines of *Odyssey*, Books 1–12, a
story also very much about the sea, *thalassa* and its compounds occur 63
times, or once every 99 lines; in the 343 lines of *Hero and Leander* they
occur 19 times, once every 18 lines, more than 5 times as frequently. In

continuance of its obsessive role in the invocation, the word *lychnos* also
occurs 19 times in the poem. And we also hear a good deal about announcement (the *angel-* root, plus the related *diactoriē, semainō*, and
sēmēion), concealment (*cryptō, cryphios,* also *lathridios*), darkness (*nyx* and
its various forms, *achlys, omichlē*), and silence (*siōpē, sigē*). Periodically
through the poem these features will condense in ways that are arresting
and occasionally, like *lychnon acouō*, almost violent in their juxtaposition:

εὐνῆς δὲ κρυφίης τηλεσκόπον ἀγγελιώτην.

[237]

[far-seeing announcer of the secret mating.]

("Oxymoron!" writes Kost in his note to the line.) There is a strong
temptation simply to collect these obsessions and interpret them cor-
porately. This would not be to dwell on tenuous and incidental congruences, but to respond directly to the immediate experience of reading.

   This sense of the stylistic thrust of Mousaios's poem can be strongly
confirmed and elaborated by seeing the poem in the specific literary
context in which, we now know, it was written. That context is not
one often considered, either for its own sake or in relation to Mousaios;
the standard treatment, or even a good introductory survey, has yet to
be written.[11] But we have for inspection an immense amount of text—
as much as we do for any other comparable phase of classical literature,
if not more—and the evidence for the relation of *Hero and Leander* to
that corpus is extensive and detailed. The main figure in the field is
Nonnos of Panopolis, primarily for his *Dionysiaca:* a 48-book, 25,000-
line *Iliad-cum-Odyssey* on the life of Dionysos and the only other Greek
epic we know begins *Eipe, thea.* . . . In fact, the rest of the first line has a
shape somewhat like that of Mousaios's first line:

Εἰπέ, θεά, Κρονίδαο διάκτορον αἴθοπος εὐνῆς . . .

[Speak, goddess, of the agent of Zeus's fiery mating . . .]

Εἰπέ, θεά, κρυφίων ἐπιμάρτυρα λύχνον ἐρώτων . . .

[Speak, goddess, of the lantern, witness of the secret loves . . .]

Four more words in both cases, a lumping of genitives around a noun
core; there may also be something to the *Cronidao / cryphiōn* alliteration.
A variant of Nonnos's strange epic noun, *diactoros*, shows up in line 6

of Mousaios (also in 301), and Mousaios's *martys* is an important member of Nonnos's *copia uerborum*. And the texture of verbal parallels between the two poems is often thicker than this. To give just one remarkably neat example, two lines of Nonnos—

οὐ θρασὺν Ὠρίωνα δυσίμερον, οὐ πρόμον Ἥρης

[20.83]

[not brave Orion, unhappy in love, not Hera's champion]

ἄξονος ἄκρα κάρηνα καὶ ἄβροχον ὁλκὸν Ἀμάξης

[23.295]

[the topmost peaks of the pole and the unwetted track of the Wagon]

—are cut and stitched together to make a line of Mousaios:

οὐ θρασὺν Ὠρίωνα καὶ ἄβροχον ὁλκὸν Ἀμάξης

[214]

[not brave Orion and the unwetted track of the Wagon]

One of the enterprises of Kost's edition of Mousaios was to make a definitive catalogue of these parallels, and his notes may be consulted almost ad lib for further examples. The one given is exceptional only in its tidiness; it is quite typical in being, not a quotation of an entire line, but a pastiche from two different passages in Nonnos. The general principle is that of the recombination of certain basic units—a principle within which Mousaios's practice is simply an extension of habits at work within Nonnos's own poem. A characteristic line of Mousaios—

μαρμαρυγὴν χαρίεσσαν ἀπαστράπτουσα προσώπου

[56]

—is only a term in a tradition already set up within the *Dionysiaca*:

μαρμαρυγὴ σελάγιζε καταυγάζουσα προσώπου

[9.104]

μαρμαρυγὴν ῥοδόεσσαν ὀιστεύουσι παρειαί

[18.353]

μαρμαρυγὴ τροχόεσσα μονογλήνοιο προσώπου

[28.227]

μαρμαρυγὴν πυρόεσσαν ἀνηκόντιζον ὀπωπαί

[30.255]

μαρμαρυγὴν στίλβουσαν ἀπημάλδυνε προσώπου

[33.24]

μαρμαρυγὴν ῥοδόεσσαν ἀπηκόντιζον ὀπωπαί

[40.414]

Note, among other congruences, that each line consists of four words of four, four, five, and three syllables respectively. Yet no two lines are quite the same; Mousaios is not so much quoting Nonnos as writing according to the same rules.

But so were several other poets; the history of my penultimate example extends into Paul the Silentiary's description of the newly renovated Hagia Sophia:

ἄλλος ἐπ' Ὠρίωνα καὶ ἄβροχον ὁλκὸν Ἁμάξης
ὄμμα φέρει

[899–900][12]

[Another turns his eyes to Orion and the unwetted track of the Wagon]

The example is merely illustrative; what is often known as the "school of Nonnos" is bound together by more than just verbal parallels. Certain extensive norms of diction, syntax, and meter define, with exceptional philological rigor, a distinct group of late classical Greek poets who were very clearly united by an agreement to write by the same striking rules. The main productions still surviving of the school are the *Dionysiaca*, Nonnos's metrical paraphrase (*metabolē*) of the Gospel according to John, *Hero and Leander*, Collouthos's brief epic on the abduction of Helen, Paul the Silentiary's eighty-odd epigrams in the Palatine Anthology, and three lengthy ecphraseis: by Paul of Hagia Sophia, by Christodoros of the statues in a public gymnasium, and by John of Gaza of an illustrated map of the heavens.[13]

The considerable inner coherence of this body of poetry is most of what is known about it. We have some general sense of the conditions under which poetry was written in the eastern Empire in the fifth and sixth centuries, but no specific external information about the "school" itself.[14] Nonnos, Collouthos, and Christodoros are all attested to be Egyptians. Paul was a functionary in the court of Justinian (527–65), and his poem on Hagia Sophia can be dated 563. Nonnos may have been the fifth-century bishop of that name; the latest educated guess for his literary *floruit* is 450–70.[15] Our Mousaios is called *grammaticos* in some of the manuscripts of his poem, and may be the addressee of two letters by Procopios of Gaza (465–528); otherwise he is totally unattested. Internal evidence, such as that offered by line 214, quoted above, makes it logical to place *Hero and Leander* after the *Dionysiaca* and before Paul's ecphrasis; more involved arguments have recently favored the period 470–510.[16]

For what led up to the school of Nonnos we have similarly scanty external evidence and considerably less text; but it is now clear that the school, for all its distinctiveness, also capped several long-term developments in Greek literature. The principal poetic texts here are the brief epic by Triphiodoros[17] (another Egyptian) on the Sack of Troy; several of the poems attributed to Orpheus, especially the *Argonautica*; the fragments of poems on Dionysos and the Giants by one Dionysios (the ninety-fifth person of that name in Pauly-Wissowa); and another fragmentary Gigantomachy, attributed to Claudian.[18] Claudian's Latin works, especially *De Raptu Proserpinae*, may also be considered, since they show stylistic features very similar to those of the Greek poems; and there are also strong analogies in late prose, particularly the Romances, both Greek (notably Achilles Tatios) and Latin (Apuleius, who of course was imitating Greek models).

In general, this body of work represents at least one strain of Greek narrative literature in that shadowy period between the Hellenistic age and the school of Nonnos. There were certainly other strains, such as that represented by Quintus of Smyrna: a consciously archaizing and even scholarly return to Homeric forms and language, and an explicit continuation of the story of the *Iliad*. But the alternative explored by Nonnos and his predecessors and followers was that of an attempted replacement of the Homeric heritage, not by the importation of something new, but by the violent rearrangement of the available poetic *données*. As a whole, the movement was an attempt to revolutionize Greek epic poetry without sacrificing the aura of its acquired décor.

Part of this effort was the rearrangement of the received *Kunstsprache*, so as to create an immediately distinctive verbal surface. A number of new words, mainly adjectives, were created by compounding. Certain basic old words disappeared (neither *agathos*, "good," nor *anthrōpos*, "man," occurs in the *Dionysiaca* or *Hero and Leander*) and certain other words, the importance of which is much less obvious, gained inscrutable currency (*blosyros*, "burly," is used 45 times in the *Dionysiaca*, 3 times in all of Homer; *anthereōn*, "chin," 77 times in the *Dionysiaca*, 4 times in Homer). This is the general context of the strangely insistent verbal iterations in Mousaios.

Particularly notable in the tradition generally is a distinct shift toward the more energetic verbs; characters habitually do not speak, they shriek (*iachō*), and are forever stretching (*titainō*), springing (*ornymi*), hurrying (*seuō, speudō*), rioting (*bacceuō*), and banging (*arassō*). Most actions are several degrees more vigorous than the story seems to account for—a tendency which, taken together with the preference for elaborate adjectives, leads to a prevalent sensation of explosions under a thickly lacquered surface:

$$αὐτοφόνῳ\ βαρύποτμος\ ἐπεσκίρτησε\ σιδήρῳ.$$

[*Dion.* 17.288]

[Heavy-fated, he skipped onto his suicidal sword.]

(Again, a four-word line.) The nobility of previous martial suicides yields to a freaked-out stoicism, the maniacal character of the gesture being to a great extent a purely nervous, twitchy reaction to *barypotmos*, "heavy-fated."

This baroque symbiosis of exorbitant energy and exorbitant elaboration obtains throughout these poems. Part of what makes them so bizarre to read is that all this stylistic vigor is not necessarily narrative energy; increasingly in the tradition there is a reliance on trancelike abstractions from the story at hand. A flashy rhetorical cleverness is triggered by the slightest excuse; the local verbal patternings in Mousaios are typical enough of the tradition, but they are only the baseline. In Nonnos in particular there is a great devotion to cataloguing, either of mythological parallels and contrasts to the action, or when possible, as in battle scenes, of the action itself. The ultimate expression of this tendency is a minor genre not found in Mousaios at all but present in Claudian and Triphiodoros, and rampant in Nonnos: the formal ecphrasis, a meticulous description of some inanimate, usually crafted object.[19] Catalogues and ecphraseis have, of course, like almost everything else in these poems, epic pedigree (the Shield of Achilles is the prime example of the latter) but are usually supposed to occur once or twice per epic. In Nonnos they have become a major part of the narrative texture, and the ecphrasis eventually takes over the whole tradition; after Mousaios and Collouthos the narrative pretension is dropped entirely.

The movement toward stasis, however, is not accompanied by any abatement of the general excitement. John of Gaza begins his ecphrasis in near hysteria:

> Πῇ φέρομαι; πτερόεις με δι' ἠέρος ἔμφρονι ῥοίζῳ
> Σειρήνων λιγύφωνος ἄγει θρόος· ἐν δὲ μενοινῇ
> Μουσάων πλήκτροισιν ἱμάσσομαι ἄρσενι κέντρῳ,
> ἕρπων ξεῖνα κέλευθα, καὶ αἰθέρι πεζὸς ὁδίτης
> λύσσαν ἔχων γονόεσσαν ἀείρομαι...

[Where am I being carried? The winged, sweet-voiced clamor of the Sirens drives me through the air with animate bustle. In my longing I am beaten with the male goad of the Muses' plectra; creeping along strange paths, a foot-traveler, having a fertile madness, I am lifted into the aether ...]

Such statements of inordinate personal excitement are a major feature of the tradition, an appropriation of the ambient stylistic violence to define the activity of the poet himself; it is the topos of vatic inspiration with an almost sadomasochistic vengeance. Something about the very intricacy and mass of the material seems to occasion the violence. Nonnos as usual gives the definitive formulation: *poicilon hymnon arassō* (*Dion.* 1.15), "I bang away at a manifold hymn," the elaboration complicitous with the violence, in answer to the poet's need to *attack* something. Triphiodoros puts it in terms of impatience:

> αὐτίκα μοι σπεύδοντι πολὺν διὰ μῦθον ἀνεῖσα
> ἔννεπε, Καλλιόπεια...
>
> [3–4]

[Right away, dispensing with long talk, speak to me, Calliope, as I hurry ...]

Let's get on with it, Muse: speed, *speudō*, poised against *polys mythos*, the big story. Claudian announces that his mind is not just full but crammed; his adjective is one that we now use for sinus trouble:

> Inferni raptoris equos afflataque curru
> sidera Taenario caligantesque profundae
> Iunonis thalamos audaci promere cantu
> mens congesta iubet.
>
> [*De Raptu* 1.1–4]

[My congested mind orders me to bring forth in audacious song
the horses of the infernal rapist, and the stars breathed upon by
hell's chariot, and the dark mating of the Juno of the underworld.]

Clarke has interpreted Claudian's declaration ingeniously: "He
claims . . . that his *mens congesta* forces him to write, and his poem is
largely an unloading of its accumulated Latin reading."[20] Cameron
calls this interpretation "strained," and refers us to a catalogue of
furores poetici in Curtius.[21] But none of Curtius's examples (including
Claudian's own lines 4–6) really parallels or explains the odd force
of "congesta"; and Clarke's reading does strikingly fit the facts of
Claudian's practice. His poems are indeed crammed with a large number of reminiscences of earlier poetry, and much of it strangely altered
and even mangled, as though stored under great pressure.[22] In this
regard he is quite typical of the late Greek tradition, in which the paraphernalia of previous work is constantly being appropriated, and
usually with a flashy elaboration or change.

Mousaios's examples of one-upmanship with phrases from Homer
and Callimachos are relatively modest in comparison with the practice
of his immediate models. Venerable formulae are alternately metaphorized (*polyphloisbos polemos*, "much-resounding war"), literalized
(*oinops botrys*, "wine-dark grape"), or inverted (Nonnos has a sea that
is *aphloisbos*, "unresounding"),[23] as the logic of progress seems to demand. In Nonnos in particular, larger units and basic issues are even
more violently and puzzlingly twisted. Crucial epic *sententiae* will
come out saying almost the reverse of what they once said; and in
general the whole heroic model of determination through adversity is
botched in being fitted to the story of a god who never really has to
work to get what he wants, although he likes to talk as if he did.[24]

But epics are supposed to be only secondarily about gods and primarily about people. The Nonnian tradition seems generally to have
been far more attracted to purely divine and even cosmological issues
exactly because, we may suspect, in so doing it overturned some of the
basic principles of the genre. The cosmic frame of reference provided,
as it were, room to turn around in, with two basic revolutionary myths:
that of Dionysos, the late-born god who converts the whole world to
his worship, and that of the Earth-giants, who challenge directly the
immemorial rule of Zeus. The later myth seems particularly common:
the subject of poems by Dionysios and (twice) by Claudian, and of the

opening and closing episodes of the *Dionysiaca*. Nonnos's Typhon, in fact, makes a good figure for these poets as a group, with their program of innovation—

> ἀντιτύπους δὲ
> κρέσσονας ὀψιγόνους πολυφεγγέι μείζονι πυρσῷ
> ἀστεροπὰς ἑτέρας χαλκεύσομαι
>
> [2.344–46]

[I will make another, different, better, newer lightning, with more sparkling fire]

—through pummeling and rearrangement:

> ἠέρι μίξατε γαῖαν, ὕδωρ πυρί, πόντον Ὀλύμπῳ.
> καὶ πισύρων ἀνέμων τελέσω δούλειον ἀνάγκην,
> μαστίζω Βορέην, κλονέω Νότον, Εὖρον ἱμάσσω,
> καὶ Ζέφυρον πλήξαιμι, καὶ ἤματι νύκτα κεράσσω
> χειρὶ μιῇ.
>
> [2.272–76]

[Mix earth with air, water with fire, the sea with Olympos. I will put a slavish constraint on the four winds. I will whip Boreas, rout Notos, beat Euros, and pound Zephyros; and I will stir night and day together with one hand.]

The violence of these poems is a violence occasioned by and directed against the entire Greek epic tradition, eventually sabotaging the whole idea of epic as storytelling. Yet ultimately the violence is wholly internal and hence suicidal; being a matter of rearrangement, the revolution can provide nothing for the genre to evolve into but a subset of itself, the ecphrasis. And in that fate these poets resemble the Earthgiants to a further term: they lose. Zeus, like Homer, still holds all the cards, and the classical epic is still the only game in town. The final destiny of the tradition in ecstatic description of static art curiously resembles that of Nonnos's Typhon some three hundred lines after the quotation just given: burned, frozen, stretched out, and buried under Mount Aetna—a massive statement of paralyzed outrage.

What is Mousaios's place in this tradition? He certainly had not given up on storytelling, not even on storytelling about people; indeed, the basis of his extensive *Nachleben* is precisely the story that he told. The seemingly non-narrative elements in his style come from his participation in the school of Nonnos, but he does not participate in that school's general drift toward ecphrasis. As has already been seen in a few details, Mousaios's use of the techniques of the school is often trimmed to less drastic and more controlled effect than is the case in Nonnos. The repetitions in *Hero and Leander*, though extensive, are only the tip of the iceberg. It is very common to find certain Nonnian verbal obsessions that will show up just once or twice in Mousaios—the large issue of *coros*, "satiety," for example (78, 285; cf. Collouthos, 259), or the smaller, more perplexing concerns with footprints (*ichnos*, 162), throats (*laimos*, 327), and backs:

πάντοθι δ᾽ ὄμμα τίταινεν ἐπ᾽ εὐρέα νῶτα θαλάσσης.

[336]

[She strained her eyes all over the wide back of the sea.]

In context, that last phrase looks like a straightforward use of a venerable Homeric metaphor (*Od.* 3.142, et al.). Mousaios can even use the figure twice (cf. 313) without calling too much attention to it, certainly not the kind of attention that the word *nōton*, "back," arouses by appearing 143 times in the *Dionysiaca* (compared with 31 occurrences in Homer's 48 books).

This selectivity with regard to Nonnian obsessions may possibly be the result of writing a poem of only 343 lines, but in at least some cases a fairly active discrimination may be detected. That odd locution *omma titainen*, "she strained her eye," for example, is another Nonnian curiosity, a typical use of one of Nonnos's most popular verbs of stress. Mousaios uses that verb one other time, where its vigor makes very literal sense: *toxa titainōn* (17), "stretching his bow." And in the later usage, the apparent strain of the diction answers to an ascertainable strain in the narrative: Hero searching for the body of her lover. In general Mousaios's diction, though it continues the adjectival thickness of the tradition, notably tones down the verbs and retains the more violent ones for specific occasions, such as a crucial moment in the courtship:

θαρσαλέη παλάμη πολυδαίδαλον εἷλκε χιτῶνα. . . .

[118]

[With a bold hand he grabbed her very elaborate dress . . .]

The characteristic Nonnian verb of speech turns up once:

νυμφίον ἀμφιχυθεῖσα φιλήνορας ἴαχε μύθους ...

[267]

[Embracing her husband, she shrieked affectionate words ...]

The occasion is Hero's first speech to Leander after his swim. The diction is still significant—Hero's words could have been quiet and soothing, just as her scanning of the sea could have been cautious and tentative—but it does, much more than in Nonnos, link the general cosmic excitement to the details of the situation at hand. Mousaios slips in a Gigantomachy without mentioning Giants: *aitheri misgeto pontos* (315), "the sea was mixed with the air"—a near-quotation not only of the Nonnian passage cited above, but also of the *Gigantias* of Dionysios: *misgeto d' ēeri pontos* (16.16). But the occasion in Mousaios is the storm that kills Leander; Mousaios naturalizes the mythology by extracting the vigor of expression which its cosmic scale has produced.

The sense, then, is one of larger forces being focused, a bit precariously, onto the story, and giving that story an arresting verbal density while still preserving its narrative outlines. Other more explicitly interpretive contexts than the Nonnian may also figure; Gelzer detects the language of neo-Platonic allegory, and such words as *angelos* and *martys* have obvious Christian resonances.[25] But they also have resonances within the narrative itself; and the ultimate distinction of the poem may be the remarkable way in which the particular Nonnian obsessions that Mousaios elects to keep *as obsessions* are integrated into the action.

For the opening concern with "announcement" glosses quite literally the central episode of the poem: the slow process by which the concealed desires of Leander and Hero are expressed, mutually recognized, and granted (86–224). The process is immensely complicated by the various constraints on speaking to the point. There are the normal games of courtship: the man's intimidating fear of rejection, the woman's obligatory demurral, and the resulting need to work around, by an elaborate rhetoric of praise and persuasion, to the essentially simple question. To these Mousaios adds certain external constraints on Hero's love life—her religious vows and her parents' concern for her social position—so that communication at each stage of the negotiations has to be relatively oblique. Even when the crucial moment has been passed, things cannot really become overt; Hero never actually says yes. Rather, there is a heavy dependence all along on concealment, and consequently on the reading of nonverbal indicators:

λοξὰ δ᾽ ὀπιπεύων δολερὰς ἐλέλιζεν ὀπωπάς,
νεύμασιν ἀφθόγγοισι παραπλάζων φρένα κούρης.

[101–02]

[Glancing obliquely, he twisted deceptive glances, seducing the girl's heart with voiceless nods.]

Hero responds:

νεύμασι λαθριδίοσιν ἐπαγγέλλουσα Λεάνδρῳ . . .

[106]

[announcing to Leander with secret nods . . .]

(Mime is itself an important Nonnian motif.) Leander interprets Hero's rhetoric of protest:

θηλείης δὲ Λέανδρος ὅτ᾽ ἔκλυεν οἶστρον ἀπειλῆς,
ἔγνω πειθομένων σημήια παρθενικάων·
καὶ γὰρ ὅτ᾽ ἠιθέοισιν ἀπειλείουσι γυναῖκες,
Κυπριδίων δάρων αὐτάγγελοί εἰσιν ἀπειλαί.

[129–32]

[When Leander heard the sting of female reproach, he recognized the signs of persuaded virgins. For when women reproach young men, their reproaches are themselves announcers of the games of Aphrodite.]

This recognition sends Leander into a highly wrought piece of rhetoric of his own that leaves Hero *aphthongos* (160), "speechless"; but

πειθοῦς γὰρ τάδε πάντα προάγγελα, παρθενικῆς δὲ
πειθομένης ποτὶ λέκτρον ὑπόσχεσίς ἐστι σιωπή.

[164–65]

[These are all announcements of persuasion, and silence is admission to the bed of a persuaded virgin.]

By this time it is clear that silence is the value, not speech; Hero's only remaining objection is that people will talk:

οὐ δύνασαι σκοτόεσσαν ὑποκλέπτειν Ἀφροδίτην·
γλῶσσα γὰρ ἀνθρώπων φιλοκέρτομος· ἐν δὲ σιωπῇ
ἔργον ὅπερ τελέει τις, ἐνὶ τριόδοισιν ἀκούει.

[182–84]

[You cannot hide shadowy Aphrodite; for the tongue of men is fond of jeering. Whatever deed someone does in silence, he hears of it at the crossroads.]

But Leander has a plan, and at this point the poem, as it were, begins to allegorize itself. What he asks for is not a declaration of consent or a pledge of faith or even affection but a signal: not a *logos*[26] but a *lychnos*, the *sēmeia pyrgou* (228), "the sign from the tower." The role of *lychnos* as an iconic obsession is recapitulated shortly thereafter, and it gives Leander the courage he needs to brave the *polyēchēs bombos* (242), "the much-echoing bombast," of the sea:

> ἀλλὰ πολυφλοίσβοιο παρ᾽ ἠιόνεσσι θαλάσσης
> ἀγγελίην ἀνέμιμνε φαεινομένων ὑμεναίων,
> μαρτυρίην λύχνοιο πολυκλαύτοιο δοκεύων,
> εὐνῆς δὲ κρυφίης τηλεσκόπον ἀγγελιώτην.
> ὡς δ᾽ ἴδε κυανέης λιποφεγγέα νυκτὸς ὀμίχλην
> Ἡρώ, λύχνον ἔφαινεν· ἀναπτομένοιο δὲ λύχνου
> θυμὸν Ἔρως ἔφλεξεν ἐπειγομένοιο Λεάνδρου·
> λύχνῳ καιομένῳ συνεκαίετο.

[234–41]

[But on the beach of the much-resounding sea, he awaited the announcer of their blazing marriage, watching for the witness of the much-mourned lantern, the far-seeing announcer of the secret mating. When Hero saw the light-leaving cloud of blue-green night, she displayed the lantern; when the lantern was kindled, Love fired the spirit of impatient Leander. He burned with the burning lantern.]

Following this signal, he swims the sea, and their marriage is consummated in silence:

> ἦν γάμος, ἀλλ᾽ ἀχόρευτος· ἔην λέχος, ἀλλ᾽ ἄτερ ὕμνων·
> οὐ ζυγίην Ἥρην τις ἐπευφήμησεν ἀείδων,
> οὐ δαΐδων ἤστραπτε σέλας θαλαμηπόλον εὐνῇ,
> οὐδὲ πολυσκάρθμῳ τις ἐπεσκίρτησε χορείῃ,
> οὐχ ὑμέναιον ἄειδε πατὴρ καὶ πότνια μήτηρ·
> ἀλλὰ λέχος στορέσασα τελεσσιγάμοισιν ἐν ὥραις
> σιγῇ παστὸν ἔπηξεν, ἐνυμφοκόμησε δ᾽ ὀμίχλη,
> καὶ γάμος ἦν ἀπάνευθεν ἀειδομένων ὑμεναίων.

[274–81]

[There was a marriage, but without dancing; there was a bridal
bed, but without hymns. No one sang the praises of Hera, goddess
of union, no marriage-attending blaze of pine flared by the couch,
no one skipped in bounding dances, no father and revered mother
sang a hymeneal. But silence, fixing the bridal bed in the marriage-
accomplishing hours, ordered the nuptial chamber, and darkness
dressed the bride, and the marriage was without sung hymeneals.]

Style and plot thus mesh in complicated ways. The elaborately obvious
rhetoric is placed by a thematic concern with the meretriciousness of
all rhetoric: language not as a trustworthy account of the situation but
as a part of the situation, a means to an end. And the stylistic reliance
on repeated, opaque verbal counters mimics the action of the characters,
holding themselves to a pinpoint obsession that they cannot or will not
make public. The poem is thus to some extent a poem about language
in a highly developed culture; against the temptation to accept the
prevailing standards of the articulate are set techniques for retaining
meaning just beyond or behind the ostensible circuit of discourse. And
that is also a diagram of Mousaios's very literal subject, human sexuality as it functions in certain social environments, as a vehicle of secrecy
and concentration amid the diffused sociability of the rest of our lives.

But in *Hero and Leander* that gulf (figured literally as the Hellespont)
has become radical and ultimately catastrophic; things are strained to
the breaking point. The specific social context of the poem is the
pandēmios heortē, the "international festival" of Aphrodite and Adonis,
an event of great conventioneering bustle—*passydiēi d' espeudon* (44),
"they hurried from all over"—but little genuine religious aura. It is
the clandestine mating of the lovers that gives the poem its moments of
near mysticism, a negative mysticism defined precisely by its denial of
public ceremony: "There was a marriage, but without dancing; there
was a bridal bed, but without hymns." In some dark joke, Hero's
sexual fulfillment is accomplished only through breaking the rules of
her public role as priestess of Aphrodite. Emotions are strung taut
across this void between civilization and sexuality—not with the
tautness of assured control, but with that of incipient hysteria and chaos.
The lovers' effort to focus their attention onto the single point of the
lychnos is simply too much; it sparks their own occasionally outsized
reactions—Leander's "grab" and Hero's "shriek"—and also underlies
in a certain way the undirected nervous energy that characterizes the

poetic texture in general. We do not need psychoanalysis to tell us what the outburst of the anonymous young man (74–83) makes explicit, that the restless activity of the *pandēmios heortē* is primarily just that of frustrated, itchy sexuality. And the storm that blows out the *lychnos* makes sense as psychological allegory: a revenge upon the private vision by the very energy required to maintain its secrecy. The lovers' privacy, we would now say, becomes psychotic. Or, more simply, they just panic.

II What did the Renaissance make of this complex little poem? On at least one important level, of course, the work was radically misconstrued. The history of Mousaios's poem in the literary culture of the Renaissance is almost exactly coextensive with its ascription to the mythical companion of Orpheus, and its popularity and prestige were intricately involved with the Renaissance readers' sense that "they were communing with the spirit of poetry at its elemental source."[27] In so doing, they perhaps sought analogues to what they hoped was their own cultural situation, a time of beginnings. *Hero and Leander* was one of the first Greek works to become widely available in the Renaissance; the *editio princeps*, ca. 1494, was one of the earliest products of the Aldine Press—possibly the first, more probably the second.[28] The manuscript to which that edition is most closely related (E in the usual sigla) is not one of those containing the telltale characterization of Mousaios as *grammaticos*; and the misdating begins here, influenced by the neat symbolism of the occasion. What better way to inaugurate western Europe's first major Greek press than with one of the earliest poems of the Greek tradition? Aldo Manuzio, in the Greek preface, hails the publication of Mousaios, "the most ancient poet," as a fitting prolegomenon to his proposed editions of Aristotle "and the other wise men"; it will also be of interest, he says, to those who want to study Ovid's sources for the *Heroides*.[29]

Not everyone was comfortable with this dating of the poem. "There are those among the learned," reports Johannes Froben in 1518, "who deny it is by Mousaios"; he goes on to note, with sadness, the skepticism of philologists concerning religious texts as well.[30] In 1566 Henri Estienne (Henricus Stephanus), hearing of the *grammaticos* heading, and having his own suspicions about the style of the poem, printed Mousaios not before Homer but after Triphiodoros in his collection of Greek epic.[31] The publication three years later of the *Dionysiaca* made more compelling arguments possible; and in 1583 Isaac Casaubon presented the decisive case.[32] He did so, however, not in any edition of Mousaios but in his notes to Diogenes Laertios, and the word was slow getting around. Chapman was still able to publish his translation of Mousaios in 1616 as the "First of all Bookes." Casaubon's arguments did not seem to have been in general circulation until the edition of Daniel Pareus (Frankfurt, 1627); coincidentally or not, only professional scholars seemed interested in the poem thereafter, and even among them its reputation plummeted. The popularity of the story, of course, continued, but it was by then available from a wide range of sources; Chapman's translation is effectively the terminus ad quem of the literary career of Mousaios's poem.

The interesting question about the misdating is how in the readers' minds this aura of priority interacted with the details of Mousaios's style. Were the more baroque features of that style instinctively discounted and perhaps not even recognized, or was the sense of a literary dawn adjusted to fit them? There is not much explicit discussion to go by; for all his popularity, Mousaios acquired only a slim body of humanist commentary, nothing like that which grew up around Homer and Ovid in the sixteenth century. Early seventeenth-century scholarship has some acute things to say, as though the solution of the dating problem had ended some kind of paralysis; but the usual starting point there is that Mousaios's style, whatever its occasional felicities or its superiority to the rest of the school of Nonnos, is essentially corrupt, a falling off from the primal simplicity and purity of Homer.[33] What we want to know is how a reader went about *liking* Mousaios with the sort of enthusiasm with which the sixteenth century seems to have liked him; and the only figure really to address this question is the intrepid Julius Caesar Scaliger, in his *Poetics*.

Scaliger is a risky guide to the consciousness of the typical Renaissance reader, but he does show that Renaissance enthusiasm for Mousaios could coexist with an intelligent and more or less accurate perception of his style. Scaliger does sense a problem in the dating question—"if it were not for the histories, you would think Mousaios more recent than Homer"—but the hinge here is not Mousaios's decadence but his ripeness: "he is more cultivated and polished."[34] Scaliger later acquired some notoriety for in fact preferring Mousaios to Homer on stylistic grounds: "I think Mousaios's style much neater and more polished than Homer's. . . . If Mousaios had written what Homer wrote, I believe he would have written it much better."³⁵ Though Scaliger may be misvaluing Mousaios's style, he is not wholly misperceiving it, and the quotations he cites in support of his judgment are almost exactly those which I used earlier for my own discussion.³⁶

What Scaliger values are elements of elaborate rhetorical display and design. "What could be more orotund, more elegant, more ornate, more melodious," he asks ("rotundius, elegantius, ornatius, numerosius"), "than this verse?"

αὐτὸς ἐὼν ἐρέτης, αὐτόστολος, αὐτομάτος νηῦς

[255]

[himself being the rower, the self-sent, self-moving boat]

He quotes lines "ob sententiam"—

παρθενικῆς δὲ
πειθομένης ποτὶ λέκτρον ὑπόσχεσίς ἐστι σιωπή.

[164–65]³⁷

[silence is admission to the bed of a persuaded virgin]

—for their rhetorical balance—

ἡ μὲν φῶς τανύειν, ὁ δὲ κύματα μακρὰ περῆσαι

[224]

[She to hold out the light, he to try the great waves]

—and simply for their verbal fullness:

μαρμαρυγὴν χαρίεσσαν ἀπαστράπτουσα προσώπου

[56]

[hurling a graceful dazzle from her face]

He expresses a fondness for *lecta uerba* ("picked terms," as they were called in English) and a thick mingling of sound and sense ("plenus numeris atque sententia"). He seems responsive to certain kinds of imitative form: he quotes from the *Odyssey* (5.291–94) a description of a storm at sea, and remarks, "This is all lovely, full, and grave, but I find nothing in it of the movement of the sea." In contrast he offers two passages from Mousaios (293–95, 314–18), including the one beginning with the escalated Homeric tag, *cymati cyma cylindeto*. He even takes tentative note of the Nonnian metrical straightjacket, the avoidance of hiatus and the preference for closing verses with bi- and trisyllables. Scaliger sees Mousaios as a self-conscious poetic virtuoso, and values him for it.

It makes a good deal of sense that Scaliger would pick up on these aspects of the Greek, especially since he was a practicing, if minor, neo-Latin poet himself. For the specific features which he appreciates are directly analogous to that widespread poetic principle for which Curtius, following the Spanish theorist Barsilaso Gracián, proposes the general term *agudeza*, "acuity" or "pointedness."[38] Indeed, Scaliger describes some lines of Mousaios (135–40) as "munda simul et acuta," "both polished and pointed"; and his son Joseph Juste ascribes his father's bad judgment in this matter to a fondness for "acumina illa et flores declamatorii," "those points and flowers of oratory."[39] In terms of classical rhetorical theory, the principle is the elevation of *ingenium* over *iudicium*, the scoring of "points"—rhetorical, metaphorical, ecphrastic, sententious—wherever the possibility arises, without burdensome attention to larger structures: *ingenium* as ingenuity. The hypertrophy of *agudeza* underlies the transformation of the earlier Renaissance literary styles into the mannerist and the baroque. The principle swamps much late sixteenth-century and early seventeenth-century verse; it is particularly noticeable in narrative, where the virtuosity is most readily experienced as an interruption of other business. The age recognized the value, even the necessity, of overtelling a story; that is the explicit form of Scaliger's appreciation of one of Mousaios's poetic kin: "That greatest of poets, Claudian, made up in ingenuity (*de ingenio*) for what he lacked in subject matter."[40] Late Renaissance readers could find in Mousaios classical precedent for their own joy in the *virtù* of poetic display: "ut nectar, ingenium."

Many of the specific tricks of the Nonnian style in general have direct analogues in late Renaissance style—sometimes very direct ones, such as the duBartasian craze for compound adjectives. There cannot be any question of large-scale causality, but there is a sense of parallel enterprise that could conceivably cause ignition in particular cases, such as Marlowe's. For encoded into the Nonnian techniques is a relation to the main body of classical literature, a relation curiously similar to that in which the Renaissance stood: hypnotized by the prestige of the great names, minutely familiar with their works, and eager to surpass them, as much as possible, on their own terms. The sixteenth century picks up where Nonnos leaves off; antique detumescence intersects

Renaissance exuberance. Gerhard Falkenburg, the first editor of the *Dionysiaca*, actually presents his author as a good example of how to use the classical tradition: "in the whole works of Homer there is nothing beautiful, nothing useful, that our author has not ingeniously (*ingeniose*) emulated."[41] And the edition carefully marks the adaptations of Homer and others so that the reader may examine the process of ingeniousness for himself.

The *Dionysiaca*, printed forbiddingly without a Latin translation (one was not supplied until 1605), admittedly sank almost without a trace;[42] but other artifacts of the school of Nonnos fared somewhat better. Triphiodoros and Collouthos (both ca. 1521), as well as Nonnos's *Metabolē* (ca. 1501), were published early and achieved a reasonable circulation. Collouthos was translated into Latin by Marlowe's friend Thomas Watson (1586), and there is even some evidence that Marlowe made an English translation.[43] The general fondness of the Renaissance for certain related authors is well known: the writers of the Greek romances, Apuleius, Claudian; Seneca might even be adduced. Sixteenth-century readers had a greater taste for the "decadence" of the classical tradition than any subsequent period did, so there are good reasons why Mousaios's popularity should not puzzle us at all.

Yet his case remains complex. Partly because of what Renaissance readers thought he was, and partly also because the taste for really rampant *agudeza* is primarily a late Renaissance affair, the history of his poem until Marlowe's version is of a pervasive if not wholly consistent dampening effect on the flashiness of the original. The process may even begin before the first edition, in the E manuscript, which contains several spot variants from the other traditions. The Homerico-Nonnian metaphor *thalassaiōn epi nōtōn* (313), "on the oceanic back," for example, is replaced by the slightly less angular *thalassaiōn hymenaiōn*, "the oceanic nuptials." If this is a conscious alteration, it may be due to something repugnant about the metaphor itself or (more likely) to its recurrence shortly thereafter (336); whatever the case, Mousaios appears in the Aldine edition shorn of one of his numerous repetitions. He also loses his one use of the Nonnian *iache* (267), Hero's shriek. E reads a nonsensical *ise* there, which has been corrected to the more reasonable *ennepe*, "she said."

The Florentine edition of Janus Lascaris, also ca. 1494, prints the correct reading for both these passages from other manuscripts, and Estienne in 1566 adopts them for his text.[44] But it was the Aldine text

that formed the basis of most of the popular editions until the seventeenth century—partly because the texts of Lascaris and Estienne were
printed without Latin translations, but also, at least in some cases, for
literary reasons as well. André de Pape considers Hero's shriek in his
notes:

> Henri Estienne reads *ennepe* for *iache*. You will not easily find that
> latter word used transitively, except in the later poets; and in this
> situation, where nothing would be less appropriate than shouting,
> it does not seem to fit at all.
>
> [p. 181]

A shriek at this point in the story, besides casting doubt on Mousaios's
early date, would also violate certain notions of emotional decorum,
at least the decorum of erotic encounters. Most of the popular texts
in the sixteenth century print *ennepe*, and most versions of the story
reflect that reading, either with noncommittal literalness—"these words
utter'd" (Chapman, 378)—or with some extra emphasis on the gentleness of Hero's speech—"Empeçole d'hablar estas blanduras" (Boscán,
2206).

This latter alternative happens to derive specifically from another
feature of the Aldine edition, the Latin translation.[45] For the whole
phrase *philēnoras ennepe mythous* the translation gives "blanda emisit
uerba"; however, from the character of the translation elsewhere it
may be gathered that "blanda" is not so much an active reinterpretation
of the emotional tenor of the scene as simply a slack equivalent for
philēnōr, "husband-fond." This is not a mistranslation, exactly; the
reference of the Greek adjective has simply been shifted from the
content of Hero's words to their style. It would seem that the translator
was thrown by the compound adjective, for which there is no obvious
Latin equivalent.

This difficulty comes up often in the poem, which was one of the
most accessible examples in the Renaissance canon of the greater
amplitude of the Greek language over Latin; Jean Vatel complains
explicitly, in an interesting use of the objection usually lodged against
the vernaculars, of the *penuria* of the Latin language for translating
Mousaios (Delamare, sigs. A8r, B4r). The Aldine translation occasionally does what seems to us to be the obvious thing and neologizes—
polyphloisboio (234) becomes "multifremi," a word unrecognized by the
Thesaurus Linguae Latinae—but generally it does not. Renaissance

dictionaries usually treat such compounds periphrastically, and the Aldine translation often does the same: *nyctigamoio gamostolon* (7) becomes "nocte nubentis nuptias ornantem," *tēlescopon* (237) becomes "procul speculantem," and so on.

Many, however, are simply debased, like *philēnoras*: *cyanopeplos* (113, 232), "in blue-green clothing," becomes *atratus*, *polydaidalon* (118), "very elaborate," becomes "uariam." And there is at times a certain blandness in the choice of Latin words where no such problem as compounding presents itself in the Greek: *odynaōn* (11), "pains," becomes "curarum"; *himeroeis* (20; Leander's epithet), "desirable," becomes "suauis." The translation often exhibits a distinct insensitivity or inattention to the specific vigor of Mousaios's diction.

Nevertheless, as the primary vehicle by which *Hero and Leander* reached Renaissance readers, the Aldine translation is a distinguished and serviceable achievement. For despite its somewhat slipshod approach to the individual words, it is almost ferociously honest and literal about something scarcely less important, the structure of statement in the poem. The translation provides for the Greek, in a way in which only Latin can, a rigorously isomorphic map:

Εἰπέ, θεά, κρυφίων   ἐπιμάρτυρα   λύχνον   ἐρώτων
Dic   dea occultorum testem   lucernam amorum

The translation preserves not only word order but also grammatical form and often even such subsidiary matters as gender. The Latin could serve as an interlinear; indeed, though unmetrical, it is printed with a lineation matching the Greek, so that the reader can move his eyes almost instantly between corresponding points in the two texts. There are even makeshift equivalents for those untranslatable Greek particles; meaning in their case is almost totally irrelevant, and the real purpose is just to hold down the place in the line. A stop-press correction reveals the extent to which this word-for-word correspondence was, even when semantically inconsequential, a matter of great concern. For line 21 the first pressrun had:

ἡ μὲν Σηστὸν ἔναιεν, ὁ δὲ πτολίεθρον Ἀβύδου

Haec quidem Sestum habitabat, uero oppidum ille Abydi

In later copies of the same edition, a meticulous alteration was made:

Haec quidem Sestum habitabat, ille uero oppidum Abydi

It is now clear that "ille" translates *ho*, and "uero" is standing in for *de*.[46]

The principles behind this achingly schematic mode of translation are not of the translator's own devising; they go back (at least) to the first entry of classical Greek literature into Renaissance culture, to the Latin Homer that Leonzio Pilato provided—*de* carefully represented by *autem*—for Boccaccio and Petrarch.[47] Because of the similarities between the two languages, the method has an obvious logic to it; yet it should be distinguished as a tradition in its own right from the later techniques of Latin verse translation, where such matters as word order are sacrificed to stylistic grace and, presumably, readability. The more literal versions, however—logical ones, after all, to be printed *en face* with the Greek—often seem to have been the more widely read, and they could, in their very freedom from the canons of neo-Latin elegance, have stylistic virtues of their own. At least one such translation has had an extraordinary *Nachleben* in our own day. Ezra Pound found Andrea Divo's literal Latin version of Homer "even singable, there are constant suggestions of poetic motion; it is very simple Latin, after all, and a crib of this sort may make just the difference of permitting a man to read fast enough to get the swing and mood of the subject, instead of losing both in a dictionary."[48] And Pound, of course, made Divo's version of Book 11 of the *Odyssey* famous as the starting text for the *Cantos*.[49] It is not generally realized that the same translation, adapted by Jean de Sponde (Spondanus) for his edition of Homer, is also the text behind Chapman's translation.[50]

Even within this tradition, however, the Aldine translation of Mousaios has certain claims to distinction and cannot be fully categorized as a Latin crib. In rendering the Greek, the translator seems to have been attuned to certain kinds of verbal patterns that would not necessarily be preserved without some conscious effort. He is fairly attentive to verbal repetitions; as noted above, he renders *cyanopeplos* rather uninterestingly as *atratus*, but does so consistently, in both of its widely spread occurrences. *Lychnos* is twice rendered as *lychnus* (212, 218), but elsewhere, including the two passages of most intense usage (1–15, 236–41), it is consistently *lucerna*. The *angel-* root is treated by variations on *nuntius*, and on at least one occasion the translation even overstates the case:

λύχνον ἀπαγγέλλοντα διακτορίην Ἀφροδίτης

[6]

Lucernam annunciantem nuncium Veneris

The duplication in the Latin violates the decorum of literal translation, but does so by following Mousaios's own rules in using an obsession obsessively.

And the translator uses even more of his own imagination in preserving for the Greekless reader a fair amount of the sonic play of the original, enough to give the Latin something of the interest and readability of patterned oratorical prose. Schoeck has remarked on the "ingenious rhetoric" of the translation in a passage playing around with the syllables *min* and *arum*:[51]

> Talia minata est conuenientia uirginibus.
> Foeminearum autem Leander ubi audiuit furorem minarum,
> Sensit persuasarum signa uirginum.
> Etenim cum iuuenibus minantur foeminae,
> Venerearum consuetudinum per se nunciae sunt minae.
>
> [128–32]

The specific disposition of the words and some of the sound patterns are traced directly from the Greek; for the rest of the aural play a few adjustments have been made to introduce effects into the Latin as though in compensation for Greek effects missed:

> τοῖα μὲν ἠπείλησεν ἐοικότα παρθενικῇσι.
> θηλείης δὲ Λέανδρος ὅτ᾽ ἔκλυεν οἶστρον ἀπειλῆς,
> ἔγνω πειθομένων σημήια παρθενικάων·
> καὶ γὰρ ὅτ᾽ ἠιθέοισιν ἀπειλείουσι γυναῖκες,
> Κυπριδίων ὀάρων αὐτάγγελοί εἰσιν ἀπειλαί.

The parallel of *arum* between lines 130 and 132 is the direct consequence of using, as the Greek demands, parallel grammatical forms; if *uirgo* were not third declension, if *puella* had been used instead, there would be a further parallel in line 130, with the lengthy Latin case-ending compensating for the more intricate jingle in the Greek (*peithomenōn/parthenicaōn*). The translator does, however, provide compensation by rendering the singular genitives in line 129 as plural, with no warrant in the Greek but also no real damage to the sense; the sonic linkage thus encompasses four lines instead of just three. Also, in line 129 he finds an equivalent for the *thēleiēs/apeilēs* parallel in the Latin "feminarum"/"minarum"; the use of plurals has the added effect of making this godsend a bit more emphatic. In lines 131–32 Mousaios changes the reference to *gynaices*; but the translation, by continuing to use *femina*, continues the play on *min*, and creates a rhyme (in this passage four of the Latin lines are rhymed, and none of the

Greek ones are). Thus, though a certain amount of local business is missed (*ēitheoisin apeileiousi, Cypridiōn oarōn*), a general texture of sonic involution is maintained. It is not hard to find other such examples:

πρὶν χαλεπὸν πνοιῇσιν ἀήμεναι ἐχθρὸν ἀήτην.

[13]

Antequàm molestum flatibus flaret inimicus uentus.

The play *aēmenai* / *aētēn* has been shifted ahead to become "flatibus flaret." A reader of the Aldine translation would get a good idea of at least one major dimension of the style of the Greek poem, and certainly some notion of its peculiarities.

The translation was a solid enough job; with appropriate local alterations, it was used in scholarly editions into the nineteenth century.[52] It was included, with the Aldine text, in the Basle edition of Aesop (1518), which went through twelve editions by 1619, and was probably the place in which most readers encountered Mousaios's poem. This was unquestionably the standard translation. Vatel's commentary draws constantly on it as well as on Delamare and the Greek; Chapman quotes it passim in the notes to his English translation as simply "the Latin."

The metrical Latin versions are less literal and more interpretive, more inquisitive about the oddities of the Greek poem and in some instances more daring in their handling of them. In comparison to the Aldine translation, they are particularly attentive to diction. For the first use of *cyanopeplos* (113), Delamare ventures the neologism *nigriuestis* (sig. B8ʳ), which does not quite capture the force of *cyan-*, but gives a literal register of the structure of the Greek word; and Pape supplies an even more ambitious sort of effect: "Ergo ut caeruleam sensit crebrescere noctem" (112). "Caeruleam" shows a return to the Greek as an indication of color. Pape, probably following the standard definition of *cyaneos*, "caeruleus, niger, uel inter nigrum, et uiridem," has seen in Mousaios's line not just a diminution of light, but a suggestive richness of shading, a richness rendered aurally in "caeruleam" / "crebrescere."

For the most part, however, the metrical translators use their interpretive freedom to file down some of the edges that the Aldine version keeps visible. The crux of *lychnon acouō*, given honestly in the Aldine translation as "lucernam audio," is a good example. Delamare mutes the effect slightly by altering the second half of the line: "Audio nanque facem, paritérque natare Leandrum" (sig. A5^r). The use of indirect discourse for Leander implies for the *fax* as well reportage of content rather than transmission of sound. On the other hand, Vatel rationalistically insists in his commentary, "Mousaios imagines that he hears the torch crackling and Leander swimming" (sig. A6^r). The other translators completely revise the statement:

> Iam mihi Leandrum uideor spectare natantem:
> Et lychnon . . .
>
> [Pape, 5–6]

> Lychnum inquam, et manibus pellentem salsa Leandrum
> [Paolini, p. 166]

Other features of the original also go against the grain. Vatel (sig. A8^v) excuses Delamare for using the word *amor* twice in one line by pointing to a similar repetition in the Greek (29); but usually the translator does not put his commentator on this particular spot. For example, Delamare reduces the six occurrences of *lychnos* in the first twenty-seven lines to five, and uses four different words to translate them. Paolini uses two different words, although he keeps all six occurrences; Pape reduces them to four, and uses three different words. None repeats his translation of *cyanopeplos* when the word recurs in the Greek. The preference for elegant variation over obsessive repetition is persistent:

> ἀγγελίην ἀνέμιμνε φαεινομένων ὑμεναίων,
> μαρτυρίην λύχνοιο πολυκλαύτοιο δοκεύων,
> εὐνῆς δὲ κρυφίης τηλεσκόπον ἀγγελιώτην.
>
> [235–37]

> *Nuncium* expectabat lucentium nuptiarum,
> Testimonium lucernae lugubris expectans,
> Lectíque clandestini procul speculantem *nuncium*.
>
> [Aldine]

> Lumina perquirens genialis *nuncia* lecti,
> Vestigánsque oculis defletae foedera thedae:
> Et *signa* occulto longe speculata cubili.
>
> [Delamare, sig. D3^v]

Dum data lucerent hymeneïa *signa*, manebas:
Luminis indicium expectans, miserabile quondam,
Pignoráque occulti procul affulgentia lecti.

[Pape]

Clara morabatur lucentis *signa* hymenaei
Obsidis expectans lachrymosae lumina testae,
Lumina furtiui quae late *nuntia* lecti.

[Paolini, p. 173]

Nor are these translators particularly keen on sonic repetition; in translating the lines cited by Schoeck, all use the *femina | mina* pair, but it comes to comparatively little:

Audiit ille libens stimulos, et uerba minarum:
Protinus agnoscens persuasae signa puellae.
Foemina nanque uiro iuueni si quando minatur,
Nuncia sunt ueneris, terrentia uerba, minaéque.

[Delamare, sig. C2ʳ]

Talibus illa minis, sibi conuenientibus, usa est.
Foemineas ergo Leander ubi audiit iras,
Protinus agnouit persuasae signa puellae.
Ardenti iuueni cùm foemina nanque minatur,
Nempe minis etiam uerum testatur amorem.

[Pape, 128–32]

His minitata, decent teneras quae uerba puellas,
Foemineas ast ille minas postquam auribus hausit,
Haud dubia agnouit uictae argumenta puellae:
Quando etenim cupido minitatur foemina amanti,
Nuntia sunt Veneris furti minitantia uerba.

[Paolini, p. 170][53]

The tradition of Latin metrical translation thus reveals throughout the century (Delamare's version was first published in 1514, Paolini's in 1587) a perception of Mousaios's style as at least partly problematic. This subtle diversion of the style toward the prevailing modes of gentility is evidenced in the vernacular versions as well. There are some very specific points of general agreement; nobody in any language seems to be able to swallow *lychnon acouō*:

> J'oy Leander desia nover, ce semble,
> Et flamboyer le flambeau tout ensemble
>
> [Marot, 11–12]

> Ecco e già parmi udir, che tu mi dica
> Del notator Leandro, e de la face
>
> [Baldi, 9–10]

> *Abydus* and faire *Sestus*, where I heare
> The Night-hid Nuptials of young *Hero* were.
> *Leanders* swimming to her; and a Light
>
> [Chapman, 7–9]

In the tradition's most radical act of surgery, the Meistersinger Hans Sachs cuts away almost all trace of the Greek text from "Die unglück-hafft lieb Leandri mit fraw Ehron" (1541). Mousaios is invoked by name at the start—

> Hört zu gar ein kleglich geschicht,
> Die uns Museus hat bericht!

—but what interested Mousaios at greatest length, the choreography of courtship, is jettisoned almost entirely, and the rest is told essentially in Sachs's own words, with graceful but unpretentious efficiency:

> Als nun die finster nacht anprach,
> Ersach Leander das warzeichen,
> Thet doch von grosser forcht erbleichen
> Ob dem grausamen meer ungstüm.
> Sprang doch darein und wend sich ümb,
> Dem liecht nach zu dem thuren schwam.
> Ero ihn freudenreich auff namb.
> Sie trücknet sein nasse gelider.
> Da er sein krefft erholet wider,
> Da pflagen sie der süssen lieb,
> Die nacht in hoher freud vertrieb.
> Vor der morgenröt urlaub numb.
> Leander wider uber schwumb.

"Finster" may be a dwindled version of Mousaios's second *cyanopeplos* (232), but the condensation is so drastic that verbal parallels are probably accidental; Sachs's first two lines here, for example, paraphrase six lines of Greek (232–37), and the whole passage corresponds to over fifty lines in the original (232–85). Sachs tells the entire story in sixty-six lines, plus a six-line "Beschluss" ("Wo noch so fleischlich liebe brend . . .") that is his only notable ornament to the simple narrative lines of the story. Mousaios's verbal fanciness is discarded without apparent regret.

Other tellers, however, involve themselves in much closer and more complex negotiations with the actual words of the original. The seminal work in many ways seems to have been Bernardo Tasso's *Favola di Leandro et d'Hero* (1537).[54] Neither a translation nor a substantially new work, it weaves continually in and out of the Greek poem during its 679 lines, with numerous substitutions, rearrangements, and inter-polations; but it always returns to some unmistakable feature from Mousaios. At the start of the narrative proper, immediately after the invocation, both poets begin with almost exactly the same words:

$$Σηστὸς ἔην καὶ Ἄβυδος . . .$$

[16]

[There was Sestos, and Abydos . . .]

Sesto et Abido . . .

[p. 356]

But Tasso stretches the exposition that follows to receive an intruded gloss:

$$γείτονές εἰσι πόλῃες. \overset{ἐναντίον ἐγγύθι πόντου·}{}$$

[opposite near the sea. They are neighboring cities.]

il mar famoso, et empio
La, dove Xerse con armati legni
Pose a l'orgoglio suo si duro giogo,
Divide con brevissimo intervallo . . .

Perhaps in compensation, Tasso ignores lines 17–19 of the Greek, and skips to lines 20–21:

$$ἱμερόεις τε Λέανδρος ἔην καὶ παρθένος Ἡρώ.$$
$$ἡ μὲν Σηστὸν ἔναιεν, ὁ δὲ πτολίεθρον Ἀβύδου . . .$$

[They were desirable Leander and virgin Hero. She dwelt in Sestos, he in the city of Abydos . . .]

These lines are condensed into one, with the rhetorical balance preserved, but not filling up the line—

> Leandro in questa, in quella Hero

—and are followed by a new exposition:

> le luci
> Sotto un'influsso di maligne stelle
> A le miserie de la vita aperse.

The omitted Greek lines recount the beginning of the lovers' passion: Tasso is emphasizing their tragedy over their pleasures by moving this bit of foreshadowing up from line 27, though he keeps Mousaios's stars from line 22. This small shift suggests a larger reorganization of the story's emotional balance; for the time being, however, Tasso returns to the original, with its encouragement to the tourist-reader to go and see Hero's tower:

> σὺ δ' εἴ ποτε κεῖθι περήσεις . . .
>
> [23]

> [And if you ever go there . . .]

> Tu, che cercando pellegrino et vago . . .

Having mentioned the tower, Tasso then skips lines 26–29 of the Greek to go directly to the description of Hero's domestic life in lines 30 ff. And so on, through the whole of Mousaios's poem.

Certain features of the original are more or less systematically dropped. Tasso generally has no direct equivalent for the more dramatic adjectival effects of the Greek; *polyphloisboio* (234) disappears altogether: "Longo il lito del mar sempre rimira" (p. 366). But the adjectival texture of the Italian is by no means spare; a parallel consideration of the two poems might lead to the conclusion that the Greek modifiers are simply diffused and spread out in the process of translation:

> παρθενικῆς δ' εὔοδμον εὔχροον αὐχένα κύσσας . . .
>
> [133]

> [Kissing the nicely smelling, nicely complexioned neck of the virgin . . .]

> Percio dal collo suo bianco et gentile
> Involandone un bascio dolce et caro . . .
>
> [p. 361]

Two overlapping strong adjectives applied to one object become four different mild adjectives applied to two objects; Mousaios's effect of convergence (*eu . . . eü . . . au*) is replaced by one of dispersal. Like the Latin metrical translators, Tasso subscribes to a theory of elegant variation: he usually succeeds in not repeating words, especially not adjectives, within hearing distance of each other. But it is probably a mistake to think of these particular adjectives as a response to this particular Greek line; rather, they, like most of Tasso's adjectives, merely drift in from the prevailing diction of Italian lyricism: *molle*, *lieto*, *gentile*, *dolce*, and so on. Such words are used at literally almost every possible opportunity; they in a sense replace *en bloc* Mousaios's own repertoire of key words, which Tasso does not keep in any systematic fashion. But Tasso's repertoire is of a different kind, not a vehicle of emphasis, but one of continual mollification. On the whole, Tasso's diction has none of the inscrutable angularity of Mousaios's terms, but instead directly supports a single, obvious emotional "tone"—and that tone itself is one of relative softness: "Mosse con lenti passi il gentil piede..." (p. 360).

Along with these adjectives, Tasso adds a good deal of interstitial decoration. There is a great concern with colors:

> Hor vedendo il Pianeta alto et sovrano
> Et di ceruleo, et di color di fiamma
> Tinto, tuffarsi a l'onde d'occidente . . .
>
> [p. 372]

Mousaios probably provides the starting point for this:

> ὡς δ᾽ ἴδε κυανέης λιποφεγγέα νυκτὸς ὀμίχλην . . .
>
> [238]

[And when he saw the light-leaving cloud of blue-green night . . .]

"Ceruleo" could have come from *cyaneēs*; it certainly does not come from the Aldine Latin: "Vt uero uidit nigrae obscuram noctis caliginem." But even recourse to the Greek does not fully account for Tasso's effect; he plays "ceruleo" off, not against the dark ("inter nigrum, et uiridem"), but against another brightness, "color di fiamma." "Tinto" is the cue: these are lines by a countryman of Botticelli.

Tasso also has an immense growth of ambient detail, especially of plants:

> La fanciulletta con le chiome d'oro,
> Ove ricchi legami Amor tessea,
> Sovra gli homeri sparse, hor di frondose
> Ghirlande fatte con sottil lavoro,
> Il crine ornava de la santa Dea;
> Hor dal bel grembo suo pioggia di rose
> Sovra l'ornato altar lieta spargea.

[p. 358]

By extrapolation of this tendency, the water through which Leander swims becomes minutely alive and itself actively erotic:

> Gli amorosi Delphini a paro a paro
> De la sua compagnia lieti et contenti
> Givan solcando il mar queto et tranquillo;
> Le figlie di Nereo per l'onde salse
> Scherzando co i Trittoni in lieta schiera,
> Sovra i lascivi pesci ivano intorno . . .

[p. 367][55]

It is as though the erotic energy that in Mousaios manifests itself as general excitation bursts out here as décor—a shift that might be said to account for the relative gentleness, even languor, of the action in Tasso's poem: "Co basci interrompendo le parole, / Disse" (p. 369). That is the equivalent to Hero's *iache*, which Tasso probably encountered as *ennepe*; it is significant that Tasso felt moved to "heighten" the scene, and also that he did so not by energizing the verb, but by surrounding it with kisses.

The most time-consuming of Tasso's interpolations, however, are of a different sort: his apostrophes to numerous addressees of varying abstractness. These are not without precedent in Mousaios (e.g., the instructions to the tourist-reader), but Tasso works them up into a major part of his narrative style. Thus the invocation, which in the Greek is simply to an unnamed *thea*, in the Italian is addressed successively to the twin cities (12 lines), the "lucerna" (8 lines), and the "Santa madre d'Amor" (13 lines). The pseudo-Christian resonance of this last is everywhere audible; here, for instance, is Hero, in a completely new but quite typical speech, praying for Leander's safety:

> O Dea, che l'ampio, et dilettoso regno
> Reggi del terzo ciel con pace eterna,

> Madre di quel diletto, et di quel bene,
> Che fa la vita qui dolce et soave . . .

> [p. 374]

But even when hewing close to the original, Tasso contrives to strike a similar note; Leander's praise of Hero as a new Aphrodite and Athena (135 ff.) becomes:

> O piu degna del Ciel, che de la terra,
> Che mortale non sei . . .

> [p. 361]

Certain of the semimystical hints in the original are seized on eagerly:

> Santo silentio de pensier celati
> De le fanciulle messaggiero accorto,
> Tu con parole tacite, et con cenni
> Dimostri il vero a le dubbiose menti:
> Luce importuna, o pur garrulo augello
> Giamai non turbi il tuo tranquillo stato.

> [p. 362]

This is Tasso's revision of lines 164–65 (see p. 78 above); the religious nimbus is intensified, and a *sententia* converted into an apostrophe.

Most of the apostrophes for which Tasso is directly responsible are from the narrator to various agents in the narrative; and in general few of these apostrophes can really be called part of the story, since no response is usually expected from the recipients. Rather, these speeches are directed *at* the story, to invest the action with a certain emotive aura—with, to use the technical term, "pathos."[56] The covert addressee all along is the reader, whose response is being instructed; and we may even be specific as to what that instruction is: *piange*. Tasso's poem is a tear-jerker:

> Cantate meco homai Sesto et Abido,
> Ah misere Citta, meco cantate;
> Anzi piangete il grave danno vostro,
> Piangete meco il vostro alto dolore . . .

> [p. 355]

That is the start of the poem, though most of the overtly lachrymose outbursts occur, understandably, toward the end. The last part of the poem, after the consummation, is particularly expanded in Tasso's version, and mostly by such apostrophes to the dawn, the winds, and

so on. Up to about line 450, which corresponds to line 288 in Mousaios, Tasso stays fairly close to the original, never digressing for more
than a dozen or so lines at a time; but while Mousaios then hurries up
the conclusion, Tasso draws it out. Leander's return to Sestos after his
first night with Hero occurs more than four-fifths of the way through
Mousaios's version, but only about two-thirds of the way through
Tasso's. Tasso extends the falling action to make it more commensurate
with the rising, and, as we have seen, alters certain local details for the
same purpose.

The shift toward the maudlin in a way underlies the entire mode of
the poem, elaboration into deliquescence. The expansions do not intensify but etiolate the central impact, vaporize it, as it were, into aura,
"tone." At the center of Tasso's *Favola* there remains the old vision of
Italian poetry, the vision going back to Dante and Cavalcanti, of an
Eros at once sexual, religious, and intellectual; but the vision in Tasso
is quieted and decorated:

> Amor, che ad ogni cosa era presente,
> Senza più ritrovar contesa o schermo,
> Per la strada de gli occhi andando al core,
> Con ombre oscure, et color chiari et vivi,
> Pinse la bella Idea del giovenetto;
> U come in specchio trasparente et bello
> L'anima pargoletta si mirava,
> Co i lumi intenti, et con la lingua muta.
>
> [p. 362]

The sweep of that opening is involuted into the wide-eyed hypnosis of
childhood—and not that of *La Vita Nuova*, but of another Dantesque
locus:

> Esce di mano a lui che la vagheggia
>   Prima che sia, a guisa di fanciulla
>   Che piangendo e ridendo pargoleggia,
> L'anima semplicetta che sa nulla,
>   Salvo che, mossa da lieto fattore,
>   Volentier torna a ciò che la trastulla.
>
> [*Purg.* 16.85–90]

Tasso's "Idea" is less a matter of the intellect than of aesthetic, indeed
painterly, effect: "Con ombre oscure, et color chiari et vivi"—as
though visual glitter and elegance had been imposed on a line from

72921

Cavalcanti, "Diafan dal lume d'una schuritade" (*Donna me prega* 17).
But then Tasso merely exemplifies the evolution of Italian erotic poetry
in general, whose Muse became "Amore, / Che concetti donasse a
l'intelletto" (p. 364)—conceptions metamorphosing into conceits.
Stylistically, Tasso's poem is a specimen of languid late Petrarchanism,
a tradition which systematized the erotic vision into motifs and effects
(the apostrophe is particularly Petrarchan). Something of the same sort
may, of course, be said for the school of Nonnos, except for the languor; the Greek tradition's approach to its own données is furious, not
limp. Tasso retells Mousaios's story so as to fit the autumnal mood of
another kind of decadence.

That mood became the starting point for a more ambitious telling of
the story, this time in Castilian:

> Canta con boz suave, y dolorosa
> O Musa, los amores lastimeros,
> Que'n suave dolor fueron criados

So begins Juan Boscán Almogáver's *Historia de Leandro y Hero*, first
published (posthumously) in 1543. It was the most substantial, if not
necessarily the most vital, part of Boscán's effort to get the Renaissance
going in Spanish literature, in particular to transplant the ambience of
"suave dolor." It is clear that Tasso's *Favola* provided both instigation
and example.[57] Boscán's *versos sueltos*, a major innovation in Spanish
poetry, obviously copy the Italian meter; and Boscán also adapts some
of Tasso's incidental decoration, such as the nymphs that surround
Leander as he swims:

> Estando en la mitad de su jornada,
> Agora, padeciendo ora, venciendo.
> Saliole Doris con sus hijas todas:
> Y todas le tomaron alli en medio,
> Por podelle valer en su trabajo.

> [2129–33]

But it is also clear that Boscán was working from Mousaios as well, and
the most important feature of Tasso's example may have been his way
of swerving in and out of the original. Like Tasso, Boscán never really
drops the original, though the digressions become longer and longer
as he progresses, much longer than the digressions in the Italian. Indeed,
the *Historia* is the prize expansion of Mousaios's poem, at 2,793 lines;

the combined Marlowe-Chapman version is only 2,376 lines, and does not really count, since it abandons the original fairly early.

Part of the reason for this great length is a local diffuseness of procedure; Boscán responds to some of the more impacted effects of the Greek by becoming very talkative:

μαρμαρυγὴν χαρίεσσαν ἀπαστράπτουσα προσώπου . . .

[56]

[hurling a graceful dazzle from her face . . .]

> Entrava con sus rayos d'hermosura,
> Aca, y alla mil gracias descubriendo:
> Mil gracias, que'ncubrir no se podian.

[127–29]

Possibly this expansion is a substitute for evocative diction, particularly adjectives. There are no adjectives (except for "mil") in the three lines above, while in the next line Boscán uses one, a mild equivalent for the one in the Greek, and seems content to pass on, thus producing a rare line-for-line translation:

οἷά τε λευκοπάρῃος ἐπαντέλλουσα σελήνη.

[57]

[such as the white-cheeked moon gives off.]

> Como salir la blanca aurora suele

[130]

Boscán, of course, lacked Tasso's stilnovist heritage—it was exactly such a heritage that he wanted to create—and it is thus not surprising that his adjectival texture is generally quite thin. Compare their handling of a typical virtuoso line of Mousaios:

> Percio dal collo suo bianco et gentile
> Involandone un bascio dolce et caro . . .

[p. 361]

> Y assi no desmayo, antes fiando
> D'un dulce enternecer, que'n si sentia . . .

[587–88]

The kiss itself has disappeared in Boscán—an interesting fact—and the whole overloaded moment has shrunk to a single "dulce," probably taken directly from Tasso.

When Boscán does use adjectives with any density, he tends to repeat himself very quickly, as with "suave" and "dolorosa" in the opening lines, or with two other adjectives shortly thereafter:

> Testigo fiel, y dulce mensagera
> De dos fieles, y dulces amadores.
>
> [8–9]

These lines are repeated almost verbatim near the end of the poem (2770–71), as though in imitation of Mousaios's *lychnou sbennymenoio* (15,338). The verbal repetition within the phrase is similarly Mousaian in principle, as is the rhetorical parallelism. Indeed, conspicuous rhetorical balance, atypical of Tasso, is one of Boscán's major tools of expansion, often from a specific analogue in the Greek:

> El yr del uno, el esperar del otro,
> El dessear, y el acudir conforme,
> La lumbre muerta, y a Leandro muerto.
>
> [17–19]

The last line is a fairly direct translation of the Greek, though somewhat cruder than the original:

> λύχνου σβεννυμένοιο καὶ ὀλλυμένοιο Λεάνδρου.
>
> [15]

[the lantern quenched and dead Leander.]

For chiastic variation Boscán has substituted parallel repetition: "muerta" / "muerto." The balance of the line seems to be exerting a magnetic effect on the previous lines, which fall into similar patterns without warrant in the Greek. A further-reaching influence seems to be exerted by three other lines, which Tasso trimmed to less than one:

> ἱμερόεις τε Λέανδρος ἔην καὶ παρθένος Ἡρώ.
> ἡ μὲν Σηστὸν ἔναιεν, ὁ δὲ πτολίεθρον Ἀβύδου,
> ἀμφοτέρων πολίων περικαλλέες ἀστέρες ἄμφω . . .
>
> [20–22]

[They were desirable Leander and virgin Hero. She dwelt in Sestos, he in the city of Abydos, both the very beautiful stars of both cities . . .]

In Boscán the vicinity not only of these lines, but of every mention of the cities in the opening paragraphs is affected:

> Canta tambien la triste mar en medio,
> Y a Sesto d'una parte, y d'otra Abydo,
> Y Amor aca, y alla, yendo, y viniendo . . .
>
> [4–6]

> Sesto, y Abydo fueron dos lugares:
> A los quales en frente uno del otro;
> Est'en Asia, y aquel siendo en Europa . . .
>
> [20–22]

> Y en ambos dio con una sola flecha:
> Dando en el coraçon d'un gentil moço,
> Y en otro coraçon d'una donzella.
> Los nombres de los quales, eran estos:
> Era Leandro el del: y el d'ella Hero:
> Iguales en linage, y en hazienda,
> En valer, en saber, y en hermosura.
> El estava en Abydo, y ella en Sesto.
> D'ambos lugares ambos eran gloria . . .
>
> [31–39]

In the later sections of the poem especially, a single rhetorical pattern, once set off, can go on for half a dozen lines almost unchanged (e.g. 510–18).

In other regards, Boscán's additions and changes are often more substantive than Tasso's. The Petrarchanization of the lovers in the *Favola* is largely a matter of tone and suggestion; Boscán, however, systematically expands and alters narrative details along lines suggested by Castiglione, whose *Il Cortegiano* Boscán had translated.[58] Boscán also makes major use of *contaminatio* from other classical sources, including the *Heroides* and, most notoriously, Vergil.[59] After the lovers' first meeting, Leander looks for Hero's signal for six nights without seeing it, and Boscán interrupts his story:

> Pero quiça querran saber algunos
> Atentos en leer toda esta istoria:
> Por donde fue, que Hero no pudiesse,
> Tan presto hazer su seña desseada.
> Yo lo dire, si con plazer me'scuchan:
> Y me dan facultad que me divierta
> Un poco, del proposito empeçado.
>
> [1112–18]

There follows (1119–1570; "un poco"?) without further explanation a fairly literal translation from the *Georgics* (4.317–529), the story of how the beekeeper Aristaeus trapped Proteus and heard the story of Orpheus and Eurydice. Then, says Boscán, Proteus went to Neptune to complain about his treatment and received in compensation a gift of prophecy, which he exercised in week-long public ceremonies at various cities. His visit to Sestos happened to come immediately after the lovers' meeting, and Hero's father forced her to participate. Around line 2000 or so, Boscán begins to reenter the story as Mousaios told it.

To some extent the digression contains its own justification, in the digression within the digression: Vergil's authority may be invoked to legitimate interpolating stories only tangentially related to the business at hand. But on a simply narrative plane the Aristaeus-Orpheus nexus —they were rivals for Eurydice, and Aristaeus unintentionally caused her death—is tighter than the Hero-Proteus nexus; and Vergil states the connection at the beginning of the digression. Boscán simply starts in with the promise that the digression will eventually reveal its own relevance.

Boscán's poem is all in all a much less assured accomplishment than Tasso's, and the comparison shows, to the disadvantage of the former, their respective cultural situations. Tasso insinuates the story into an existing if somewhat flaccid tradition; exactly because he is translating *into* something, he can do this by numerous small but cumulatively insidious alterations. Boscán, wanting to create a literary ambience by imitation, gets fouled by the manifest externality of his effects. Almost all effects seem external when new; they only appear inevitable when they have been in use for awhile. Genius provides some exceptions to this rule, but Boscán does not. Still, clanking artificiality can be worked with poetically (anything can), as it is, after all, in Mousaios's poem; in certain ways Boscán's telling is much closer to the Greek than Tasso's is.

But Boscán's specific problem is that his foregrounding of machinery suits so badly with the proclaimed "tone" of "suave dolor" (itself an importation). The location of his major digression shows, perhaps, an unarticulated awareness of this. By putting it shortly before the consummation, he reversed Tasso's tendency toward equalizing the rising and falling actions, the pre- and the postcoital. The very interruption heightens the glitter of the sexual act, and not the aftermath, as the point of reference—so much more appropriately, in a way, for a poem intended to start a literary tradition. In his uneven, creaky manner, Boscán, more than any other sixteenth-century teller of the story, looks forward to Marlowe.

Tasso and Boscán also anticipate Marlowe in a more obvious way. Marlowe's poem is written at least partly in a similar relation to the original text, which is subjected to abridgements and expansions, but to which the author is nevertheless always returning. Partly in reaction to such practice, another tradition developed of careful literalism, of more or less direct translation of the original. Bernardino Baldi, by his own account, had already completed a version of Mousaios's poem when a look at Tasso's *Favola* pricked his conscience as a translator: "Havendola ... con diligenza veduta, e confrontata con la Greca, mi accorsi chiaramente, che non solo egli non traduce, ma (trattone alcuni concetti ch'egli prende dal Poeta) la forma à suo modo." Baldi then revised his own version according to a new principle:

> cioè di premere quanto più per me si potesse le pedate del Poeta Greco, e stringermi al possibile à lui, accioche in questo modo potessero i nostri vedere piu d'appresso le bellezze native, delle quali cotanto abondantemente egli adornò questo leggiadrissimo Poema suo . . . .

Baldi's earlier translation has not survived and may not have really existed; in any case, the translation that Baldi did publish in 1585 seems directly dependent on Tasso, and can often be interpreted simply as an editing of that version according to a criterion of lexical fidelity:

> παρθενικῆς δ' εὔοδμον ἐύχροον αὐχένα κύσσας,
> τοῖον μῦθον ἔειπε πόθου βεβολημένος οἴστρῳ.
>
> [133–34]

[kissing the nicely smelling, nicely complexioned neck of the virgin, he spoke these words, stung by the goad of desire.]

> Percio dal collo suo bianco et gentile
> Involandone un bascio dolce et caro,
> In tai parole la sua lingua sciolse.
>
> [Tasso, p. 361]

> Da stimoli d'Amor percosso, e punto,
> Baciando il bianco, et odorato collo
> Di lei, sciolse la lingua, e cosi disse.
>
> [Baldi, 206–08]

"Bianco," it would seem, is retained as an interpretive but reasonable equivalent of *euchroon* (color replacing evaluation). "Dolce," as an equivalent for *euodmon*, is sharpened to "odorato" and applied to the correct noun; indeed, Tasso's "bascio" is not even there to be modified any more, since Baldi imitates the grammatical structure of the first line of the Greek exactly. Tasso's adjectives of general pleasance, "gentile" and "caro," which have no specific justification in the Greek, disappear entirely here and throughout the translation. It is a fairly effective principle of Baldi's version that there is no important word in it without some specific source in Mousaios.

If Baldi does not "contaminate" the Greek with anything of his own, at least on a lexical level, there are nevertheless certain qualifications to his claims of fidelity. One of these he admits in his preface:

> E vero nondimeno che molte volte io non mi sono in tutto obligato
> à gli epiteti Greci, e ciò parte per non haverli potuti trasferire con
> vaghezza nella nostra lingua, parte per non haver io giudicata
> necessaria questa diligenza quasi superstitiosa.

Baldi's general response to this problem is debasement or, sometimes, complete omission: *polydaidalon* (118) becomes "ricco" (184), *polyphloisboio* (234) becomes "fremente" (365); *cyanopeplon* (113) becomes "profonda" (176), and the second occurrence of the same adjective (232) disappears entirely (it should be in or around 361). The effect of the Greek adjectives thus simply fades throughout Baldi's version.

Despite the pruning, moreover, Baldi manages to be as wordy as Tasso, if not more so. We may refer back to the lines quoted above, where Baldi and Tasso both take three lines of Italian to translate two lines of Greek. Baldi's whole translation is 524 lines—not notably shorter than Tasso's, in view of the latter's interpolations. At the time of the example given, in fact, Baldi is more than forty lines out in front. Baldi does have in this particular casea requirement which comes up periodically, that of including from the Greek something Tasso omits: "Da stimoli d'Amor percosso, e punto." Such instances, however, are not overly common, and this one gives evidence of a more compelling reason for the length of Baldi's translation, his use of doublets: "percosso e punto" for *bebolēmenos*. With elision, Baldi is using the same number of syllables as the Greek word, and the two Italian words do serve the legitimate lexical purpose of stating two distinguishable nuances of the original term. Two lines later, though, the same habit serves a much slacker purpose: "sciolse la lingua, e cosi disse." The first phrase is really the best evidence in these lines for Baldi's primary reliance on Tasso's wording; it is hard to see what else the locution is doing here, especially when its narrative content is immediately restated. One is tempted to try to redo the lines:

> Da stimoli d'Amor punto, baciando
> Il bianco et odorato collo, disse.

Baldi's criterion of literalness does not compel him to sacrifice a fairly leisurely quality to his style; and since, unlike Tasso, he has nothing special to add to the original, the result is simple dilution. Mousaios's rhetorical balances are particularly subject to expansion, as in the lines immediately following those quoted above:

> Κύπρι φίλη μετὰ Κύπριν, Ἀθηναίη μετ᾽ Ἀθήνην
>
> [135]

> Ciprigna, à me dopò Ciprigna cara,
> Minerva à me dopo Minerva amica
>
> [209–10]

"Cara" and "amica" are legitimate explications of the Greek phrases, and not the automatic dosage of sweetener that they would be in Tasso. Still, like Poe's glory and grandeur, they hover uncertainly between parallelism and contrast, and do little to intensify the rhetoric in compensation for the expansion. Compare what Clément Marot does with almost exactly the same strategy:

> Chere Venus, apres Venus la gente,
> Noble Pallas, apres Pallas prudente
>
> [245–46]

Marot has a *use* for the antithesis; Baldi really does not. Elsewhere Baldi's expansions of Mousaios's balances are unemphatically asymmetrical:

> L'un di lor gratioso hebbe Leandro
> Nome, e la verginella appellossi Ero.
>
> [32–33]

And in the related matter of verbal repetitions, Baldi subscribes to the same canons as do Delamare, Pape, and Paolini:

λύχνον ἀπαγγέλλοντα διακτορίην Ἀφροδίτης,
Ἡροῦς νυκτιγάμοιο γαμοστόλον ἀγγελιώτην . . .

[6–7]

De la face cortese apportatrice
De le novelle di Ciprigna, ed'Ero,
Notturna sposa pronuba, e messaggia

[11–13]

Apangellonta is "apportatrice," while *angeliōtēn* is "messaggia"; *nycti-gamoio* is "Notturna sposa," while *gamostolon* is "pronuba." Shortly thereafter, *angeliēn* (12) is translated as "ambasciatrice" (21). In the course of the first paragraph, *lychnos* is successively "foco," "face," and "facella."

The cumulative effect is that Baldi takes more away from Tasso's version than he restores. Some of the vigor of the action in the original is reintroduced as a result of Baldi's superior scholarship; he unmistakably translates *iache* (267), if a bit mildly: "indi proruppe / In queste dolci, et amorose note" (411–12). And in an example given above he restores the agitation of Leander *pothou bebolēmenos oistrōi*, even if his placement of the Italian phrase keeps it from implying, as strongly as the Greek does, Leander's actual style of speech. But this is not enough to restore anything like the full stylistic vigor of the original, and Baldi has nothing of Tasso's own resources to compensate.

Marot's version (1541), which I have already had occasion to use as a counterexample, is a consistently firmer accomplishment, and shows what could be done even within Baldi's own ground rules. Marot does not announce his intentions as Baldi does; but internal evidence, reinforced by external probability, suggests that Tasso was behind this translation as well. There are numerous small but cumulatively impressive parallels between Marot's and Tasso's phrasing, particularly with regard to adjectives. *Euchroon* (133) is "blanc" (242), as though from Tasso's "bianco" (p. 361); *eustephanou* (220), "well-garlanded," becomes "bell," in the Italian (p. 365), "gratieuse et belle" in the French (396); Hero's *pyrgos ouranomēcēs* (187), "heaven-high tower," is called a "gran torre" by Tasso (p. 364), a "grand tour" by Marot (341), and both poets are taken enough by that phrase to use it elsewhere without prompting in the Greek (Tasso, p. 357; Marot, 8). Also like Tasso, Marot drops *polyphoisboio* (234): "sur le bord de la mer" (421). On occasion the verbal parallels are thick and rather complex:

αὐτὰρ ὁ θαρσαλέως μετεκίαθεν ἐγγύθι κούρης,
ὡς ἴδε κυανόπεπλον ἐπιθρώσκουσαν ὀμίχλην.
ἠρέμα δὲ θλίβων ῥοδοειδέα δάκτυλα κούρης
βυσσόθεν ἐστενάχιζεν ἀθέσφατον.

[112–15]

Sed ipse audacter adibat prope puellam,
Vt uidit atratas insurgere tenebras,
Tacite quidem stringens roseos digitos puellae,
Ex imo suspirabat uehementer.

[Aldine]

[Then he marched boldly up to the girl when he saw spring up
the cloud clothed in blue-green. Quietly squeezing the roselike
fingers of the girl, he groaned deeply and inexpressibly.]

Da le tenebre cui fatto securo
Il desioso amante, sospirando
La bianca man de la fanciulla strinse

[p. 360]

Parquoy, voyant le jouvenceau Leandre
De toutes parts les tenebres s'espandre,
Plus hardiment d'elle s'approcher ose,
Et luy serra les doigtz plus blancz que rose,
Et souspirant

[207–11]

"Tenebres" and "souspirant" may, of course, have come from the Latin.
Marot and Tasso, however, both omit "uehementer"; and what about
Hero's white hand? It looks there as if Marot, sharing the sexual taste
of his contemporary for the marmoreal, adopted the alteration while
still retaining a link to the original text: "plus blancz que rose."

The apparent sympathy with the motives behind Tasso's alterations
is important; for though Marot's version is, like Baldi's, a more or less
"straight" translation, it is not done, as Baldi's is, in a spirit of antagonism
toward the more paraphrastic tradition represented by Tasso. Some of
Tasso's smaller habits of expansion and alteration have quite direct
analogues in Marot; the French writer, for example, has no scruples
about introducing certain simple adjectives ad lib:

τοῖα μὲν ἠιθέων τις ἐφώνεεν ...

[84]

[One of the young men said this . . .]

> Ainsi disoyent maintz gratieux et doulx
> Jeunes amants.
>
> [157–58]

ἀνδράσιν ὕπνον ἄγουσα καὶ οὐ ποθέοντι Λεάνδρῳ.

[233]

[bringing sleep to men, but not to lusting Leander.]

> Et les humains rendoit par tout dormants,
> Fors Leander, le plus beau des amants
>
> [419–20]

(The list of favorite terms is roughly the same as Tasso's, though Marot has little use for *vivace* and *santo*, and shows a new interest in *riche* and *grand*.) More often than Tasso does, however, Marot contrives to have his added adjectives attach to some definite suggestion in the Greek:

Ἡρὼ μὲν χαρίεσσα, διοτρεφὲς αἷμα λαχοῦσα . . .

[30]

[Graceful Hero, descended from noble blood . . .]

> Hero jadis, pleine de bonne grace,
> Née de riche et de gentille race . . .
>
> [57–58]

ἔσχατα τιμήεντος ἄγων ἐπὶ κεύθεα νηοῦ.

[119]

[leading into the farthest depths of the venerated temple.]

> la menant adoncq
> A l'un des bouts du temple, grand et long
>
> [217–18]

The addition of "bonne" to "grace" is objectionable only on grounds of redundancy, not inaccuracy. "Riche" and "gentille" give two nuances of *diotrephes*; the first is perhaps more suspect than the second, but not indefensible in the context of the poem (cf. Mousaios, 125). More daringly, Marot makes the Greek temple into a French cathedral; he may almost be said to imply that the building is holy because it is so impressive architecturally. But this alteration does demonstrably explicate, in contemporary terms, something in the original text.

Of similar import is Marot's diction when translating individual
words more directly. As may be seen in the parallels cited above, Marot
follows Tasso's lead in deescalating many of the more elaborate and
energetic words in the original. In the same way that *eustephanou* becomes
"bell'," so *himeroeis* (20) becomes "aggreable" (38), *polydaidalon* (118)
becomes "riche" (216; like Baldi's "ricco"); *daidaleon* (340), like *polyphloisboio*, disappears altogether (595). And as in Tasso, something more
serious is going on than simply an inability to translate certain terms.
In her addresses to Leander, the Greek Hero calls him *xeinos* (123, 174),
guest and stranger, to remind him, in case he has forgotten, of how
desperate his unexpected advances are. "You're crazy," she tells him:

ξεῖνε, τί μαργαίνεις; τί με, δύσμορε, παρθένον ἕλκεις;

[123]

[Stranger, why are you raving? Why, wretch, do you grab me,
a virgin?]

Hero asks more or less the same questions in Marot, but the offense
against *xenia* has been changed subtly into a much more manageable
faux pas:

Estes vous insensé,
Mon gentilhomme? Entreprenez vous bien
D'ainsi tirer une fille de bien?

[222–24]

A *xeinos* is an outsider, but a "gentilhomme" is already a solid member
of one's own society, and certainly a far less dangerous creature to
receive attention from. This shift is emblematic of Marot's shifts of
diction in general: the overstated gaucheries of the original are being
trimmed to fit a much tidier and comfortable universe. As Tasso's idiom
has a visionary dimension, so Marot's has a social one: the world of
the poem is made polite.

It has been the fame of the French language, from the sixteenth
century on, to have encoded a whole system of social decorum into
its linguistic norms. The genteel and seemingly fragile style of Marot's
translation is actually quite durable stuff; it is still instantly recognizable
as a basic French mode: "la succulence de notre vieille langue," writes
a twentieth-century critic, "rend plus savoureuse encore aujourdhui."[60]
And the same critic, when he describes the Greek poem, is really reading
back into it the spirit of Marot's version: "Ce n'est point un aède qui

chante, c'est un conteur qui dit joliment une histoire." [61] The art of speaking "joliment"—detached and easy in polite company, amused but certainly not mocking—is a fairly inclusive accomplishment, a way of dealing with intensities without actually having to fight them:

> ἡ δὲ θεῆς ἀνὰ νηὸν ἐπῴχετο παρθένος Ἡρὼ
> μαρμαρυγὴν χαρίεσσαν ἀπαστράπτουσα προσώπου ...
>
>   [55–56]

[Virgin Hero went through the goddess' temple, hurling a graceful dazzle from her face ...]

> Dedans le temple où se faisoit la feste,
> Hero marchoit en gravité honneste,
> Rendant par tout de sa face amyable
> Une splendeur à touts yeulx aggreable
>
>   [101–04]

Like Tasso, but to a much greater degree, Marot is translating *into* something. It is worth noting that Marot does not, like Boscán and Baldi, follow Tasso's precedent of using pseudoclassical *versi sciolti*, but puts the story into his native rhymed verse—"en rithme françoise," according to his title page. Like Baldi, Marot takes his time—the whole translation runs to 602 lines, almost twice as long as the original—but here the expansiveness seems merely an extension of the diction, a technique for controlling the energy. Marot, for example, can translate *iache* without breaking stride: "Auquel encor bien fort battoit le poulx" (480). Adjectives not directly debased are similarly treated periphrastically, so that their force is spread out:

> πολυμήχανον ἔννεπε μῦθον.
>
>   [202][62]

[He spoke a very cunning speech.]

> Va dire un mot plein de grand artifice.
>
>   [364]

Leander is no longer tricky and dangerous, just clever and elegant. Simple length may account for Marot's willingness to take over some of Mousaios's verbal repetitions unaltered; throughout the first paragraph "flambeau" appears consistently for *lychnos*, five times, with a variation of Marot's own thrown in gratis: "Et flamboyer le flambeau tout ensemble" (12). But then, Mousaios's opening paragraph is fifteen lines long, Marot's is thirty.

The ultimate significance of Marot's relative fidelity to the original text may thus be in how it reveals the strength of his medium, which can absorb so much of what the original has to offer without getting too excited. Much more than Tasso does, Marot is able to shift the emotional thrust of the poem almost entirely by nudges from within the lexical sense, without the aid of changes or interpolations. And there is, in addition, something about his style that is simply more appropriate to narrative poetry than the style of any previous adapter, perhaps even more appropriate in its way than Mousaios's Greek. For with the sense of social and linguistic decorum comes a real sense of social behavior, and of the role of language in that behavior. In Marot's version we see, as never before in the tradition, people in action—a limited style of action, perhaps, but still recognizably real:

> Adoncq Hero, honteuse de rechef,
> Vers son manteau baissa un peu le chef,
> Et en couvrit sa face illustre et claire,
> Pensant en soy: Hero, que veulx tu faire?
>
> [349–52]

This delicate balance of the external pressure of the occasion—"illustre et claire," the way Leander sees her—and Hero's flickering introspection is barely hinted at in the Greek:

> ὣς φαμένη ῥοδέην ὑπὸ φάρεϊ κρύπτε παρειήν,
> ἔμπαλιν αἰδομένη, σφετέροις δ' ἐπεμέμφετο μύθοις.
>
> [194–95]

[So speaking, she hid her rosy cheek under her cloak, ashamed again, and blamed her words.]

And Tasso is crudely aesthetic and selfish by comparison:

> Et qui tacendo, col bel lembo adorno,
> Come pentita del suo ardir, nascose
> Le guancie cinte di purpurea rosa.
>
> [p. 364]

"Come pentita": merely an outsider's assessment, and no real counter to the lover's fixation on Hero's "bel lembo adorno" and her rosy blush.

Tasso's idiom is that of personal erotic vision, Marot's that of a social fabric.

Marot's translation is in a way the most accomplished version of Mousaios's poem, but it is not, even within the genre of self-consciously literal translation, the most interesting or most ambitious. Chapman's translation, like Baldi's, is prefaced with a critique of his predecessor's more liberal version:

> When you see *Leander* and *Hero*, the Subjects of this Pamphlet; I perswade my self, your prejudice will encrease to the contempt of it; eyther headlong presupposing it, all one; or at no part matcheable, with that partly excellent Poem, of Maister *Marloes*. For your all one; the Workes are in nothing alike; a different Character being held through, both the Stile, Matter, and invention. For the match of it; let but your eyes be Matches, and it will in many parts overmatch it. In the Originall, it being [judged?] by all the most Learned, the incomparable Love-Poem of the world. And I would be somthing sorry, you could justly taxe me, with dooing it any wrong in our English; though perhappes it will not so amble under your seasures and censures, as the before publish't.

Marlowe's was a pretty poem, but you cannot call it Mousaios, let alone "the incomparable Love-Poem of the world." Chapman offers to provide, through his more responsible scholarship, the real thing. Some of this scholarship is displayed for us in a moderately elaborate apparatus of notes, where the Aldine translation is measured against the Greek, and Chapman's own renderings explained and defended (another documented case of reading by triangulation).

But Chapman's attitude toward Marlowe's liberties is by no means as simple as Baldi's toward Tasso's; obviously they could not be, since Chapman was himself implicated in Marlowe's poem. And furthermore, Chapman was not the kind of man to efface his own genius before mere *Wissenschaft*; indeed, he was one of those Renaissance figures whose personal vision realized itself precisely through its own arcane researches. Chapman's individual note is sounded in the first line: "Goddesse relate, the witnesse-bearing-light...." "Light" for *lychnos* echoes the beginning of Chapman's continuation of Marlowe's poem: "New light gives new directions, Fortunes new." "Light" is, in general, one of Chapman's most resonant terms, with special associations: not the

bright expanse of day, but light (rhymes with "night") secret and
guarded within darkness, the "inner light" of poetic inspiration, a
thing that can break out and disrupt the surface, at times with great
energy. The poem itself is called, in the dedication, a "little Light"
shining to "passing few" in the darkness of "Moderne *Barbarisme*."

Chapman follows the Greek faithfully in the repetitions of this key
word throughout the first paragraph of the translation; but he has done
so after picking a word that is, to his mind, worth repeating so emphat-
ically. "Light," in its abstractness, lacks the latent, semimechanical
absurdity of Mousaios's *lychnos*; for the same reason Chapman cannot
maintain this translation throughout the poem, and at the next appearance of the Greek word (25), the object in question has become, more
specifically, a "Torch" (39; still more romantic than a "lantern"). But
"light" thereafter alternates with "torch" as a translation of *lychnos*,
and the two words are occasionally juxtaposed:

> But (deere) take heed, that no ungentle blo're
> Thy Torch extinguish, bearing all the Light
> By which my life sailes

[306–08]

> ἀλλά, φίλη, πεφύλαξο βαρυπνείοντας ἀήτας,
> μή μιν ἀποσβέσσωσι—καὶ αὐτίκα θυμὸν ὀλέσσω—
> λύχνον, ἐμοῦ βιότοιο φαεσφόρον ἡγεμονῆα.

[216–18]

[But, dear, guard against the heavy-blowing winds, lest they extin-
guish—and my heart would also die—the lantern, the light-
bearing commander of my life.]

And Chapman also works his central term into the poem in other
places, to express his characteristic sense of human behavior sustained
by inner illumination:

> every way shee wan
> A following minde in all Men: which their eyes
> Lighted with all their inmost Faculties
> Cleerely confirm'd

[108–11]

> ἡ δ᾽ ἄρα, καλλιθέμεθλον ὅπη κατὰ νηὸν ἀλᾶτο,
> ἑσπόμενον νόον εἶχε καὶ ὄμματα καὶ φρένας ἀνδρῶν.

[71–72]

[Wherever she went through the beautifully built temple, she held men's minds and eyes and hearts following her.]

giving yet some Light
Even by her darke signes, of her kindling fire

[160–61]

νεύμασι λαθριδίοισιν ἐπαγγέλλουσα Λεάνδρῳ.

[106]

[announcing to Leander with secret nods.]

Chapman "allegorizes" Mousaios in roughly the same way that, according to Lord, he "allegorizes" Homer: by minute adjustments of the available Greek words so as to intersect a more systematic terminology without disrupting the narrative sense.[63] Chapman's obsessional use of "light" duplicates to some extent the obsessional use of *lychnos* in the Greek, and also explicates, in a more sanguine and overt way than Mousaios does, the role of such obesssions in the mind's economy.

Chapman's sense of the secrecy of his own inspiration also meshes with his extravagant and tortuous verbal style—being hidden, the light must break out—so that, partly on his own momentum and partly through receptivity to these aspects in the original, he parallels Mousaios's stylistic vehemence to an unprecedented degree. "Light" is not (as Marot's "flambeau" is) the only repetitive emphasis in the opening paragraph: "The Night-hid Nuptials of young *Hero*" (8) for *gamon ennychon Hērous* (4); "Night-wedding *Heroes* Nuptiall Offices" (12) for *Hērous nyctigamoio gamostolon* (7). The repetition in the Greek is not, in context, particularly striking, being confined to Hero's name and the *nyct-* root; but Chapman's elaboration of the parallel partly compensates for his loss of the *angel-* repetition in lines 6 and 7. The handling of the adjectives shows a similar pattern: "Night-wedding" directly translates *nyctigamoio* as a compound adjective, while "Night-hid" steps up the simpler *ennychon* into a compound.

Chapman's treatment of adjectives is, in general, one of the most interesting features of his translation. In a note on *ouranomēcēs* (187), which the Aldine translation gives as "altissima," Chapman observes that the adjective—"because it is a compound, and hath a grace superiour to the other"—requires some special extravagance in English. Here he uses periphrastic hyperbole: "Hous'd in an all-seene-Towre, whose tops touch heaven" (265). Similarly, for *polydaidalon* (118): "her elaborate Robe, with much cost wrought" (175). But Chapman is alert to other forms of heightening as well, and he applies them even to uncompounded adjectives. *Thyoentos* (48), "redolent," is Englished from the Aldine translation as the inkhorn term "odorifferous" (72). *Cyanopeplon* (113) becomes the occasion for exploiting resonances within English poetry:

> And as he saw the Russet clouds encrease . . .
>
> [169]

> But looke, the Morne in Russet mantle clad . . .
>
> [*Hamlet* 1.1.166]

(Curiously, the clothing, *peplos*, implied in Mousaios's adjective but missing in Chapman's line, is preserved in Shakespeare's.)

Often Chapman simply uses his wit to try to imagine what the adjective might mean in other terms. The second *cyanopeplos* (232) yields, unexpectedly, both a new sense of urgency and a return to one of the poem's major areas of imagery, the sea: "And now, Nights sooty clowdes clap't all saile on" (327). The *hygros acoitēs* (207), "wet bed-fellow"—i.e., Leander in the sea—is seen with increased literalness and suggestiveness: "All hid in weeds, and in Veneran fome" (295). And puzzling over *helcesipeplos* (286), "long-robed," produces a previously unsuspected element in the plot; Hero, for the first time in the tradition, becomes pregnant:

> *Hero* kept all this from her parents still;
> Her Priestly weede was large, and would not fill . . .
>
> [404–05]

Most of these examples involve expansions, but by way of articulating specific points in the original, and not (as in Marot and Baldi) a general thinning out and quieting. At 480 lines, Chapman's translation is, except for Sachs's encapsulated telling, the shortest of the vernacular versions; because of the nature of most of its expansions, it also makes for the densest reading. And this density is often spiked by something like Mousaios's vigorous brand of verbs:

> And all day after, No desire shot home,
> But that the Chamber-decking Night were come.
>
> [325–26]

> πολλάκις ἠρήσαντο μολεῖν θαλαμηπόλον ὄρφνην.
>
> [231]

[Many times they wanted the marriage-attending darkness to come.]

Up, on the rough backe of the high sea, leapes

[440]⁶⁴

δυσκελάδων πεφόρητο θαλασσαίων ἐπὶ νώτων.

[313]

[he was carried on the shrill-screaming oceanic back.]

The particular vigor in these examples is Chapman's own doing; *pephorēto*, in the second case, is actually a passive construction. But "leapes," like "rough" (applied directly to the back, not to the sea) and "high," is Chapman's way of dealing openly with the ungainliness of the Greek *thalassaiōn epi nōtōn*, rather than, like the editor of E, deleting it, or, like Marot, toning it down:

> Estoit porté des bruyantes et grosses
> Vagues de mer . . .
>
> [552–53]

It is curious that Chapman does not translate *iache*; in its place he has merely "these words utter'd" (378). Marot does translate the correct Greek, but in a way that does not agitate his verbal surface. The moral may be that intuition over a long haul counts for more than accurate scholarship about details.

Chapman's translation has been harshly criticized; it is by no means a sustained accomplishment, even on its own terms, and it has some bizarre lapses:

> His throat was turn'd free channel to the flood,
> And drinke went downe, that did him farre from good.
>
> [461–62]

But in his knotty unloveliness Chapman offers something important that the more polished continental and later English versions cannot provide, something other than the "favour and prettiness," the "sentiment, grace, and pathos" which Maclure seeks.⁶⁵ Chapman's Mousaios is a poet of aggressive overwriting, in whom every word is trying to spread its influence as far as it will go; Chapman nurses rather than prunes these exfoliations, to crowded and even clotted effect. The very practical reasons behind this approach may be sought in his attitude toward the original and its subject matter; he writes, in the dedication of his continuation of Marlowe, of "being drawne by a strange instigation to employ some of my serious time in so trifeling a subject, which yet made the first Author, divine *Musaeus*, eternall. . . . But he that shuns trifles must shun the world. . . ."

No continental version is based on so sharp a tension: what is the strange instigation that lures the free mind to the things of this world? In the continuation of Marlowe, Chapman eases his mind with explicitly intellectual and moral additions, but in the translation he has to face the way in which Mousaios himself turned the story to account. Chapman writes in his dedication there of "No lesse esteeming this, woorth the presenting to any Greatest, for the smalnes of the worke; then the Authour himselfe hath beene helde therfor of the lesse estimation: having obtain'd as much preservation and honor, as the greatest of Others: the Smalnesse beeing supplyed with so greatly-excellent Invention and Elocution." "Smalnesse" presumably covers both length and subject matter. Verbal extravagance—"Invention and Elocution"— preempts a latent absurdity of pretension; and Chapman is exactly the writer to respond to this aspect of the original, that epic about a *lychnos*. Upgrading *lychnos* to "light" does mark a certain inability to handle directly the humorous potential, which nevertheless remains, making itself felt clumsily on occasion. But Chapman is at least responding to the problem, and for the most part in something very like the way in which Mousaios does. And if the result does not quite click in English, it nevertheless remains as a ferocious defense against the more usual attempt to translate *Hero and Leander* as if it were *Aucassin et Nicolette*.

III A genteel translation of Mousaios in 1616 would have been a difficult matter anyway, since the principal activity in the tradition by then was open parody. In Spain, Góngora, the Renaissance poet with, one would think, the closest affinities to the school of Nonnos, took aim at Boscán and told the story of two absurdly poor lovers, grubby but pretentious, "No menos necios que illustres," who become "En amores i firmezas / Al mundo exemplos comunes" (75.86–88).[66] In England Nashe and Jonson began a similar tradition, which lasted into the Restoration.[67] Their burlesques derive historically from Marlowe's poem, but not in quite the same way in which Góngora derives from Boscán. Nashe and Jonson are not really making fun of Marlowe; Nashe actually pays him a handsome compliment, and Marlowe is closer in many ways to being their kindred spirit than being their target.

A good deal in his poem reads very much like parody; Hero, for
example, having squeaked out a two-word answer to one of Leander's
aggressive questions, starts to cry:

> as shee spake,
> Foorth from those two tralucent cesternes brake,

Hero's eyes as cisterns could easily pass, except that what comes out of
them in not just water:

> A streame of liquid pearle,

This metaphor is one that Góngora uses as a joke;[68] but Marlowe feels
compelled to top it with another

> which downe her face
> Made milk-white paths,

—and then another:

> wheron the gods might trace
> To *Joves* high court.
>
> [1.295–99]

As the gods begin to troupe across Hero's face we may begin to suspect
mockery; at other times the conclusion is all but impossible to avoid:

> Even as delicious meat is to the tast,
> So was his necke in touching, and surpast
> The white of *Pelops* shoulder.
>
> [1.63–65]

That could be simple Petrarchan praise of marmoreality, a bit clumsily
integrated into a synaesthetic comparison; Pelops's ivory shoulder is
a standard bit of poetic small change in the Renaissance. But anyone
who stops to remember why Pelops had an ivory shoulder is in for a
shock; and that kind of intelligence, at least, we are used to taking for
granted in Marlowe.

These suspiciously pretentious conceits go along with a general
texture of exorbitant claims: "far above the loveliest, *Hero* shin'd"
(1.103). One critic has likened Marlowe's characters to "huge balloons
in a Mardi Gras parade."[69] A sense of the mock-heroic begins to stir;
there is even one scene oddly like *The Rape of the Lock:*[70]

> So at her presence all surpris'd and tooken,
> Await the sentence of her scorneful eies:
> He whom she favours lives, the other dies.

> There might you see one sigh, another rage,
> And some (their violent passions to asswage)
> Compile sharpe satyrs ...
>
> [1.122–27]

These suspicions are strongly reinforced in the later part of the poem, when we get to see these famous characters in action. Leander, having finally gotten Hero's consent, puzzles over what to do with it:

> Albeit *Leander* rude in love, and raw,
> Long dallying with *Hero*, nothing saw
> That might delight him more, yet he suspected
> Some amorous rites or other were neglected.
>
> [2.61–64]

Hero, similarly out of it, rushes downstairs the next night to meet her "lover"—

> She stayd not for her robes, but straight arose,
> And drunke with gladnesse, to the dore she goes.

—without quite taking stock of the situation:

> Where seeing a naked man, she scriecht for feare,
> Such sights as this, to tender maids are rare.
>
> .   .   .   .
>
> The neerer that he came, the more she fled,
> And seeking refuge,

(What else?)

>   slipt into her bed.
> Whereon *Leander* sitting, thus began,
> Through numming cold, all feeble, faint and wan ...
>
> [2.235–38, 243–46]

And so on, as the whole consummation turns into something very close to slapstick. In one of its dimensions Marlowe's *Hero and Leander* is a travesty on the whole tradition.

But it is also much more than that. The most cogent recent discussions of the poem have recognized that its comic absurdities are merely expressions of a more pervasive and basic kind of energy.

The Marlovian style serves first of all to mock rhetorical habits of hyperbolic compliment and idealization. But it also suggests, more seriously, that behind the façade of rhetorical and social decorum there is concealed a whole world of bacchanalian impulses too shocking and chaotic to be admitted into polite society.[71]

The rhetorical excesses of the narrator (and Leander) and the knockabout clumsiness of the characters are spun off from a central mad bustle of erotic power:

> Even as, when gawdie Nymphs pursue the chace,
> Wretched *Ixions* shaggie footed race,
> Incenst with savage heat, gallop amaine,
> From steepe Pine-bearing mountains to the plaine:
> So ran the people foorth to gaze upon her ...
>
> [1.113–17]

If Marlowe's poem is a travesty of its tradition, it also goes back to the source of that tradition, to reproduce for the first time in the Renaissance something like Mousaios's sense of pervasive agitation.

The poem, for example, ends with a strangely brutal sunrise, as Hesperus mocks "ougly night" with his beams,

> Till she o'recome with anguish, shame, and rage,
> Dang'd downe to hell her loathsome carriage.
>
> [2.333–34]

But an earlier sunrise is scarcely less violent:

> Now had the morne espy'de her lovers steeds,
> Whereat she starts, puts on her purple weeds,
> And red for anger that he stayd so long,
> All headlong throwes her selfe the clouds among
>
> [2.87–90]

"Throwes her selfe": as if from Mousaios's *epithrōiscousan* (113), used of the onset of night. But there is more to Marlowe's effects than just unexpectedly excited verbs. The conceit of this last example allows him to depict this natural energy in explicitly erotic terms, in a way Mousaios does not; and Marlowe's range of effects is simply larger than that of the Greek. Here is Marlowe's night:

> The aire with sparkes of living fire was spangled,
> And night deepe drencht in mystie *Acheron*,
> Heav'd up her head, and halfe the world upon,
> Breath'd darkenesse forth ...
>
> [1.188–91]

Not abrupt violence, but something deep and slow: "Heav'd" pulling out of "drencht." Jove can go within one couplet from "for his love *Europa*, bellowing loud," to "tumbling with the Rainbow in a cloud" (1.149–50). "Tumbling" suddenly reacquires the fullness of its physical as well as its erotic implication: the king of gods in free fall. Marlowe is full of surprises:

> A dwarfish beldame beares me companie,
> That hops about the chamber where I lie
>
> [1.353–54]

And as though taking their cues from this environment, Hero and Leander act out a love that Marot would never have dared put into his poem:

> *Leander* now like Theban *Hercules*,
> Entred the orchard of *Th'esperides*,
> Whose fruit none rightly can describe, but hee
> That puls or shakes it from the golden tree
>
> [2.297–300]

The metaphor should not obscure the fact that it is Hero who is being pulled and shaken:

> Even as a bird, which in our hands we wring,
> Foorth plungeth, and oft flutters with her wing,
> She trembling strove
>
> [2.289–91]

Those last two words are almost definitive; their love is not a love of gentleness and sweetness, but a love of strife[72]—

> Therefore unto his bodie, hirs he clung,
> She, fearing on the rushes to be flung,
> Striv'd with redoubled strength
>
> [2.65–67]

—and, from the very first, trembling: "He toucht her hand, in touching it she trembled" (1.183).

This energy, of course, is Marlowe's own; he did not get it by imitating stylistic features from Mousaios. Certain aspects of Mousaios's *agudeza* he does respond to, particularly the fondness for sententiae and antithesis; but most of the details of their respective stylistic excitations are different. Marlowe's strong verbs are not symbiotic, as Mousaios's are, with a thick, elaborate adjectival overlay; most of Marlowe's adjectives are short and Anglo-Saxon, with no wholesale use of aureate or compound diction. The major locus of Marlowe's excesses is not diction but statement, his hyperboles of description and metaphor. And, with the possible exception of "strive," there is nothing in Marlowe like Mousaios's emphatic repetition of key terms. Chapman provides a much closer match to the specific texture of Mousaios's style.

But Marlowe is a much more assured writer than Chapman, and on an important level provides, by indulging his own genius, a work of much the same *kind* as Mousaios's: a simple love story dramatically overwritten. And in that overwriting both authors are making a statement about human sexual behavior, that area of our lives most notable for combining anxious elaboration with simple intent. Those statements are not the same, but their forms are similar enough to imply deep affinities and even a dialogue of sorts. Marlowe is closer to Mousaios than any of the other Renaissance adapters are, and he is also in many ways closer to Mousaios than he is to any of them.

Certainly nothing of importance has been proved about Marlowe's specific indebtedness to other sixteenth-century versions, although he must certainly have been aware of their existence in general. The few suggestions that have been advanced may be reviewed briefly. For the striking description of Hero as "*Venus* Nun" (1.45) Marot has been adduced: "nonnain à Venus dediée" (59).[73] But the English phrase could be obtained directly by making a literal translation, via Renaissance dictionaries, of the corresponding phrase in either Mousaios (*Cypridos hiereia*, 31) or the Aldine Latin ("Veneris sacerdos"); and when the same phrase recurs in the Greek (141), Marlowe translates it the same way (1.319), though Marot does not ("fille à Venus consacrée," 255; though cf. 230).[74] For good measure, the English phrase seems to have been available slang for "whore."[75]

Tasso's Nereids have been proposed as the source of some decoration at an analogous point in Marlowe's story: "Sweet singing Meremaids, sported with their loves" (2.162).[76] There is obviously some real similarity of spirit in this sexualization of the sea; Tasso's "scherzando" could be behind "capring *Triton*" (2.156). And the whole Neptune episode in Marlowe may be simply an extension of that god's amplified role in the *Favola*, possibly as a literalization of "vasto, horribil grembo di Nettuno" (p. 377). But substantially the same decorations may be found in Boscán's *Historia*. Fraunce's citation of the Spanish poem

shows that it had at least some currency in England; in addition to the
well-known locus with which this essay began, Fraunce also uses the
Historia as a source of examples in his *Arcadian Rhetoric* (1588).[77] And
Boscán's is the version that, as a whole, Marlowe's telling most resembles: in the extensiveness of its interpolations, including *contaminatio*
from the *Heroides*,[78] and also in the presence of a major etiological
digression before the consummation. The digressions come at slightly
different points in the story, but they are introduced in something of
the same spirit:

> Yo lo dire, si con plazer me'scuchan:
> Y me dan facultad que me divierta
> Un poco, del proposito empeçado.
>
> [1116–18]

> Harken a while, and I will tell you why . . .
>
> [1.385]

Neither digression is tied in with the main narrative until the end,
and then only tenuously. In the absence of further evidence, however,
none of these parallels is compelling; they can be explained without
trouble in terms of general Renaissance narrative practice.

Marlowe's only firmly established ancillary sources of any importance are Ovidian: the *Heroides*, apparently in Turberville's translation,[79]
and the *Amores*, in Marlowe's own translation.[80] Mousaios is indis-
putably the principal and direct source; his very wording provides
Marlowe with, almost literally, his starting point:

> On *Hellespont* guiltie of True-loves blood,
> In view and opposit two citties stood,
> Seaborderers, disjoin'd by *Neptunes* might:
> The one *Abydos*, the other *Sestos* hight.
>
> [1.1–4]

The first line is Marlowe's own, but the next three work almost entirely
from hints in the Greek:

> Σηστὸς ἔην καὶ Ἄβυδος ἐναντίον ἐγγύθι πόντου·
> γείτονές εἰσι πόληες.
>
> [16–17]

[There was Sestos, and Abydos opposite near the sea. They are
neighboring cities.]

Marlowe's phrasing is close enough to the original to allow Baldwin to draw some conclusions about the use of Latin translations.[81]

> Sestus erat et Abydus è regione, prope mare
> Vicinae sunt urbes.
>
> > [Aldine]

> Oppositae stabant prope Pontum, Sestus, Abydos,
> Vicinae inter se non longis tractibus urbes,
>
> > [Delamare, sig. A7ʳ]

> Stabant oppositae, ponti discrimine paruo,
> Sestos Abydenaéque domus
>
> > [Pape]

> Sestus erat, pelagíque aduerso in litore Abydus,
> Non longe diuisae urbes
>
> > [Paolini, p. 166]

Delamare and Pape collapse the Sestos / Abydos polarity into a list. Like Marlowe, Paolini, whose translation was used by Martin in his notes and acquired a brief reputation as Marlowe's probable text, expands the opposition but loses the nuance of "in view," which Marlowe would have had to get from either the Aldine translation or the Greek itself. As Baldwin points out, Cooper defines *e regione* as "Streight over against: in sight"; Estienne and Scapula define *enantios* as "Aduersus, Qui est in conspectu seu coràm, Qui est eregione, Oppositus." If anything, the evidence favors Marlowe's direct use of the Greek "in conspectu . . . Oppositus," "In view and opposit."

This conclusion is reinforced slightly by the use in Marlowe's text of the Greek forms of the two proper names. Sixteenth-century spelling being what it is, that evidence is hardly trustworthy in itself; and indeed, "*Abydos*" later becomes "*Abidus*" (1.53) and "*Abydus*" (2.112). But "*Sestos*" is consistently "*Sestos*" throughout Marlowe's text; Chapman, in both his continuation and his translation, consistently uses the Latinized forms of the two names. It seems safe to claim that if Marlowe did not actually read the Greek text, he at least looked at it.

Marlowe's one substantial addition to Mousaios here is also worthy of comment: "disjoin'd by *Neptunes* might." The phrase is not really, like Tasso's gloss about Xerxes, an interpolation into the Greek text, but rather grows directly out of the Sestos / Abydos polarity that Marlowe heightens in other ways as well. The introduction of Neptune's might is a characteristic instance of Marlowe's pervasive concern with power, and it also reflects on the formal import of the rhetorical antithesis. As the cities have to be held apart, so the formal disposition of line 4 is an indicator of underlying tension, and not just genial euphuistic balance. And by inserting this gesture, of course, Marlowe is topping Mousaios in the way in which Mousaios tops Homer.

From this point Marlowe begins, in his use of the original, to proceed after the manner of Tasso and Boscán, alternately improvising and returning to the text for guidance. The next eighty-six lines look like an elaboration of two lines of Mousaios:

> ἱμερόεις τε Λέανδρος ἔην καὶ παρθένος Ἡρώ.
> ἡ μὲν Σηστὸν ἔναιεν, ὁ δὲ πτολίεθρον Ἀβύδου . . .
>
> [20–21]

> Suauísque Leander erat, et uirgo Erò.
> Haec quidem Sestum habitabat, ille uero oppidum Abydi . . .
>
> [Aldine]

[They were desirable Leander and virgin Hero. She dwelt in Sestos, he in the city of Abydos . . .]

Marlowe reverses the order of the names, and follows each with a long descriptive passage:

> At *Sestos*, *Hero* dwelt . . .
>
> [1.5]

> Amorous *Leander*, beautifull and yoong,
> (Whose tragedie divine *Musaeus* soong)
> Dwelt at *Abidus* . . .
>
> [1.51–53]

Baldwin assumes that Marlowe's "amorous" is a translation of Mousaios's *himeroeis*;[82] if so, it is further evidence of Marlowe's direct recourse to the Greek. Of the Latin translators, only Delamare provides a real equivalent: "cupiendus amore" (sig. A7^r). Pape and Paolini give no modifier at all here, and the Aldine's "suauis" is an example of its habitually detumescent diction. The presence of two other adjectives in Marlowe's line, and the absence of an answering epithet for Hero, fuzz the analogy and make the argument less convincing. Still, "yoong" might be from *ēitheon* in line 19, and Hero's epithet *parthenos* might simply have been transferred to Leander: though Hero is called "*Venus*

Nun" (1.45), nothing is specifically said here about her chastity, whereas for Leander,

> Some swore he was a maid in mans attire,
>
> .   .   .   .
>
> And such as knew he was a man would say,
> *Leander*, thou art made for amorous play:
> Why art thou not in love, and lov'd of all?
> Though thou be faire, yet be not thine own thrall.
>
> [1.83, 87–90]

At the beginning of the description of Leander, Marlowe touches base again briefly with the Greek:

> since him, dwelt there none,
> For whom succeeding times make greater mone.
>
> [1.53–54]

> πορθμὸν Ἀβύδου,
> εἰσέτι που κλαίοντα μόρον καὶ ἔρωτα Λεάνδρου.
>
> [26–27]

[the strait of Abydos, still mourning the fate and love of Leander.]

Again with a kind of Mousaian one-upmanship, Marlowe makes his statement a shade more hyperbolic. He then slips past Mousaios's description of Hero's home life (an omission worth noting) to the account of the festival:

> The men of wealthie *Sestos*, everie yeare,
> (For his sake whom the goddesse held so deare,
> Rose-cheekt *Adonis*) kept a solemne feast.
> Thither resorted many a wandring guest,
> To meet their loves; such as had none at all,
> Came lovers home, from this great festivall.
>
> [1.91–96]

> δὴ γὰρ Κυπριδίη πανδήμιος ἦλθεν ἑορτή,
> τὴν ἀνὰ Σηστὸν ἄγουσιν Ἀδώνιδι καὶ Κυθερείη.
> πασσυδίη δ' ἔσπευδον ἐς ἱερὸν ἦμαρ ἱκέσθαι,
> ὅσσοι ναιετάασκον ἁλιστεφέων σφυρὰ νήσων.
> ...ἦ γὰρ ἐκεῖνοι
> αἰὲν ὁμαρτήσαντες, ὅπη φάτις ἐστὶν ἑορτῆς,

οὐ τόσον ἀθανάτοισιν ἄγειν σπεύδουσι θυηλάς,
ὅσσον ἀγειρομένων διὰ κάλλεα παρθενικάων.

[42–45, 51–54]

[Then came the international Cyprian festival that they put on in Sestos for Adonis and Aphrodite. They hurried from all over on the holy day, those who lived at the feet of the sea-girt islands. . . . Always rushing off together, wherever there is report of a festival, they hurry not so much to make sacrifices to the gods, as for the beauty of the assembled virgins.]

Verbal parallels are becoming more scattered; "wealthy" may reflect the proximity of *perictionōn* (49), and "Rose-cheekt" may owe something to white-cheeked Hero's rosy blush a few lines later (58–59). Yet Marlowe's reliance on the original text is still clear enough for us to observe that he has completed the secularization of the festival: there is not even the theoretical alternative of attending to the *athanatoisi thyēlai*.

Next in both the Greek and the English is a description of Hero's effect on the crowd; Marlowe seems to be condensing Mousaios:

> But far above the loveliest, *Hero* shin'd,
> And stole away th'inchaunted gazers mind
>
> [1.103–04]

ὡς ἡ μὲν περὶ πολλὸν ἀριστεύουσα γυναικῶν,
Κύπριδος ἀρήτειρα, νέη διεφαίνετο Κύπρις.

. . . .

ἡ δ' ἄρα, καλλιθέμεθλον ὅπῃ κατὰ νηὸν ἀλᾶτο,
ἑσπόμενον νόον εἶχε καὶ ὄμματα καὶ φρένας ἀνδρῶν.

[67–68, 71–72]

[Thus, far excelling among the women, Aphrodite's priestess seemed to be a new Aphrodite . . . . Wherever she went through the beautifully built temple, she held men's minds and eyes and hearts following her.]

Like Mousaios, Marlowe compares Hero to the moon, but with a difference:

> Nor that night-wandring pale and watrie starre,
> (When yawning dragons draw her thirling carre,
> From *Latmus* mount up to the glomie skie,

Where crown'd with blazing light and majestie,
She proudly sits) more over-rules the flood,
Than she the hearts of those that neere her stood.

[1.107–12]

μαρμαρυγὴν χαρίεσσαν ἀπαστράπτουσα προσώπου,
οἷά τε λευκοπάρῃος ἐπαντέλλουσα σελήνη.

[56–57]

[hurling a graceful dazzle from her face, such as the white-cheeked moon gives off.]

If "crown'd with blazing light and majestie" is a translation of line 56 of Mousaios, it is the first and only remotely adequate translation in the tradition (cf. the Aldine Latin: "Splendorem gratum emittens facie"). To be sure, "majestie" overstates *chariessan*, but only to the extent that Marlowe's whole comparison overstates the Greek simile by relating it to the description, not of Hero herself, but of her effect on those around her: Mousaios's moon gives off light, Marlowe's controls the tides. This concern with power works deeply into Marlowe's "lyricism" and provides something of a thematic equivalent for the intimidating formal ornateness of the Greek diction.

The two poems next intersect, briefly, in slightly different sententious passages on the relation of seeing and love:

What we behold is censur'd by our eies.
Where both deliberat, the love is slight,
Who ever lov'd, that lov'd not at first sight?

[1.174–76]

ὀφθαλμὸς δ᾽ ὁδός ἐστιν· ἀπ᾽ ὀφθαλμοῖο βολάων
ἕλκος ὀλισθαίνει καὶ ἐπὶ φρένας ἀνδρὸς ὁδεύει.

[94–95][83]

[The eye is the path. By the eyes' rays the wound slides and passes into a man's heart.]

Then comes the lovers' first interview, where Marlowe's account uses numerous details from Mousaios. There is in both poems an initial touching of hands, notably more gentle in Marlowe—

He toucht her hand, in touching it she trembled

[1.183]

ἠρέμα δὲ θλίβων ῥοδοειδέα δάκτυλα κούρης
βυσσόθεν ἐστενάχιζεν ἀθέσφατον· ἡ δὲ σιωπῇ,
οἷά τε χωομένη, ῥοδέην ἐξέσπασε χεῖρα.

[114–16]

[Quietly squeezing the roselike fingers of the girl, he groaned
deeply and inexpressibly. She, in silence, as though angered, pulled
back her rosy hand.]

—a good deal of reliance on tacit signals—

Love deepely grounded, hardly is dissembled.
These lovers parled by the touch of hands,
True love is mute, and oft amazed stands.
Thus while dum signs their yeelding harts entangled,
The aire with sparkes of living fire was spangled

[1.184–88]

λοξὰ δ᾽ ὀπιπεύων δολερὰς ἐλέλιζεν ὀπωπάς,
νεύμασιν ἀφθόγγοισι παραπλάζων φρένα κούρης.
αὐτὴ δ᾽, ὡς συνέηκε πόθον δολόεντα Λεάνδρου,
χαῖρεν ἐπ᾽ ἀγλαΐησιν. ἐν ἡσυχίῃ δὲ καὶ αὐτὴ
πολλάκις ἱμερόεσσαν ἑὴν ἐπέκυψεν ὀπωπήν,
νεύμασι λαθριδίοισιν ἐπαγγέλλουσα Λεάνδρῳ...

[101–06]

[Glancing obliquely, he twisted deceptive glances, seducing the
girl's heart with voiceless nods. And she, when she sensed the de-
ceitful desire of Leander, rejoiced in her attractiveness. And quietly
she often bent her longing glance, announcing to Leander with
secret nods...]

—and a dramatic onrush of night:

And night deepe drencht in mystie *Acheron*,
Heav'd up her head...

[1.189–90]

ὡς ἴδε κυανόπεπλον ἐπιθρῴσκουσαν ὀμίχλην...

[113]

[when he saw leap up the cloud clothed in blue-green...]

As the line numbers show, Marlowe uses these elements out of their
order in the Greek, in ways that will concern us later, as will certain

changes in the dialogue. Hero's first speech, which in the Greek begins the dialogue (123–27), is eliminated, and Leander's first speech (Mousaios, 135–57) greatly expanded and broken up into three speeches (1.199–294, 299–310, 315–28) by very brief, primarily wordless reactions from Hero. Leander's arguments are mostly imported by Marlowe from other sources, but the underlying "text," as Baldwin puts it, is from Mousaios, and is at one point directly translated:

> Then shall you most resemble *Venus* Nun,
> When *Venus* sweet rites are perform'd and done.
>
> [1.319–20]

> Κύπριδος ὡς ἱέρεια μετέρχεο Κύπριδος ἔργα.
>
> [141]

[As priestess of Aphrodite, perform Aphrodite's works.]

Hero's reaction to Leander's speech occasions a condensed version of a sententia from an earlier point in Mousaios:

> Women are woon when they begin to jarre.
>
> [1.332]

> καὶ γὰρ ὅτ' ἠιθέοισιν ἀπειλείουσι γυναῖκες,
> Κυπριδίων ὅάρων αὐτάγγελοί εἰσιν ἀπειλαί.
>
> [131–32]

[For when women reproach young men, their reproaches are themselves announcers of the games of Aphrodite.]

Hero's subsequent speech is almost a *cento* of various bits from Mousaios. She begins by picking up on the wording of the analogous speech in the Greek:

> Who taught thee Rhetoricke to deceive a maid?
>
> [1.338]

> τίς σε πολυπλανέων ἐπέων ἐδίδαξε κελεύθους;
>
> [175]

[Who taught you the ways of very circuitous words?]

Leander tries to embrace her, and she makes a request that the Greek Hero had made much earlier:

> Gentle youth forbeare
> To touch the sacred garments which I weare.
>
> [1.343–44]

ἐμὸν δ᾽ ἀπόλειπε χιτῶνα.

. . . .

Κύπριδος οὔ σοι ἔοικε θεῆς ἱέρειαν ἀφάσσειν.

[124, 126]

[Let go of my tunic. . . . It is not right for you to attack the priestess of the goddess Aphrodite.]

She then returns to the later speech for an arresting rearrangement of the Greek account of her domestic situation:

> Upon a rocke, and underneath a hill,
> Far from the towne (where all is whist and still,
> Save that the sea playing on yellow sand,
> Sends foorth a ratling murmure to the land,
> Whose sound allures the golden *Morpheus*,
> In silence of the night to visite us,)
> My turret stands, and there God knowes I play
> With *Venus* swannes and sparrowes all the day.
> A dwarfish beldame beares me companie,
> That hops about the chamber where I lie,
> And spends the night (that might be better spent)
> In vaine discourse, and apish merriment.
>
> [1.345–56]

πύργος δ᾽ ἀμφιβόητος ἐμὸς δόμος οὐρανομήκης,
ᾧ ἔνι ναιετάουσα σὺν ἀμφιπόλῳ τινὶ μούνῃ
Σηστιάδος πρὸ πόληος ὑπὲρ βαθυκύμονας ὄχθας
γείτονα πόντον ἔχω στυγεραῖς βουλῇσι τοκήων.
οὐδέ μοι ἐγγὺς ἔασιν ὁμήλικες, οὐδὲ χορεῖαι
ἠιθέων παρέασιν· ἀεὶ δ᾽ ἀνὰ νύκτα καὶ ἠῶ
ἐξ ἁλὸς ἠνεμόεντος ἐπιβρέμει οὔασιν ἠχή.

[187–93][84]

Turris autem circumsona, mea domus altissima,
Qua inhabitans cum ancilla quadam sola
Sestiensem ante urbem, supra profundas undas

Vicinum mare habeo inuisis consiliis parentum.
Neque me prope sunt coetaneae, neque choreae
Iuuenum adsunt. semper autem nocte et die
Ex mari uentoso insonat auribus sonitus.

[Aldine]

[A noise-surrounded tower is my heaven-tall home, where, living
with a single attendant, before the city of Sestos, above the deep-
water rocks, I have the sea as a neighbor because of the hateful
wishes of my parents. In that place I have no age-mates, and there
is no chorus of young men. But always, night and day, the racket
of the windy sea roars in my ears.]

The Aldine translation is defective in line 189. Seventeenth-century
editors added "habentia litora," so that "profundas undas habentia"
would correspond to *bathycymonas*, and "litora" to *ochthas*. Some of
the later sixteenth-century printings of the Aesop edition read "ripas"
for "undas"; that apparently is the text that Chapman translates: "a
steepe shore" (266). Hero's rock and hill in Marlowe may have come
somehow from this reading, perhaps by mistaking "ripas" for "rupes."
Or Marlowe could have had direct recourse to *ochthē*—and even better,
he could have mistaken it for *ochthos*. The two Greek words actually
differ only in gender, but Renaissance dictionaries awarded somewhat
more dramatic definitions to the latter. For *ochthē*, for example, Constantin has "ripa . . . locus praeruptus ripae," and for *ochthos*, "rupes,
salebrosus locus et praeruptus, onus, tumulus prominens, collis, locus
inuius et asper." "Upon a rocke and underneath a hill"—"rupes . . .
collis."[85]

The "dwarfish beldame" is generally thought to descend from the
nutrix or *anus* in the *Heroides*, which Turberville translates "Hag" or
"Beldame." With her, Marlowe has vivified Hero's home-life at the
same time that he takes away some of its narrative contours: Marlowe's
Hero is not out there by parental edict. If anything, she seems held
in her tower by a kind of trance sustained by the sound of the sea;
"golden *Morpheus*" gives mythic form to the hypnotic effect of that
sound. Hero's isolation is not an externally ordained imprisonment,
but a state of mind, permeated by a kind of white noise. The specific
character of the effect in question—"Sends foorth a ratling murmure
to the land"—is accordingly softer than the Greek, which, as part of

Mousaios's general concern with ambient racket and danger, describes the booming (*epibremei*) of a sea stirred up by the wind:

> Day and Night, the windy Sea doth throw
> Wilde murmuring cuffes about our deafned eares.
>
> [Chapman, 272–73]

However, Marlowe is at least translating aural virtuosity with aural virtuosity; and this particular display, fittingly enough, concludes Marlowe's principal use of Mousaios as a direct tool of composition. In her very next words Marlowe's Hero does what it is important that Mousaios's Hero does not do: she issues, however accidentally, an invitation:

> Come thither; As she spake this, her toong tript,
> For unawares (*Come thither*) from her slipt,
> And sodainly her former colour chang'd . . .
>
> [1.357–59]

The poem changes too, as Marlowe begins to direct the plot by himself. In the Greek Leander is about to bring up the subject of the *lychnos*, which Marlowe began by omitting when he omitted Mousaios's invocation. In the English poem, Hero begins to faint, and there follows the digression about Mercury; when we return to the main story, it is to the uncanonical first visit to the tower. There are some possible echoes of Mousaios in the latter part of Marlowe's poem:

> Love alwaies makes those eloquent that have it.
>
> [2.72]

> οἷσι δ' ἀνάσσει,
> αὐτὸς ὁ πανδαμάτωρ βουληφόρος ἐστὶ βροτοῖσιν.
>
> [199–200]

[To those mortals whom he commands, the all-ruler is a bringer of plans.]

Leander's "Love I come" (2.154) could easily have been prompted by *deuro moi eis philotēta* (248); and it may even be that the famous "unknowne joy" (2.293) of the final consummation is a distilling of the long series of negatives at the analogous place in the Greek (274–81). But these parallels are much less extensive and convincing than those in the earlier parts of Marlowe's poem; and at least one important part of Marlowe's dealings with Mousaios comes decisively to an end with Hero's invitation and swoon.

This catalogue, however, does not exhaust the relation between the two poems. Marlowe's hyperbolic style, and particularly his habit of insinuating hyperbole into the texts that he is imitating, suggest deep analogies of literary intent, not merely with Mousaios, but also with the even more extravagant tradition of which Mousaios was a relatively meek part. Oddly enough, there are in Marlowe's poem certain scattered details distinctly reminiscent of motifs from the school of Nonnos, motifs that Mousaios eliminates or tones down. A common form of erotic compliment in Mousaios, whereby Hero rivals or replaces an established mythological figure—she is *allē Cypris anassa* (33), "another reigning Aphrodite," *neē Cypris* (68), "a new Aphrodite"—is a deescalation of a much more serious topos in Nonnos. There *neos* and *allos*, "new" and "other," are important terms in the revolutionary program of the rebellious Earth-giant, who will replace the gods with his own cronies, and make himself *gnēsion . . . neon scēptouchon Olympou* (*Dion.* 1.479), "the legitimate, new ruler of Olympos," and reform the very structure of the universe:

> ἀντιτύπους δὲ
> κρέσσονας ὀψιγόνους πολυφεγγέι μείζονι πυρσῷ
> ἀστεροπὰς ἑτέρας χαλκεύσομαι, εὐρύτερον δὲ
> ὄγδοον οὐρανὸν ἄλλον ὑπέρτερον ὑψόθι τεύξω
> ἄστρασι φαιδροτέροισι κεκασμένον.
>
> [2.344–48]

[I will make another, different, better, newer lightning, with more sparkling fire; and I will build another, wider, higher heaven, the eighth, better than the others with its shinier stars.]

Like Mousaios, Marlowe adopts this kind of rhetoric to serve a minor erotic context, but, unlike Mousaios, he does so in a way that unmistakably preserves the revolutionary dimensions. Mercury, attempting to seduce the country maid, "would needs discover / The way to new *Elisium*" (1.410–11); and Hero, in bed with Leander, mimics Typhon's struggles in microcosm:

> She trembling strove, this strife of hers (like that
> Which made the world) another world begat
>
> [2.291–92]

There is even in Marlowe's poem a brief deposing of the Olympians and restoration of the rule of the Titans (1.451–64), as if in imitation of the Gigantomachies so common in the school of Nonnos, though present only by allusion in Mousaios.

The likelihood, however, of any direct connection between Marlowe and the other Nonnians besides Mousaios is very slight. There is the tantalizing report of Marlowe's translation of Collouthos; but if it really existed, it has completely disappeared, and there is no other evidence of any appreciable firmness linking Marlowe to any part of the school of Nonnos except Mousaios. The parallels just given scarcely count, and even within themselves do not quite mesh. The Titans are mythologically distinct from the Giants, and in Marlowe at least are not even observed fighting. They simply slip into and out of office at the command of the Destinies, with a docility probably accounted for by the fact that they came to Marlowe through the myth of the Golden Age; it is the Olympians ("Murder, rape, warre, lust and trecherie," 1.457) who are violent. Similarly, Hero is an Earth-giant only by analogy; the text behind her exertions is almost certainly Empedocles' account of the war of the elements (though Empedocles may be the ultimate source of the topos in Nonnos et al.). Arcane sources are certainly not needed to explain Marlowe's use of "new" and "another."

Still, this upcropping of similar motifs is interesting, and perhaps even more so for being independently motivated, as though Marlowe were instinctively attuned to certain implications of Mousaios's style that receive from Mousaios only a somewhat curtailed expression. Marlowe restores some of the overtly cosmic, apocalyptic dimension to what is going on. In so doing he moves in the opposite direction from Mousaios and decodes stylistic tension into explicit declarations of power or excess.

But not all of Marlowe's apparent involvements with the school of Nonnos at large are thematic. Marlowe's first substantial digression from the Mousaian text is into a genre very important to the school but carefully absent from Mousaios: the ecphrasis. There are three major ecphraseis in Marlowe's poem: the descriptions of Hero (1.9–50), Leander (1.55–90), and the church of Venus (1.135–57). To include descriptions of people under the rubric of ecphrasis is to stretch the term slightly, though there are such descriptions in Nonnos (usually, as here, in an erotic context); architecture is a more characteristic subject, and thus Marlowe's third exercise comes the closest to fitting into the classical tradition. The historical connections are less tenuous here than was the case with the Earth-giants; Martin cites an analogous passage in Apuleius's *Metamorphoses*:

> nam summa laquearia citro et ebore curiose cauata subeunt aureae columnae, parietes omnes argenteo caelamine conteguntur bestiis et id genus pecudibus occurrentibus ob os introeuntium. mirus prorsum homo, immo semideus uel certe deus, qui magnae artis suptilitate tantum efferauit argentum. enimuero pauimenta ipsa lapide pretioso caesim deminuto in uaria picturae genera discriminantur: uehementer, iterum ac saepius beatos illos, qui super gemmas et monilia calcant.
>
> [5.1][86]

> For the enbowinges above weare of Cytern, and Yvery, propped and undermined with pillors of Golde, the walles covered and seeled with Silver, divers sortes of beastes weare graven and carved, that seemed to encounter with such as entred in: al thinges weare so curiously and finely wrought, that it seemed either to be the worke of some demigod, or God him selfe, the pavement was al of pretious stone, devided and cut one from an other, whereon was carved divers kindes of pictures, in such sorte that blessed and thrise blessed weare they whiche might goe upon such a pavement ...[87]

Maclure replaces Martin's note with references to the palace of the Sun and Arachne's tapestry in Ovid (*Met.* 2.1 ff., 6.103 ff.), and to the erotic tapestry, itself derived from Ovid, in Busirane's castle (*FQ* 3.11.28–46). The references are pertinent, and Marlowe's catalogue of the divine lusts clearly owes much to at least one of these last two passages. However, Apuleius's curious detail of floor illustrations (cf. Marlowe, 1.141 ff.) also qualifies him for consideration as a direct source; and, as Martin shows in another note (to 1.117–18), the placement of the ecphrasis in Apuleius rhymes in an intriguing way with the Marlovian context. A few lines earlier (1.103–30) Marlowe had been describing Hero's stunning effect on the festival crowd; a few paragraphs earlier, Apuleius had been describing an analogous scene with Psyche:

> uero puellae iunioris tam praecipua, tam praeclara pulchritudo nec exprimi ac ne sufficienter quidem laudari sermonis humani penuria poterat. multi denique ciuium et aduenae copiosi, quos

eximii spectaculi rumor studiosa celebritate congregabat, inaccessae formonsitatis admiratione stupidi et admouentes oribus suis dexteram primore digito in erectum pollicem residente eam ut ipsam prorsus deam Venerem religiosis uenerabantur adorationibus. iamque proximas ciuitates et attiguas regiones fama peruaserat deam, quam caerulum profundum pelagi peperit et ros spumantium fluctuum educauit, iam numinis sui passim tributa uenia in mediis conuersari populi coetibus, uel certe rursum nouo caelestium stillarum germine non maria, sed terras Venerem aliam uirginali flore praeditam pullulasse.

[4.28]

Yet the singuler passinge beautie and maidenly Majestie of the yongest daughter, did so farre surmounte and excell them twoo, as no earthly creature coulde by any meanes sufficiently expresse or set out the same, by reason whereof (after the fame of this excellent maiden was spred abrode in every part of the Citie,) the Citizens and straungers there, beinge inwardly pricked by zelous affection to beholde her famous person, came daily by thousandes, hundreds and scores to her fathers Pallaice, who as astonied with admiration of her incomperable beautie did no lesse woorshippe and reverence her, with crosses, signes and tokens, and other divine adorations, accordinge to the custome of the olde used rites and ceremonies, then if she weare Ladie Venus in deede: And shortly after the fame was spredde into the next Cities and borderinge Regions, that the Goddesse whome the deepe seas had borne and brought foorth, and the frothe of the spurginge waves had nourished, to the intent to showe her highe magnificencie and divine power in earth, to suche as earst did honour and woorshippe her: was now conversant emongst mortall men, or els that the earth and not the seas, by a newe concurse and influence of the celestiall Planetes, had budded and yelded foorth a newe Venus, endewed with the flower of virginitie . . .

The coincidence of the two passages in Apuleius and the two passages in Marlowe is remarkable enough; but more important is the common psychology that in both writers links sexuality and ecphrasis. Apuleius himself diagrams the nexus: "mirantur quidem diuinam speciem, sed ut simulacrum fabre politum mirantur omnes" (4.32), "Every one merveled at her divine beautie, as it were at some Image well painted and sette out." As one builds a building or paints a picture, so one converts oneself into an erotic object; in this exercise of artistic skill one rivals the gods, becomes *alia Venus*, "a newe Venus," or "mirus prorsum homo, immo semideus uel certe deus." One aims to create what Nonnos calls *thaumata*, "miracles," things drastically different from the normal range of experience, things which bring the ongoing processes of life to a dead halt. It is by this almost paralytic effect that such objects may be recognized: they replace action with astonishment, and one simply stares.

Indeed, the faculty of sight, on whose tyrannous force both Mousaios and Marlowe provide *sententiae*, seems to be an important term in the equation: *Ophthalmoi, ti to thauma?* (*Dion.* 1.93), "eyes, what is this miracle?" The ecphrasis is in a way the formal embodiment of this pattern of astonishment, the insertion of a static visual field into the narrative, an interruption of the story to dwell on something that is standing still. That, of course, is not all that description can do as part of a narrative, but it is a fair enough account of at least Marlowe's case. Tuve claims that a contrast with Spenser is in order: Marlowe's descriptions do not qualify as allegory, subtly advancing the argument through seemingly static details, but must be labeled *amplificatio*, the aim of which, in the terms of Renaissance theory, is the production of *meraviglia*.[88] Marlowe works this formal proposition back into his story, where disabling *meraviglia* is exactly the mode of everybody's reaction to Hero:

> So ran the people foorth to gaze upon her,
> And all that view'd her, were enamour'd on her.
> And as in furie of a dreadfull fight,
> Their fellowes being slaine or put to flight,
> Poore soldiers stand with fear of death dead strooken,
> So at her presence all surpris'd and tooken,
> Await the sentence of her scorneful eies
>
> [1.117–23]

She is herself an ecphrastic object, notoriously artificialized—and not just because the poet chooses to treat her that way, but to a great extent because she has fixed herself up that way:

> Buskins of shels all silvered, used she,
> And brancht with blushing corall to the knee;

> Where sparrowes pearcht, of hollow pearle and gold,
> Such as the world would woonder to behold
>
> [1.31–34]

Ecphrasis frustrates narrative progress, and erotic glamor has a way of frustrating erotic fulfillment (Venus's priestess as nun). A lover too overwhelmed to move is of little use to anything but the ego, and Hero's very impressiveness as a sexual object is part of what limits her functioning as a sexual agent. Intimidating splendor is one of the things in which her prospective divine lover is most interested; Apollo

> offred as a dower his burning throne,
> Where she should sit for men to gaze upon.
>
> [1.7–8]

Her human lover eventually rebels against the whole routine: "Nor heaven, nor thou, were made to gaze upon" (1.223). Yet moving from gazing to acting—transforming sight into touch, as it were—is no simple matter; and the intimidation of Hero's lovers is merely the first stage in an intricate and difficult process of seemingly endless and systematic frustration: "The neerer that he came, the more she fled . . ." (2.243).

In fact, to Mousaios's story Marlowe adds three unconsummated sexual encounters—Mercury and the country maid, Neptune and Leander, and Hero and Leander in their first night at the tower—and also details considerably the problems of the final success:

> Yet ever as he greedily assayd
> To touch those dainties, she the *Harpey* playd,
> And every lim did as a soldier stout,
> Defend the fort, and keep the foe-man out.
>
> [2.269–72]

And this frustration continues to rhyme with some of the more notorious formal processes in the poem, as the intruded episodes themselves not only interfere with the story at hand, but even treat of the narrative digression as a factor in the situation; sexual frustration, it seems, is very fruitful of storytelling:

> *Leander* made replie,
> You are deceav'd, I am no woman I.
> Thereat smilde *Neptune*, and then told a tale . . .
>
> [2.191–93]

Similarly, Mercury, about to lose the country maid, traps her attention
with a story:

> Herewith he stayd his furie, and began
> To give her leave to rise: away she ran,
> After went *Mercurie*, who us'd such cunning,
> As she to heare his tale, left off her running.
> Maids are not woon by brutish force and might,
> But speeches full of pleasure and delight.
>
> [1.415–20]

Yet Mercury's talk does not exactly "win" her; what it does is, briefly,
freeze the situation into something like Keats's Grecian urn, where,
if nothing is gained, at least nothing is lost. The maid,

> knowing *Hermes* courted her, was glad
> That she such lovelinesse and beautie had
> As could provoke his liking, yet was mute,
> And neither would denie, nor graunt his sute.
>
> [1.421–24]

Again, as with the ecphraseis, "art" is the image and instrument of a
kind of paralysis, a diversion of kinetic sexual energy into certain
static patterns. With the reliable help of human ingenuity, the sexual
impulse threatens to end, not in orgastic release, but merely in its own
elaboration.

The dilemma here is both a millennial one in the minds of the characters—how to translate adoration into action—and a more specific one
in the technique of the poem—how to give a digressive, baroque
work, constantly diverted by its own *agudeza*, palpable unity of intent.
And both aspects of the dilemma are resolved when the frustrations
and digressions fall into place as part of a general strategy of gratification.
On the fourth try in the poem, coition is achieved, spectacularly—
spectacularly enough to imply that it was not just worth the wait but
considerably enhanced by it. Such a strategy had been implied all
along:

> The mirthfull God of amorous pleasure smil'd,
> To see how he this captive Nymph beguil'd.
> For hitherto hee did but fan the fire,
> And kept it downe that it might mount the hier.
>
> [2.39–42]

The provocative role of delay and interference is a recurrent motif, in increasingly vehement statements, from Hero's discreet coyness in the first interview—

> Thereat she smild, and did denie him so,
> As put thereby, yet might he hope for mo.
> Which makes him quickly re-enforce his speech . . .
>
> [1.311–13]

—to the agony of physical separation that drives Leander into the Hellespont:

> So beautie, sweetly quickens when t'is ny,
> But being separated and remooved,
> Burnes where it cherisht, murders where it loved.
>
> [2.126–28]

Hero, in her first meeting with Leander, "Strove to resist the motions of her hart" (1.364); but,

> Thus having swallow'd *Cupids* golden hooke,
> The more she striv'd, the deeper was she strooke.
>
> [1.333–34]

This strife of resistance eventually merges directly into the rhythms of sexual intercourse:

> She trembling strove, this strife of hers (like that
> Which made the world) another world begat,
> Of unknowne joy.
>
> [2.291–93]

Something like the same principle informs the unity of much baroque art:

> By using variety and ornament cumulatively . . . the Baroque artist aimed at responses that could be emotional as well as aesthetic and intellectual. The "piling" or cumulative technique produced a tension that sought—and eventually was rewarded with—release (which is why the technique is not precisely the same thing as the *blason* or "catalogue-making" of poets of an earlier time).[89]

Notions of the "sensuality" of the baroque relate partially to that art's exploitation of this principle of building incrementally to an explosion, for the basic pattern is neither psychological nor artistic, but neurological. A later author much concerned with these matters has made some of the connections almost explicit:

> In point of style, fault is often found with the continual, slightly modified repetition. The only answer is that it is natural to the author; and that every natural crisis in emotion or passion or understanding comes from this pulsing, frictional to-and-from which works up to culmination.[90]

The form and content of Marlowe's poem similarly resolve into directly sexual rhythms, and the whole work might be characterized as an essay in the creative use of friction.

Sexual intercourse can at least provide a paradigm for opposition that is actually intimate cooperation toward a fairly simple end by a fairly roundabout way. It is similarly conventional to distinguish baroque from mannerist art by the illusory nature of the former's diversity; the oppositions are matters of effect, not signs of genuinely Manichean forces. The central conflict of Marlowe's story—the "winning" of Hero—shows this pattern. Chaucer's Criseyde gives the secret perhaps its most memorable expression:

> This Troilus in armes gan hir streyne,
> And seyde, "O swete, as evere mote I gon,
> Now be ye kaught, now is ther but we tweyne!
> Now yeldeth yow, for other bote is non!"
> To that Criseyde answerde thus anon,
> "Ne hadde I er now, my swete herte deere,
> Ben yold, ywis, I were now nought heere!"
>
> [*Troilus and Criseyde* 3.1205-11]

Thus Hero in bed with Leander:

> Treason was in her thought,
> And cunningly to yeeld her selfe she sought.
> Seeming not woon, yet woon she was at length,
> In such warres women use but halfe their strength.
>
> [2.293-96]

The decision to yield actually occurred when the two lovers were mutually enamored by the same look (1.161-66), and the process of yielding while seeming not to began then. Even before Hero begins interrupting Leander's speeches (1.195–96), she has secretly and explicitly decided to hear him out. And the first meeting at the tower gives Marlowe a chance to reverse the roles several times, as Leander retires and Hero pursues; the game remains the same.

Significantly, the conflict consists almost entirely of these psychological oscillations. Marlowe removes most of the external impediments to the consummation when he further secularizes Hero's religious role and deprives her of her parents; as if to emphasize the change, he gives Leander a fairly benign father:

> *Leanders* Father knew where hee had beene,
> And for the same mildly rebuk't his sonne,
> Thinking to quench the sparckles new begonne.
>
> [2.136–38]

Even this gentle reproof infuriates Leander and leads Marlowe to the simile of the horse enraged by the bit. Leander is supplementing the force of external interference with his own emotions, which are learning to use frustration as a springboard: "love resisted once, growes passionate" (2.139). There remains, of course, the actual sea separating the two lovers. But it has not caused much trouble up to this point (Leander apparently returns home from his first night with Hero by boat; see 2.113); and when Leander does get around to swimming it, Marlowe turns the episode into another treatment of the dynamics of flirtation.

Marlowe's poem, in other words, is not about the opposition of love to something else—except, in the Neptune episode, other love. The principal topic is the internal machinery of erotic behavior, machinery which can create certain oppositions for strategic purposes but is ultimately not bound by them. This is subtly but decisively different from the situation in Mousaios's poem, where the sense is of love tightly and firmly surrounded by danger, the silence perilously maintaining itself against the ambient noise (*pyrgos amphiboētos*). In Mousaios's own terms, it is *Erōs* and *Moira*, love encircled by fate (27, 307, 323). The Mercury story in Marlowe involves an etiology for the hostility of the "Adamantine Destinies" toward Love (1.463); but at least in the poem as we have it that opposition is not made good.

This may simply be due to the "incompleteness"—if that is what it is—of Marlowe's poem, since he never got to the point in the story where Fate would make itself felt in its malign aspect. But it may,

on the other hand, be significant that the Destinies enter Marlowe's
poem only in a digression, as though they themselves were somehow
just part of the entertainment, and that what they are primarily observed
doing is changing their minds. "The point of the tale" according to
Turner, "is clear: if by destiny one means an immutable law of fate,
it does not exist."[91] And a further comparison of certain details in
Mousaios's and Marlowe's respective treatments of the main story up
to the point Marlowe did reach suggests that the truncation of the
story in Marlowe is not really inappropriate. Mousaios continually
acknowledges a surrounding menace in ways Marlowe often does not,
and the latter's telling of the tale projects a distinctly less tense, less
panicky ambience.

   Examples of this contrast on the verbal level have already come up:
the difference between "ratling murmure" and *epibremei ēchē*, between
touching Hero's hand and squeezing it. The general excitation of the
actions in Marlowe's poem can assume much more varied forms,
probably because it does not always seem to be fighting back against
something. Marlowe can suggest the Mousaian sense of energy straining
against décor—

> the ground
> Was strewd with pearle, and in low corrall groves,
> Sweet singing Meremaids, sported with their loves
> On heapes of heavie gold
>
> [2.160–63]

—but the torsion between sporting and heavy gold, compared with
that between *heilcē* and *polydaidalon*, is a relatively casual business; the
mermaids, Marlowe goes on to say,

> tooke great pleasure,
> To spurne in carelesse sort, the shipwracke treasure.
>
> [2.163–64]

   There is nothing in Marlowe quite like the more Mousaian moments
in Chapman: "Up, on the rough backe of the high sea, leapes" (440).
Marlowe's Leander does "leap" into the Hellespont, but with a rather
different spirit:

> With that hee stript him to the yv'rie skin,
> And crying, Love I come, leapt lively in.
>
> [2.153–54]

Marlowe's character does not leap into or onto or at something, he just leaps lively. Chapman's words trace a tense entry into recognized danger, Marlowe's an uncalculated and rather comic explosion of adolescent energy. The passages admittedly are not quite parallel, since Chapman's line refers to Leander's plunge on the fatal night, when the sea was especially rough and high; but his translation of the precisely parallel passage makes the same contrast, though less strikingly:

> Lept from the Shore, and cast into the Sea
> His lovely body . . .
>
> [353–54]

The contrast extends into the plot: Marlowe retains only vestiges of Leander's anxieties about the sea; he

> pray'd the narrow toyling *Hellespont*,
> To part in twaine, that hee might come and go,
> But still the rising billowes answered no.
> With that hee stript him . . .
>
> [2.150–53]

In Mousaios, Leander is much more concerned with the risk of what he is doing (245–50), and his worries assert the danger of the *pontos ameilichos* at even this point in the story. In Marlowe, Leander, more excited by the thought of Hero ("*Hero, Hero*, thus he cry'de full oft," 2.147) than concerned about or even cognizant of the sea, just jumps in on a crest of erotic impulse. In defiance of some of the most important imagery in the Greek poem, he does not even wait for night.

Hurriedly, he discards his clothes, where Mousaios has him carefully tie them in a bundle on his head. This sets up another joke in Marlowe's poem, and also allows an even closer comparison with the Greek. Hero responds to Leander's appearance after the swim with the same verb that Mousaios's Hero uses in the original text:

> drunke with gladnesse, to the dore she goes.
> Where seeing a naked man, she scriecht for feare
>
> [2.236–37]

"Scriecht" exactly translates *iache*. However, the likelihood of Marlowe's using Lascaris or Estienne is slight, and the parallel is particularly suspect because Marlowe has already departed so far from Mousaios's plot for so long. It seems reasonably clear that Marlowe arrives at the verb on his own, through his recasting of the whole scene; for Hero's screech makes very direct and obvious sense as a punch line. The fear expressed in Mousaios's verb is not tied to anything so specific as the sight of a naked man; Hero's *iache* springs from a much more diffuse anxiety and is a much more unexpected reaction. Also, Marlowe's Hero simply screeches and then runs, while Mousaios's screech has a direct object: Hero screeches a speech, *iache mythous.* The Greek verb pushes against something, specifically against Hero's very medium of expression; it manifests a stress that the English verb, an unaimed outburst, does not. Mousaios's lovers are jumpy about something, whereas Marlowe's are just flailing, arms akimbo; the courtship of Marlowe's characters is largely that of unencumbered adolescence. The occasional vehemence of their actions is not a serious fighting back against their environment, but simply emotional extravagance and display, the gaudiness of youth first trying out its adult sexual roles.[92]

Marlowe's lovers are a bit crazy, but they are not obsessed to anything like the degree that the Greek lovers are obsessed. Marlowe begins his use of the Greek text by cutting from the story their principal iconic obsession, the *lychnos* (since Marlowe's Leander makes his swim in broad daylight, he has no need for it). And with the *lychnos*, and the example of the first fifteen lines, Marlowe drops Mousaios's technique of emphatic verbal repetition. These repetitions in Mousaios serve a desire to retain a center of reference away from the surface of normal discourse, and they index an aggressive distrust of language, even hostility toward it: *iache mythous.* Marlowe would seem not to share that hostility, as is clear enough from his willingness to thematize much that Mousaios keeps tightly implicit in his verbal style.

Though Marlowe takes over Mousaios's concern with silent communication, he tampers with it in revealing ways. To complement the successful reading of nonverbal signs in the first interview, he adds a comic scene of the misreading of such signs in the Neptune episode (2.213–24). And in the earlier scene, he eliminates most of Hero's speeches, which contain the denials that Leander has to interpret: in other words, there is simply less lying going on in the English. In addition, Marlowe violates certain principles of Mousaios's inner tension by indicating unreported speeches (1.192–96, 329) and, of course, primarily by allowing Hero her explicit invitation. That "Come thither" slips out as a flutter somewhere between purpose and accident, an area of speech not covered by Mousaios's rhetorical tradition, which insisted on either intention or silence. The distinction between the uttered and the unuttered, the utterable and the unutterable, is not being so carefully drawn in the English as in the Greek, nor is the distinction between speech and nonspeech:

> And now begins *Leander* to display
> Loves holy fire, with words, with sighs and teares
>
> [1.192–93]

The final assault on Hero in bed is similarly accompanied:

> Wherein *Leander* on her quivering brest,
> Breathlesse spoke some thing, and sigh'd out the rest;
> Which so prevail'd, as he with small ado,
> Inclos'd her in his armes and kist her to.
>
> [2.279–82]

A species of suasive oratory thus moves directly into what for Mousaios is the heart of silence—but oratory that grades immediately through inarticulateness into action. Speech in Marlowe, despite its elaborateness, is a much more casual matter than in Mousaios; and silence, accordingly, is a term of no particular importance.

Marlowe's poem thus lacks much of the specific tension which eventually shatters the happiness of Mousaios's lovers, so it makes a good deal of sense that the English version ends where it does. The proposition that Marlowe's *Hero and Leander* is a finished work has been argued in detail by Martz;[93] in particular, he suggests that Marlowe covertly makes his own comparison with the original in the line about Leander, "Whose tragedie divine *Musaeus* soong" (1.52): since Mousaios has already done that, Christopher Marlowe will sing of Leander's comedy.[94]

Against this tidy notion must be set some clear foreshadowings of the tragic dénouement—the first line, for example: "On *Hellespont* guiltie of True-loves blood." Even stronger language is used just before the lovers' first meeting:

> On this feast day, O cursed day and hower,
> Went *Hero* thorow *Sestos*, from her tower
> To *Venus* temple, where unhappilye,
> As after chaunc'd, they did each other spye.
>
> [1.131–34]

And of course there is the story of the Destinies, who would seem intended to participate in some retributive machinery; the same role has been suggested for the injured Neptune.[95] Marlowe certainly did not intend to change the eventual end of the story in the way in which, say, Petowe did, and probably he at least set out to cover the whole of Mousaios's plot. Yet it remains intriguing that he stopped writing exactly where he did, at so satisfying a close, rather than trailing off, as though he realized that he had reached some sort of logical conclusion. Certainly "finishing" the poem with a tragic end after what had gone before would have required some poetic strategies that we cannot easily extrapolate from what we have.

That Marlowe's abbreviation of the plot is part of a serious revision of the meaning of the Greek poem is suggested by some interesting parallels in the conclusions as they stand. Both poems end with a woman falling: Mousaios's with Hero hurling herself onto the rocks, Marlowe's with "ougly night" hurling "downe to hell her loathsome carriage." And both poems end at dawn. But they are different dawns; Mousaios's (*ēlythe d' ērigeneia*, 335) is the cold light of external knowledge, which reveals the wreckage done during the night; it is the birth of day as the traditional enemy of love. That is the dawn that Marlowe's Hero fears:

> For much it greev'd her that the bright day-light,
> Should know the pleasure of this blessed night
>
> [2.303–04]

But her attempt to slip away and hide in a kind of further darkness is foiled by Leander, who grabs her and will not let her go. Trapped, she draws herself up to the full dignity of her erotic presence, initiating a dawn not from outside the bedroom, but from inside:

> Thus neere the bed she blushing stood upright,
> And from her countenance behold ye might,
> A kind of twilight breake, which through the heare,
> As from an orient cloud, glymse here and there.
> And round about the chamber this false morne,
> Brought foorth the day before the day was borne.
> So *Heroes* ruddie cheeke, *Hero* betrayd,
> And her all naked to his sight displayd.
>
> [2.317–24]

The "real" day comes as an extension of this:

> By this *Apollos* golden harpe began,
> To sound foorth musicke to the *Ocean*,
> Which watchfull *Hesperus* no sooner heard,
> But he the days bright-bearing Car prepar'd.
> And ran before, as Harbenger of light,
> And with his flaring beames mockt ougly night,
> Till she o'recome with anguish, shame, and rage,
> Dang'd downe to hell her loathsome carriage.
>
> [2.327–34]

Mousaios's dawn is the check of knowledge on human desire; Marlowe's is the radiation of that desire, and his poem's conclusion celebrates love's courage to come out into the daylight.

Hero and Leander get rid of night, which has served them well enough but is ultimately just a heuristic device of courtship, and not a term in an absolute antithesis. An earlier onset of night anticipates the pattern of the later dawn in following rather than directing human desire. In Mousaios, Leander must wait until night to make his first overt approach to Hero:

> ὄφρα μὲν οὖν Λείανδρος ἐδίζετο λάθριον ὥρην,
> φέγγος ἀναστείλασα κατήιεν εἰς δύσιν Ἠώς,
> ἐκ περάτης δ᾽ ἀνέφαινε βαθύσκιος Ἕσπερος ἀστήρ·
> αὐτὰρ ὁ θαρσαλέως μετεκίαθεν ἐγγύθι κούρης,
> ὡς ἴδε κυανόπεπλον ἐπιθρῴσκουσαν ὀμίχλην.
> ἠρέμα δὲ θλίβων ῥοδοειδέα δάκτυλα κούρης
> βυσσόθεν ἐστενάχιζεν ἀθέσφατον.
>
> [109–15][96]

[And as Leander sought the secret hour, Dawn, hauling down the light, went to her setting, and the deep-shaded Evening Star appeared on the horizon. Then he marched boldly up to the girl when he saw leap up the cloud clothed in blue-green. Quietly squeezing the roselike fingers of the girl, he groaned deeply and inexpressibly.]

In Marlowe the sequence is reversed:

> He toucht her hand, in touching it she trembled,
> *Love deepely grounded, hardly is dissembled.*
> These lovers parled by the touch of hands,

> True love is mute, and oft amazed stands.
> Thus while dum signs their yeelding harts entangled,
> The aire with sparkes of living fire was spangled,
>
> [1.183–88]

These erotic fireworks suddenly become stars, and themselves bring on the night:

> And night deepe drencht in mystie *Acheron*,
> Heav'd up her head, and halfe the world upon,
> Breath'd darkenesse forth (darke night is *Cupids* day.)
>
> [1.189–91]

Night and day are both mere extensions of the lovers' own impulses, as the various hindrances to consummation are merely means to an end. At the conclusion of Marlowe's poem the whole context in which Eros operates is revealed as, in some deep sense, our own creation, built to serve an ancient strategy of gratification that most of us have forgotten or only incompletely mastered.

There is a deeply anthropocentric cast to the world of Marlowe's poem; and the center specifically is man as an erotic agent. Human sexual energy projects itself outward onto the inanimate world. Thus the sea, caressing and restraining, becomes a troublesome suitor. On a simpler level, Hero's place in bed, still warm from her body, arouses Leander (2.253–58). Things inert take vitality and value from people, not from any independent reality:

> About her necke hung chaines of peble stone,
> Which lightned by her necke, like Diamonds shone.
>
> [1.25–26]

Even speech is valued, not for what it says, but for who says it, and why:

> Aye me, such words as these should I abhor,
> And yet I like them for the Orator.
>
> [1.339–40]

Leander's presence sexualizes his speech as Hero's presence sexualizes her décor; even seeing is an act of erotic aggression:

> There *Hero* sacrificing turtles blood,
> Vaild to the ground, vailing her eie-lids close,
> And modestly they opened as she rose:

> Thence flew Loves arrow with the golden head,
> And thus *Leander* was enamoured.
> Stone still he stood, and evermore he gazed,
> Till with the fire that from his count'nance blazed,
> Relenting *Heroes* gentle heart was strooke,
> *Such force and vertue hath an amorous looke.*
>
> [1.158–66]

This force and virtue explain why gazing astonished is not ultimately an act of paralysis, for under such scrutiny things come alive and respond. Early in his continuation, Chapman describes the phenomenon in a way inclusive of most of Marlowe's poem:

> Love-blest *Leander* was with love so filled,
> That love to all that toucht him he instilled.
> And as the colours of all things we see,
> To our sights powers communicated bee:
> So to all objects that in compasse came
> Of any sence he had, his sences flame
> Flowd from his parts, with force so virtuall,
> It fir'd with sence things meere insensuall.
>
> [3.83–90]

The world as love's body. Marlowe not only engages Mousaios's poem on a deep level, he also, as Martz says, turns it inside out,[97] and with it some basic premise of the classical tradition of which Mousaios is still, despite the revolutionary ambitions of his colleagues, a part. Marlowe in a way fulfills those ambitions, even as Mousaios withdraws from them. The dawn spreading from Hero's face is a heady, extravagant conclusion, romantic in an almost Blakean sense: not the light that shines on men, but the light that shines from them.

3 ROBERT HERRICK AND CLASSICAL LYRIC POETRY

I Robert Herrick's *Hesperides* is a very long book of very short
poems, the image of a long life of short moments, of a poetic
impulse quickly roused and quickly expended.

> Fain would I kiss my *Julia's* dainty Leg,
> Which is as white and hair-less as an egge.
>
> [H-349 / 139.3]

An entire poem: a swift dilation on a single wonder, ticklish rapture
achieved as a minutely explosive rhyme. In a fuller context that rhyme
might be funny. It *sounds* funny, and we probably laugh; but the joke,
if there is one, does not quite have time to mobilize itself. Rather, the
poem supplies the force of a punch line without the content—and that
turns out to be the graph of a serious erotic event: a potential swoon
("Fain would I kiss . . .") unexpectedly rescuing itself by an act of
precise concentration ("as white and hair-less as—an egge!") It is a
definitive instance of bright, nervous sexuality realizing itself in brittle
décor.

What love and décor have to do with one another is a central concern
of Herrick's. He speculates on the meaning of the gifts that he offers
to his "mistresses":

> Why I tye about thy wrist,
> *Julia*, this my silken twist;
> For what other reason is't,

154

> But to shew thee how in part,
> Thou my pretty Captive art?
>
> [H-322/128.2/1–5]

Such trinkets in general do psychologically what the bracelet does physically as well: surround, define, limit within a miniature space. Early in his book, Herrick even identifies one such bracelet as his own very classically styled *fatum*:

> Three lovely Sisters working were
> (As they were closely set)
> Of soft and dainty Maiden-haire,
> A curious *Armelet*.
> I smiling, ask'd them what they did?
> (Faire *Destinies* all three)
> Who told me, they had drawn a thred
> Of Life, and 'twas for me.
>
> [H-47/18.3/1–8]

And toward the close of the book, that same *telos* reappears, disturbingly, as a noose proffered by Eros himself:

> The Halter was of silk, and gold,
> That he reacht forth unto me:
> No otherwise, then if he would
> By dainty things undo me.
>
> [H-863/279/5–8]

An atypical poem ("in the manner of George Herbert," says Patrick), one of Herrick's very few attempts to see outside his own fate. The *Hesperides* is, for the most part, a book about dainty things lived with more or less on their own terms; and to understand Herrick is to understand what those terms are—what his particular kind of daintiness is and how his emotions are organized around it.

"Her Legs" is perhaps Herrick's basic, molecular poem. Its mode becomes at times even a structural principle, for the longer poems have a way of proceeding as accumulations of similar instances:

> And next to these two blankets ore-
> Cast of the finest *Gossamore*.
> And then a Rug of carded wooll,
> Which, *Spunge-like* drinking in the dull-

> Light of the Moon, seem'd to comply,
> Cloud-like, the *daintie Deitie.*
>
> [H-443/167/94–99]

Again, the context is erotic, Oberon going to Mab's bed; the sexual impulse in Herrick habitually expresses itself as décor. Here this process operates mainly on the setting, but it can also abstract and transform facets of the woman herself:

> How rich and pleasing thou my *Julia* art
> In each thy daintty, and peculiar part!
> First, for thy *Queen-ship* on thy head is set
> Of flowers a sweet commingled Coronet:
> About thy neck a Carkanet is bound,
> Made of the *Rubie, Pearle* and *Diamond:*
> A golden ring, that shines upon thy thumb:
> About thy wrist, the rich *Dardanium.*
> Between thy Breasts (then Doune of Swans more white)
> There playes the *Saphire* with the *Chrysolite.*
> No part besides must of thy selfe be known,
> But by the *Topaz, Opal, Calcedon.*
>
> [H-88/30.1]

So the end of the poem, its point of rest. As with Julia's leg, the issue is not just content—the connotations of expense and exoticism in those last three words—but the writing itself. Those words cut the very sound of the poem into tangible shape:

> Topaz
> Opal
> Calce-
> don

The basic pattern is one of vowels (*AB, AB, BxA*); but there are also the parallels of "p" and "l," and the doubly chiastic "t"/"z"/ / /"c"/ "d" (*A* unvoiced/*B* voiced/ /*B* unvoiced/*A* voiced). The words are foci of aural as well as thematic attention. Here they form a single block poised against the texture of the previous line and a half; perhaps more characteristic of Herrick is the use of contrastive vowels and consonant clusters to make the individual words flash out against one another:

This *Camphire, Storax, Spiknard, Galbanum:*
These *Musks,* these *Ambers*...

[H-414/157.2/2–3]

Reading Herrick out loud, one finds one's voice picking these moments out, seizing upon them as aural points of reference. And one soon notices that the technique involved does more than simply underscore significant nouns. The lines quoted from "*Oberons* Palace" exemplify the way in which Herrick's poetics can convert his words in general into a kind of prickly aural décor, a texture of minute fixations. Herrick's hyphenations across line endings seldom come so thick as they do there, but they are common enough and, like his frequent, seemingly pointless enjambments, part of a general effort to have his words stick out. Rhymes cut across rhythmic momentum (note the hidden pentamenter: "Drinking in the dull-light of the Moon") and spangle themselves arrestingly throughout the lines ("like"—"light"—"comply"—"like"—and, in the next line, "lies") to give what are ostensibly tetrameters something of the choppy, piquant movement that is Herrick's trademark:

> Happy day
> Make no long stay
> Here
> In thy Sphere;
> But give thy place to night,
> That she,
> As Thee,
> May be
> Partaker of this sight.

[H-633/220.3/5–13]

Herrick probably averages the shortest lines of any important English poet. The rhythmic edges cut the words into objects; the movement never builds but is always encountering some arrest to the attention. The voice learns to move among these objects with the kind of erotic, fingertip agility—touch and disperse—that is occasionally the content of the poem:

> But since It must be done, dispatch, and sowe
> Up in a sheet your Bride, and what if so

> It be with Rock, or walles of Brasse,
> Ye Towre her up, as *Danae* was;
>   Thinke you that this,
> Or hell it selfe a powerfull Bulwarke is?
> I tell yee no; but like a
> Bold bolt of thunder he will make his way,
>   And rend the cloud, and throw
> The sheet about, like flakes of snow.
>
>   [H-283/116/141–50]

The tricky turn between the seventh and eighth lines (syncopated accent around a line ending) is not inadvertent, but a repeated feature of this particular poem (cf. 3–4, 15–16, 67–68, 129–30, not to mention numerous more navigable enjambments). The last two lines come apart like the bedsheet:

> And rend the cloud,
> and throw
> The sheet about,
> like flakes of snow.

Indeed, this "Pindaric ode" comes closer than any other seventeenth- or eighteenth-century specimen in English to the rhythmic dexterity of classical Greek lyric. The variable line lengths in Jonson's much better-researched endeavors, for example, merely pace an orderly presentation of solidly iambic material. Herrick's lineation, extracting energy at odd junctures, becomes a tool for showing us impatience as a dance.

It is exactly by means of such agility that one lives, rather than dies, amid one's chosen décor. The movement is that of childlike discovery and amazement, a short but bright faculty of attention continually distracted by something new:

> Me thought, her long small legs and thighs
> I with my *Tendrils* did surprize;
> Her Belly, Buttocks, and her Waste
> By my soft *Nerv'lits* were embrac'd:
> About her head I writhing hung,
> And with rich clusters (hid among
> The leaves) her temples I behung . . .
>
>   [H-41/16.2/5–11]

The eroticism here is almost a polymorphous perversity, an act of prepubescent exploration, wide-eyed and for the time being innocent.

A whole stance toward life is implied by that innocence and the verbal texture that supports it. For example, that bugbear of seriousness for the Augustans, the disyllabic rhyme, helps fix in some of Herrick's "somber" moments an emotion in which comprehension and regret cannot be dissociated from a certain simple surprise that things should turn out just so:

> Yet though thus respected,
>   By and by
>   Ye doe lie,
> Poore Girles, neglected.
>
> [H-205/83.1/13–16]

That very emotion is a crucial one in Herrick's economy: the precise acceptance of loss as conversion into décor.

> In this little Urne is laid
> *Prewdence Baldwin* (once my maid)
> From whose happy spark here let
> Spring the purple Violet.
>
> [H-782/262.1]

Again, as with Julia's leg, an incipient elegiac languor is reversed: first, by the unexpected volitional thrust given to these funereal strewings by the lineation—"let / Spring," as though the giving of this permission were an important act on our part—and second, by the newly salient final rhyme that will not permit us to read "Violet" as (to use the technical term) a dying fall. It is a small but precise redemption: one dies *into* something. This pattern underlies Herrick's thematic concern with funereal ceremony, particularly the almost obsessive placing of minute memorial objects ("smallage") on the tomb. But the issues are as much personal as they are ritualistic. The tomb in question is, more often than not, Herrick's own, and the pattern involved is a basic one in his psychology. The acceptance of death that it seems to make possible for him is one instance of a general strategy of effacement, since his décor not only memorializes but simultaneously displaces. One's general sense of the curious obliqueness of Herrick's love poetry, oblique without seeming devious, can be made specific: his eroticism is, precisely, decorous—even about such a matter as hymeneal blood:

> Dispatch your dressing then; and quickly wed:
> Then feast, and coy't a little; then to bed.
>
> .   .   .   .
>
> Fall down together vanquisht both, and lye
> Drown'd in the bloud of Rubies there, not die.
>
> [H-618/216.2/7–8, 15–16]

Similarly, in the passage from the Crew epithalamium, the conversion of the bedsheet into a flurry of snowflakes *is* the consummation; by the time one reaches the next stanza it is all over. In both cases the sexual drive at the crucial moment suddenly transforms itself into a swarm of objects. The last line above suggests a reason for wanting to have it this way, since in displacing the climax one might also hope to displace the *tristesse*. Death is a psychological as well as a physical fact, and one can provide for it with exact consolation:

> Ah, cruell Love! must I endure
> Thy many scorns, and find no cure?
> Say, are thy medicines made to be
> Helps to all others, but to me?
> Ile leave thee, and to *Pansies* come . . .
>
> [H-191/74.3/1–5]

Herrick's décor is, in its fullest sense, his way of saying goodbye— important for a poet of many short poems, who must do so so often. Many of his poems conclude with explicit gestures of leave-taking, in the tact of which his special verbal techniques play their role:

> Thus I
> Passe by,
> And die:
> As One,
> Unknown,
> And gon:
> I'm made
> A shade,
> And laid
> I'th grave,
> There have
> My Cave.
> Where tell

I dwell,
Farewell.

[H-475/178.2]

The short lines (disyllabic triplets!) interfere with the emotional resonances of the subject matter. The content of Herrick's verse is only
moderately "spiritual," but it projects nevertheless a definite discipline
for the soul; and he shares with his fellow West-country clergyman,
George Herbert, whom he resembles in few other ways, a concern
with the poetic strategies of self-effacement.

That is one way of talking about a group of lyric poems: attempting
to see repeated in them, on various levels and occasions, some basic
pattern or signature, some genetic encoding that governs the placement
of so many words so lightly carried. And behind all of what I have said
waits something of a linguistic allegory, as though Herrick's very
medium punned on his habitual content: the word itself as seized
moment, lighting up and disappearing—the lesson and discipline being
to let it do both. "Carpe diem," we might say, is not just a convenient
paraphrase of much of Herrick's "meaning," but is a proposition acted
out in the writing of the poems.

Insofar as origins are concerned, however, and insofar as we really
have to choose, it is probably more plausible to see Herrick as beginning
with his aural temperament, his trick of using words, and working
out from there the consequences, psychological and otherwise, of such
a style. The poems, read as a whole, support the sense of a man with
nothing really new to say or find out or in general to get at, but with a
keen disposition, quickly expended and quickly renewed, to write in
a certain way. This approach is more in key with our larger sense of
the enterprise of lyric poetry—poetry whose paraphrasable content
seems so often banal or even nonexistent, and whose power has to be
explained by mysterious reference to "style" or "sound." A lyric
oeuvre, at least of a certain kind, might be described as a group of poems
that collectively realize and make intelligible the nature and implications
of their common stylistic habits.

One way to describe the *Hesperides* would thus be to say that it picks
up a specific inflection in British poetry, for which the *fons* may be
Arthur Golding, unconcernedly rhyming "rape" and "grape" and
describing the Golden Age as a time when men

> Did live by Raspis, heppes and hawes, by cornelles,
>   plummes and cherries,
> By sloes and apples, nuttes and peares, and lothsome
>   bramble berries
>
>   [I.119–20]

But Herrick probably took the inflection, in a more sophisticated form, directly from his master, Ben Jonson:

> The faery beame uppon you,
> The starres to glister on you,
>   A Moone of light
>   In the Noone of night,
> Till the firedrake hath oregon you.
>   [*The Gypsies Metamorphosed* 262–66; 7:573]

Or even:

> Goe little Booke, Goe little *Fable*
>   unto the bright, and amiable
> LUCY of BEDFORD . . .
>
>   [8:662]

The *Hesperides* is a codification of that note. In Jonson the note is one possibility among many, and Jonson's oeuvre is a journey among possibilities. Herrick's oeuvre is that single definition made good, a determination of the periphery, as though by a bracelet, within which almost all of his poems take place. We do not even really want to speak of his oeuvre but of his "World."

Herrick particularly invites such attention by being the only important English poet to publish essentially all of his work in one definitive act, within his own lifetime and at least to some extent under his own supervision. Moreover, the individual poems themselves, approaching so closely and often to latter-day notions of "pure poetry" (there are two of them in George Moore's anthology), imply even in isolation some closed and specially poetic system of which they are part. Anything that Herrick picks up becomes curiously transformed, passing into some special zone where it no longer resembles the same things in our own world—a common experience with poetry, but especially strong and not always pleasant with poetry such as Herrick's.

Indeed, it is a matter of particular interest how his system assimilates

foreign objects (and all objects are initially foreign), for in such assimilation any system is quickly placed, its intentions put on the line. And
it is of even more particular interest that one of Herrick's largest sources
of foreign objects is classical literature—a fact widely recognized but
still needing to be related to the specific and even peculiar demands
of Herrick's own brand of poetry. As befits a writer of the last phase
of the English Renaissance, Herrick's use of the classics is both eccentric
and sophisticated; and as further befits a writer with his own well-
developed "world" to live in, that use, though respectful, is often
curiously unawed.

We need, for example, in assessing Herrick's "paganism" to consider
how little, in a certain sense, the classical gods mean to him. A characteristic minor genre of his is the "hymn" to a Roman deity, but it tends
to be the vehicle not so much for worship as for a kind of wistful business
transaction:

> Mighty *Neptune*, may it please
> Thee, the *Rector* of the Seas,
> That my Barque may safely runne
> Through thy watrie-region;
> And a *Tunnie-fish* shall be
> Offer'd up, with thanks to thee.
>
> [H-325/129.2]

An object is simply plucked from the god's traditional domain and
presented to him, not with solemn deference but with denotative
efficiency. Even within the cultural terms under which Herrick operated,
there are other possibilities. Though literal worship may be out of the
question, the invocation of a substantial presence is not; and that sort
of invocation can be made through décor, the sensual manifestation
of the deity's potency: the way Sappho summons Aphrodite to the
apple orchard. But Herrick's devolution onto a single propitiatory
object, chosen more for identification than emphasis (as is usual in these
poems, and unlike Julia's leg, the object is not even a rhyme word), has
the contrary effect of simply locating and taming.

This is, of course, Herrick's characteristic gesture, and elsewhere the
proffered object can be the familiar snippet of greenery with which
he customarily decks his tombs. But that gesture is neither intended
nor fitted to evoke potency; quite the contrary, it crystalizes a dying
energy into careful consolation. The gods in Herrick are radically

reduced, subjected to a bland reification occasionally made explicit by prefacing the god's name with the indefinite article: "You can make a *Mercury*" (H-569/204.4/16). The continuing sense is of light vegetable garnish on an impassive statue.

It might be objected that this is to judge Herrick in terms of literary models (Sappho?) to which he did not have access. But there were available models for bringing these particular dead back to life; Herrick does not follow them, at least not in his "hymns." Jonson's "Execration upon Vulcan" (*Underwood* 45; 8:202–12) makes a good point of comparison: Jonson reversed the trend toward a kind of mild allegorization (Vulcan as fire) by simply *addressing* himself to it, at large, until the object in question could not help but assume the intelligible lineaments ("a cloddish forge-tender who can only smart with multiple disgraces, and destroy things")[1] of an addressee. Herrick's own hymn to Vulcan (H-613/214.3) derives from the same allegory and even concerns the same relation to the poet—the burning of his works—but finds four rather indifferent lines to say on a subject that keeps Jonson going memorably for 216. Nor did Jonson's mode lie beyond Herrick's powers. Herrick uses that mode, and successfully, but not with a classical deity; he applies it to Sack (H-128/45.1, H-197/77.2).

There are exceptions to the general inefficacy of the classical gods in Herrick, but there are also particular reasons for these exceptions. Most instructive are the only deities who actually seem vivified by the style of worship they receive—namely, Herrick's "Closet-gods":

> It was, and still my care is,
> To worship ye, the *Lares*,
> With crowns of greenest Parsley,
> And Garlick chives not scarcely:
> For favours here to warme me,
> And not by fire to harme me.
>
> [H-674/234.4/1–6]

Such worship is essentially the same that all the others receive, but here it fits: the small talismanic presence giving a center to the domestic situation. How a man anchors his mind within the drawn circle of his own home has generally, especially in England, been his own business. The *lar* is precisely the god within the drawn circle, acceptable to others because he has no territorial ambitions; you know you are home when you have nowhere else you have to get to. And the loss of potency that affects the Olympians in Herrick is essentially a process of domestication; they all become *lares*, little figurines over the fireplace.

Elsewhere in dealing with these matters, Herrick seems to be poetically most vital when relieved of the actual classical names. On, for example, "the gods" in general—the undifferentiated plural, the idea or odor, not the details, of paganism—Herrick has a number of attractive and even original things to say. His highly pertinent allegorization of pagan sacrifice—their "easie natures like it well, / If we the roste have, they the smell" (H-66 / 22.4 / 3–4)—has lately been singled out for discussion.[2] The allegory even seems to lead, via that carefully chosen adjective, to articulation of a more general recommended disposition:

> The Gods are easie, and condemne
> All such as are not soft like them.
>
> [H-132 / 47.2 / 13–14]

In a somewhat similar manner, the "Graces" are literal classical gods, but their name transfers effortlessly into English abstraction, from which Herrick can derive guidance in shaping his poem. His hymn to them explores the actual mode of their power in a way in which the hymns to the other deities do not:

> When I love, (as some have told,
> Love I shall when I am old)
> O ye Graces! Make me fit
> For the welcoming of it.
> Clean my Roomes, as Temples be,
> T'entertain that Deity.
> Give me words wherewith to wooe,
> Suppling and successefull too:
> Winning postures; and withall,
> Manners each way musicall:
> Sweetnesse to allay my sowre
> And unsmooth behaviour.
> For I know you have the skill
> Vines to prune, though not to kill . . .
>
> [H-569 / 204.4 / 1–14]

And their power thus, pointedly enough, includes the fashioning of their fellow gods into décor:

> And of any wood ye see,
> You can make a *Mercury*.
>
> [15–16]

The Graces have a reality that Mercury does not. One could, if one wanted, pretend that they are not foreign gods at all, but capitalized attributes of an English personality.

This example is a minor one, but the principle is not: classical paraphernalia tend to energize themselves in Herrick as they become more nearly invisible. Indeed, the largest and most important group of classical "borrowings" in Herrick is, to the unsuspicious, wholly invisible in a way that, like so much else, Herrick seems to have picked up from Jonson. And it is to Jonson that we may go for a definitive example and tour de force:

> Drinke to me, onely, with thine eyes,
>   And I will pledge with mine;
> Or leave a kisse but in the cup,
>   And Ile not looke for wine.
> The thirst, that from the soule doth rise,
>   Doth aske a drinke divine:
> But might I of *Jove's Nectar* sup,
>   I would not change for thine.
> I sent thee, late, a rosie wreath,
>   Not so much honoring thee,
> As giving it a hope, that there
>   It could not withered bee.
> But thou thereon did'st onely breath,
>   And sent'st it backe to mee:
> Since when it growes, and smells, I sweare,
>   Not of it selfe, but thee.
>
> [*The Forest* 9; 8:106]

This is one of Jonson's most Herrick-like pieces, even to the concern with the transfer of bodily odors onto erotic décor; and one of Herrick's poems is in fact a miniature of lines 9–16 (H-144 / 51.3). Herford and Simpson call Jonson's poem "the one supreme success among his songs" (2:385); it is certainly one of the most durable products of the whole Elizabethan song tradition, and in fact one of the very few examples that everyone still recognizes. (An American historian, on being tested, said she had always thought it was a temperance pledge, but, yes, she knew the song.) Its popularity for three centuries comes from the way in which it suits everybody's ideal of what a civilized drinking song should be: graceful and trivial, neat but effortless, the inspiration (surely)

of the moment, a bubble. Not until more than a century and a half
after its publication did anyone note publicly that the poem is virtually
a *cento*, closely translated, of a number of separate bits of widely unknown Greek prose: the bubble was cunningly and deceitfully stitched
together out of pieces from several old inner tubes.

The investigator in question does not seem to have been tipped
off by anything in Jonson's poem itself; it is more likely that Richard
Cumberland was rooting around in the papers of his grandfather
Richard Bentley when he made the discovery he subsequently reported
in *The Observer* in 1785:

> I was surprised the other day to find our learned poet Ben Jonson
> had been poaching in an obscure collection of love-letters, written
> by the sophist Philostratus in a very rhapsodical stile, merely for
> the purpose of stringing together a parcel of unnatural far-fetched
> conceits, more calculated to disgust a man of Jonson's classic taste,
> than to put him upon the humble task of copying them, and then
> fathering the translation.[3]

Bentley had worked on an edition of Philostratos, and Cumberland
simply found that the Greek at which he was looking suddenly sounded
strangely familiar. For it is the very familiarity of Jonson's song that
constitutes the marvel which Cumberland interprets as an affront:
"The little poem he has taken from this despicable sophist is now
become a very popular song."

Cumberland's disequilibrium, the evident shock of his discovery,
is interesting, especially so because it is only the beginning of a minor
tradition among British men of letters. Others, not affected by Cumberland's eighteenth-century literary hauteur or his hereditary taste
for poet-baiting, have been more willing to see the case as testimony
to Jonson's talent. But the tremor of recognition, variously displayed
as amazement or outrage, remains, occasionally reported in the press,
as a kind of *rite de passage* for readers of Jonson.[4] In one recent article,
a classicist considers the manuscript version of the poem, concludes
that the later folio version represents an attempt at increased literalness,
and argues, tentatively ("This is the sort of judgement which classical
scholars are often ill-equipped to appreciate—I could as easily convince
myself of the reverse . . ."), that the earlier version is superior for
being "freer and more spontaneous."[5]

Behind this conclusion is the desire to save ground for freedom and spontaneity as essential elements of poetic composition; a bubble, somehow, should not have a history. Certainly one wants some sort of term between Jonson and Philostratos, some term of "inspiration" or "transformation" or "revision" to account for the success of the English poem. But Jonson's whole intent and—one may argue— accomplishment lie in reducing the paraphrasable differences between his poem and Philostratos's prose to almost nothing.

I quote the texts in literal translation, and in about the order of Jonson's use of them:

> So put the cups down and say good-bye to them, especially for fear of the fragility of their material, and drink to me with your eyes only—Zeus tasting such a drink carried off the beautiful wine-pourer. Or if you want, do not waste wine, but put in only water, and taking the cup to your lips, fill it with kisses and give it to those who need them.
>
> [*Epistolai erōticai* 33]

> Your eyes are clearer than wine-glasses, so one can see the soul through them. . . . I immediately, when I see you, am thirsty and stand still, unwilling, and hold the cup away; and I do not put it to my lips, but know I am drinking you.
>
> [32]

> But if you ever take a sip, everything left becomes warmer with your breath, and sweeter than nectar.
>
> [60]

> I have sent you a garland of roses—not to honor you (though that too), but to please the roses themselves, so that they might not wither.
>
> [2]

> If you want to please a lover, send back the remaining flowers, no longer smelling just of roses, but also of you.
>
> [46][6]

The parallels are striking enough, but the use in modern editions of Kayser's nineteenth-century numbering of the letters makes even Jonson's activity of choice and arrangement look more vigorous than it really is. In Renaissance editions the letters quoted would be 24, 25, 23, 30, and 31, respectively. And since 60/23 is actually only a collateral source, it would seem that Jonson took the Greek in almost exactly the order in which it presented itself to him—as though he had opened his book, transcribed a few letters, flipped a couple of pages, transcribed two more, and strung his notes together to make a "poem." Suspiciously, there is a close correspondence between the individual letters and the formal divisions of Jonson's song: 33 informs the first four lines, 32 and 60 the second, 2 the third, and 46 the fourth. Certainly Jonson is not, to use his own metaphor, digesting Philostratos whole and then refashioning him, and Symonds's description of the achievement will not do: " 'To Celia' is a lyrical outcome of Jonson's admiration for these curious and singularly beautiful sophistic compositions in general."[7]

But what exactly does Jonson do? Some small changes are made; homosexual suggestions, for example, are elided throughout. Forty-six is inscribed to a boy, though there is characteristically no specific indication of this in the text itself (a few letters in the collection are inscribed to a woman in some manuscripts and to a boy in others). An inauspicious reference to Zeus and Ganymede is suppressed in 33 and replaced by "I will pledge with mine"; 2 and 46 are deftly linked by Jonson's use of "growes" in line 15. In 46 the wreath simply comes back smelling of its recipient, with no hint of the life-preserving powers adumbrated in 2; Jonson unobtrusively converts the two conceits into one. His main "creativity" is exercised in the second four lines, where the source is not exact. Jonson's invention, though, works scrupulously in terms of available details: thirst and the soul, separately, from 32, nectar from 60, and Jove, with interesting economy, from the unused clause in 33. These detachable bits are fitted into a conceit difficult to distinguish in kind from those of the surrounding lines. It has never been seriously suggested that lines 5–8 represent Jonson's "real" voice breaking momentarily through the Philostratean static;[8] and if that were even the intention, why would they be medial instead of climactic? Rather, if the rest of the poem is taken as in some sense "given," what these lines suggest is a textual critic's careful, conjectural reconstruction of a lacuna. The other major "improvisation"—"And I will pledge with mine"—looks in retrospect like much the same thing: a reasonable and convincing extrapolation of the Greek's *men-de* texture, even though that is not the specific character of the suppressed original at this point.

It all implies a demanding literary game: punch holes in a text, and then fill them in again in such a way that nobody can guess what you have done. In an age when textual criticism was a central cultural endeavor, this would not seem as silly as it might today. It was the game that Spenser played (though he did not, like Jonson, punch his own holes) when he slipped two carefully made-up names into his catalogue of the Nereids (FQ 4.11.48–51); the reader is not likely to guess which ones they are without taking out his Hesiod. Jonson is not "creatively transforming" the ancient text, but mastering the range of appropriate context which his donnée sets up: given lines 1–4 and 9–16, what would it make sense for lines 5–8 to say? In this peculiar Jonsonian way the professions of scholar and writer converge.

In that convergence is one of the few kinds of literary study that does not have to worry about being impertinent to its object, since it replies on a comparable level of activity. Study of the text is precisely by means of further writing: how might one, on one's own and in English, find oneself saying just these words? The goal here is the very undetectability of the source, its total effacement into the present occasion, since that is exactly the sign that a viable English literary possibility has been realized—that we now know, in at least one very specific sense, what these words mean. It is a curious but effective way of expanding English literature by lifting the burden of the past: decomposing the original in this manner, rather than trying to assimilate or answer it as a whole, converts it, at least for the moment, from *daimōn* into resource. One works this way up or back to the starting point, to the place where one begins, again, from scratch.

Other relationships to one's literary past are of course possible—in fact more common and certainly easier to discuss. We may distinguish the epic style of allusion, in which a *perspective* on the past is exactly what is wanted: "Compare Milton's invocation of the Muse to Vergil's," etc. There is an important sense in which one cannot read *Paradise Lost* without knowing the *Aeneid*, or read the *Aeneid* without knowing Homer. But one can certainly read "Drinke to me, onely," without knowing Philostratos, or even who he was; most people, even professionals, do, and without missing much. The mode of allusion here— a lyric mode, if you will—does not put the past in perspective but makes it if anything copresent, enables one to pretend that the congruences between the past and present are but happy accidents, two living minds meeting in the same words.

"Drinke to me, onely," is a limiting case in several ways, in its nearly complete verbal absorption in its source, and also in the relative obscurity of that source, obscurity which would exclude even a normally well-trained seventeenth-century reader from following the game as he could when the source was Catullus or Ovid.[9] But the principles involved are valid for much of Jonson's general program of classical quotation: sententiae and turns of phrase so adjusted to their English context, or their English context so adjusted to them, that the reader is never quite sure without checking the notes (some of them, of course, supplied by Jonson himself) what sort of ground he is walking on. And, as with the famous drinking song, the reader has often complained:

> mais l'ennui avec Jonson, c'est qu'on ne sait jamais, en l'admirant, si l'on n'est pas la dupe d'une fraude innocente ou plutôt de sa propre ignorance . . . qui nous dit que certains vers charmants ne viennent pas en droite ligne de Catulle ou d'Anacréon, que tel passage admiré par nous n'est pas une simple traduction bien faite ou une ingénieuse adaptation?[10]

And again, that is exactly the point, as at least one Renaissance writer openly admitted: "combien audacieusement j'entreprens moy mesmes à tous coups de m'esgaler à mes larrecins, d'aller pair à pair quand et eux, non sans temeraire esperance que je puisse tromper les yeux de juges à les discerner" (Montaigne, *Essais* 1.26). This is how one gets oneself to write well.

If anything, the same "ennui" pertains even more extensively in Herrick than in Jonson. The most famous line Herrick ever wrote is only the latest term in a clearly defined tradition that reaches back through four languages:

Gather ye Rose-buds

[H-208 / 84.1 / 1]

Gather therefore the Rose

[Spenser, *FQ* 2.12.75]

Cogliam la rosa

[Tasso, *Gerusaleme Liberata* 16.117]

Cueillez dés aujourdhuy les roses

[Ronsard, 2:287][11]

Collige, uirgo, rosas

[*De Rosis Nascentibus* 49][12]

Such intermediaries, though, are relatively rare;[13] the available evidence usually points to a direct tracing of Latin phraseology into English. And this tracing can often be spotted as a crucial part of the way in which the poem was written. The importation is an irritant, a stimulus to establishing an appropriate English context. It is worth noting that the rules here do not require that the English context have too much to do with the Latin one:

> Goe happy Rose, and enterwove
> With other Flowers, bind my Love.
>
> [H-238/98.2/1–2]

> I, felix rosa, mollibusque sertis
> nostri cinge comas Apollinaris.
>
> [Martial, 7.89.1–2]

[Go, happy rose, and with soft garlands bind the hair of our Apollinaris.]

The proper name is glossed over, and with it the homosexual context; but otherwise the source is quite exact and unmistakable—certainly more literal than Waller's famous dealings ("lovely" instead of "happy") with the same lines. After this the poems diverge:

> Tell her too, she must not be,
> Longer flowing, longer free,
> That so oft has fetter'd me.
>
> [3–5]

> quas tu nectere candidas, sed olim,
> sic te semper amet Venus, memento.
>
> [3–4]

[And remember to wreathe that hair when, though a long time from now, it will be white—so may Venus always love you.]

Yet this divergence does not leave Herrick's quotation stranded. He has fixed on "cinge," sensed in this word an intersection with his own special concern for encircling décor, and spun out of this juncture a very Renaissance and relatively un-Roman thing, a "conceit." In retrospect one can spot the seam ("too"), but it itself matches with the casual, paratactic way in which Herrick's "conceits" tend to proceed. The thematic issue of binding is so gracefully and unemphatically developed that it comes as something of a surprise to learn that the first two lines were written by someone else, without this particular metaphor in mind. But to "change" Martial's lines this way has been a matter of paying very literal attention to what they *say*, to their status as a specific verbal configuration radiating specific possibilities. Herrick merely shifts the emphasis onto "cinge" so that, within the context of both this stanza and the *Hesperides* as a whole, the borrowed lines come across to someone equipped to follow both parts of the game with new and unexpected force: the love-gift as noose. The treatment of the quotation, in Stanley Cavell's phrase, brings the words home— which is to say, within the circuit of one's own *lar*.

Spotting these quotations was perhaps the major enterprise of nineteenth-century criticism of Herrick, of which Martin's edition is the culmination. That enterprise was more pertinent than for many poets because this style of quotation is demonstrably so basic a part of the way in which Herrick went about his business. Pollard, in 1898, gives what is within its own terms a fair statement of the case:

> Herrick, the most spontaneous of poets, perhaps by virtue of his very spontaneity, acquired a trick of throwing into verse the ideas which met with his approval in his desultory reading—he may be said, indeed, to have kept a poetical commonplace book, his authors supplying the commonplaces and he himself the poetry.[14]

If anything, Pollard does not go far enough, for it is not only or even primarily "ideas" that Herrick borrows. The sententiae are simply the most apparent, sometimes even attributed on the spot—

> *Vertue conceal'd* (with *Horace* you'l confesse)
> *Differs not much from drowzie slothfullnesse.*
> [H-459/173/13–14]

—and often, as here, italicized as a cue. That cue misled Pollard into assuming that italicized visibility is the norm: "in the final edition of his works every italicised line will have to be traced to its original, together with numerous others, as to the source of which his memory must have failed him when he was seeing his book through the press." For one thing, Herrick's typographical practice shows some real perversity in this regard:

> Shame is a bad attendant to a State:
> *He rents his Crown, That feares the Peoples hate.*
> [H-488/182.2]

That first, unitalicized line translates Seneca quite literally (*Hippolytus* 430), while the second line, in italics, is a pastiche sentiment varyingly suggestive of no less than four sources.[15] Here the italics punctuate the poem; they are not a tip to the researcher.

It is, moreover, not a very good poem (it is quoted entire), for reasons worth considering. The italics are intended to give clout to a discursive conclusion, but poetic argument is simply not one of Herrick's vital modes. Sententious borrowings should, as indeed they do in Jonson, provoke one to a discursive aggressiveness of one's own; there is even a valid nonscholarly reason then for italicizing, since what is going on in English is a conversation, made up by definition of different voices, deploying themselves with varying emphasis. In this regard—the development of the argumentative couplet—Herrick is outside the main line of English neoclassicism. His genius was almost premental, and explicit statements of wisdom remain most viable in his work when allowed to float at the level of avuncular commonplace: "Old Time is still a flying" (H-208 / 84.1 / 2). Insomuch as *Quellenforschung* leads us to dwell on the imported "thought" as a point of poetic emphasis, it is merely distracting.

And in any case, a very large class of Herrick's borrowings are not sententious at all, but much more minutely verbal. A line quoted above—"Longer flowing, longer free"—provides a good example; its phrasing and structure obviously owe a lot to Jonson: "Robes loosely flowing, haire as free" (*Epicoene* 1.1.99; 5:167). That Herrick borrowed this way from Jonson is not surprising; in the general context of contemporary writing, small gestures of diction and cadence are bound to catch in the ear and reassert themselves. But Herrick derives such sub-sententious smatterings from the Romans even more frequently than he does from his contemporaries. The presence of these borrowings is quite difficult to detect, but the sources usually turn out to be unambiguous and often quite literal. A reference, for example, to "the old Race of mankind" (H-377 / 147 / 38) looks perfectly bland, except that it could serve as an interlinear translation of Horace, "prisca gens mortalium" (*Epod.* 2.2). The "easy" gods mentioned earlier derive from a special use of *facilis* in Ovid (*Heroides* 16.282) and Martial (1.103.4). There is a strong reliance on cognates: "The golden pomp is come" (H-201 / 80.2 / 4, 5), "aurea pompa uenit" (Ovid, *Amores* 3.2.44); "Stars consenting with thy Fate" (H-106 / 35 / 33), "consentit astrum" (Horace, *Carm.* 2.17.22).

Sometimes these habits seem to lead to clumsy English, as in Herrick's "*supremest* kisse" (H-14/9.1/6; also H-327/129.4/2 and H-1028/315.4/1), which looks like a schoolboy's version of Ovid's "oscula . . . suprema" (*Met.* 6.278). But Herrick tenaciously makes "supremest" a part of his *copia uerborum* (see H-838/274.2/6), and the usage is further camouflaged by the jazzy character of so much of his Latinate diction. As a neologism "supremest" is no crazier than "circum-walk" (H-35/14.3/5), and as a "Latinism" it is no more intrusive upon the native tongue than "liquefaction" (H-779/261.2/3), both of which seem to be Herrick's own inspiration. And at any rate, this Poundian willingness to be even childishly literal is part of what is meant by paying attention to the specific possibilities of specific verbal configurations.

In a similar example, Herrick writes "The Extreame Scabbe take thee" (H-6/7.1/6) under the evident influence of Horace's recommendation, "occupet extremum scabies" (*Ars Poetica* 417), "let the mange take the hindmost." (An interesting example for several reasons; what casual reader is likely to think of "scab" as a "Latinism"?) Martin calls this a "blurred reminiscence," but it is in its way a very specific reminiscence. Herrick has forgotten or ignored the grammar of the passage—"extremum," aside from not really meaning "extreme," is not modifying "scabies"—but has exactly remembered the way in which the words are arranged with respect to each other. A genuinely blurred reminiscence would recall the "sense" of the passage, and maybe even some of the particular words used, but not how they went down together on the page. Herrick is simply less interested in what his poets mean than in what they say.[16]

This last is important. Nothing in the rules of the game especially commits Herrick to the context from which his quotation is fetched. Occasionally his borrowing will almost reverse the thrust that obtains in the original. "*Corinna's* going a Maying" is not prima facie likely to make anyone think of Persius—

> So when or you or I are made
> A fable, song, or fleeting shade
>
> [H-178/69/65–66]

—but there it is: "cinis et manes et fabula fies" (5.152), "you will become dust and shade and fable." Herrick is so fond of that locus that he uses it again, with much the same phrasing:

> We must be made,
> Ere long, a song, ere long, a shade.
>
> [H-336/133/29–30]

And the injunctions in the previous line of the Latin—"indulge genio, carpamus dulcia," "indulge the genius, let us take the sweets"—similarly find their places in his work: "Gratifie the *Genius*" (H-231 / 96.3 / 6), and (probably) from the same stanza in "*Corinna*," "take the harmlesse follie of the time" (58). Thus isolated, the Latin looks, in fact, like a two-line précis of the *Hesperides*. But in the original the passage is all placed as part of a somewhat bitchy harangue by "sollers Luxuria," and constitutes one horn of a complicated moral dilemma that involves a matching harangue from Avarice. Source-hunting that brings context to bear can make Herrick seem at least unguarded, and possibly worse; Sidney, for example, who remembered the context of Persius's lines, might immediately have pegged Herrick as one of "those harde harted evill men who thinke vertue a schoole name, and knowe no other good but *indulgere genio*, and therefore despise the austere admonitions of the Philosopher, and feele not the inward reason they stand upon." [17]

But to remember the original context is clearly in some sense to miss the point. Herrick's response is primarily to moments of verbal grace rather than to structures of meaning, and his attention to the phrases of his originals is not effectively matched by an attention to the individual poems as wholes. There are, considering the bulk of the whole and the general ambience of classical quotation, notably few translations and imitations of complete poems in the *Hesperides*. The exceptions are important and helpful, and will be considered later; but the principle remains that while Herrick seems very interested in classical poetry, he is not comparably interested in classical poems.

Of course, his own notions of structure are relatively simple, if rigorous. For Herrick, it does not take much to make a poem; he has relatively modest standards for what Gascoigne calls the "invention," the *aliquid salis*, that sets a poem off from its surroundings. Several of the shorter poems in the *Hesperides* are actually translations lifted from the middle of some classical work:

> prisca iuuent alios, ego me nunc denique natum
>   gratulor: haec aetas moribus apta meis
>
> > [Ovid, *Ars* 3.121–22]

> Praise they that will Times past, I joy to see
> My selfe now live: *this age best pleaseth mee.*
>
> > [H-927 / 292.6]

Such moments are always isolating themselves for Herrick; he does not generally respond to them as stages in a larger process. He was certainly not alone in this; the prevailing and distinctive Renaissance mode of classical study, to read with pen in hand and notebook open, ready for entries, was pitched to encourage just such a kind of attention.[18] Herrick's long book of short poems merely carries the process to some sort of limit, almost to an aesthetic.

All we can safely say that Herrick "got" from the classics in this way is a certain Latinate firmness of statement—the heft or timbre of his authors' voices but none of their specific intentions. Yet the prejudice persists that deeper congruences somehow obtain. It is interesting that the other major tradition of nineteenth-century Herrick criticism, developing alongside the source-hunting, concerns itself with the suggestive matter of equating oeuvre with oeuvre. "Perhaps there is no collection of poetry in our language which, in some respects, more nearly resembles the *Carmina* of Catullus."[19] That is Nathaniel Drake, 1804, in a document central to the early nineteenth-century rediscovery of Herrick. In context all he is specifically referring to ("some respects") is the juxtaposition of bitter and sweet in the arrangement of the poems; but the notion activated an entire century of interest.

Drake's remark, in quotation marks but unattributed, out of context and with "perhaps" omitted, found its way into S. W. Singer's preface to the Pickering edition of the *Hesperides* (1846), thence to Carew Hazlitt's edition (1869), and was widely circulated throughout nineteenth-century discussion of Herrick. By the time of James Russell Lowell, Herrick had become, as though by common consent, the "most Catullian of poets since Catullus."[20] The gradual movement from the *Carmina* to "Catullus" should not distress us. It is part of the business of a lyric poet to attach a literary personality to his own proper name, and in so doing he helps delineate the nature of a lyric oeuvre: a specific disposition participating in a series of concrete events but not really determined by them. The lyric center is more in the "personality," realized as style, than in the poems. One could have a wholly different set of poems that somehow added up to the same oeuvre. One could have an "English Catullus."

One could, but Herrick no longer strikes us as much of a contender for that title (we now prefer Burns). Perhaps in the nineteenth century Catullus ("pedicabo ego uos et irrumabo") seemed much tamer (Herrick himself refers to "soft *Catullus*," H-575 / 206 / 43) or Herrick much more daring than they do today. The number of Catullan references in Herrick is not even so high, and one scholar has tellingly suggested that the reason Herrick acquired the reputation he did was because he simply touched the old favorites: the sparrow poems (H-256/103.3), the elegy on his brother (H-186/73.1), and the kissing routine from *Viuamus mea Lesbia* (H-74/24.2).[21] Touched but not really imitated; on inspecting the last, for instance, we find the old story of decontextualization, but with a rather special vengeance:

> Ah my *Anthea!* Must my heart still break?
> (*Love makes me write, what shame forbids to speak.*)
> Give me a kisse, and to that kisse a score;
> Then to that twenty, adde an hundred more:
> A thousand to that hundred: so kisse on,
> To make that thousand up a million.
> Treble that million, and when that is done,
> Let's kisse afresh, as when we first begun.
> But yet, though Love likes well such Scenes as these,
> There is an Act that will more fully please:
> Kissing and glancing, soothing, all make way
> But to the acting of this private Play:
> Name it I would; but being blushing red,
> The rest Ile speak, when we meet both in bed.

Catullus's kisses are clearly synecdoche for full sexuality; they are certainly not of the type that would ever threaten to displace actual copulation. But Herrick trifles with the idea of a sexuality that is all foreplay, and when he does try to go further has a very un-Catullan trouble saying just what is on his mind. Indeed, the poem traces a complete circle of embarrassment: it begins by substituting writing for speech, and ends by substituting speech for writing. Herrick's evasiveness shows that, paradoxically, his mind really is wholly on sex, while what is on Catullus's mind in the original is not coition but mortality:

> soles occidere et redire possunt:
> nobis cum semel occidit breuis lux,
> nox est perpetua una dormienda.
>
> [5.4–6]

[Suns can set and rise again; but with us, when the brief light has
once set, night is endless, unbroken, and must be slept out.]

Therefore:

> da mi basia mille, deinde centum . . .   [7]

[Give me a thousand kisses, then a hundred . . .]

—the kissing a frantic, baroque gesture to confound fate. Herrick is
aware enough of mortality, and even echoes the Catullan passage—

> Our life is short; and our dayes run
> As fast away as do's the Sunne:
> And as a vapour, or a drop of raine
> Once lost, can ne'r be found againe
>
> [H-178/69/61–64]

—but elsewhere, where it is not a lead-in to so manic and desperate a
burst of energy as is the case in the original.

This example merely points up with useful neatness the general
absence from Herrick of that vehemence which sustains so much of
Catullus's lyricism—his "intense levity," in Eliot's phrase—and which
constitutes for us his special inflection. But not only for us; it is not
necessary to go outside the seventeenth century for a genuinely assimi-
lative reading. Marvell, in "To his Coy Mistress," is neither manic nor
desperate, and is not mimicking Catullus's phraseology nearly so closely;
but he nevertheless maintains Catullus's underlying tension quite well
in placing exaggerated numerical rhetoric against ineluctable fact:

> My vegetable Love should grow
> Vaster than Empires, and more slow.
> An hundred years should go to praise
> Thine Eyes, and on thy Forehead Gaze.
> Two hundred to adore each Breast:
> But thirty thousand to the rest.
>
> .   .   .   .
>
> But at my back I alwaies hear
> Times winged Charriot hurrying near:
> And yonder all before us lye
> Desarts of vast Eternity.
>
> [11–16, 21–24]

It is Herrick who needs to dismember the Catullan poem before he can safely introduce it into his world.[22]

The first real disagreement with the Herrick-Catullus identification came from Edmund Gosse, who, however, instead of suggesting another approach, simply proposed replacing Catullus with Martial, and in so doing established the rules for much subsequent discussion. Grosart replied, defending Catullus. One scholar suggested Tibullus, and in the twentieth century the debate died down into a general consensus for Horace.[23] All this sounds, certainly, like some parlor game: "I am a free-born *Roman*," Herrick himself says (H-713/242.1/11), and we are to guess which one. But there is underneath a serious possibility that the classical models as oeuvres furnished Herrick with a steadying sense of his own enterprise, of how to sustain a lyric impulse until it becomes an oeuvre. And worth particular scrutiny for that role are the three poets whose poems Herrick does with any frequency address as wholes: Martial, Anacreon, and Horace.

II   Herrick's imitation of Martial, whatever deeper affinities may be lacking, is the most persistent and overt. No less than twelve poems in the *Hesperides* (a record) are direct translations or adaptations of specific poems of Martial's,[24] and the Roman epigram is clearly the strongest single genre-concept operative in Herrick's writing in general. His haplessness with that genre should not obscure, indeed should emphasize, its hold over his imagination; as a poet, he wanted to be Martial in a more direct way than he wanted to be anybody else in particular. And Martial provides the closest model for the overall shape of Herrick's poetic enterprise: of all the classical oeuvres, the *Epigrammata* is the one that Herrick's book most resembles as book, both in its general layout and in the kind of attention with which a reader is likely to approach it.

Both are, that is, very long books of very short poems. Both are organized into a large, inclusive group (the *Hesperides*, 1,130 poems; the *Epigrammata* 1–12, 1,187 poems)[25] that everyone knows something about, and a smaller section, tucked away at the end (the *Noble Numbers*, 272 poems; the *Xenia* and *Apophoreta*, 350 poems), of more specialized interest. Each poem, no matter how short, is provided with its own title, usually a denotation of subject or addressee, though there is no rule against several poems having the same title.[26] The entries, at least in the larger groups, seem to be shuffled according to local criteria of variety and contrast, with occasional thematic clusters; but the impression on reading them straight through is likely to be one of simple accumulation.[27]

But then, who reads them straight through? Both books are, in a certain sense of the word, unreadable.[28] Both invite, even demand, anthologizing; Martial himself seems to have made at least one such selection, an authorized abridgement of Books 10 and 11 (see 12.4). Indeed, the Roman poet is consistently quite clear-headed about the underlying paradox of his book:

> Disticha qui scribit, puto, uult breuitate placere.
>   quid prodest breuitas, dic mihi, si liber est?
>
> [8.29]

[Whoever writes couplets, I suppose, wants to please with his brevity. But what good is brevity, tell me, if it makes up a book?]

Stylistic brevity, by its very nature, exhausts the attention, both of reader and of writer, instead of sustaining it; one is always starting over again, only to go not very far. The result over a long haul tends to be a collection of generally interchangeable poems, largely independent of each other while being, as their titles sometimes confess, curiously similar. And Martial recognizes, with complicated defensiveness, the need for special kinds of strategy in approaching such a collection:

> Si nimius uideor seraque coronide longus
>   esse liber, legito pauca: libellus ero.
> terque quaterque mihi finitur carmine paruo
>   pagina: fac tibi me quam cupis ipse breuem.
>
> [10.1]

[If I seem too big, a long book with a delayed conclusion, just read selections, and I'll turn into a booklet. Quite a few pages end with a short poem—make me as small as you like.]

Several of Martial's most important literary habits converge in this little poem. It is, for one thing, addressed to the reader, with whose impatience and even hostility Martial carries on a lengthy run of negotiations. And the poem is spoken by the book itself, which is one of Martial's most common protagonists; when not actually speaking, it is forever being encouraged and cautioned. The level of reference can often be quite literal. There is a very physical sense to the word "pagina" above: not synecdoche for the printed medium, but a specific material object whose constraints put particular poems into particular positions. Elsewhere (1.2) Martial gives a more detailed account of paper and binding, as well as the location of the bookstore where this vendible object may be obtained.

To imitate the formal disposition of the *Epigrammata* is thus to imitate one of the aspects of Martial's poetry to which the poet himself draws somewhat detailed attention. And the *Hesperides* shows a similar concern in Herrick's mimicry, at one point or another, of most of Martial's routines of self-reference. Though Herrick's *liber* does not actually speak for itself, there are numerous personifications and objectifications of it (eleven poems are entitled "To his Booke"), continual encounters with the sour or generous reader, and even a brief acknowledgment of the likelihood of spot-reading ("If thou dislik'st the Piece thou light'st on first . . ." H-6/7.1/1). The tour de force in this regard, a very specific application of the assumptions of Martial 10.1, comes in the poem to Michael Oldisworth (H-1092/329.1/5–6). Herrick there refers to "The pillar of Fame" (H-1129/335.2) as being on the "next sheet," and in so doing makes a complicated pun on the makeup of sig. CC: after gathering and cutting, the pillar (CC7^v, p. 398) would indeed be physically on the next sheet of paper, even though formally eight pages away from the Oldisworth poem (CC3^v, p. 390). But the specificity of this instance is actually quite unusual for Herrick; the level of reference is more commonly not to "this" *pagina*, but to the *paginae* at large:

> Who with thy leaves shall wipe (at need)
> The place, where swelling *Piles* do breed . . .
>
> [H-5/6.3/1–2]

And there is in general a certain distance and softness to Herrick's imitation of Martial's way of making thematic material of his book's formal design.

Part of the problem is simply that the *Hesperides* does not really copy the layout of the *Epigrammata* very closely, not nearly so closely as Herrick's contemporaries often did. There are no internal book divisions in the *Hesperides*, nor are the poems numbered. Herrick's collection resembles, rather, the earlier Renaissance books of epigrams; by the end of the sixteenth century, the double-integer frame of reference had become almost an unquestioned part of the genre. Indeed, Jonson and Sir John Davies produced only one book of epigrams apiece, but each has come down to us labeled as the "first" book.[29] The book divisions in the *Epigrammata* are Martial's own; the poem numbers were added by editors in the mid-sixteenth century, though in so doing they were only expanding Martial's own occasional habit of accounting for his poems in terms of simple arithmetic:

> Cui legisse satis non est epigrammata centum,
> nil illi satis est, Caediciane, mali.
>
> [1.118]

[If reading a hundred epigrams isn't enough for someone, Caedicianus, he'll never have enough trash to satisfy him.]

That is how Book 1 ends. All of Martial's principal books contain about a hundred entries (the average for 1–12 is 97.8),[30] so that it indeed looks as if he knew it was time to publish when he had accumulated up to about that level. *Satis*, as of something reaching the top and clicking off, is a continual note:

> iam lector queriturque deficitque,
> iam librarius hoc et ipse dicit
> "Ohe, iam satis est, ohe, libelle."
>
> [4.89.7–9]

[Now the reader gripes and gives up, and now even the publisher says, "Whoa, that's enough, whoa, book!"]

And at the level of the book, Martial's sense of gauging his work's sufficiency by a numerical grid is even more elaborate:

> Quinque satis fuerant: nam sex septemue libelli
> est nimium: quid adhuc ludere, Musa, iuuat?
>
> [8.3.1–2; cf. 3.1, 5.15, 6.1]

[Five books were enough, and six and seven are too much. What do you want to keep it up for, Muse?]

Such reports on the progress of formal time often serve, along with the other references to the *liber* and the audience, to begin and end Martial's individual Books. These poems are themselves formal announcements, declarations of an externalized structure of presentation. Herrick, with no book numbers or quotas to play against, can imitate such routines only with some vagueness: "The bound (almost) now of my book I see" (H-1019/313.3/1; cf. H-983/305.3). His dealings with his *liber*, most of their salience as an ongoing part of the work gone, have tended to accumulate simply at the beginning and the end—eight in each case. The *Noble Numbers* are officially anticipated—"Part of the worke remaines; one part is past" (H-1126/334.4/1)—and the book's last line is labeled as its last line—"To his Book's end this last line he'd have plac't" (H-1130/335.3/1)—and, in one display of real cleverness, a quatrain from Martial (2.8.1–4) is made into part of the book's corporate structure by being used to introduce the errata. But for the most part there is no equivalent in the *Hesperides* for the numerical snappiness of the *Epigrammata*'s self-descriptions.

This loss is more significant than might first appear, for the sense of humor behind Martial's number poems is also missing from Herrick's work. Herrick never seriously acknowledges the problems of writing a long book of short poems, nor does his sense of the struggle between writer and reader ever reach that spooky level on which things have to be mediated by pure mathematics. The point is not that the *Hesperides* is more "formless" than the *Epigrammata*—it is certainly more symmetrical—but that Herrick fudged in a way Martial did not on certain practicalities regarding the shape of his oeuvre. The ridiculous string of digits that has to follow every quotation from Herrick's book, as opposed to the brief double integer that we use in references to Martial, is evidence of that: history's revenge for the fact that Herrick did not provide a canonical grid for poems that we have trouble keeping track of any other way.

And in so doing Herrick also missed or ignored the joke, a joke that makes sense in the whole context of Martial's work. Martial's flashy subjection of his poems to these arithmetical constraints implies mockery in several directions: not only against himself for not being able to write anything but epigrams, but also against his public for needing to be coddled, and further against himself for shamelessly desiring a public. The objectification of the *liber* is part of a general objectification of the poet and his work as well, a placing of him in his context as a man writing for an audience: "Non scribit, cuius carmina nemo legit" (3.9.2), "he isn't a writer if nobody reads his poems." Writer and reader are linked in a deep complicity:

> Seria cum possim, quod delectantia malo
>   scribere, tu causa es, lector amice, mihi,

qui legis et tota cantas mea carmina Roma:
sed nescis quanti stet mihi talis amor.

[5.16.1–4]

[I could write seriously, but I prefer being entertaining—and the reason for that is you, dear reader, who read and recite my poems all over Rome. But you don't know what your affection costs me.]

The usual literary act of which Martial treats is not the mental one of composition but the physical one of *editio*, publication, that process by which the poem itself becomes a physical object and factor in the world. Hence the interminable concern with grubby matters of literary politics; and to the assertion that the poet should be above such things, the appropriate reply is to ask why he should pretend to be. For that is the kernel of the sense of humor that we call urbane, or at least urban: combining a "derisive acceptance of oneself as part of a mass" with the appropriate "techniques for bringing down those who would deny their membership in that mass."[31]

Martial's poems are indeed profoundly urban, in an almost modern way, an account of life in a mass. The formal landscape itself is precisely an urban landscape: an overwhelmingly large array of small bits, minutely different and numbingly similar, among which one simply has to walk and pick, often according to the flimsiest of criteria. The *Libri* rise like giant, hundred-unit apartment blocks, providing each poem with a numerical address—a necessary acknowledgment of the fact that, in the case of any particular poem, one is more likely to have to look it up than to run into it on one's own.

And such a situation similarly informs the *modus* of the poems themselves. The epigrammatic technique of efficient, reductive insult is itself a very practical urban skill, a way of coping quickly with the endless number of people whose lives jostle and impinge upon yours; but the aesthetic of Martial's Muse has a deeper base than that. It is the aesthetic of isolation at close range:

Vicinus meus est manuque tangi
de nostris Nouius potest fenestris.
quis non inuideat mihi putetque
horis omnibus esse me beatum,

iuncto cui liceat frui sodale?
Tam longe est mihi quam Terentianus,
qui nunc Niliacam regit Syenen.
non conuiuere, nec uidere saltem,
non audire licet, nec urbe tota
quisquam est tam prope tam proculque nobis.
Migrandum est mihi longius uel illi.
uicinus Nouio uel inquilinus
sit, si quis Nouium uidere non uolt.

[1.86]

[Novius is my neighbor, and I could touch him from my window. Who wouldn't envy me and think me lucky, with the advantage of such a companion around the clock? But he's as far away from me as Terentianus, who is now governor of Syene on the Nile. I can't eat with him or even see him or hear him; nobody in the whole city is so close and so far away from me. One of us is going to have to move. If you don't want to see Novius, try being his neighbor or his tenant.]

We need only a slight extrapolation to reach a very modern aesthetic moment: the man seen framed and lighted in his apartment window is already something of an objet d'art, and his tacit agreement to avoid eye contact with his neighbor introduces aesthetic distance, behind glass. He is a glimpsed specimen, of which the cityscape, virtually built out of glimpses and specimens, is full—in his very minuteness and isolation remarkable and even wonderful, like an insect in amber:

Dum Phaethontea formica uagatur in umbra,
    inplicuit tenuem sucina gutta feram.
sic modo quae fuerat uita contempta manente,
    funeribus facta est nunc pretiosa suis.

[6.15]

[While an ant wandered in the shade of a poplar, a drop of amber covered the little beast. And so, contemptible while he was alive, he becomes precious in his tomb.]

("*Fourmillante cité. . . .* ") The insect in amber is a significant image: it is common in Martial (cf. 4.32, 59), and is used twice in the *Hesperides* (H-497/185.4, H-817/269.4), though the definitive instance is in another, later corpus of major urban poetry:

> Pretty! in Amber to observe the forms
> Of hairs, or straws, or dirt, or grubs, or worms;
> The things, we know, are neither rich nor rare,
> But wonder how the Devil they got there?
>> [Pope, *Epistle to Dr. Arbuthnot* 169–72]

The intersection of distaste and delight in "Pretty" is an important node—the knot, which Martial himself does not so clearly show, that ties together the "lyric" and "satiric" parts of his work. The former now tends to slip from memory, even though it provided the source for some of the most famous "pure" English lyrics of the seventeenth century— not only Waller's rose, but also Jonson's lily:

> Have you seene but a bright Lillie grow,
>> Before rude hands have touch'd it?
> Have you mark'd but the fall o'the Snow
>> Before the soyle hath smutch'd it?
>> [*Underwood* 2.4.21–24; 8:134]

In a sense, Jonson merely expands "niuesque primas liliumque non tactum" (5.37.6), "first snow, and a lily untouched." Probably the reason this side of Martial has not made a bigger impression, and certainly the reason why this particular poem, from which Herrick also borrows (H-375/145.1), is not better known, is the continuity of this impulse with Martial's particular brand of irony. After several similarly "delicate" remembrances of his dead *puella*, Martial slips without warning into the parallel case of his neighbor:

> et esse tristem me meus uetat Paetus,
> pectusque pulsans pariter et comam uellens:
> "Deflere non te uernulae pudet mortem?
> ego coniugem" inquit "extuli et tamen uiuo,
> notam, superbam, nobilem, locupletem."
> Quid esse nostro fortius potest Paeto?
> ducentiens accepit et tamen uiuit.
>> [18–24]

[My friend Paetus refuses to let me mourn, while he beats his breast and tears his hair the same way. "Aren't you ashamed to cry over a little slave?" he says. "I've lost my wife, and still live—a wife famous, proud, noble, wealthy." Who could be tougher than our friend Paetus? He takes his millions and still lives.]

And that is the end of the poem.[32]

Elsewhere Martial's preciosity and sarcasm, instead of just jostling each other in this way, come into stereoscopic alignment; there is, for example, a farm that might be run by Herrick's fairies—

> finis mus populatur et colono
> tamquam sus Calydonius timetur,
> et sublata uolantis ungue Prognes
> in nido seges est hirundinino;
>
> .   .   .   .
>
> uix implet cocleam peracta messis,
> et mustum nuce condimus picata.
>
> [11.18.17–20, 23–24]

[A mouse pillages the frontier and is feared by the farmer as if it were the Calydonian boar. The crop is carried off to a bird's-nest in the claw of winged Procne. . . . The finished harvest hardly fills a snail-shell, and we store the vintage in a nutshell sealed with pitch.]

—might, except that the very purpose of the miniaturization is spiteful. Martial has been given the farm as a gift, and is commenting acidly on the donor's generosity:

> Errasti, Lupe, littera sed una:
> nam quo tempore praedium dedisti,
> mallem tu mihi prandium dedisses.
>
> [25–28]

[You made a mistake, Lupus—but only by one letter. When you gave me an "estate" (*praedium*), I wish you'd given me dinner (*prandium*).]

Again, end of poem. A pretty place, but you cannot call it a farm.

Herrick, it might be said, simply removes the first half of that last sentence from the context of the second half: a pretty place. The satiric strain in his Oberon poems ("Part Pagan, part Papisticall," H-223/91/25) is vestigial in comparison with Martial's. The preciosity in which the two poets meet remains a vital mode in each, but the lesson learned by comparing them here helps to explain some of Herrick's failures else-where. For in depriving the preciosity of its sarcasm, Herrick also deprives the sarcasm of much of its brightness; and this is fatal to his attempt to imitate not only Martial's book, but also his poems.

However much the *Hesperides* may resemble a collection of epigrams, it is, notoriously, the entries labeled "epigram" that have the least success in justifying their existence. The other poems can be much more genuinely "epigrammatic" in effect, since there is something to the very musculature of Herrick's verse that suggests the neurophysiological if not the intellectual force of a good Roman epigram. A modern poet has seen in the particular nexus of rhyme and diction surrounding Julia's leg an effective way of translating Martial:

> nunc sunt crura pilis et sunt tibi pectora saetis
> horrida, sed mens est, Pannyche, uolsa tibi.
>
> [2.36.5–6]

> As it is, your trouble
> Is that despite the virile stubble
> That mats your chest and furs your leg,
> Your mind's as hairless as an egg.[33]

(The proximity of "hairless" precludes accident.) Yet Herrick has serious difficulty parlaying his indisputable aural talent into more explicit modes of wit. The distaste behind his satiric epigrams has a way of presenting itself as its own justification, lumpishly, without the transis-torized formal order—the busy urbanite's joy at sizing things up fast—that is a basic part of Martial's aesthetic. In other words, Herrick does not know how to tell a joke:

> Of foure teeth onely *Bridget* was possest;
> Two she spat out, a cough forc't out the rest.
>
> [H-419 / 158.4]

The point of this is so blunt that it is almost tempting to see the poem as something other than a joke, some strange Beckettian symbiosis between an old *clocharde*, her body falling apart, and Herrick, poet and vicar, sitting there, watching and keeping track. That will not do, of course—it *is* supposed to be a joke, though the mental operation that presents itself as "wit," literally that of adding two and two, is a good

example of Herrick's modest standards for the *aliquid salis*. He is fond
enough of the story, however, to try to tell it again, with somewhat
better results:

> *Franck* wo'd go scoure her teeth; and setting to't,
> Twice two fell out, all rotten at the root.
>
> [H-728 / 247.3]

Addition has become multiplication, and there is another point besides:
you brush your teeth to keep them healthy, so if they fall out while
you're brushing them, that's funny. Or at least Herrick has done some
intellectual structuring of the event to that end.

But not very much; the vitality of his thought here is not nearly
enough, especially since this is the second version of the anecdote, to
lighten the obsessional weight of those teeth. What is it, one ends up
wondering, with Herrick and rotten teeth? The body is not just decaying
(acceptable memento mori), but coming to pieces, turning into perverse
décor; Madame Ursly makes a necklace out of her ex-teeth (H-668 /
232.4). Is this fetish somehow related to Herrick's persistent interest in
hardened bodily secretions, such as rheum turned, as he puts it himself,
to amber (H-816 / 269.3)? His disgust, that is, shows signs of being as
childlike as his delight: hypnosis by bric-à-brac.

The teeth story is derived from an epigram of Martial's, which
Herrick significantly stops translating as soon as Martial begins to get to
his proper business:

> Si memini, fuerant tibi quattuor, Aelia, dentes:
>   expulit una duos tussis et una duos.
> iam secura potes totis tussire diebus:
>   nil istic quod agat tertia tussis habet.
>
> [1.19]

[If I recall, Aelia, you used to have four teeth. One cough got rid
of two of them, and another cough two more. Now you can cough
all day without worrying: there's nothing a third cough could do.]

Not one of Martial's finest moments, but a recognizable and even
typical joke. Herrick took only the first step, the presentation of a closed
set of données. The second is the play of intelligence with those données,
rearranging them, as though in a box, until a formal unity appears, a
sudden and somewhat frightening sense of completeness. The lady in

803 coughs all the time. It's her whole life. She used to worry about coughing her teeth out, but they're all gone now, so I guess she's happy. *Tussis* as *psychē*: a soul finally freed from the constraints of the body.

It is the geometry of those constraints, and not really the material out of which they are made, that so fascinates Martial. His business is not really picking at foibles but the manufacture of coherent oddities. There are serious human dimensions to this; though the teeth-poem is meant as a put-down of Aelia, it draws on the very real fact that people, especially people in a city, will indeed accept and even welcome such reduction, or rather concentration, of their being into some minute obsession—in the name of *securitas*. The underlying vision of Martial's work is that of human life beset by and accommodating itself to an immensely intricate system of perfectly specific limits to its behavior.

Hence the rampant concern with sex, where the limits are quite literal and come into the most immediate contact with our desires, and are therefore subject to the most extraordinarily persistent ingenuity on the part of both participants and observers:

> Cum futuis, Polycharme, soles in fine cacare.
> cum pedicaris, quid, Polycharme, facis?

[9.69]

[When you fuck, Polycharmus, you're used to shitting at the end.
When you're buggered, Polycharmus, what do you do?]

A reasonable question, really, since we may feel sure that Polycharmus, that name notwithstanding, has a body constructed in essentially the same way as our own. There are enough first-person adventures in the *Epigrammata* to let us know that Martial shares our certainty. We are all made of the same clay, or rather machinery: the delight in the poem is that of watching a clearly defined system pursue its own logic into a nexus of frustration, like a vacuum cleaner getting hold of its own cord.

Martial's "obscenity" is thus, like the mathematical structures of his book, a basic part of his subject matter: man's eternal engagement with the formal possibilities of the literal. Herrick's vulgarities are something else—usually, as with Bridget's teeth, a direct register of revulsion—but in the nineteenth century they were often blamed on Martial's example. That is probably in general true, though on those few occasions on which we can parallel specific wording, Herrick may be observed consistently toning things down:

una pudicitiae mentula nota meae.

[10.63.8]

Contented with the bed of one.

[H-116/41.1/8]

sed nemo potuit tangere: merda fuit.

[3.17.6]

But none co'd eate it, 'cause it stunk so much.

[H-131/47.1/6]

The modern impression, in fact, may be that Herrick is not obscene enough for his own artistic good, since with the loss of explicitness, diagrammatic splendor becomes overshadowed by simple ill-nature. Even the closest thing to an exception is a bit fuzzy:

> Since *Gander* did his prettie Youngling wed;
> *Gander* (they say) doth each night pisse a Bed:
> What is the cause? Why *Gander* will reply,
> *No Goose layes good eggs that is trodden drye.*
> [H-636/223.1]

I take this to be a joke about a bumpkin, full of rustic lore but with little understanding of his own body, who blunderingly substitutes urine for semen. If that is it, there is something to admire in the way in which Herrick has finessed the issue of diction by making misinterpretation of a euphemism his subject matter. But the real issue is not diction, as can be seen by turning to poetry that unmistakably maintains Martial's essential vision while staying scrupulously chaste in its terminology:

> Could you directly to her Person go,
> Stays will obstruct above, and Hoops below,
> And if the Dame says yes, the Dress says no.
>
> . . . .
>
> And will you run to Perils, Sword, and Law,
> All for a Thing you ne're so much as *saw*?
> [Pope, *Sober Advice from Horace* 130–32, 135–36]

It is that kind of memorable externality about the absurd but very definite limits to similarly absurd but definite human endeavor that Herrick never achieves.

We should, of course, not be surprised to find a rural clergyman not writing secular urban poetry. Herrick's failure to "do" Martial has reasons and precedents outside his own work; there is even a minor tradition in English (e.g. Thomas Bastard) of flat epigrams written by West-country ministers. And also standing between Herrick and Martial is the huge corpus of Renaissance epigram, in which the Roman form is generalized to purposes that do not have much to do with the original specimens—purposes that, for example, Herrick's sententious epigrams, which have little precedent in Martial, are intended to serve. It is in terms of other traditions than the Roman that Herrick's epigrammatic practice is best, or at least most charitably, discussed.[34]

But there are also important issues involved that concern Herrick's own specific work and temperament. He does not, unlike most of the city-wits writing "epigrams" at the time, seem even to want to face people down, but shrinks from encounters fairly consistently. A bit of literary politics copied from Martial is interestingly altered in this direction:

> Miraris ueteres, Vacerra, solos
> nec laudas nisi mortuos poetas.
> ignoscas petimus, Vacerra: tanti
> non est, ut placeam tibi, perire.

[8.69]

[You only admire the old poets, Vacerra, and never praise anyone who isn't dead. Excuse me, Vacerra, if I don't, just to please you, die.]

> I ask't thee oft, what Poets thou hast read,
> And lik'st the best? Still thou reply'st, The dead.
> I shall, ere long, with green turfs cover'd be;
> Then sure thou't like, or thou wilt envie me.

[H-174 / 66.2]

Martial refuses to die; Herrick all but offers to. Martial's joke is adapted to fit Herrick's fondness for imagining his own death, and in the process all but loses its point: this we-aim-to-please gesture is not really ironic but merely another instance of Herrick's habitual self-effacement. Also, Martial names his addressee, twice; Herrick is just speaking to "the Detracter." There is little probability, of course, that "Vacerra" (meaning "log," i.e. "blockhead") is really the man's name, but the word itself aims the gesture in a definite way; "To the Detracter," like "To the soure Reader," sounds like "To whom it may concern." And even within the obvious conventions of epigrammatic names, there are strange things at work in the *Hesperides*: when Herrick does give a target a name (as in examples quoted earlier), he seldom addresses him directly. This tendency cuts him off from one of the great thrills of writing epigrams, that moment of putting the question: "cum pedicaris, quid, Polycharme, facis?" Question marks (as in the Gander poem) still abound in Herrick's epigrams, but the absence of an immediate addressee deprives them of much of their purpose. Herrick's real moments of direct address are in contexts of praise and friendship; the satiric targets are a world apart, and with them Herrick is unwilling to sully, or risk, his vocative.

Mid-century Cavalier verse is governed by a general movement of social retirement,[35] and Herrick's gesture of retreat into the circle of his friends is a miniature example of that movement. But the gesture has a special meaning in Herrick, where it is only the most explicitly social aspect of his habit, already referred to here so many times, of decontextualization. If the *Hesperides* is a coherent world, the mode of its coherence is not that of external social interaction, since nobody will even speak to a large part of the population.

A naïve generalization, perhaps, but supported by deeper principles: the retreat is a retreat inward, an internalization which preserves the objects of the external world but not the specific structure of their relationships—one way of describing the process by which functional realities are converted into décor (decoration). Bridget the teeth-woman inhabits the same book as Bridget Herrick (H-562 / 203.2), but not the same society. They are not going to talk to each other on the street. We are certainly not likely to guess, as would be clear in Martial, that they are made of the same clay. Wit—"a recognition, implicit in the expression of every experience, of other kinds of experience which are possible"—is a knowing exploitation of context, a reminder of not wholly controllable realities outside the poet. But to consider similar moments in Herrick and in his contemporaries, as Leavis points out, is to realize how "Herrick's game, Herrick's indulgence . . . is comparatively solemn; it does not refer us outside itself."[36] "Solemn," perhaps, does not go quite to the mark, but there is a definite tendency, as with Julia's leg, to ward off explicit humor, to let the object at hand completely occupy the field of vision until it becomes almost a hallucination, setting up its own rules.

> Her pretty feet
> Like snailes did creep
> A little out, and then,
> As if they started at Bo-peep,
> Did soon draw in agen.
>
> [H-525 / 194.1]

Another complete poem, and again one that for all its ticklish effect
is not quite a joke—certainly not when compared to its commonly
adduced analogue in Suckling:

> Her feet beneath her Petticoat,
> Like little mice stole in and out,
> As if they fear'd the light
>
> [76.43–45] [37]

The quotation comes from the middle of a 132-line poem, in the course
of which the parameters of mockery are made clear: both the hick
impressionability of the narrator and the titillating pretensions of the
wedding ceremony itself. Other moments distinctly reminiscent of
Herrick are, like Martial's miniature farm, controlled by their larger
context:

> The maid, (and thereby hangs a tale,
> For such a maid no Whitson-ale
>   Could ever yet produce)
> No Grape that's kindly ripe, could be
> So round, so plump, so soft as she,
>   Nor half so full of Juyce.
>
> [31–36]

The satire is "gentle," to be sure, but the poem culminates in an unmistakable demystification of the whole epithalamial tradition:

> At length the candles out, and now
> All that they had not done, they do:
>   What that is, who can tell?
> But I beleeve it was no more
> Then thou and I have done before
>   With *Bridget*, and with *Nell*.
>
> [127–32]

Herrick does not demystify; he stares. Suckling's air of locker-room
conversation—two guys comparing notes—is distinctly absent from

Herrick's work. Herrick's retirement is not just into the friendly circuit of his fellow Cavaliers; it is a much more inward and private affair.

III There was in Herrick's classical library, however, literature which suited that inwardness much better than Martial did; and for more cogent and fruitful analogies to Herrick's own poetic enterprise we can turn to one of the most thoroughly decontextualized lyric *corpora* in Western literature, the so-called "poems of Anacreon." The originals in this case are no longer widely read, certainly not taken seriously, even by classicists; and it requires some historical reconstruction to understand why the Renaissance took them very seriously indeed. They did, for one thing, have in common with most Greek literature a certain freshness as text; the calendar of availability made the Greek writers the most current as well as the oldest writers in the classical tradition. The Renaissance "rediscovery" of Anacreon was not, as in the case of Horace and Martial, the reactivation of a generally continuous line of transmission, but a specific event, occurring less than a half-century before Herrick's birth. What had been continuously available, as with most Greek writers, was Anacreon's name and vita and reputation; in 1554, Henri Estienne unexpectedly provided the poems to go with them.[38]

Moreover, he was wrong—and the whole affair presents an even more complicated and interesting case of mistaken identity than that involving Mousaios. The poems which the Renaissance knew as the essential corpus of Anacreon were not written by him or by anyone of his period, and in fact do not belong to any one writer or even period. They were composed by several poets, none of whom can be identified,[39] over a period of at least two centuries, and probably more. Interestingly enough, Estienne's *editio princeps* does include some of what are now taken to be genuine fragments of Anacreon, but Estienne placed them in an appendix reserved for doubtful attributions, without the Latin translations that were provided for the other poems: the real Anacreon was not considered to be of interest to the general reader.

A serious scholar, Estienne was not just being perverse. The poems now known as the Anacreontea come down in their own manuscript, with a reasonably unambiguous heading: *Anacreontos Teiou symposiaca*, "Drinking Songs of Anacreon of Teos." The real Anacreon survives in fragmentary quotations by grammarians and the like; Estienne considered their testimonies prima facie less pertinent than that of a manu-

script. And his initial caution may have been turned into suspicion by
the stylistic and other differences between the two sets of poems. It is
exactly these differences, interpreted in the context of a wider understanding of Greek literary history, that now lead us to mark the
Anacreontea as unmistakably late classical.

They are undemanding little poems, perhaps most importantly not
strange. When Estienne, anxious to demonstrate the worth of what he
is publishing,[40] quotes Sophocles—

κἂν ἦ γέρων,
ἐν τοῖσι δεινοῖς θυμὸν οὐκ ἀπώλεσεν.

[*Electra* 25–26]

[Even though an old man, he has not lost heart in these harsh times
(*deinois*).]

—and then compares, as though of equal merit, "Anacreon"—

ἂν δ᾽ ὁ γέρων χορεύῃ,
τρίχας γέρων μέν ἐστιν,
τὰς δὲ φρένας νεάζει.

[39.3–5]

[When an old man dances, his hair may be old, but he is young in
spirit.]

—he makes it unintentionally easy to specify what has been left out:
deinotēs, that classical Greek sense of the sharpness encircling man's life,
a sense combining the lexical functions of wonder, terror, and shrewd-
ness. Within such a convergence of qualities the tradition of tragedy
becomes possible—a tradition, however, rejected in the Anacreontea
in favor of one in which impulses have no consequences:

θέλω, θέλω μανῆναι.
ἐμαίνετ᾽ Ἀλκμαίων τε
χὠ λευκόπους Ὀρέστης
τὰς μητέρας κτανόντες·
ἐγὼ δὲ μηδένα κτάς,
πιὼν δ᾽ ἐρυθρὸν οἶνον
θέλω, θέλω μανῆναι.

[9.3–9]

[I want, I want to go mad. Alcmaion and white-footed Orestes went mad and killed their mothers. I don't kill anyone, but when I drink red wine, I want, I want to go mad.]

Alcmaion was the subject of one of Euripides' final trio of plays, so that the examples here span the history of Greek tragedy. Two lines later, in reference to another parallel from the stage, occurs the only use of *deinos* in the collection. Epic similarly eludes these poets:

> Θέλω λέγειν Ἀτρείδας,
> θέλω δὲ Κάδμον ᾄδειν,
> ἁ βάρβιτος δὲ χορδαῖς
> Ἔρωτα μοῦνον ἠχεῖ.

[23.1–4]

[I want to tell of the sons of Atreus, I want to sing of Cadmos; but my lyre plays only Love on its strings.]

"Anacreon's" way of defining his art is consistently negative, even when less apologetic:

> Δότε μοι λύρην Ὁμήρου
> φονίης ἄνευθε χορδῆς.

[2.1–2]

[Give me Homer's lyre without its bloody strings.]

Lyric is what is left after removing mortality from tragedy and epic. "Anacreon" occasionally alludes to death vaguely as the limit of pleasure, but the torsion thus derived is slight:

> ὅτ᾽ ἐγὼ πίω τὸν οἶνον,
> τοῦτό μοι μόνον τὸ κέρδος,
> τοῦτ᾽ ἐγὼ λαβὼν ἀποίσω·
> τὸ θανεῖν γὰρ μετὰ πάντων.

[50.25–28]

[When I drink wine, that's the only good I've got. That's what I'll hold on to. For death comes after all.]

As that last line implies, death fades into simply the future, about which "Anacreon" is fond of saying that we know nothing:

> Ἐπειδὴ βροτὸς ἐτύχθην
> βιότου τρίβον ὁδεύειν,

χρόνον ἔγνων, ὃν παρῆλθον·
ὃν δ᾽ ἔχω δραμεῖν, οὐκ οἶδα,
μέθετέ με, φροντίδες·
μηδέν μοι καὶ ὑμῖν ἔστω.
πρὶν ἐμὲ φθάσῃ τὸ τέλος,
παίξω, γελάσω, χορεύσω
μετὰ τοῦ καλοῦ Λυαίου.

[40]

[Since, being mortal, I was made to travel life's road, I know about the time that's past, but not what I have ahead of me. Good-bye cares; we have no business together. Before the end gets me, I'll play and laugh and dance with my lovely wine.]

Variations on *ouc oida*, "I don't know," run all through the collection. The real Anacreon makes no such claims to ignorance, but has quite specific and frightening ideas about death and the future and what it means to be mortal:

πολιοὶ μὲν ἡμὶν ἤδη
κρόταφοι κάρη τε λευκόν,
χαρίεσσα δ᾽ οὐκέτ᾽ ἤβη
πάρα, γηραλέοι δ᾽ ὀδόντες,
γλυκεροῦ δ᾽ οὐκέτι πολλὸς
βιότου χρόνος λέλειπται·
διὰ ταῦτ᾽ ἀνασταλύζω
θαμὰ Τάρταρον δεδοικώς·
Ἀίδεω γὰρ ἐστι δεινὸς
μυχός, ἀργαλῆ δ᾽ ἐς αὐτὸν
κάτοδος· καὶ γὰρ ἑτοῖμον
καταβάντι μὴ ἀναβῆναι.

[LGS 322]

[My temples now are gray, and my head white. Graceful youth is gone. My teeth are old. There is not much time for sweet life left. Because of this I cry often, afraid of Tartaros. The depths of Hades are terrible (*deinos*), and the road there is hard, since there is no coming back for one who has gone down.]

Non facilis descensus Auerno. The poem that Estienne recommends derives from a culture more successful at insulating its participants against *to deinon.*

The Anacreontea are undemanding in more immediate ways as well. Anacreon himself lived in a time when mythology was part of a viable and often complicated and very local religion; the poem that, according to Hephaistion, came first in the Collected Anacreon is a prayer to Artemis on what sounds like some unknown ceremonial occasion (*LGS* 295). The gods in the Anacreontea, by comparison, though they are all over the place, lack any serious religious aura—much like the pagan gods in Herrick. The bust on the mantelpiece turns out to be a common term, when one of the Anacreontic gods comes on like a plastic Jesus:

> Ἔρωτα κήρινόν τις
> νεηνίης ἐπώλει·
> ἐγὼ δὲ οἱ παραστὰς
> "πόσου θέλεις" ἔφην "σοὶ
> τὸ τευχθὲν ἐκπρίωμαι;"
>
> [11.1–5]

[A young man was selling an Eros made out of wax. I went up to him and said, "How much do you want me to pay for this thing?"]

More generally, and similarly in accord with the practice of Herrick and many other Renaissance poets, the gods are just genial rhetorical decorations, partly salvageable as metaphor, but not with any great incisiveness:

> ὁ δ᾽ Ἔρως ὁ χρυσοχαίτας
> μετὰ τοῦ καλοῦ Λυαίου
> καὶ τῆς καλῆς Κυθήρης
> τὸν ἐπήρατον γεραιοῖς
> κῶμον μέτεισι χαίρων.
>
> [43.12–16]

[Golden-haired Eros, with beautiful Lyaios and beautiful Cythera, gladly plays the game dear to old men.]

Lyaios (wine) and Cythera (sex) are not even being set in relief against each other; they are blended by the exactly parallel placement of *calos*, "beautiful," into a general haze of pleasurability. (The haze envelopes the whole collection; l. 13 is identical with 40.9, quoted above.) The appearance of the gods here is simply a permutation of accepted poetic decoration, a recitation of names that seem to reinforce the prevailing mood.

Eros does make an interesting career for himself as an independent character elsewhere in these poems; they are a major source for the figure that we know as Cupid, and I shall be coming back to him. But even at his liveliest he is a secular character: secular, meaning that he is not an object of anything so embarrassing or inscrutable as worship; and a character, meaning that his attributes are developed and demonstrated in these poems themselves. The poems are in general self-explanatory, even to the point of employing the Intruded Gloss:

> Οὔ μοι μέλει τὰ Γύγεω,
> τοῦ Σάρδεων ἄνακτος.
>
> [8.1–2]

[My concern is not for the stuff of Gyges, ruler of Sardis.]

Archilochos, in the very probable original of this,[41] describes Gyges as *polychrysos*, "very rich" (which is the point), but does not, like "Anacreon," feel he has to tell us who Gyges was. It is almost as if the Anacreontea were written to be "timeless," with an eye on Renaissance publication; there is certainly nothing in them like the topical satire found in fragments of the real Anacreon (e.g. *LGS* 318). The very absence of historical contingencies in these poems is part of what makes them so impossible to date. We are in general not referred outside them to lost systems of belief or communal understanding; indeed, the recurrent content is precisely the relaxation of all tightly held sensibility:

> Ἐπὶ μυρσίναις τερείναις
> ἐπὶ λωτίναις τε ποίαις
> στορέσας θέλω προπίνειν . . .
>
> [32.1–3]

[Stretched out on soft myrtle, on lotus leaves, I want to drink . . .]

An important part of this effect of facility is metrical. All of the Anacreontea are written, with certain minor variations, in one of two closely related meters, the "Anacreontic" (⏑⏑‒⏑‒‒) and the "hemiambic" (⏑‒⏑‒⏑⏑);[42] and within these meters they show remarkably little rhythmic invention. In the genuine Anacreontic fragments we find, in some cases, an actual mixing of different metrical lines in the same poem, and even in others (e.g. *LGS* 322, a poem wholly in Anacreontics) a forceful awareness of the rhythmic possibilities of, for example, enjambment (*mychos, catodos*). The Anacreontea are timid by comparison. They derive from a time of metrical insecurity, as Greek rhythm moved slowly toward the accentual and the old quantitative rules lost their aural reality. Several poems cannot distinguish long and short alpha or iota—a giveaway that the rules are being followed on orthographic grounds alone—and some appear to be composed according to purely isosyllabic criteria.[43] This underlying chaos, however, is compensated for by a very bland regularity on other levels. Line endings consistently intersect sense units, a fact which is particularly important because the lines are so short. Almost every poem is paced as a series of self-contained seven- or eight-syllable units, with little of the involved syntactic development that characterizes much classical literature:

> Χαλεπὸν τὸ μὴ φιλῆσαι,
> χαλεπὸν δὲ καὶ φιλῆσαι,
> χαλεπώτερον δὲ πάντων
> ἀποτυγχάνειν φιλοῦντα.

[29.1–4]

> [It is hard not to love,
> it is hard to love,
> and hardest of all
> is to lose your love.]

The effect is reinforced by distinct suggestions (see especially 38) of rhyme as a structural principle. Similar in many ways to medieval Latin lyric, the Anacreontea are, for one trained in the more demanding traditions of high classical poetry, curiously easy to read.

Some such considerations were in Estienne's mind when he recommended Anacreon (and, in passing, Sappho) to those who are *philomousoi* but not *philoponoi*, fond of poetry but not of work. The distinction, it should be made clear, is intended to be favorable to Anacreon, and refers both to readers and to the poet himself. Estienne goes on to develop this distinction in terms of the stylistic virtues of "flowery" smoothness and ease, culminating in a Greek term for effortless pleasure: "we must see that of all the nine melic poets, Anacreon received the easiest life (*tryphain*) from the Muses."[44] *Tryphē*: grace in the lap of luxury, the poetic Good Life. Estienne uses that virtue, as his mention of the nine *melopoiētai* suggests, to rewrite previous understanding of the Greek lyric tradition.

For the primary victim of his distinction between poetry and work is Pindar, a notoriously difficult poet whose odes had hitherto constituted the only substantial body of classic Greek lyric available. They still do; but the clarion tone of Estienne's introduction ("For look, Anacreon of Teos, contrary to every human expectation, has come to light, breaking the adamantine bonds with which he had been held, slaughtering the myriad guards by whom he had been kept," etc.)[45] derives from the momentary illusion of having discovered an alternative, and better, lyric tradition. As though to begin consolidating this breakthrough, he included in the *editio princeps* not only the Anacreontea and a gathering of fragments, but also five bits of Alcaios and two poems of Sappho; he was later able to make the "poems of Anacreon" the centerpiece of his full edition of the Greek lyric fragments. This, it should be emphasized, was the habitual company the Anacreontea kept in the Renaissance; Miner's misleading remark that for seventeenth-century readers "Anacreon could be found in editions of the Planudean *Greek Anthology*"[46] reflects our own association of "Anacreon" with Hellenistic and later literature. But in the Renaissance the Anacreontea were valued for providing contact with something especially pure and primal:

> Quis Anacreonta blandum
> Mihi quis senem elegantem
> Suscitabit ad choreas
> Non elaboratum ad pedem?
> Age comites Lyaei
> Soluite iugum Camoenis,
> Vt amore liberali
> Repetamus illa prisca
> Concinendi mysteria . . . [47]

[Who will rouse gentle Anacreon, that elegant old man, to dance to his uncomplicated measure? Come, friends of Bacchus, loosen the Muses' yoke, so that with generous love we may rediscover those ancient mysteries of song . . .]

Estienne's judgment, of course, was surprisingly bad scholarship from a man whose instinct in these matters elsewhere enabled him to see through the mistaken ascription of *Hero and Leander*. Yet, as in the case of Mousaios, the misattribution showed good sense of an important kind and constituted a useful and alert bit of literary propaganda. For in the France of the Pléiade the reading of Greek lyric was not preeminently an academic concern; and Estienne's appeal for gratitude from the *philomousoi* (this edition, he doesn't mind telling them, was a lot of work) was in fact directly answered in a fruitfully appropriate fashion by Ronsard:

> Verse donc et reverse encor
> Dedans ceste grand' coupe d'or,
> Je vais boire à Henry Estienne,
> Qui des enfers nous a rendu
> Du vieil Anacreon perdu
> La douce Lyre Teïenne.
>
> A toy gentil Anacreon
> Doit son plaisir le biberon,
> Et Bacchus te doit ses bouteilles:
> Amour son compagnon te doit
> Venus et Silene qui boit
> L'Esté dessous l'ombre des treilles.
>
> [3:366]

An Anacreontic poem, and a successfully Anacreontic poem, in honor of the rediscovery of Anacreon, by a poet who had spent much time and ingenuity trying to imitate Pindar.[48] That Ronsard would try to imitate Greek lyric was, because of its prestige, sight-unseen, really a given. The publication of Estienne's edition early in Ronsard's career provided a stylistic model much more tractable than Pindar to the specific business that French poetry was about at the time; "l'Anacréon chez nous," wrote Sainte-Beuve of the period, "était comme pré-existent."[49]

It is, for one thing, clear just from the examples quoted how much more adaptable, even to the point of inevitability, French rhymed syllabic verse is to the rhythmic effects of the Anacreontea ("Non elaboratum ad pedem") than to the torsions of the choral ode. More generally, the simplicity of "Anacreon's" verbal surface suited one of the major evolving concerns of both French and English neoclassicism, that of fitting the exertions of writing to a norm of elegant limpidity, of clear and distinct ideas. It was primarily on such grounds that Ronsard, further following Estienne, later staged his own *certamen Pindari et Anacreontis*:

Me loüe qui voudra le replis recourbez
Des torrens de Pindare à nos yeux desrobez,
Obscurs, rudes, fascheux, et ses chansons cognües
Que je ne sçay comment par songes et par nües,
Que le peuple n'entend: le doux Anacreon
Me plaist . . .

[7:191][50]

Pindar could not be of much service in developing means of being effortlessly articulate, of never betraying oneself by seeming to try very hard. "Anacreon," on the other hand, people could understand. That the simplicity of the Anacreontea is really a matter of thinning out rather than of concentration—not *vers faciles* but *vers facilement faits*—need not concern us. It certainly did not concern Ronsard, because, thanks to the scholarly cachet that had been bestowed upon these poems, he did not know.

But there is more here than a simple case of usefully mistaken identity. For what does it mean to take the Anacreontea seriously as the oeuvre of one man: sixty poems written by several poets over several centuries, and gathered together under the name and reputation of a man who wrote none of them? Exactly what kind of authorial presence does such a situation produce? Estienne, in order to make his ascription of the collection, did have to relegate to his appendix or suppress entirely some poems in which the speaker is perfectly conscious of not being Anacreon —indeed, in which the process of becoming Anacreon is the business at hand:

τὸν Ἀνακρέοντα μιμοῦ,
τὸν ἀοίδιμον μελιστήν.

[60.30–31]

[Imitate Anacreon, the famous singer.]

And the point about this *imitatio* is not just that it is self-conscious, but that it is meant to be easy; the opening lines of the poem, though corrupt, seem to describe a very clubbable, non classical sort of literary brotherhood, in which *aethlos men ou proceitai* (60.2), there is no contest going on but everyone who enters will get a prize. This uncompetitiveness may in part be explained very simply: the only name to be made has already been made, and presides over everybody's work, good or bad. The collection's opening poem describes an appropriately casual scene of instruction:

Ἀνακρέων ἰδών με
ὁ Τήιος μελῳδὸς
ὄναρ γέλων προσεῖπεν,
κἀγὼ δραμὼν πρὸς αὐτὸν
περιπλάκην φιλήσας.
γέρων μὲν ἦν, καλὸς δέ,
καλὸς δὲ καὶ φίλευνος·
τὸ χεῖλος ὦζεν οἴνου,
τρέμοντα δ᾽ αὐτὸν ἤδη
Ἔρως ἐχειραγώγει.
ὁ δ᾽ ἐξελὼν καρήνου
ἐμοὶ στέφος δίδωσι·
τὸ δ᾽ ὦζ᾽ Ἀνακρέοντος.
ἐγὼ δ᾽ ὁ μωρὸς ἄρας
ἐδησάμην μετώπῳ·
καὶ δῆθεν ἄχρι καὶ νῦν
ἔρωτος οὐ πέπαυμαι.[51]

[Anacreon, the poet of Teos, saw me in a dream, and laughed and said hello. I went up and hugged and kissed him. He was an old man, but beautiful, beautiful and lecherous. His lips smelled of wine. Cupid led him tottering along. He took a garland off his head and gave it to me. It smelled of Anacreon. Like a fool I took it and put it on my head; and ever since, even now, I have not stopped loving.]

As an act of bardic investiture, this is at least as serious as the poems it prefaces. There is no encounter with an actual Muse, nor is anything even said about the writing of poetry. Rather, what is described is the Anacreontizing of the speaker's own emotions; the vocation here initiated is not that of writing like Anacreon or in the same tradition in which Anacreon wrote—these poets do not really do either, or even try very hard—but that of just *being* Anacreontic. That may sound, in its emphasis on life rather than art, like the more serious alternative, but it is not. For it is not tied to anything so specific and demanding and available for inspection as a poetic *technē*, but serves instead merely a dead man's reputation, the classical stock figure "Anacreon," with the quotation marks already encircling his name.

The speaker of these poems is intelligible mostly as a convergence of repeated clichés: he is old and usually broke, fond of dancing and roses and young boys and girls, and especially liquor, which is valued mainly for the quick relief it provides from the vaguely defined menace of *merimna*, anxiety. He is given to observing that we know nothing about the future and little about anything else and advocating a philosophy of the "present moment." It seems stuffy to call this anything so sharply etched as a persona; it is a repertoire of bits, like that of a clown. "Anacreon" is the gestalt of these routines, and as such is immortal without even having to try; hence the absence in these poems of any specific (as opposed to sententious) awareness of mortality or, for that matter, goal.

For the "personality" of the speaker is just an analogue of the characteristic mode of operation in the poems, the quick gathering of Anacreontic décor:

> Στεφάνους μὲν κροτάφοισι
> ῥοδίνους συναρμόσαντες
> μεθύωμεν ἁβρὰ γελῶντες.
> ὑπὸ βαρβίτῳ δὲ κούρα
> κατακίσσοισι βρύοντας
> πλοκάμοις φέρουσα θύρσους
> χλιδανόσφυρος χορεύει.
>
> [43.1–7]⁵²

[Let's fit rosy garlands on our heads and drink, laughing softly. A girl with pretty ankles is holding the luxuriant, ivy-haired *thyrsoi* and dancing to the lyre.]

By my count there are four words there (*men*, *de*, *hypo*, and *pherousa*) not directly evocative of the corporate motifs of the collection. This reservoir includes not only specific objects (garlands, roses, lyres, girls, hair) and actions (drinking, laughing, dancing), but also such affects as that provided by *habros*, "soft." Drop down to the next poem:

> τὸ ῥόδον τὸ καλλίφυλλον
> κροτάφοισιν ἁρμόσαντες
> πίνωμεν ἁβρὰ γελῶντες.
>
> [44.3–5]

[Let's fit the rose with its beautiful leaves on our heads and drink, laughing softly.]

The very phrasing recirculates (though the Greek does use two different words for "drink"). The only really new element here is the slight abstraction provided by the *calli-* compound—one instance of a class of terms (*terpnos*, *hēdys*) that register a general sense of enjoyment without having to be too specific about the stimulus. Setting these terms in motion would of course be the quickest way for a poet to establish his poem's Anacreontic pedigree, but it also informs their general theme of undirected loitering among pleasantries:

> Τὶ καλόν ἐστι βαδίζειν,
> ὅπου λειμῶνες κομῶσιν,
> ὅπου λεπτὴν ἡδυτάτην
> ἀναπνεῖ Ζέφυρος αὔρην . . .
>
> [41.1–4]

[How lovely it is to wander where the meadows are growing, where Zephyros breathes a light, sweet wind . . .]

And further, this interminable familiarity of décor allows us to specify what kind of collection this is, and what it might have to say to a practising poet. Taken as a whole, the Anacreontea propose a lyric oeuvre as a closed system of motifs, as though the writing of poetry were merely the display, over and over again, of the intrinsically poetic. There was a good deal of this going on in late classical Greek poetry; the *Dionysiaca* is an epic written on such principles, though with an increasing, obsessive violence that almost transforms its données into something different. The Anacreontea, on the other hand, allow their poeticisms to remain in a deliquescent repose, never really challenging their own validity.

This bland systematization, a principle easy to learn and teach, accounts for the collection's large time span; and indeed, as the last poem seems to claim, the rules are such that pretty much anyone who wanted to could pick them up, and also that no one could really do anything exceptionally competent within them. The Anacreontic tradition might thus be described as a kind of miniature Petrarchanism—another poetic leveler, distinction within which we now tend to associate with sabotage ("My Mistres eyes are nothing like the Sunne"). And just as the Anacreontea, both as a whole and as individual poems, center on no potent voice, but on the Silenoid stock-figure of "Anacreon," so Petrarchanism condenses around a modish image of the "Petrarchan lover," which does no justice either to the historical Petrarch or even to his purely literary personality.

There are more interesting and subtle parallels as well, for the Greek poems show a process something like the internalization of reference so familiar in Petrarch ("Di pensier in pensier, di monte in monte ..."). The passage quoted earlier about wanting to rave like Orestes without actually killing anyone transfers interpersonal dramatic action to the plane of psychological allegory; and other poems similarly metamorphose the mythic subjects of earlier poetry:

> Σὺ μὲν λέγεις τὰ Θήβης,
> ὁ δ᾽ αὖ Φρυγῶν αὐτάς,
> ἐγὼ δ᾽ ἐμὰς ἁλώσεις.

[26.1–3]

Edmonds, in his Loeb translation, for once rises to the occasion:

> Thebes doth your verse employ,
> Another's, frays of Troy;
>   My tale shall be
>   The Sack of Me.

Of course the context here is the familiar topos of love as a military operation, a psychomachy, available at least in embryo as far back as Sappho. But the topos is not just a static simile; its meaning, both historically and literally, is the displacement of external action by inner, of communal event by personal.[53] And the process of internalization acquires at times in the Anacreontea a bizarre emphasis. Cupid shoots his arrows at the speaker:

> ἔβαλλ᾽, ἐγὼ δ᾽ ἔφευγον.
> ὡς δ᾽ οὐκέτ᾽ εἶχ᾽ ὀιστούς,
> ἠσχάλλεν, εἶτ᾽ ἑαυτὸν
> ἀφῆκεν εἰς βέλεμνον·
> μέσος δὲ καρδίης μευ
> ἔδυνε καί μ᾽ ἔλυσεν·
> μάτην δ᾽ ἔχω βοείην·
> τί γὰρ βάλωμεν ἔξω,
> μάχης ἔσω μ᾽ ἐχούσης;

[13.12–20]

[He shot, and I jumped out of the way. So when he had no more arrows, he got mad and threw himself at me like a weapon. He plunged into the middle of my heart and undid me. My shield is useless. How can I fight on the outside when my battle is within?]

Elsewhere (6) the speaker catches Cupid, dunks him in wine, and swallows him, and then reports a tickling sensation in his stomach.

Such moments have particular significance because they help to explicate the psychological consequences of this kind of poetry. As the motifs continue to repeat themselves and become totally possessed and familiar, and as they take over the situation to exclude all possibility of surprise, they cease to be agents of a linguistic or other reality independent of the speaker and become instead, like the wax Cupid, compliantly fetishized elements in a personal fantasy. A certain thematic concern with dreaming—three of the poems (1, 30, 37) claim to describe dreams—partially crystalizes this; but the key term is the collection's habitual verb *thelō*, "I want," "I wish." The process in question is not the potent and unpredictable self-revelation of actual dreaming, but a waking fantasy or reverie keyed to the effects of the collection's primary stimulus:

> Διὰ νυκτὸς ἐγκαθεύδων
> ἁλιπορφύροις τάπησι,
> γεγανυμένος Λυαίῳ
> ἐδόκουν ἄκροισι ταρσῶν
> δρόμον ὠκὺν ἐκτανύειν
> μετὰ παρθένων ἀθύρων . . .

[37.1–6]

[Lying down at night on my sea-purple blankets, and happy with wine, I thought I was running quickly on tip-toe, playing with the little boys . . .]

Relevant to the whole modus of these poems, with their self-made clichés, is one of liquor's primary gifts to the race: the sudden adequacy of the banal, the sufficiency and appropriateness of our *conscious* desires, as rendered in a hundred commonplace and otherwise vapid declarations and images. Being young again and dancing with the kids is what, as it were, the Anacreontic tradition has been trying to persuade the speaker that he really wants; the poem describes a state (drunkenness) in which wanting those things is somehow enough. Such images of life as suddenly having become undemanding may be distinguished from genuine vision—a nexus of intelligibility to be grasped and held in the mind. By its very nature the Anacreontic *onar* has nothing to get at—"nothing at the limits of dream, the dream simply ends"—and presupposes the maudlin regret of its own dispersal:

> ἐθέλοντα δὴ φιλῆσαι
> φύγον ἐξ ὕπνου με πάντες·
> μεμονωμένος δ' ὁ τλήμων
> πάλιν ἤθελον καθεύδειν.

[37.11–14]

[When I wanted to kiss them, they all ran out of my dream. Unhappy, remembering this, I wanted to lie down again.]

Such evanescent velleity is different from serious erotic intent, the frustration of which is a matter of purposeful thwarting, not disappearance. But none of the sexual objects in the Anacreontea have sufficient vitality to put up active human resistance. The rules of the tradition prevent the speaker from ever concerning himself with anyone his own age—the hopeless gap between himself and youth is part of the point. Other traditions of erotic poetry may be compared here—the Roman elegy, for example, where the mistress is felt as an independent force that alternately yields and fights back. Even the real Anacreon poses his own desire as only one element in a precisely cantilevered structure:

> σφαίρῃ δηὖτέ με πορφυρῇ
> βάλλων χρυσοκόμης Ἔρως
> νήνι ποικιλοσαμβάλῳ
> συμπαίζειν προκαλεῖται·
> ἡ δ', ἐστὶν γὰρ ἀπ' εὐκτίτου
> Λέσβου, τὴν μὲν ἐμὴν κόμην,
> λευκὴ γάρ, καταμέμφεται,
> πρὸς δ' ἄλλην τινὰ χάσκει.

[LGS 302]

[Golden-haired Eros throws a purple ball my way and calls me to play with a fancy-sandaled little girl. But she's from Lesbos, with its beautiful buildings, and doesn't like my hair because it's white, and is gawking after another little girl herself.]

But that kind of clear-headedness about externals, including cultural externals (those girls from Lesbos!), is not "Anacreontic"; the endless boys and girls of the tradition are not realized as participants in specific situations but are simply supposed into existence. Their very numerousness emphasizes the marginal nature of their reality, the casualness of the act that calls them into being:

> Εἰ φύλλα πάντα δένδρων
> ἐπίστασαι κατειπεῖν,
> εἰ κυματῶδες εὐρεῖν
> τὸ τῆς ὅλης θαλάσσης,
> σὲ τῶν ἐμῶν ἐρώτων
> μόνον ποῶ λογιστήν.
> πρῶτον μὲν ἐξ Ἀθηνῶν
> ἔρωτας εἴκοσιν θὲς
> καὶ πεντεκαίδεκ᾽ ἄλλους.
> ἔπειτα δ᾽ ἐκ Κορίνθου . . .

[14.1–10]

[If you can count all the leaves of the trees, if you can number the sands of the entire sea, I will make you alone the accountant of my loves. First, from Athens, put down twenty loves, and fifteen more. Then, from Corinth . . .]

"Anacreon's" loves are not concretely desired objects, but rather images of desire, perhaps with a capital *D*:

> Ἄγε ζωγράφων ἄριστε,
> γράφε, ζωγράφων ἄριστε,
> Ῥοδίης κοίρανε τέχνης,
> ἀπεοῦσαν, ὡς ἂν εἴπω,
> γράφε τὴν ἐμὴν ἑταίρην.

[16.1–5]

[Come, best of painters, paint, best of painters, master of Rhodian art, paint my girl friend (who's not here) just as I say.]

The two halves of line 4 are interdependent; the speaker actually wants her absent, for otherwise she could not be just as he says. The goal of such sexuality is not orgasm but meditation on the inert. The cult of untouchability, eventually drawing the lover's imagination to heaven, is perhaps the opposite number in Petrarchanism. In both cases the systematized imaging of desire acts to exclude unpredictable presences and so becomes a very private and, ultimately, tame affair— as we would now say, masturbative fantasy moving toward impotence.

That conclusion may seem an intentionally outrageous "modern" interpretation, but I am actually being guided by Herrick, who introduces the issue of sexual incapacity into his adaptation of the opening poem of the Anacreontea:

> Me thought I saw (as I did dreame in bed)
> A crawling Vine about *Anacreon's* head:
> Flusht was his face; his haires with oyle did shine;
> And as he spake, his mouth ranne ore with wine.
> Tipled he was; and tipling lispt withall;
> And lisping reeld, and reeling like to fall.
> A young *Enchantresse* close by him did stand
> Tapping his plump thighes with a *mirtle* wand:
> She smil'd; he kist; and kissing, cull'd her too;
> And being cup-shot, more he co'd not doe.
> For which (me thought) in prittie anger she
> Snatcht off his Crown, and gave the wreath to me:
> Since when (me thinks) my braines about doe swim,
> And I am wilde and wanton like to him.
>
> [H-1017 / 313.1]

The Greek *tremonta* has been expanded on several fronts into a general account of the effects of drunkenness; this Anacreon is not up to handing the garland over on his own, or for that matter even to noticing the speaker. And Herrick (like the Porter in *Macbeth*) shows a grasp of what is now taken to be the physiological role of alcohol in human sexuality. Though it does perform the vital function of releasing inhibitions, it also reduces male capacity, so that a seduction with liquor is really an occassionally tricky exercise in timing. The moment missed, one is left with the very Anacreontic situation of emotional longing out of control in a context of physical incompetence. The issues here can be easily metaphorized, as is always done when we speak of poetic "intoxication"; the Anacreontic tradition kept in sight the physical bases of a certain kind of bardic inspiration. Where one may speak of "the drugged or tranced melancholy of the *Rime*,"[54] in the case of "Anacreon" one can specify the chemical make up of the drug.[55]

Herrick would not have known that this was the opening poem of the collection; his rescuing of it from the appendix where sixteenth-century scholarship had put it—Thomas Stanley, for example, in translating the "complete" Anacreon, ignores it—shows an interesting attunement to the Anacreontea not just as a collection of poems but as a self-perpetuating—indeed, a helplessly self-perpetuating—tradition. And because of this attunement, Herrick's poem claims attention not only as an interpretation of the original but also as an entry in the *Hesperides*. It is, for one thing, the only act of bardic investiture to occur in Herrick's book. Of all the poets that Herrick so persistently quotes, Anacreon is the only one with whom he overtly "identifies" himself; much of the appropriateness of this identification should be clear by now. Certainly the routines of that stock character are used widely through the *Hesperides*, and are in fact the terms in which Herrick's literary personality is generally recalled; "il baigne dans l'atmosphère anacréontique toute son oeuvre." [56] And there are also the implications of an even stronger act of explicit identification, when Herrick's "Mistress" tells him that in Elysium,

> Ile bring thee *Herrick* to *Anacreon*,
> Quaffing his full-crown'd bowles of burning Wine,
> And in his Raptures speaking Lines of Thine
>
> [H-575 / 206 / 32–34]

Anacreon, *in afflatu*, recites Herrick—very possibly because, in a way that does not hold for Herrick's relations to the other classical poets, these two write the same kind of poems. For once no structural complexities intervene, since Herrick can handle easily the two major modes of the Anacreontea: the telling of a simple story and the relaxed rehearsal of Anacreontic motifs. There are nine more or less direct translations of Anacreontea in the *Hesperides*,[57] and it is, significantly, on the level of the motif rather than of the phrase that much of the translating is done:

> I feare no Earthly Powers;
> But care for crowns of flowers:
> And love to have my Beard
> With Wine and Oile besmear'd.
> This day Ile drowne all sorrow;
> Who knowes to live to morrow?
>
> [H-170 / 65.1]

The first ten lines of Anacreontea 8 have been sectioned, condensed, and rearranged:

> Οὔ μοι μέλει τὰ Γύγεω,
> τοῦ Σάρδεων ἄνακτος·
> οὐδ᾽ εἷλέ πώ με ζῆλος,
> οὐδὲ φθονῶ τυράννοις.

[Herrick, l. 1]

> ἐμοὶ μέλει μύροισιν
> καταβρέχειν ὑπήνην,

[3–4]

> ἐμοὶ μέλει ῥόδοισιν
> καταστέφειν κάρηνα·

[2]

> τὸ σήμερον μέλει μοι,
> τὸ δ᾽ αὔριον τίς οἶδεν;

[5–6]

[My concern is not for the stuff of Gyges, ruler of Sardis. No ambition takes me. I do not envy tyrants (1). My concern is for my beard to be wet with myrrh (3–4). My concern is for my head to be wreathed with roses (2). Today concerns me; who knows anything about tomorrow (5–6)?]

The motifs have been reduced to a kind of shorthand, two of them switched around, and another one—drinking to end sorrow—grafted onto the reference to "this day." Herrick clearly feels at ease here to improvise within a certain field. His translation of Anacreontea 40 (see above, pp. 198–99) follows the original line for line—

> Borne I was to meet with Age,
> And to walke Life's pilgrimage.
> Much I know of Time is spent,
> Tell I can't, what's Resident.
> Howsoever, cares, adue;
> Ile have nought to say to you:

—until it reaches the catalogue of Anacreontic pleasures:

> But Ile spend my comming houres,
> Drinking wine, and crown'd with flowres.

[H-519 / 191.4]

In neither case do the changes alter the original poem in any significant way, since the Greek modus is itself that of easy improvisation from a repertoire: *paixō, gelasō, choreusō*. Herrick is not primarily imitating "Anacreon's" words but rather his basic procedures.

In the most extensive instance of this symbiosis, Herrick completely reverses his usual habits to copy structure directly and let details fall where they may:

> ὅτ' ἐγὼ πίω τὸν οἶνον,
> ἀπορίπτονται μέριμναι
> πολυφρόντιδές τε βουλαὶ
> ἐς ἁλικτύπους ἀήτας.
> ὅτ' ἐγὼ πίω τὸν οἶνον ...
>
> [50.4–8; the first "stanza" is corrupt]

[When I drink wine, anxieties and careful plans are thrown to the sea-winds. When I drink wine, etc.]

The slot after each refrain is filled in ad lib from the repertoire. Herrick simplifies the entries and does not bother to have them match the original too closely, makes the refrain concluding rather than introductory, varies its wording, and keys it (lightly) to the entry it follows. But he nevertheless preserves the poem's basic "idea" essentially intact: an inoffensively efficient display case for the routines of the system.

> Brisk methinks I am, and fine,
> When I drinke my capring wine:
> Then to love I do encline;
> When I drinke my wanton wine:
> And I wish all maidens mine,
> When I drinke my sprightly wine ...
>
> [H-996 / 309.1 / 1–6]

With "Anacreon," Herrick's rules on borrowing seem to be altered. Browsing through Martin's notes turns up little from "Anacreon" in Herrick's characteristic style of spot-quotation. This may be the result of the linguistic barriers (Delattre concludes that Herrick relied at least partly on Estienne's Latin translation),[58] but is, perhaps as a consequence, compensated for by what is in Herrick an atypical style of "deep" assimilation. Besides the translations themselves, there are a number of other obvious but independent "imitations." Two poems (in addition to one translation) are actually called "Anacreontic,"[59] and the conversion of the name into adjective is itself revealing— Herrick writes no "Horatian Odes." Several other poems not so explicitly labeled nevertheless quite obviously repeat Anacreontic poems with different details—notably in a series giving, as it were, the further adventures of Cupid.[60] And Herrick's involvement with that character is so serious that he does with it what he does with very few classical motifs—dissolves it back into something like what must have been its original meaning:

> It is an active flame, that flies,
> First, to the Babies of the eyes;
> And charmes them there with lullabies;
> And stils the Bride too, when she cries.
>
> Then to the chin, the cheek, the eare,
> It frisks, and flyes, now here, now there,
> 'Tis now farre off, and then tis nere;
> And here, and there, and every where.
>
> [H-329 / 130.2 / 8–15]

The antecedent of "it" is "kiss"; Herrick has for once seen through the mythology, back to the kind of quick, tentative, slightly perverse ("every where") eroticism that originally led the Hellenistic poets to represent Love as a little boy with wings.

There are other signs of such special relationships to the Anacreontic world. The two most heartfelt love poems in the *Hesperides*, for example, are not addressed to women but to Sack, the Anacreontic Muse. In an important way, that Muse is more real to Herrick than his "mistresses" are; Sack manifests herself as an independent presence who must be confronted and dealt with in negotiations of some delicacy:

> Prethee not smile;
> Or smile more inly; lest thy looks beguile
> My vowes denounc'd in zeale, which thus much show thee,
> That I have sworn, but by thy looks to know thee.
>
> [H-128 / 46 / 45–48]

Sack's smile implies somebody else besides the speaker who wants something out of this situation, and makes that situation thereby volatile and tricky. Her aggressiveness, however oblique, is a rare thing in Herrick's women, and she shows up the unreality of most of the other females in the *Hesperides*, at least as sexual agents. Julia, Anthea, and the rest may or may not have had some biographical reality, but in the serious games of emotional involvement they are as oblivious as children. Sack's sister figure, the Anacreontic "Enchantresse," though described as "young," is, in her impatience, one of the very few sexually mature women in Herrick's work; and even there any such impatience against the speaker is left implicit. The translation of Horace's duet with Lydia (H-181 / 70.1, *Carm.* 3.9) also stands out as a dialogue of an experienced man and woman carefully and gradually acknowledging their mutual attraction; its dramatic validity as dialogue may be gauged by comparing Herrick's own encounter with Elizabeth Wheeler "under the name of *Amarillis*" (H-1068 / 323.4).[61]

Herrick's own women seem curiously impassive under his erotic scrutiny. His speculations, like those of "Anacreon," have the air not of serious proposals, which try to take into account the probable response, but of uninterrupted fantasy. What most memorably occupies his attention is not, as in much Cavalier love poetry, the woman's will, but her body, often some very specific and peculiar part of it, or even just the scenery:

> How fierce was I, when I did see
> My *Julia* wash her self in thee!
>
> [H-939 / 294.4 / 1–2]

The addressee is the river, which is, even on an erotic level, at least as important to Herrick as Julia:

> Into thy streames my self I threw,
> And strugling there, I kist thee too
>
> [7–8]

The whole poem, moreover, about unachieved intercourse, simply retells a story from Martial (4.22), though with characteristic elision of context. The woman in Martial is a nervous virgin avoiding her husband on their wedding night. Herrick suppresses this, and by not replacing it with anything, leaves the woman with, in effect, no will of her own at all, no share in the responsibility for the outcome of the episode.

Herrick sends a few trinkets, makes a few easy persuasions to enjoy; but except for the Sack poems and the Horatian translation, none of the erotic poems in the *Hesperides* really dramatizes an encounter with an active presence. Indeed, the occasion of much of his direct address is the absolute imperviousness of the woman, her refusal to recognize that he is alive. You will notice me, he says more than once, when I'm dead—hence those interminable funeral instructions. Herrick's eroticism is directed across a void, one only bridged by those intricate psychologies of courtship with which he is largely uninvolved. This is, in its directly human dimensions, the Anacreontic void: age lusting after youth, Herrick and the teenybops, old Anacreon and young Cupid. And Herrick's "mistresses" have the same characteristics as "Anacreon's" loves: passive, unreal, and evanescent, as absurdly numerous as shadows:

> I have lost, and lately, these
> Many dainty Mistresses:
> Stately *Julia*, prime of all;
> *Sapho* next, a principall:
> Smooth *Anthea*, for a skin
> White, and Heaven-like Chrystalline:
> Sweet *Electra*, and the choice
> *Myrha*, for the Lute, and Voice.
> Next, *Corinna*, for her wit,
> And the graceful use of it:
> With *Perilla:* All are gone;
> Onely *Herrick's* left alone,
> For to number sorrow by
> Their departures hence, and die.
>
> [H-39/15.3]

"Upon the losse of his Mistresses" is, in fact, a telling Anacreontic poem that is not in the Greek collection; Herrick brings the erotic catalogue into alignment with the disappearing fantasy. Only Herrick's left alone: the women are never anything but images of his own desire. The same pattern appears elsewhere, interpreted directly as part of the psychology of the Anacreontic Muse:

> Whither dost thou whorry me,
> *Bacchus*, being full of thee?
> This way, that way, that way, this,
> Here, and there a fresh Love is.
> That doth like me, this doth please;

> Thus a thousand Mistresses,
> I have now; yet I alone,
> Having All, injoy not *One*.

> [H-415/157.3]

The effective presences in Herrick's mind are the agents of imagining; the sustained engagement of the Sack poems is matched not by the "real" erotic poems but by the farewell to "Poetry" (S-4/410.1). This very distinction may and should animate certain old suspicions about that last word: "Poetry" cuts one off from reality, incapacitates one for life.

> This sweet inchaunting knowledge turnes you cleene
> Out from the fields of naturall delight,
> And makes you hide unwilling to be seene
> In th'open concourse of a publike sight:
> This skill wherewith you have so cunning beene,
> Unsinewes all your powres, unmans you quite.

> [Samuel Daniel, *Musophilus* 494–99]

Much of Herrick's work does come very close to suiting the conception of poetry against which such objections are lodged. What the "poems of Anacreon" provided Herrick with, partly through illusion and partly through decadence, was a model for a self-contained lyric world whose principal activity is the casual permutation of its own décor. It has often been said that Herrick eschewed Petrarchanism, but he did so only to adopt another system of much the same sort.

The underlying notion here of the business of lyric poetry is the sustenance of mood, of an undisturbed and private enchantment with something called "the poetic"—the creation of a dream-world. That notion is so familiar that it is good to remember it has no genuine classical precedent and was not fully consolidated until the nineteenth century. That was, however, the century that rediscovered Herrick, and exactly because its readers saw in him an early precedent for their image of "the typical poet, the man who, if not a lyrist, would be nothing— the birdlike creature whose only function was to sing in a cage of trammelling flesh." [62] To see Herrick as such, of course, they had to ignore or even remove ("as one removes a snail from a lily's heart") [63] many other things in his work, but there is no point in denying their insight. What I want to claim in response is that this version of the

Poetical Character exists in the *Hesperides* with a much clearer sense of its own place, its ramifications and possibilities, especially on the sexual level, than Herrick's nineteenth-century readers could see, or at least talk about. It was, for example, an act of some clarity on Herrick's part to make his favorite poet-figure into an impotent, drunk old man.

In a sense, Herrick's alterations in the opening poem of the Anacreontea really change nothing, but merely make some of the underlying assumptions a bit more visible: the reliance on the psychology of alcohol, the essential inefficacy of the poet-figure, and therefore the general autonomy, via the Enchantress, of the onward flow of the tradition. But to make these things explicit translates them from their world into ours, where the unreality of Anacreontic eroticism shows up as senile incapacity. And one of the more tantalizing implications in the poem is the continuance of this flow into (or onto) Herrick, a definition of a kind of personal helplessness. The alterations in the body of the poem would seem to be by way of specifying the kind of *erōs* mentioned in the last line of the Greek, enough so to give a strange spin to the end of Herrick's version:

> Since when (me thinks) my braines about doe swim,
> And I am wilde and wanton like to him.

If "like to him" is taken not as slack filler but at face value, as a restrictive modifier referring back to the figure of Anacreon as presented in the poem, then the sexually itchy Enchantress is following a strategy of desperation, perhaps not fully aware of the systematic error that the Anacreontic crown is introducing into her search.

Yet there is, in the context of Herrick's other poems, more to this impotent poet-figure than one might guess. Several original poems deal with the senile lover, the "drie-decrepid man" still longing pathetically after his "mistresses":

> Old I am, and cannot do
> That, I was accustom'd to.
>
> [H-19/10.4/3-4]

But at times his condition does not seem quite so pathetic:

> Young I was, but now am old,
> But I am not yet grown cold;
> I can play, and I can twine
> 'Bout a Virgin like a Vine:

> In her lap too I can lye
> Melting, and in fancie die:
> And return to life, if she
> Claps my cheek, or kisseth me . . .
>
> [H-43/17.2/1-8]

The vegetation anticipates the crawling vine on the head of the impotent Anacreon. Here, though, one is likely to assume from the standard innuendo of "die" that the speaker can actually manage intercourse— though why "in fancie" ("infancy")? Perhaps the phrase is only a (redundant) indication that "die" is to be taken "metaphorically." But the word "fancy" occurs at an analogous moment in "The Vine," a very similar poem which closely precedes this one. In "The Vine," after some more elaborate viticultural foreplay, the term "fancy" again comes up in connection with the woman's genitals. That word is the pivot on which the poem swerves away from actual consummation:

> But when I crept with leaves to hide
> Those parts, which maids keep unespy'd,
> Such fleeting pleasures there I took,
> That with the fancie I awook . . .
>
> [H-41/17/18-21]

Earlier I called the sexual activity in "The Vine" prepubescent, and the conclusion of the poem bears out that characterization: a child suddenly scaring himself awake when he touches on the adult mysteries.

Certainly the retreat from full coition is an integral part of the poetic business. In a comparable poem by Suckling, the wakening conclusion is an obvious joke, a purely arbitrary interruption of even the rhyme and meter. The activity in question is well on its way to its usual finish:

> I not content
> With that, slipt to her breast, thence lower went,
> And then—I awak'd.
>
> [12.29-31]

End of poem. Herrick, however, implies real causality ("Such . . . That"); and there is also something about the character of the sexual behavior in the first part of the poem that seems to lead to the "fleeting" approach to the genitalia themselves.

One of the deductions that might be drawn from the collection of motifs in the Anacreontea is the congruity of the senile and the prepubescent. Both are periods of erotic energy without genital organization and control; and a good deal of the rather peculiar erotic activity in the *Hesperides* makes sense as that of either a wide-eyed ten-year-old or of a dirty old man. The emphasis on foreplay and nongenital, especially oral, gratifications, the fixation on affects (smells, textures) and details (Julia's leg), and the general voyeuristic preference of perception to action (Herrick has been called "the Peeping Tom of English poetry")[64] are all intelligible as a wide diffusion of erotic energy denied specifically orgastic focus and release.

What is missing in the *Hesperides* is aggressive, genital, in other words, "adult" sexuality. The retreat from intercourse is pervasive, and especially notable in a poet whose concerns are so often explicitly sexual. Almost always when Herrick encounters the matter of actual intercourse, there is some buckling effect not explained by mere decorum; indeed, by drawing attention to themselves, such moments are among Herrick's most ungainly. The major "consummation poems"—the Epithalamia —dwell at extraordinary length on the psychology of delay:

> Night now hath watch'd her self half blind;
> Yet not a Maiden-head resign'd!
>
> [H-149A / 54 / 31–32]

A hundred lines later (!) we get to the impatient bed:

> And (oh!) had it but a tongue,
> Doves, 'two'd say, yee bill too long.
>
> [139–40]

More importantly, Herrick's own adventures, or fantasies, tend to go haywire at suspicious moments.

> How fierce was I, when I did see
> My *Julia* wash her self in thee!
> So *Lillies* thorough Christall look:
> So purest pebbles in the brook:
> As in the River *Julia* did,
> Halfe with a Lawne of water hid,
> Into thy streames my self I threw,
> And strugling there, I kist thee too;
> And more had done (it is confest)
> Had not thy waves forbad the rest.
>
> [H-939 / 294.4]

Herrick's changes here from the source in Martial shift responsibility for the "failure" away from Julia—and hence, by implication, onto Herrick—and also ("I kist thee too") bring the setting explicitly into the erogenous zone, as simultaneous interference and compensation. Actual propositioning in the *Hesperides* is almost never really unambiguous:

> More white then whitest Lillies far,
> Or Snow, or whitest Swans you are:
> More white then are the whitest Creames,
> Or Moone-light tinselling the streames:
> More white then *Pearls*, or *Juno's* thigh;
> Or *Pelops* Arme of *Yvorie*.
> True, I confesse; such Whites as these
> May me delight, not fully please:
> Till, like *Ixion's* Cloud you be
> White, warme, and soft to lye with me.
>
> [H-105/34.2]

Ixion's cloud is one of the great sexual frauds in Western literature, Zeus's strategy for diverting uppity male drive into harmlessness. It is even something of an emblem for the internalization of the procreative impulse, since the offspring of this union was not another human being, or even a demigod, but the Centaurs—the creations of a poet's fancy, his *chimères*, of which those paradigms of exorbitant whiteness, so typical of Herrick's eroticism, are good examples.

Such internalization, while merely and perhaps unintentionally suggested in this example, is a persistent motif; many of the erotic poems are openly labeled as mere dreams or wishes. And one such poem carries this reticence even further in a way that offers an exceptionally good opportunity to triangulate Herrick's position:

> I dream'd we both were in a bed
> Of Roses, almost smothered:
> The warmth and sweetnes had me there
> Made lovingly familiar:
> But that I heard thy sweet breath say,
> Faults done by night, will blush by day:
> I kist thee (panting,) and I call
> Night to the Record! that was all.
> But ah! if empty dreames so please,
> Love give me more such nights as these.
>
> [H-56/20.3]

The conclusion is Anacreontic in sentiment: when I waked, I cried to dream again. But the actual tag is Ovidian, and from one of the most hauntingly direct episodes in the *Amores*:

> singula quid referam? nil non laudabile uidi,
>   et nudam pressi corpus ad usque meum.
> cetera quis nescit? lassi requieuimus ambo.
>   proueniant medii sic mihi saepe dies.
>
> [1.5.23–26]

[Why go into details? I saw nothing to complain about, and I pressed her naked against my body. Who doesn't know what followed? Tired, we both rested. Let me have many mid-days like this.]

The whole Latin poem is a good example of the kind of erotic poetry, the poetry of adult lust mutually confronted and gratified, that Herrick does not even try to write. The second half of line 25 describes an erotic moment significantly missing from Herrick's repertoire; when dealing with coition, he looks forward to it, not back on it. The allusion can be pinned down with some certainty because Herrick appears to be imitating the phrasing of Marlowe's translation; and the otherwise bizarre appropriation of this tag to Herrick's poem may owe something to Marlowe's curious rendering of the penultimate line of the Latin:

> Judge you the rest, being tyrde she bad me kisse.
> *Jove* send me more such afternoones as this.

Marlowe might seem to have changed a straightforward poem about coitus into an oblique poem about kissing—kissing, in fact, as an apparently adequate substitute for coitus.[65]

And as another middle term, there is a remarkable poem of Campion's, set in the same time of day as the Ovidian poem and keyed by the same tag, that introduces a different kind of obliquity:

> It fell on a sommers day,
> While sweete Bessie sleeping laie
> In her bowre, on her bed,
> Light with curtaines shadowed;
> Jamy came, shee him spies,
> Opning halfe her heavie eies.
>
> . . . .

> Jamy then began to play,
> Bessie as one buried lay,
> Gladly still through this sleight
> Deceiv'd in her owne deceit;
> And, since this traunce begoon,
> She sleepes ev'rie afternoone.[66]

An early, urbane version of "The Eve of St. Agnes": copulation becomes acceptable, probably to both parties, when it is as though uncon-
scious, as though a dream. ("Traunce" is a good translation for the
Anacreontic *onar*.) Herrick continues this inward movement, characteristically erasing the awareness of daylight context ("Deceiv'd in her
owne deceit"—like Cymochles in Spenser's Bower of Bliss, *FQ* 2.5.34)
and making this a "real" dream, and in fact moving the whole scene
from noon to night.

This last is an important change from the Latin; Ovid's poem is in a
Roman tradition, along with Catullus 32 ("nouem continuas futu-
tiones") of explicit daytime sexual speculation. It cannot be distinguished from Herrick's poem by calling the latter a "fantasy," for they
are both "fantasies." But Ovid's, in its setting and aggressiveness, is a
fantasy much more attached to the will; and its plot is in fact the materi-
alization of fantasy. The companion piece to the *Amores* is, after all, a
versified seduction manual, with instructions on positions, etc. What
Ovid would act out in the daylight world, Herrick would deescalate in
content, and locate within the shadows of his own brain.

The major implication of all this is that we should take seriously, and
not only on a biographical level, the declaration that Herrick makes
part of the formal design of his book:

> To his Book's end this last line he'd have plac't,
> *Jocond his Muse was; but his Life was chast.*
>
> [H-1130/335.3]

That last line, which indeed is the last line of the *Hesperides*, is a commonplace of the Roman poets. The ultimate source (at least it is cited
as such by Pliny the Younger and Apuleius) is Catullus:

> nam castum esse decet pium poetam
> ipsum, uersiculos nihil necesse est
>
> [16.5–6]

[For the pious poet ought to be chaste himself, but his verses don't have to be.]

But Herrick's neat, one-line pointing of the thought is itself part of a long tradition:

uita uerecunda est, Musa iocosa mea

[Ovid, *Tristia* 2.254]

[My life is discreet, my Muse playful.]

lasciua est nobis pagina, uita proba

[Martial, 1.4.8]

[Our page is lecherous, our life proper.]

lasciuus uersu, mente pudicus eras

[Hadrian][67]

[You were lecherous in verse, continent in mind.]

The last is perhaps closest to Herrick's line; it is in fact what Herrick proposes his line to be—a funerary inscription, a summation of a man's life—and is also the least disingenuous of the group. But all of them seem legalistically evasive in comparison to Herrick's flat statement about the content of his sex-life. Catullus, the only one to use the unambiguous term *castus*, is positing a standard ("decet"), not making a personal statement. Ovid commits himself only to a contrast of styles— "uerecunda" just means he kept the blinds closed—and is suspect for other reasons, as an exile hoping for recall. Martial's "proba" only claims that he has conducted himself like a gentleman; Hadrian seems to be contrasting two areas of the life of the mind. Not only does the *Hesperides* not provide the appropriate context for a genuinely ironic, Roman apologia, but Herrick's line is simply much more literal than any of its antecedents. And it is anticipated often enough in his book, with a directness and lack of ambiguity that contrast with the curlicued nature of his amatory adventures:

> Go I must; when I am gone,
> Write but this upon my Stone;
> Chaste I liv'd, without a wife,
> That's the Story of my life.
>
> [H-546 / 199.2 / 1–4]

The note of semicomic resignation in that last line is a modern inflection; as seventeenth-century English, it has much more the character
of simple statement, and maybe even a declaration of the kind of art
form, of *fabula*, that Herrick would prefer his life to realize. Elsewhere
he even calls himself a "maid" (H-235 / 97.3 / 2). *Recusationes* abound,
and one of them even makes the point that Herrick is not cutting himself off from erotic activity, but simply reorganizing it:

> I could wish you all, who love,
> That ye could your thoughts remove
> From your Mistresses, and be,
> Wisely wanton (like to me.)
>
> [H-289 / 117.4 / 1–4]

The alternative to the troubles of sexual involvement is not asceticism
but being "wisely wanton." Probably the stress should fall on the first
word: a *kind* of wantonness—like that of Anacreon, perhaps, or the
"cleanly-*Wantonnesse*" of the "Argument" (H-1/5.1/6)?

Chastity, of course, is an intentional virtue, not merely a matter of
incapacity or inexperience. Some of the results, however, may be much
the same; and there are reasons, I think, for suspecting that Herrick
might have been attracted by the game of disguising intention as accident. The figure of the aged lover is a simple Anacreontic convention,
and there is no particular reason to take it as biographical fact and hence
genuine constraint. Certainly more convincing and realistic are the
occasions on which Herrick may be observed *looking forward* to being
old as the appropriate time for a special kind of erotic activity (H-336/
132.3, H-569 / 204.4). There is something privileged about the erotic
perspective of old men; in "*Connubii Flores*" it is a "Chorus Senum"
that offers advice on the consummation:

> Go to your banquet then, but use delight,
> So as to rise still with an appetite.
> Love is a thing most nice; and must be fed
> To such a height; but never surfeited.
> What is beyond the mean is ever ill:
> *'Tis best to feed Love; but not over-fill:*
> Go then discreetly to the Bed of pleasure;
> And this remember, *Vertue keepes the measure.*
>
> [H-633 / 220.3 / 18–25]

The advice is not surprising—old men have always counseled *medio-critas*—but the application to what to do *after* you get into bed with someone is. This is a good example of Herrick's tendency, discussed by Jenkins, to shift the classical virtue of Moderation from moral discipline to aesthetic strategy.[68] And exactly what sort of activity is being recommended? As in the other nuptial poems, the consummation is not being exactly denied, but it is in some peculiar sense being elided or displaced, to the end of avoiding postcoital depression. And the concern with surfeit echoes a far more explicit sexual strategy advocated within Herrick's hearing by Jonson, translating "Petronius," where surfeit is equated with orgasm:

> Doing, a filthy pleasure is, and short;
> And done, we straight repent us of the sport:
> Let us not then rush blindly on unto it,
> Like lustfull beasts, that onely know to doe it:
> For lust will languish, and that heat decay.
> But thus, thus, keeping endlesse Holy-day,
> Let us together closely lie, and kisse,
> There is no labour, nor so shame in this;
> This hath pleas'd, doth please, and long will please; never
> Can this decay, but is beginning ever.
>
> [*Underwood* 88; 8:294][69]

As a justification for continence, this is quite practical and amoral. Not too surprisingly, it shows up elsewhere in the Cavalier tradition;[70] it is such a conclusion as an experienced adult might come to. The Petronian poem, however, is the most explicit about the compensatory role of other kinds of sexual play, of reticence not just as a way of avoiding *tristesse*, but of actively recapturing something of the innocence of childhood sexuality. As such, the poem may have provided precedent or reinforcement for Herrick's own frequent sense of kissing as an alternative kind of sexuality that threatens or promises to displace actual coition:

> Give me a kisse, and to that kisse a score;
> Then to that twenty, adde an hundred more:
> A thousand to that hundred: so kisse on,
> To make that thousand up a million.

Treble that million, and when that is done,
Let's kisse afresh, as when we first begun.

[H-74 / 24.2 / 3-8]

The strategy advocated by "Petronius" supplies a middle term between childhood and old age, a way of getting from one to the other, of realizing a complete life in which somatic energies would not get so thoroughly absorbed into the psychological demands and responsibilities of specific genital intent:

A Bachelour I will
Live as I have liv'd still,
And never take a wife
To crucifie my life:
But this I'le tell ye too,
What now I meane to doe;
A Sister (in the stead
Of Wife) about I'le lead;
Which I will keep embrac'd,
And kisse, but yet be chaste.

[H-31 / 13.4]

That may have been the biographical form of the sexual imagination projected elsewhere. Certainly it "fits," placing Herrick in the long underground tradition of celibate clergy working out accommodations with their libidos without actually breaking the rules: Elizabeth Herrick as *agapēta*. Generally, Herrick does at least propose to go beyond kissing, but with a coyness, even cuteness ("Name it I would; but being blushing red . . . "—H-74/24.2/13), that keeps Herrick's poem from really standing up as an answer to "Petronius's" arguments:

Begin with a kisse,
Go on too with this:
And thus, thus, thus let us smother
Our lips for a while,
But let's not beguile
Our hope of one for the other.

This play, be assur'd,
Long enough has endur'd,
Since more and more is exacted;

> For love he doth call
> For his Uptailes all;
> And that's the part to be acted.
>
> [H-727 / 247.2]

(Did "thus, thus, thus" grow from "thus, thus" in Jonson's translation? The adverbs describe the same activity in both cases.) Herrick's very starting point is an assumed unwillingness to go beyond kissing, and something about the conspiratorial first-person plural implies that not only the addressee has to be convinced and encouraged. In advocating intercourse, Herrick's stance is still that of anticipation, not experience, and he does not reply to the Petronian poem on its own adult grounds, in the way that Waller and Henry Bold attempt to answer Suckling's poems "Against Fruition."[71] Rather, Herrick locates himself exactly where Suckling says one should locate oneself if one has a choice—in the realm of expectation. The sexual activity in the *Hesperides* is by and large precoital; it never quite seems to go over the edge. One suspects that Herrick was following the advice of "Petronius" and Suckling without admitting it.

But the very fact that he would not admit it makes sense as well. Seriously preserving expectation means not being too aware of that preservation as a trick, a choice; to betray it into thematic visibility is to weaken its effectiveness by showing it up as one possibility among many. The dream-world, a meticulous pretense of completeness and inevitability, is in a way the logical vehicle for Suckling's advice. Indeed, "he wakes himself that does enjoy" (40.6)—out of context, a curiously Blakean *gnōmē*; but Suckling's advice is to avoid waking up. To say so, however, he has to bring into the scope of his poem the sort of experience which occasioned his argument, and with that come irony and cynicism.

If nothing else, to know that your life is a choice means that you will have to spend a lot of energy defending that choice, both to others and in your own mind, and also fending off thoughts about what you might be missing. The sexual world of the *Hesperides*, I am proposing, is held in place by a choice that for the most part intentionally disguises itself as innocence or incompetence or ignorance. The biographical and emotional fates of the other Cavaliers suggest why one might want to do such a thing. The *Hesperides*, that is, makes sense as the work of one man with a stake in what is going on and is, in that respect, the opposite of the Anacreontea, which converge on no particular mortality. The Greek poems offer a model for a kind of mindless generality of desire; Herrick imitates much of the emotional texture of that world, but in a way that offers something which the most important lyric Oeuvres offer, and which the Anacreontea clearly cannot: the image of a possible life.

Which brings us to Horace.

IV   From Horace, a sense of strategy—for, among other things, not wondering what you are missing:

> mitte sectari, rosa quo locorum
> sera moretur.
>
> [*Carm.* 1.38.3–4]

[Leave off looking for where the late rose waits.]

There is something sinister about the *rosa sera*, exotic and poignant beauty that one cannot, in simple terms, handle. It evokes the nervous discontent of the horizon, the endless restiveness, both theirs and ours, at the borders of empire:

> Quid bellicosus Cantaber et Scythes,
> Hirpine Quincti, cogitet Hadria
> diuisus obiecto, remittas
> quaerere . . .
>
> [2.11.1–4]

[What the warlike Cantabrian and Scythian are planning, separated from us by the intervening Adriatic, stop asking, Quinctus Hirpinus . . .]

It is not just a matter of "keeping within one's limits"—put things that way and one already has the components of a very serious discontent—but more basically of not quite letting oneself find out what those limits are, whether political or, in a more vague, Anacreontic way, personal:

> quid sit futurum cras fuge quaerere . . .
>
> [1.9.13]

[What will be tomorrow, avoid asking . . .]

Which is not to deny that there are Cantabrians or Scythians, or even that they are likely to affect our lives sometime in "the future." Indeed, it is Horace's way of honoring the *fines* of our existence not to test them; he knows very well that they are there.

> Tu ne quaesieris, scire nefas, quem mihi, quem tibi
> finem di dederint
>
> [1.11.1–2]

[Do not ask, it would be wrong to know, what end the gods give me, to you.]

So begins one of Horace's most famous poems, certainly one of his most clichéd poems, and in its way a poem about clichés. A poem about not finding things out; wisdom is not always knowledge:

> sapias, uina liques, et spatio breui
> spem longam reseces. dum loquimur, fugerit inuida
> aetas: carpe diem, quam minimum credula postero.
>
> [6–9]

[Be wise, strain the wine, and for a brief space cut off long hope. While we talk, envious time runs on. Pluck the day, trust as little as possible to the future.]

Rather, a poem about *spatia breuia*, short phrases and moments, a gentle tentativeness of breathing and utterance: "ut melius, quidquid erit, pati" (3), "better, whatever it will be, to endure." In a sense, it is a poem about the choriamb, –◡◡–, of which every line contains three in a row. Put two choriambs together and the juncture of long syllables will tend to preserve rather than, as in iambics and trochaics, dissolve the outlines of the individual feet. Horace in general does not resist this pull in his phrasing, and several of his choriambs are single words— "quaesieris"—or independent phrases—"scire nefas." And this rhythmic hesitancy rhymes with a mental process that yields not purposed argument, but what a recent critic has called a "heaping up" of "old saws." [72] They certainly sound like old saws, and indeed "carpe diem" (a choriamb) has become the definitive Horatian cliché.

As so often in Horace, however, the verb is curiously precise: not "take"—too vague, though the standard English equivalent, as if from *capio*[73]—or "seize" or "grab"—excessively crude expenditures of energy, unsure of what resistance will be encountered—but "pluck," as of a flower:

> meliusne fluctus
> ire per longos fuit, an recentis
> carpere flores?

[3.27.42–44]

[Was it better to go through the wide waves, or to pluck fresh flowers?]

A matter, again, of what you can handle: "fluctus" / "flores," "ire" / "carpere," the vague and the calculable. The sea, whose indeterminate vastness and energy make similarly indeterminate demands on our resources—"ire" can, in practical terms, mean just about anything—is a consistently lurid image; in the Leuconoe poem, the discursive flutter of the opening and closing poises against the only line that drives straight through, the one about winter

> quae nunc oppositis debilitat pumicibus mare

[5]

[which now wears out the sea upon the opposing rocks]

Rhetorical aggressiveness as an emblem of the relentless processes of the universe: that is what you will find out if you insist on finding things out. Horace's poem here declines to become what it beholds. What it *says*, more or less literally, is that only knowing distraction offers us a place in which to do our living—space to breathe, how short so ever.

Herrick, who sings of Heaven and hopes to have it after all, would not assent to Horace's conclusion, "minimum credula postero." Nevertheless, as a treatment of mortality, indeed, of human limitation in general, Horace's poem comes quite close to the sense of things in the *Hesperides*:

> But thou at home, blest with securest ease,
> Sitt'st, and beleev'st that there be seas
>
> [H-106 / 36 / 69–70]

It is not a matter, as in Catullus, of confronting or confounding our *fines*, but of ascertaining, with some cunning, how to live with them—indeed, by means of them, deriving a quiet pressure from our awareness of their presence somewhere on the other side of our particular hill. That is part of what is implied by the modest range of classical lyric "subject matter" or discourse: the significance of such poetry is not

what it says, but what it takes into account. Of "Anacreon" it may
be stated that he says many of the same things Horace says but seems
to take much less into account. The Anacreontea lack cunning. Their
regnant intellectual gesture is *ouc oida*, "I don't know"; Horace's is,
"Don't ask."

It is of course unfair to compare these two groups of poems. Horace
(who would have had access to the original Anacreon as well as, probably, some of "Anacreon") certainly does not invite such a comparison
himself. He does mention Anacreon, several times, with some affection;
but his own sense of precedent and endeavor is tied to the tradition
of Lesbian lyric, and in particular the example of Alcaios. Horace, for
whom, as for all classical poets, the emblematic value of meter was
very high, writes no poems in "Anacreontics," but writes many in
Alcaics and Sapphics. Yet the comparison of Horace and "Anacreon"
is invited by Herrick, who makes the two of them constant traveling
companions in the *Hesperides*, where they are bound together in service
to the same Muse that Herrick himself serves, Sack. He tells her:

> *Horace, Anacreon* both had lost their fame,
> Had'st thou not fill'd them with thy fire and flame.
>   [H-128 / 45.1 / 31–32; cf. H-544 / 198.1 / 7–18]

Merely to make this pairing, in the Renaissance context, is to perform
something of a reinterpretation of Horace, who becomes thereby not
the sober *ethicus* of the conversation poems, but the author of the Odes;
Herrick's Horace, friend of Anacreon, is a step in the seventeenth-
century rediscovery of the Roman as a specifically lyric poet.[74] But
Horace's famed reasonableness can also be seen as a way of placing and
justifying the Greek poet's drinking habits:

> Rouze *Anacreon* from the dead;
> And return him drunk to bed:
> Sing o're *Horace;* for ere long
> Death will come and mar the song
>   [H-111 / 39.3 / 9–12]

That abrupt appearance of death is in fact a specifically Horatian effect,
like the famous unannounced entry of "pallida Mors" into a description
of spring (1.4.13).[75]

The tension is one that the Anacreontea try to state several times but
never quite realize. Realizing it requires the un-Anacreontic sense of

the mass and importance of the ambient reality surrounding our festivities like the future or the sea:

> o fortes peioraque passi
> mecum saepe uiri, nunc uino pellite curas;
> cras ingens iterabimus aequor.
>
> [1.7.30–32]

[Oh brave men, you who have often endured worse with me, drive away your cares now with wine. Tomorrow we set out again on the huge sea.]

End of poem. What is un-Anacreontic about that last line is not just the special heft given to the actual by that carefully placed adjective, "ingens," but also the awareness of work out there to which we must and will return. As Nisbet and Hubbard observe, the sentiment is almost Homeric:[76]

> ἀλλ᾽ ἄγετ᾽ ἐσθίετε βρώμην καὶ πίνετε οἶνον
> αὖθι πανημέριοι· ἅμα δ᾽ ἠοῖ φαινομένηφι
> πλεύσεσθ᾽ . . .
>
> [Od. 12.23–25]

[But come, eat food and drink wine all day today; at the first light of dawn, you sail . . .]

Horace's lines, to be sure, are set in a dramatic context—they are Teucer's exhortation to his comrades—but that is itself part of the point. Wine, like food, is a functional element in a larger human endeavor, and drinking in Horace is in general not a release from at least certain kinds of responsibility. Drinking is, like everything else, a skill; and there is a repeated concern in the *Carmina* with learning how to get drunk without becoming violent or clumsy (e.g. 1.27, 3.8). That is a concern which Horace shares with Anacreon (*LGS* 300) and to some extent with Herrick, who diagrams the issue in quite Horatian terms:

> *Bacchus*, let me drink no more;
> Wild are Seas, that want a shore.
> When our drinking has no stint,
> There is no one pleasure in't.
>
> [H-304 / 122.3 / 1–4; cf. H-988 / 307.1]

We appreciate drinking, like life, only if it ends. In the Anacreontea, on the other hand, despite a couple of vague references to drinking "gracefully" (2.6, 53.14), the prevailing mood is that of the Bacchic rout—"I want, I want to go mad" (for practical applications, see 59)— circumscribed only by the promise that no actual murder is going to result. Horace does welcome an alcoholic *mania*, but only under the sign of an occasion.

> non ego sanius
> bacchabor Edonis: recepto
> dulce mihi furere est amico.
>
> [2.7.26–28]

[I will riot no more reasonably than the Edonians. It is sweet to rave when a friend has come back.]

A friend presumed dead turns up alive: what other response would even begin to seem adequate? The deciding factor may be that Horace is celebrating another's good luck rather than just cheering himself up; in another ode (3.19) there is a similar response ("insanire iuuat," 18, "it is good to go mad") to a friend's appointment to the College of Augurs. In general, "dulce est desipere in loco" (4.12.28), "it is sweet to go crazy in the right place." This is not a matter of "controlling oneself," but of grounding one's exuberance in the facts of one's life: of keeping the *mania* from being merely a private fantasy, of making it instead a response to an appropriate stimulus.

Horace is similarly very concerned with the locus of a poem, its role as part of a situation. There are, for example, occasions on which the thing to do is to read Anacreon:

> hic in reducta ualle Caniculae
> uitabis aestus et fide Teia
> dices laborantis in uno
> Penelopen uitreamque Circen
>
> [1.17.17–20]

[Here in this recessed valley you will avoid the heat of the dog-days, and sing on a Teian lyre of Penelope and crystalline Circe longing for the same man.]

And this concern, itself uncharacteristic of "Anacreon," who is never too specific about the *melos* of his pleasure, is involved in Horace's development of another Anacreontic gesture—the negative, antiheroic definition of what exactly the territory of lyric poetry is. The example

of Alcaios, a busy politico by day, is used to show how lyric is antiheroic
only in being complementary:

> age dic Latinum,
>   barbite, carmen,
>
> Lesbio primum modulate ciui,
> qui ferox bello, tamen inter arma
> siue iactatam religarat udo
>   litore nauim,
>
> Liberum et Musas Veneremque et illi
> semper haerentem puerum canebat
> et Lycum nigris oculis nigroque
>   crine decorum.
>
> [1.32.3–12]

[Come, give a Latin song, lyre first tuned by the citizen of Lesbos,
who, ferocious in war, would still, between battles, or tying up
his battered ship on the wet shore, sing of Bacchus and the Muses
and Venus and the boy who is always at her side, and of Lycus,
beautiful for his black eyes and black hair.]

Here poetry is interstitial to business, implying its own context as
otium implies *negotium*. The assessment of kinds of poetry is made
according to similar notions of appropriateness:

> Quantum distet ab Inacho
> Codrus pro patria non timidus mori,
>   narras et genus Aeaci
> et pugnata sacro bella sub Ilio:
>   quo Chium pretio cadum
> mercemur, quis aquam temperet ignibus
>   quo praebente domum et quota
> Paelignis caream frigoribus, taces.
>
> [3.19.1–8]

[You tell of the lineage from Inachus to Codrus, who was not afraid
to die for his country, and of the family of Aeacus and of the wars
fought at sacred Troy. But as for what to pay for a jar of Chian
wine, and who will heat the water on the fire, and in whose house
and when I can avoid the Paelignian cold, you say nothing.]

Just a minute, the *lares* ("Who's got money for the wine?") are asking for logistical attention. Twelve lines later the lyre and flute are brought down off the wall, and epic is displaced by lyric. What sets such moments apart from the artistic proposals in the Anacreontea is the appeal to context: all that is in effect said to the rhapsode is, "Not now." Elsewhere, when pressed to write heroic poetry himself, Horace pleads his own incompetence (*culpa ingeni*, 1.6.12) or the superiority of other available genres, such as the prose chronicle (2.12). All these are ways of putting things by—and not with any tightly woven strategy, since Horace does handle political and military themes when occasion (or commission) warrants.

None of this awareness of alternatives can be felt in "Anacreon," who reports a wholly internal psychomachy, a struggle between the heroic and erotic themes for his own poetic soul (23), which results in an attempted metamorphosis (internalization) of the epic mode— Homer without the blood (2). This is, if we care to extrapolate, a much more ambitious program than Horace's; the Roman does not propose a metamorphosis of the Homeric, but his own accommodation into an array of independent possibilities of which Homer is only the most prestigious:

> non, si priores Maeonius tenet
> sedes Homerus, Pindaricae latent
>   Ceaeque et Alcaei minaces
>   Stesichoriue graues Camenae;
>
> nec, si quid olim lusit Anacreon,
> deleuit aetas; spirat adhuc amor
>   uiuuntque commissi calores
>   Aeoliae fidibus puellae.

$$[4.9.5-12]$$

[If Maeonian Homer holds the highest seat, still the Muse of Pindar is not hidden, nor that of Simonides or of threatening Alcaios, or of grave Stesichoros. Nor has time erased what Anacreon once played. The love of Sappho still breathes, and her passions confided to the lyre still live.]

Indeed, it is that very array of names that seems to hold possibilities open, allows them to coexist in friendship. One of the epistles contains a picture of Horace's relation to Propertius, a very different kind of poet:

carmina compono, hic elegos . . .
discedo Alcaeus puncto illius; ille meo quis?
quis nisi Callimachus? si plus adposcere uisus,
fit Mimnermus et optiuo cognomine crescit.

[*Epis.* 2.2.91, 99–100]

[I write lyrics, he writes elegiacs . . . When I leave, I am Alcaios by
his vote. And who is he by mine? Who but Callimachos? If he seems
to want more, let him be Mimnermos and swell with his longed-
for name.]

With this discrimination of talent, compare "Anacreon":

Ἡδυμελὴς Ἀνακρέων,
ἡδυμελὴς δὲ Σαπφώ·
Πινδαρικὸν τόδε μοι μέλος
συγκεράσας τις ἐγχέοι.

[20.1–4]

[Anacreon is a sweet swinger, and Sappho a sweet singer. Somebody pour me a song, mixing in something Pindaric.]

The final sense here, through *syncerasas*, the technical term for mixing
wine, is of some omnibus lyric Sangria. On the other hand, part of
the very theory of the Horatian lyric is that one need not try to be
everything, that one is better off sticking to one's genre, keeping to
one's limits. Distinguishing himself from Pindar, Horace calls himself
"paruus" (4.2.31); his writing of "Alcaic" lyrics is his way of establishing his niche.

Niches imply both an edifice and a certain desire to hide from it.
Frank Lloyd Wright, on a visit to Yale, is said to have asked to be
housed in Harkness Tower so he would not have to look at it; and
there is to Horace's situation a similar intrinsic paradox. In superficial
paraphrase, "all" that Horace wanted was to stay detached from this
business of politics and power and just retire to his Sabine farm and
take his time; but to get that farm, and keep it, he had to be friends
with the emperor. There is evidence that the relationship made him
uncomfortable, in a way only exacerbated by Augustus's attempts to
be even friendlier: "Are you afraid," the emperor wrote, "that you will
lose credit with posterity for seeming to be my friend?"[77] We may

be sure, emperors being emperors, that Horace replied the thought had never crossed his mind—though in historical fact, his *fama*, which was very important to him, has indeed suffered for just this reason.

Horace's appeal to an image of politico-lyric unity in the figure of Alcaios is a bit devious, since Horace's own case hardly realized such a unity; his situation was, if anything, closer to that of Anacreon, expelled and depoliticized by the Asian conquest of his homeland and dependent on the patronage of a series of local Greek *tyrannoi*. It was not just Horace's verse that was interstitial to politics but his whole life. And his use of Alcaios is not so much direct identification or analogy as part of a general strategy to validate the place of the lyric poet. The picture of the Lesbian poet tying up his ship and bursting into a song about Bacchus or Cupid comes in a poem whose starting point is an outsider's request: "Poscimur" (1.32.1). Horace is concerned to establish, in a semiofficial way, just what is (and is not) to be expected of him.

Hence the great importance in the Odes of lyric poetry itself as subject matter. That is the plane on which Horace ignores his own warnings elsewhere against *spes longa*; he trims his aspirations to the enterprise of professional advancement:

> quodsi me lyricis uatibus inseres,
> sublimi feriam sidera uertice.
>
> [1.1.35–36]

[If you place me among the lyric poets, I will touch the stars with my towering head.]

The words *lyricus uates* are Horace's armor, the structural bracing for his niche; the Muses, he says in one of his most ambitious odes (3.4.9 ff.), have always protected him—a claim given in its practical form later on:

> Romae principis urbium
> dignatur suboles inter amabilis
>   uatum ponere me choros,
> et iam dente minus mordeor inuido.
>
> [4.3.13–16]

[The sons of Rome, first of cities, see fit to put me among the lovely chorus of poets, and I am now less gnawed by the tooth of envy.]

Whose *inuidia*? Horace's against others, or others' against him? Probably the latter, but acceptance by Augustus of Horace's semiofficial post of *uates* could have helped fend off both. The "plot" of *Carmina* 1–3 is to a great extent Horace's installation into the College of the *Melo-poiētai*: from *Maecenas atauis* (1.1) to *Exegi monumentum* (3.30) by way of *Descende caelo* (3.4). Book 4 is permeated with the sense of this achieved goal:

> nupta iam dices "ego dis amicum,
> saeculo festas referente luces,
> reddidi carmen, docilis modorum
> uatis Horati."

[4.6.41–44]

[Soon, as a bride, you will say, "As the age brings around the festival days, I repeat a song dear to the gods, for I was trained in the verses of the poet Horace."]

In an Indian summer, there is an awareness of the extent to which the *carmina* have been the means by which his life has been organized:

> age iam, meorum
> finis amorum—

> non enim posthac alia calebo
> femina—condisce modos, amanda
> uoce quos reddas: minuentur atrae
> carmine curae.

[4.11.31–36]

[Come now, last of my loves—for after this I will warm to no other woman—learn verses to repeat with your lovely voice. Dark cares will fade with song.]

The fading erotic impulse reaches to song for its sustenance; and in earlier books, it is with wine that cares are diminished. The *carmen* has become the center; the last word of the last ode is "canemus." And in Book 4 Horace arrives at his most interesting artistic self-characterization:

> operosa paruus
> carmina fingo.

[4.2.31–32]

[Small, I confect laborious songs.]

The context is the simile of a bee making cells (niches). From the very knowledge of one's finitude ("paruus") one draws great energy of attention ("operosa") to, for instance, the way in which one word can condense out of another by pulling in its vowels—

opero sa
paruu s

—or to the way in which four words, syntactically cross-hatched and twisted around a line ending, can generate, out of the air, a small drama of their own:

oper o sa
paruus
car   mina
fin

go

The explicit concern with the hieratic term "lyric" and its applications is part of what makes the Odes *the* classical model for a lyric oeuvre, and might do so even if all the others were not in ruins. Certainly it is the only one that we have in essentially the form in which its author wanted us to have it; there has never been any serious debate about the canon, or lacunae, or even the order of the poems. Indeed, that order is one of the most intriguing and satisfying aspects of the collection. The poems are not grouped, as Catullus's poems are and as most of the Greek oeuvres seem to have been, by a combination of overt metrical, generic, and thematic criteria, but are disposed according to more subtle contrasts and linkages that encourage us to read them straight through. As noted above, there is something like a plot to follow—certainly a tension of ongoing development and change.

This is in part made possible by the sensible ratio of poem length to book length: not Martial's 1,200 short poems, but 103 somewhat longer poems. Even Horace's individual Books can be read as units; they seem shaped by their contents, not by a grid (the allocation is 38, 20, 30, 15). For technical purposes we refer to Horace's odes, as to Martial's poems, by a double integer (2.14); but informally we more commonly use the first half-line (*Eheu fugaces*). The poems are few enough, and distinct enough, to make that practicable; and Horace provides one of the best formal models for a book of lyrics. Ronsard, though still imitating

Pindar in his individual poems, was almost certainly paying homage to Horace's collection when he published, as a unit, *Les Quatre premiers livres des Odes* in 1550, 94 poems distributed 20, 29, 27, 18.

Herrick followed other models in the disposition of his book, but he did maintain Horace's underlying interest in lyric poetry as a profession, a way of defining one's life. *Exegi monumentum* (3.30) was frequently on Herrick's mind, with its pyramids less durable than lyrics (H-201 / 80.2 / 45–48, H-211 / 85.1 / 21–24) and its strikingly phrased boast, "non omnis moriar," "Thou shalt not All die" (H-366 / 143.1 / 1; cf. H-554 / 200.4 / 1). Indeed, the poem from which this last quotation comes—one of those "Upon himself"—goes on to make explicit the rhyme that may have had something to do with shaping Herrick's notion of his own fate:

> for while Love's fire shines
> Upon his Altar, men shall read thy lines;
> And learn'd Musicians shall to honour *Herricks*
> Fame, and his Name, both set, and sing his Lyricks.

Herrick uses that rhyme elsewhere (H-604 / 213 / 6, 8); it also, intriguingly, shows up in one of the earliest references to Herrick, and the first example we have in the tradition of equating Herrick with a specific classical poet:

> And then *Flaccus Horace*,
> He was but a sowr-ass,
> And good for nothing but *Lyricks:*
> There's but One to be found
> In all English ground
> Writes as well; who is hight *Robert Herick*.[78]

Herrick's primacy ("There's but One to be found") apparently extends to the whole effort of fitting classical precedent to contemporary practice; in the entire poem, a survey of the bigger names in Greek and Latin poetry, no other modern is brought in for this kind of analogy. And specifically, Herrick and Horace meet under the sign of "lyric," that title for trivial poems saved from inconsequence, it would seem, by being written well—what Auden in his poem on Yeats calls "this strange excuse." The ambivalent respect that the anonymous author accords these two poets is only one example in a millennial uncertainty about the "value" of lyric poetry, an uncertainty against which that semimagical title "lyric" is itself one of the chief hedges.

The primary usefulness of the label in both poets is its way of helping them organize an image of a possible life in a given situation. In their hands, the lyric enterprise becomes that of the proper maintenance of hedges in general, of establishing a system of habits that can be a defense without being a prison. The *Carmina* and the *Hesperides* both resemble the Anacreontea in projecting a self-contained lyric "world" in which a large number of customary things go on but not very much really happens. Indeed, they share with each other (and with the Anacreontea) a good deal of that particular décor: young girls, older men, herbage of various sorts, wine, music, domestic gods to be honored, a decent admixture of the grotesque, and an occasional, admiring glimpse of royalty about its business. And in both poets these motifs circulate within a system of sententiae about mortality, equanimity, and the good life.

What keeps this systematization from being merely Anacreontic is our sense, derived partly from the presence of literal information in the poems themselves, and partly from pressures and intensities not otherwise explicable, that all this "poeticizing" is really an integral part of a very specific human situation. Lyric poetry is a vehicle for worshipping not exactly oneself, but one's *lar*. The most important congruence between Herrick and Horace reaches from their work into their lives: two aging bachelors piddling around in their rustication, celebrating moments of pleasurable transiency while being made keenly aware of the menace of civil disruption to all such havens. The writing of "lyric poetry" brings coherence to such a life, both by treating thematically of its emotional dynamics, and also by providing a career and title appropriate to both the writer's ambition and his place.

This congruence, of course, does have its historical dimension, especially if, as is often assumed, many of Herrick's poems were written before he went to Devonshire. The similarity of situation would then simply have been one of the later terms of Herrick's involvement with Horace—life imitating, as though by accident, art. Certainly that involvement was long-standing and complicated; Horace is one of Herrick's primary sources for his characteristic habits of quotation, but in ways that, uncharacteristically, sometimes suggest a special sort of intimacy:

Now is the time for mirth

[H-201 / 80.2 / 1]

Nunc est bibendum

[1.37.1]

It is probably an accident that the next line of Herrick's poem ends "be dumbe," echoing "bibendum." It is probably not an accident that a tag from Horace is used to start a poem about poets. Other poets are quoted in the course of the poem, and more exactly and at greater length; if statistics settled these issues, the presiding spirit would seem to be Ovid. His "aurea pompa uenit" (*Amores* 3.2.44) gets double play in lines 4 and 5; and *Amores* 3.9 supplies the injunction to trust to good verses ("carminibus confide bonis," 39), the "text" on Tibullus (Herrick, 41–44; Ovid, 39–40), and, via Marlowe's translation (where the poem is numbered 3.8), Herrick's striking conclusion:

> hunc quoque summa dies nigro submersit Auerno;
>   defugiunt auidos carmina sola rogos.
>
> [27–28]

> Him the last day in black *Averne* hath drownd,
> Verses alone are with continuance crown'd.

> And when all Bodies meet
>   In *Lethe* to be drown'd;
> Then onely Numbers sweet,
>   With endless life are crown'd.
>
> [49–52]

(Line 28 of the Latin appears in a slightly modified form on the title page of the *Hesperides*.) In general the occasion of Herrick's poem is closer to that of Ovid's than it is to that of *Carmina* 1.37—except, importantly, for the drinking, the conviviality. For exactly those Horatian and non-Ovidian habits convert Ovid's minor key into Herrick's major: as though Herrick were giving us Ovid's poem as it would have been written by Horace.

Horace does appear once more—his pyramids turn up in the penultimate stanza—and he has another interesting distinction as well: he is not mentioned by name. Moorman interprets this as evidence of Herrick's particular regard for Horace, an unwillingness to involve so sober a poet in so unseemly a bash. "In his Bacchanalian lyrics he looks not to Horace, but to Anacreon."[79] Anacreon, however, is not mentioned either, nor is Martial; and in any case, as noted earlier, Herrick's Horace is not so starchy a figure as Moorman's evidently is. It makes more sense to say that Horace is not mentioned because, in some way, Horace is speaking.

The more substantial Horatian quotations have a similar way of occurring at the beginning[80] and at the end.[81] The frequent use of italics in the latter cases indicates an explicit sense of the Horatian quotation as the goal of Herrick's poem: coming on his own to a conclusion that someone else has already reached. Yet, as with most of the other poets that Herrick quotes, the structural influence of these borrowings generally stops at their own borders. They do not lead Herrick into anything like the discursive volatility of the true "Horatian ode"; they are instead forever condensing into simple *gnōmai*. One attempt to go somewhat further than usual merely proves the rule:

> No wrath of Men, or rage of Seas
> Can shake a just mans purposes:
> No threats of Tyrants, or the Grim
> Visage of them can alter him;
> But what he doth at first entend,
> That he holds firmly to the end.
>
> [H-615 / 215.1]

> Iustum et tenacem propositi uirum
> non ciuium ardor praua iubentium,
>   non uultus instantis tyranni
>   mente quatit solida neque Auster,
>
> dux inquieti turbidus Hadriae,
> nec fulminantis magna manus Iouis:
>   si fractus illabatur orbis,
>   impauidum ferient ruinae.
>
> [3.3.1–8]

[The depraved frenzy of imperious citizens does not shake the just man, strong of purpose, from his determined mind; nor does the face of the threatening tyrant, or the South Wind, the violent master of the restless Adriatic, or the great hand of thundering Jove. If the cracked heavens were to fall on him, the ruins would strike him unmoved.]

The examples have been rearranged; that is no big matter, but the deescalation of the last two lines of the Latin is. Horace's unnamed global disaster is not only more "dramatic" than Herrick's "the end," but also sets the frame of reference for the rest of the ode. The next stanza introduces, among the other heroes, Augustus, who ended worldwide civil war; and the poem's second main movement, Juno's speech, begins with the destruction of Troy (18 ff.). Indeed, what Juno's speech—attaching to Roman success the condition that Troy not be restored—has to do with the opening of the poem is one of the classic problems of interpretation in the *Carmina*. Herrick, however, gets nowhere near this issue. By cutting where he does, and shrinking the scale of events as it threatens to extend beyond the personal and moral, he simply, and characteristically, extracts from one of Horace's most demanding poems a tidy little six-line maxim.

Still, on at least two occasions, Herrick does address Horatian poems as wholes. The only explicitly labeled translation in the *Hesperides* (H-181/70.1) is of a Horatian ode (*Donec gratus eram*, 3.9). More ambitious and interesting, however, is one of Herrick's few long poems, "His age, dedicated to his peculiar friend, Master *John Wickes*, under the name of *Posthumus*" (H-336/132.3). Horace, again, is not mentioned in it, but the title fixes the allusion, with some certainty, to the famous opening of *Carmina* 2.14:

> Eheu fugaces, Postume, Postume,
> labuntur anni . . .

Indeed, Herrick's opening line is an almost exact quotation:

> Ah *Posthumus!* Our yeares hence flye . . .

To this Herrick immediately gives his own special shading:

> And leave no sound . . .

The insidious silence of time is one of Herrick's more personal and striking motifs, and shows up elsewhere as his addition to a source (H-62/21.6/5–6). But instead of continuing to move away from the Horatian poem, he returns to it, similarly interleaving some more of his own contributions:

> nor piety,
> Or prayers, or vow
> Can keepe the wrinkle from the brow . . .
>
> [2–4]

> nec pietas moram
> rugis et instanti senectae
> adferet . . .
>
> [2–4]

Herrick's addition—"Or prayers, or vow"—again neatly excerpts. The first twelve lines of Herrick's poem constitute a telescoped translation of the first twenty-four lines of the original. One could argue that nothing really crucial is left out; even the celebrated dying fall of the repeated name, though Herrick misses it in the first line, is caught later in a kind of miniature:

> none,
> None, *Posthumus*, co'd ere decline . . .
>
> [6–7]

(The proper name is not repeated here in the original; note also Herrick's choice of verb.) What is scrapped is a good deal of mythological data, in general amounting to a vision of hell, here reduced to "cruell *Proserpine*" (8), a slack phrase not in the original, though possibly deriving from another Horatian ode (1.28.20). The larger arc of the Latin poem, however—general regret focusing onto death—is preserved; and judicious cutting allows Herrick to realize this as a devolution onto a potent bit of funereal décor:

> no one plant found
> To follow thee,
> Save only the *Curst-Cipresse* tree . . .
>
> [10–12]

> neque harum quas colis arborum
> te praeter inuisas cupressos
> ulla brcucm dominum sequetur . . .
>
> [22–24]

That repositioning of the cypress is one way of converting a poem by Horace into a poem by Herrick; it was not all that hard.

After line 24, Horace gives, in a four-line coda, a parting glimpse of Postumus's *dignior heres* looting his predecessor's carefully preserved wine-cellar; Herrick picks up from this a hint leading him out of his original:

> A merry mind
> Looks forward, scornes what's left behind:
> Let's live, my *Wickes*, then, while we may,
> And here enjoy our Holiday.
>
> [13–16]

The transformation of Posthumus into Wickes signals that the translation itself is over. Still, though Herrick's sentiment here is not strictly in the original, it may be said to be implicit there, in the merry-minded heir with his own ideas about what to do with what's left behind. And the sentiment is certainly explicit in the context of the whole of the *Carmina*; it is indeed the deduction that Horace might make from the presented situation, though he does not happen to do so in this particular poem. Herrick leaves *Eheu fugaces*, but stays within the general Horatian context as his poem moves out from its starting point.

Herrick's poem as a whole is particularly rich in classical allusions. There are unusually numerous bits of salient classical decoration— Iülus and Baucis, Anchus and Tullus, and Pollio's lampreys—though the most memorable is as always the least obvious: a 1700-year-old condiment dispenser fulfilling something of the function of a *lar*:

> we can meet, and so conferre,
> Both by a shining Salt-seller . . .
>
> [49–50]

That is, "splendet in mensa tenui salinum" (*Carm.* 2.16.14). Over the course of the next seven stanzas, Herrick, in his articulation of a norm of equanimity, continually touches classical bases: Catullus ("Let's live," 15; "the white and Luckie stone," 40)[82] and Persius ("Ere long, a song, ere long, a shade," 30), but most especially Horace. Some of the Horatian moments are exact (the waxing and waning moon, 19–20); some collateral (the quotation from Persius overlaps onto "puluis et umbra sumus," *Carm.* 4.7.16, which Martin cites as the only source); and some more general and thematic: stanza eight ("Well then, on what Seas we are tost," 57) reads to the suspicious like a graft of *Integer uitae* onto the Ship of State, with the former's sense of humor preserved.

What is most to the point is, again, the way in which Herrick stays within Horace's orbit. The opening of stanza four (25–27) rewrites in a major key the vision of hell slighted in the translation of *Eheu fugaces*— the underworld, but not Tartaros—yet does so by having recourse to another Horatian ode about death (4.7.14–15; note the reference to line 16 above). And there being in general nothing Herrick says that goes outside Horace's *copia sententiarum*, the first nine stanzas (1–72) constitute something of an allusion to the whole of the *Carmina*.

With stanza ten the poem becomes less sententious and ("as for my selfe") more personal and specific, as Herrick begins to visualize him-

self actually handling the sense of lost time in his old age. And the first
nine stanzas of the poem snap into place when we realize that the
primary activity Herrick envisions for himself is reading his own
poetry, some of which we have just read:

> At which I'le reare
> Mine aged limbs above my chaire:
> And hearing it,
> Flutter and crow, as in a fit
> Of fresh concupiscence, and cry,
> *No lust theres like to Poetry.*

[107–12]

(Very much like William Carlos Williams in his old age, a poet whom
Herrick resembles in other ways as well.) This poem about the lost past
has suddenly ceased to be a poem about memory. What Herrick is
doing, first of all, is *imagining* a future act of remembering. That wife
and child, Baucis and Iülus, are not serious anticipations, but blatant
bits of (classical) poetic scenery; and Herrick is postulating precisely
the assumption in old age of all his concerns (lust, for example) to the
level of imagination. The basic statement made about old age is that
what is going to be remembered is not a person or object or event—
these things pass—but a poetic act, one of the class of things which
remain continuously available, news that stays news. Such is one of the
services poetry performs for the race as a whole; good writing is one
of the few things that grow rather than decay with acquaintance and
use. Herrick simply applies this lesson to his own life: the past he will
endeavor to recall, like modern man reading Homer, will be that of his
imagination. Emotion is poetry recollected in excitement.

Herrick, as I have said, does not mention Horace by name. But the
central image of Herrick rereading Herrick enters the poem only after
we have seen that to reread Herrick is in a certain definite sense to reread
Horace. The tacit analogy goes something like this: Old Herrick is to
Young Herrick as Robert Herrick, seventeenth century A.D., is to
Flaccus Horace, first century B.C. In each case, roughly, the latter
writes, the former reads. And the special excitability of that reading
probably derives from the coexistence of both parts of the analogy: it
is, as D. S. Carne-Ross has remarked, exactly in a time of great contemporary poetry that all great poetry feels contemporary. Or, to come
at it another way, with the availability of the past, present and future

open up. Certainly the mere prospect of rereading his own poems had given Herrick no comfort only a few pages earlier:

> What can I do in Poetry,
> Now the good Spirit's gone from me?
> Why nothing now, but lonely sit,
> And over-read what I have writ.

[H-334 / 132.1]

But because the first half of "His age" makes contact with Horace's words as contemporary resource, the second half looks forward to the use of Herrick's own poetry; the poem is the most precise and practical of Herrick's numerous dealings in the matter of poetic immortality. Elsewhere Herrick's focus is on the marmoreal self-sufficiency of the product; here it is on the unexpected vitality that inspection of such a product—for instance, of *Carmina* 2.14, in all of its Latinate, funereal rigor—can release in the beholder. And specifically what the poem says is that a man's life can be pulled together across time in the same sense—no less, no more—that the race is pulled together, by occasional access to just that vitality.

Insomuch as Herrick's use of Horace puts the Roman poet into any historical perspective, that is it. There is, however, another recess, one not suggested in any particular way in the Wickes poem, but one which Herrick may well have known about, and which may even have shaped his own sense of procedure. For Herrick's relation to Horace superimposes startlingly onto Horace's relation to the Greek lyricists, within whose college the Roman poet was so eager to be enrolled. There is a tendency to forget how strange a collection the *Carmina* was in the context of Latin literary history, that Horace faced his own classical tradition across a linguistic and cultural void not much narrower than that across which Herrick faced his. And it seems that one of Horace's principal techniques for bridging that void was what in a way is the quickest and most obvious: the wholesale importation of spot-quotation, without any particular regard for context.

Herrick's "Now is the time for mirth" follows Horace's example not only in sentiment but also in being a borrowed phrase used to start a poem: "Nunc est bibendum" merely translates the opening of a poem by Alcaios, *nyn chrē methysthēn* (*LGS* 152). That happens so often in Horace that nineteenth-century scholarship developed a technical term for it: the borrowing of a "motto." This example and several others

were commonplaces of Renaissance criticism.[83] They are identified in
the notes of many sixteenth-century editions and occasionally collected
for inspection as a group. The elder Scaliger cites a half-dozen instances
in his discussions of Horace in the *Poetics* and guesses that the list would
be longer if more of the Greek had survived.[84] Estienne gives a similar
catalogue in the notes of his first edition of "Anacreon."

Subsequent scholarship has not contradicted Scaliger's guess, nor has
it implied that Horace's quotations are consistently controlled by context, in the way in which, say, Vergil's quotations of Homer are.
Pasquali, in the standard modern treatment of the issue, writes of "Nunc
est bibendum": "la citazione al principio compie l'ufficio di motto;
non si può parlare di imitazione nel senso commune della parola, ma
al più di un prender le mosse da un poeta greco e più ancora di con-
trasto voluto. In Orazio è sempre cosi...."[85] We may, of course, be
missing larger congruences, both because of the general destruction of
the Greek lyric corpus and through our own inattention. The *bibendum*
poems of Horace and Alcaios do seem to be united by political concerns
(the defeat of Cleopatra and the assassination of the tyrant Myrsilos) in
a more intimate way than either is linked to Herrick's poem. And
Fraenkel notes with some amazement that a serious dialogue between
Carmina 3.4 (*Descende caelo*) and Pindar's first Pythian, a dialogue that
helps make structural sense out of the difficult Latin poem, had never
been explored during the four centuries in which both texts had been
available.[86] Yet the bulk of the evidence, as it stands now, and even
more so as it stood in the Renaissance, still suggests that the baseline of
such congruences was a widespread habit of mere spot-quotation; and
the twin example of Herrick may encourage us to wonder if such a
habit is not somehow central to at least a certain kind of lyric poetry.

Quotation from an older language and culture can be an effective
distancing device, increasing our alertness to words, not as compul-
sions to be indulged or resisted, but as objects whose structural possibilities are to be studied. The practical lesson of such a technique may be
that words are, like everything else we have, borrowed, and that the
measure of our freedom and contentment is our detachment from them,
and hence our awareness of them: it is by objectifying language that we
may hope to keep it from running our lives. The act is that which converts a given situation into a home, by alignment of décor; and the
corporate attempt of both Horace's *Carmina* and Herrick's *Hesperides*
is a definition of "home," that place where, when you are there, you

have nowhere else you need to get to. What both oeuvres allow us to say is that such a state is neither an unearned gift nor a matter of effortless "acceptance," but a meticulous training of one's aspirations to intersect, as though on their own, with the lineaments of the given.

That is the opposite of the epic quest, the search for a home somewhere else, for a way to say what you mean; the lyric enterprise is, by comparison, an attempt to fulfill the obvious, to learn carefully how to mean what you say. And the argument of the borrowed content is perhaps at its most articulate, as in the Leuconoe poem, when it considers its own status in saying that one does not really want to commit oneself too closely to argument, but is better off ("ut melius") noting the momentary surprises to which life, speech, and the other arguments in which we participate incidentally give rise. That such poetry "of the present moment" should be so intricately linked to the past is another part of what it has to say: that the world has been lived in before, and may, with skill and luck, be lived in again. Bubbles have no history, but they do have precedents.

APPENDIX: HERRICK'S EDITION OF "ANACREON"

Except for a handful of poems that also appear elsewhere, the Anacreontea are known to us today from a single MS—the same MS that contains, separately, the Palatine Anthology. The discovery of this MS was first announced by Claude de Saumaise (Salmasius) in 1606, but its contents were not edited and published for another two centuries. Estienne's 1554 edition of "Anacreon" is thus of particular historical importance as the sole source of most of these poems until Giuseppe Spalletti's edition from the Palatine MS in 1781. We are not sure of the source of Estienne's own text; the details of the question may be found in Preisendanz. Estienne writes of having consulted at Louvain (where he is known to have been in 1551) a MS of Greek "epigrams" owned by Thomas More's friend John Clement; this could have been the Palatine MS, or a part of it. In any case, Estienne's transcript of the Anacreontea, now at Leyden, makes it clear that whatever MS he did use was virtually identical in its contents with the one that we have now, and certainly did not represent a separate tradition. The important differences between Estienne's edition and the Palatine MS are thus Estienne's own doing, and we can partially reconstruct the process of alteration.

Estienne, as he admits in his own notes, completely reordered the poems. This order, duly translated into numbers, became the standard mode of reference until Spalletti; since it has occasionally caused trouble for scholars, Estienne's order seems worth reprinting (see the accompanying table). Also, Estienne evidently decided that since 1 and 20

Estienne's Canon of the Anacreontea

Estienne	Modern eds.	Estienne	Modern eds.	Estienne	Modern eds.
1	23	21	18A	41	38
2	24	22	18B	42	42
3	33	23	36	43	34
4	32	24	40	44	30
5	44	25	45	45	28
6	43	26	48	46	29
7	31	27	49	47	39
8	37	28	16	48	2
9	15	29	17	49	3
10	11	30	19	50	56
11	7	31	9	51	57
12	10	32	14	52	59
13	12	33	25	53	55
14	13	34	51	54	53
15	8	35	54	55	27
16	26	36	52		
17	4	37	46		
18	5	38	47		
19	21	39	50		
20	22	40	35		

mention Anacreon in the third person, and since 6 is attributed to "Julian" in the Planudean Anthology, they could not possibly be genuine, and suppressed them from his edition altogether. For less obvious reasons, 41, 58, and 60 (the last of which also mentions Anacreon in the third person) were removed from the canon proper to an appendix, which also included some of what are now known to be genuine fragments of Anacreon, as well as some dubiously attributed epigrams from the Anthology and some anonymous but "Anacreontic" drinking songs. Anacreontea 18 was printed as two poems, so that Estienne's final canon consisted of fifty-five poems instead of the current sixty.

For his first edition, Estienne also provided a Greek preface, a Latin verse translation of thirty-one of the canonical Anacreontea, two poems attributed to Sappho, and four fragments of Alcaios. A second edition appeared in 1556, without the preface. A complete Latin verse translation of the fifty-five-poem canon by Elie André (Helias Andreas) appeared in 1555, was reprinted (with the two Sappho poems added) in 1556, and often bound with Estienne's edition. In 1560 Estienne incorporated his canon and appendix of the Anacreontic poems into his *Carminum poetarum nouem, lyricae poëseωs principum fragmenta*; this was a companion volume to Estienne's Pindar, and together the two books constituted a complete collection of the Greek lyric remains. For this edition Estienne restored his old preface in a Latin translation and plugged the holes in his translation of the Anacreontea with André's versions, even though they are appreciably freer than his own. The doubtful and fragmentary poems were also translated, with a few decorous exceptions (e.g. *LGS* 302; see above, p. 211). Also, in an appendix ("Anacreontia carmina diuersorum") to the whole volume, Estienne printed Anacreontea 1, with his own translation, and 6, with an already available translation by Philip Melancthon (20 was not printed anywhere until Spalletti). The collection was reprinted in this form, at various locations, in 1566, 1567, 1586, 1598, 1600, 1612, and 1624.[1]

Ben Jonson owned a copy of the 1598 Heidelberg edition of this book,[2] and it is almost certain that Herrick also owned or at least worked from some edition of it. It is certainly the logical book to suspect, since there was little competition. Fulvio Orsini's collection of Greek lyrics (Antwerp, 1568) makes no use of Estienne's discoveries and prints only those poems and fragments available from other sources. The most likely alternative source for the Anacreontea until the mid-seventeenth century would have been Eilhard Lubin's edition (Rostock, 1597); Lubin provides a Latin verse translation that uses occasional phrases from Estienne-André but is basically a new effort, and notably more literal. The specific influence, however, of Estienne's Latin has been traced in Herrick's versions of several of the Anacreontea and of a fragment attributed to Simonides (H-121 / 42.3, *LGS* 444) that is also in the *Carminum poetarum nouem*.[3] There is further the fact that Herrick also produced versions of Anacreontea 1 and 6—both noncanonical but available in the appendix to the same book. We may even detect in Herrick the influence of Melancthon's Latin translation of the latter. The Greek ends with what would seem to be a very Herricksy effect: "And now within my marrow he tickles (*gargalizei*) with his wings." Herrick completely misses that onomatopoetic verb: "Hence then it is, that my poore brest / Co'd never since find any rest" (H-229/96.1/ 5–6). This curious loss of contact with the specific action of the wings may be due to Melancthon: "Nunc ille saeuit imis / Puer mihi in medullis." Anacreontea 6 and Melancthon's translation were both easily obtainable elsewhere, but Anacreontea 1 was harder to find. Casaubon prints it, untranslated, in his notes on Athenaios (Lyons, 1600, et al.),[4] but otherwise it is, as far as I know, available in the Renaissance only in the *Carminum poetarum nouem*.

I have found no hard evidence in all of this that Herrick knew Greek; still, his library would have contained at least one other book of Greek poetry. His apparently abbreviated version of Anacreontea 8 may be explained by assuming that he was reading it in the Planudean Anthology, where the Greek is similarly curtailed; and the only other Greek poems that he takes over entire are also from the Anthology: H-271/109.4 and Palatine 7.182; H-431/162.5 and 10.28.

NOTES

CHAPTER 1: GOLDING'S OVID

For my text of Golding's translation I have used *Shakespeare's Ovid*, ed. W. H. D. Rouse (1904; reprint ed., Carbondale, Ill., 1961; there is also a paperback reprint, New York, 1966). The more accessible edition is that of John Frederick Nims (New York, 1965), but on even superficial examination it seems to be the less reliable, with obvious misreadings (beginning at I.2: "ywrought" for "y^t wrought"), misprints, transposed lines, etc. For Ovid's Latin, I have used Rudolf Ehwald's text, as reprinted in the Loeb edition of the *Metamorphoses*, ed. Frank Justus Miller (London and New York, 1916). References with an uppercase Roman numeral are to Golding, those with a lowercase Roman numeral are to the Latin. Quotations from Sandys's translation are taken from the edition of Karl K. Hulley and Stanley T. Vandersall (Lincoln, Nebr., 1970); since Sandys's lines are not numbered, reference is given to page in this edition.

1   Introductory verses by "T. B."—probably Thomas Blundeville—to John Studley's translation, *The eyght tragedie of Seneca. Entituled Agamemnon* (London, 1566; *STC* 22222), sig. A1^r.
2   Peend says this in the preface of his translation, published late in 1565, of Ovid's story of Hermaphroditus. However, the translation shows signs of being influenced by Golding's version and hence not, as claimed, a fragment from an independent effort preempted by Golding's publication. See A. B. Taylor, "Thomas Peend and Arthur Golding," *N&Q* 214 (1969): 19–20.
3   1567, 1575, 1584, 1587, twice in 1593, 1603, 1612.
4   A few examples are reported by Harriet Manning Blake, "Golding's Ovid in Elizabethan Times," *JEGP* 14 (1915): 93–95; and by Taylor, "George Peele and Golding's *Metamorphoses*," *N&Q* 214 (1969): 286–87. For a full catalogue, however, one must consult M. W. S. Swan's Ph.D. dissertation, "A Study of Golding's Ovid" (Harvard University, 1942), pp. 258–300. Swan's study, unfortunately somewhat difficult of access, is the most useful work on the subject so far; my own sense of the validity of the examples I discuss was greatly steadied by Swan's

much longer and more thorough catalogues of Golding's verbal habits as a translator. A more easily available dissertation by William Myron McIntyre, "A Critical Study of Golding's Translation of Ovid's *Metamorphoses*" (Berkeley, 1965; *DA* 26:1045–46), utilizes some of Swan's work, but is in general less valuable.

5   William Webbe, *A Discourse of English Poetrie* (1586); in G. Gregory Smith, ed., *Elizabethan Critical Essays* (London, 1904), 1:243. Also in Smith are similar homages by Nashe (1:315) and Puttenham (2:63, 65–66), and briefer praise by Harington (2:196) and Meres (2:322).

6   Pound, *Literary Essays*, ed. T. S. Eliot (Norfolk, Conn., 1954), p. 238 n. (a remark dated 1929); *The ABC of Reading* (1934; reprint ed., Norfolk, Conn., 1951), p. 127.

7   Nims, p. xxxi.

8   Pound, *The ABC of Reading*, pp. 126–27.

9   Webbe, in Gregory Smith, 1:262.

10 Lowell, "The Muses Won't Help Twice," *Kenyon Review* 17 (1955): 317–24.

11 John Dover Wilson, "Shakespeare's 'Small Latin'—How Much?" *ShS* 10 (1957): 18.

12 Louis R. Zocca, *Elizabethan Narrative Verse* (New Brunswick, N.J., 1950), p. 215.

13 James Wortham, "Arthur Golding and the Translation of Prose," *HLQ* 12 (1949): 339–67. For a more thorough survey of comment on Golding—most of it incidental—see McIntyre, "Critical Study," pp. 36–84.

14 T. W. Baldwin, review of the Nims edition, *JEGP* 66 (1967): 125.

15 Our one piece of external evidence, however, supports the former possibility: a Latin text of the *Metamorphoses* signed "Wm She" on the title page. Forgery, though, is strongly suspected; see S. Schoenbaum, *William Shakespeare: A Documentary Life* (New York, 1975), p. 57.

16 The results have never been fully collected; many of them are scattered through editions of individual Shakespearean plays, particularly those of H. C. Hart, who had a thing about Golding, in the older Arden series (*Love's Labor's Lost*, 1 and 2 *Henry IV*). Leo Rick, "Shakespeare und Ovid," *SJW* 55 (1919): 46–47, conveniently prints out some of the best examples on two facing pages; for a similar gathering, see H. R. D. Anders, *Shakespeare's Books* (Berlin, 1904), pp. 22–25. The whole question is fully reargued, with new evidence, by Baldwin, *William Shakspere's Small Latine and Lesse Greeke* (Urbana, Ill., 1944), 2:430–51. For further discussion of individual *loci*, see my Bibliography below, pp. 281–82.

17 Anders, pp. 24–25.

18 Baldwin, *Shakspere's Small Latine*, 2:430–32.

19 *The Port Folio* (Philadelphia), n.s. 2 (1806): 248–49. The anonymous contributor, ignorant of Golding, anticipates one of Baldwin's arguments by assuming that Shakespeare was making an almost literal translation of the Latin. See Albert van Rensselaer Westfall, *American Shakespearean Criticism 1607–1865* (New York, 1939), p. 274.

20 Baldwin, *Shakspere's Small Latine*, 2:445–46. For a recent and more sophisticated discussion of the matter, see Marion Trousdale, "Recurrence and Renaissance," *ELR* 6 (1976): 172–74.

21 For these last two details, including a list of membership in Parker's society, see Louis Thorn Golding, *An Elizabethan Puritan: Arthur Golding* (New York, 1937), pp. 67, 266–69.

22 Ibid., pp. 194–95. Three of Golding's original works are reprinted there, pp. 164–201.

23 Douglas Bush, *Mythology and the Renaissance Tradition in English Poetry* (1932; reprint ed., New York, 1957), p. 110.

24 Thomas Stapleton, *A fortresse of the faith* (Antwerp, 1565; *STC* 23232), sig. LL2ᵛ; see Leonard J. Trinterud, *Elizabethan Puritanism* (New York, 1971), p. 7. The earliest citation in the *OED* is from 1572.

25 Louis Golding, pp. 191–92.

26 Ibid., p. 193.

27 From the title page of *Thabridgment of the histories of Trogus Pompeius* (London, 1564; *STC* 24290).

28 Ibid., sig. *3ᵛ.

29 *The psalmes of David and others. With M. John Calvins commentaries* (London, 1571; *STC* 4395), sig. *2ʳ.

30 Ibid., sig. *2ᵛ–3ʳ.

31 Ibid., sig. *3ʳ.

32 The two figures show up in the introductory material to the *Metamorphosis:* see the epistle to Leicester, ll. 552 ff., and the preface to the reader, l. 218.

33 Louis Golding, p. 123.

34 On this manuscript, now at Columbia, see William Nelson, "A Morall Fabletalke," *CLC* 9, no. 1 (1959): 26–31. The work has been dated no earlier than 1579 by David G. Hale, "The Source and Date of Golding's 'Fabletalke,'" *MP* 69 (1972): 326–27.

35 Wortham, "Arthur Golding," p. 359.

36 From the preface to Drant's translation of the *Sermones* (1566); quoted by Otto L. Jiriczek, "Der elisabethanische Horaz," *SJW* 47 (1911):49. The application of the biblical passage (Deut. 21:11–13) to the handling of pagan literary texts is a common topos in the Middle Ages and, as Drant indicates on his title page, goes back ultimately to Jerome.

37 Text for Stanyhurst from *Richard Stanyhurst's Aeneis*, ed. Dirk van der Haar (Amsterdam, 1933).

38 *The nyne fyrst bookes of the Eneidos of Virgil* (London, 1562; *STC* 24800). This is a posthumous publication—including some of Book 10—of as much of the poem as Phaer had been able to finish. He had published Books 1–7 in 1558; a completion by Thomas Twyne appeared in 1573.

39 Quoted by Grundy Steiner, "Golding's Use of the Regius-Micyllus Commentary upon Ovid," *JEGP* 49 (1950): 320.

40 On Regio's edition and its place in the Renaissance tradition, see Davis P. Harding, *Milton and the Renaissance Ovid* (Urbana, Ill., 1946), pp. 18–20.

41 In addition to Steiner, see Swan, "A Study of Golding's Ovid," pp. 44–50. Steiner, p. 317, promised "a detailed study . . . of the bibliographic sources employed by Golding . . . and of his techniques in using them"—a study which could, among other things, lead to a specification of Golding's text, or at least some clarification of the vast and complicated editorial history of Ovid in the Renaissance. Steiner's effort, however, apparently faltered after two articles on Ovidian incunabula, and no further work has been done on the question.

42 From dedicatory verses to John Baret's *Alvearie* (1573); Louis Golding, p. 201.

43 Philippe de Mornay, *A woorke concerning the trewnesse of the Christian religion* (London, 1587; *STC* 18149), sig. *4ᵛ.

44 See R. F. Jones, *The Triumph of the English Language* (Stanford, Calif., 1953), pp. 122–23.

45 See Veré L. Rubel, *Poetic Diction in the English Renaissance from Skelton through Spenser* (New York and London, 1941), pp. 138–39.

46 "Thee description of *Liparen*," l. 6 (a fragment from Book 8 of the *Aeneid*); van der Haar, p. 136.

47 Knud Sørensen, *Thomas Lodge's Translation of Seneca's De Beneficiis Compared with Arthur Golding's Version* (Copenhagen, 1960), p. 128.

48 See A. T. P. Byles, "William Caxton as a Man of Letters," *The Library*, 4th ser. 15 (1934): 12–14.

49 The Latin is *Aen*. 2.307, "praecipitisque trahit siluas"; the example is H. A. Mason's, from *Humanism and Poetry in the Early Tudor Period* (London, 1959), p. 252. Surrey's relation to Douglas is most fully detailed in Florence H. Ridley's edition of Surrey's *Aeneid* (Berkeley and Los Angeles, 1963).

50 *Surrey's Fourth Boke of Virgill*, ed. Herbert Hartman (Purchase, N.Y., 1933), p. 3.

51 George Puttenham, *The Arte of English Poesie* (1589), Bk. 3, chap. 23; Gregory Smith, 2:178.

52 C. S. Lewis, *English Literature in the Sixteenth Century, Excluding Drama* (Oxford, 1954), p. 248.

53 Golding could not have known it, but his version of the Dionysiac does come close to that of a genuine classical writer—namely, Aristophanes in the opening lines of *Lysistrata*:

> Announce a debauch in honor of Bacchos,
> a spree for Pan, some footling fertility fieldday,
> and traffic stops—these streets are absolutely clogged
> with frantic females banging on tambourines.

Trans. Douglass Parker (Ann Arbor, Mich., 1964).

54 Quotations of Chapman's translation are from *Chapman's Homer*, ed. Allardyce Nicoll, 2d ed. (Princeton, 1967).

55 Lewis, p. 249.

56 Nims, p. 30n.

57 For a general account of Sandys's translation, see Richard Beale Davis, *George Sandys, Poet Adventurer* (London, 1955), pp. 198–226; see pp. 208–09 for Sandys's direct use of Golding.

58 On the place of Sandys's verse in this tradition, see Ruth Wallerstein, "The Development of the Rhetoric and Metre of the Heroic Couplet," *PMLA* 50 (1935): 186–93; and William Bowman Piper, *The Heroic Couplet* (Cleveland and London, 1969), pp. 69–75.

59 See Wallerstein, p. 190.

60 There is a narcissus in *The Two Noble Kinsmen* (2.2.119), but the scene is invariably attributed to Fletcher, and the flower is introduced to bring up the myth, not as a genuinely familiar natural object. The English daffodil is a member of the genus *Narcissus*, but it does not fit Ovid's description; the two-colored flowers usually called "narcissus" are mainly Mediterranean, although they transplant easily.

61 Text from *Elizabethan Narrative Verse*, ed. Nigel Alexander (Cambridge, Mass., 1968); on the question of authorship, see p. 316. The original introductory material to the translation identifies the flower as a "daffadylly."

62 Richard Mulcaster, *Positions* (1581), ed. Robert Hebert Quick (London and New York, 1888), p. 166.

63 Fraunce, *The Countesse of Pembrokes Yvychurch* (London, 1591; *STC* 11340), sig. M1^{v}.

64 See also the account of Brian Gibbons, "Unstable Proteus," in *Christopher Marlowe*, ed. Brian Morris (London, 1968), pp. 29–32.

65 Lewis, *English Literature in the Sixteenth Century*, p. 251.

66   Lowell, "The Muses Won't Help Twice," p. 320.
67   Benjamin, "The Storyteller," in *Illuminations*, trans. Harry Zohn, ed. Hannah
     Arendt (New York, 1969), pp. 91–92.
68   Lowell, p. 323.
69   E.g., E. J. Kenney, "The Style of the *Metamorphoses*," in *Ovid*, ed. J. W. Binns
     (London and Boston, 1973), pp. 116–53; see especially the contrast with Vergil,
     p. 119. Thickly annotated, this article is a good introduction to stylistic criticism
     of Ovid's poem.
70   L. P. Wilkinson, *Ovid Recalled* (Cambridge, 1955), pp. 150–51.
71   W. R. Johnson, "The Problem of the Counter-classical Sensibility and its Critics,"
     California Studies in Classical Antiquity 3 (1970): 123–51. See also Richard A.
     Lanham's discussion of Ovid in *The Motives of Eloquence* (New Haven and London,
     1976), pp. 48–64.
72   Benjamin, p. 83.

CHAPTER 2: "THE DIVINE POEM OF MUSAEUS"

Quotations of both Marlowe's poem and Chapman's continuation of it are from
Bowers's edition of Marlowe. The references are, as is traditional, to Sestyad and
line number, though I would have preferred to encourage the printing of Marlowe's
poem as an undivided and independent unit. In my discussion I have made use too
extensive to localize of the two major annotated editions of Marlowe's poems, those
of L. C. Martin (London, 1931) and of Millar Maclure (London, 1968). Maclure's
notes are based on, supplement, but do not quite replace Martin's.

For the text of Mousaios I have generally used the edition of Karlheinz Kost (Bonn,
1971), except where the need to follow Renaissance readings intervened; Kost's
voluminous notes have also been put to extensive use. I have profited as well from
the recent work of Thomas Gelzer: "Bemerkungen zu Sprache und Text des Epikers
Musaios," *MH* 24 (1967): 129–48, and 25 (1968): 11–47; and his recent Loeb edition
of the poem, bound with the fragments of Callimachos, ed. C. A. Trypanis (London
and Cambridge, Mass., 1975). This edition, with a detailed introduction by Gelzer
and an English translation by Cedric Whitman, is by far the most convenient text
for the interested English-speaking reader.

For the Latin translations of Mousaios, I have used the following texts:

The Aldine translation: I quote from the version in *Aesopi Phrygis uita et fa-
bellae* (Basle, 1518), sigs. T3ʳ–U8ʳ, on the assumption that this is the form in which
the translation had its widest circulation. I have tried, however, to keep an eye
on earlier and later readings.

Guillaume Delamare (Gulielmus de Mara): *Musaei opusculum de Herone et
Leandro* (Paris, 1538), which I have found printed separately but bound between
the Aldine Latin and the Greek text (both also Paris, 1538). Jean Vatel's commentary is interwoven with Delamare's translation. I have not been able to
consult the earlier editions of 1514 and 1526.

André de Pape (Andreas Papius): *Dionysii Alexandrini de situ orbis liber* (Antwerp, 1575), pp. 156–83.

Fabio Paolini (Fabius Paulinus): *Centum fabulae ex antiquis scriptoribus acceptae*
(Venice, 1587), pp. 159–78.

Pape gives a line-for-line translation and also numbers his lines, so that (with one
exception, duly rectified) the Greek line numbers will serve for references to his
translation. Paolini gives a line-for-line translation but no line numbers; for him
and Delamare I give page references. Since my principal concern was with Marlowe,

I have limited my attention to these four; we also have preserved in MS an early sixteenth-century Latin metrical version by Giovanni Battista da Monte (Montanus; 1498–1551), and later Latin translations were published by Eilhard Lubin (Rostock, 1594), Florent Chrestien (with selections from the Greek Anthology, Paris, 1608), and Kaspar von Barth (Hamburg, 1608).

For the vernacular versions other than Marlowe's I have used:

Hans Sachs, ed. Adelbert von Keller and Edmund Goetze (1870–1908; reprint ed., Hildesheim, 1964), 2:195–97.

Bernardo Tasso, I tre libri de gli amori (Venice, 1555), pp. 353–78. Reference is given to page in this edition. The poem was first published in 1537; the most recent printing, as far as I know, is in Pierantonio Serassi's eighteenth-century edition of Tasso's poems (Bergamo, 1749), 2:83–102.

Juan Boscán Almogáver, Las obras de Boscan y algunas de la Vega (Barcelona, 1543; facsimile reprint, San Sebastián, 1936), sigs. M1ᵛ–R6ᵛ; line numbers are from the text in Obras poéticas, ed. Martín de Riquer et al. (Barcelona, 1957–), 1:245–318.

Bernardino Baldi, Versi e prose (Venice, 1590), pp. 591–614; line numbers are from the text in Versi e prose scelte, ed. Filippo Ugolini and Filippo-Luigi Polidori (Florence, 1859), pp. 271–89.

Clément Marot, Les Oeuvres, ed. Georges Guiffrey (Paris, 1876–1931), 2: 417–38.

George Chapman, The divine poem of Musaeus. First of all bookes (London, 1616; STC 18304); line numbers are from the text in Elizabethan Minor Epics, ed. Elizabeth Story Donno (New York and London, 1963), pp. 70–84. Donno's text is the most accessible but unfortunately does not include Chapman's interesting prefatory material, which must be sought either in the original or in nineteenth-century editions of Chapman: Homer's Batrachomyomachia, Hymns and Epigrams, ed. Richard Hooper (London, 1858), pp. 211–16; or Poems and Minor Translations, introduction by A. C. Swinburne (London, 1875), pp. 93–95.

This constitutes a list only of direct and sustained encounters with Mousaios's ext; for a fuller account of Mousaios's Nachleben, see Kost, pp. 69–85.

1   Fraunce, The third part of the Countesse of Pembrokes Yvychurch (London, 1592; STC 11341), sig. M4ʳ.

2   M. C. Bradbrook, "'Hero and Leander,'" Scrutiny 2 (1933): 60.

3   These are an Argonautica in which Orpheus plays an unusually large role, a number of short hymns to various gods, and a treatise on the magical properties of certain stones (Lithica). The poems are, of course, much later than the Renaissance supposed, mostly A.D.; more on them below. The Orphica were occasionally printed with Mousaios, e.g., by the Aldine Press in 1517.

4   For the text, with some speculative reconstructions of the lacunae and an English translation, see the Loeb volume, Greek Literary Papyri: Poetry, ed. Denys L. Page (London and Cambridge, Mass., 1942), pp. 512–15. That the fragment deals with the story of Hero and Leander has been disputed; see Gelzer in his edition, pp. 305–06 n.

5   Bush, Mythology and the Renaissance Tradition, pp. 129–30. The first sentence is adapted from John Addington Symonds; see the discussion in his Studies of the Greek Poets, 3d ed. (London, 1893), 2:344–60.

6   Bush, p. 127.

7   In the preface to his commentary on the Aeneid; see Servius, In Vergilii Carmina Commentarii, ed. Georg Thilo and Hermann Hagen (Leipzig and Berlin, 1881–

1902), 1:5. The rule was not iron-clad in early Greek practice and may actually have been codified only by Latin *imitatio*. Hesiod begins his two main poems with the Muses, and Apollonios of Rhodes and the author of the *Batrachomyomachia* begin with the process of beginning (*Archomenos*, "Taking it from the top . . ."). But a glance through the Homeric hymns, which provide our only statistically significant sample of epic invocations, reveals an overwhelming preference for starting with an important noun, usually the god's name.

8   The only close analogue in early Greek literature is the line that may have begun Antimachos's *Thebaid: Ennepete*, "Tell, daughters of great Zeus, son of Cronos. . . ." See *Epicorum Graecorum Fragmenta*, ed. Gottfried Kinkel (Leipzig, 1877), p. 276. The commentator who preserves the line for us says it is done *Homēricōi zēlōi*, "in competition with Homer." The line is certainly an escalation rather than a direct imitation of the Homeric calls to the Muse; the enterprise of topping Homer apparently began very early.

9   See Kost's excursus, "Die Lampe in der Liebesdichtung," in his edition, pp. 126–32.

10 Other four-word lines: 34, 36, 106, 122, 130, 161, 223, 226, 235, 236, 261, 292, 294, 302, 303, 310, 334. Near misses: 12, 155, 168, 225, 270, 331, 333. In the first 343 lines of the *Odyssey*, by comparison, there are three four-word lines.

11 Albert Wifstrand, *Von Kallimachos zu Nonnos* (Lund, 1933), gives several highly specialized cross-sections of the whole field. A detailed account of Nonnos's linguistic and metrical peculiarities, as well as a list of works on late Greek epic in general, may be found in the introduction to Rudolf Keydell's edition of the *Dionysiaca* (Berlin, 1959; my quotations of Nonnos are from this edition). Albin Lesky gives a broader and less technical survey in *A History of Greek Literature*, trans. James Willis and Cornelis de Heer (New York, 1966), pp. 807–19; for a more current bibliography, see the third German edition, *Geschichte der griechischen Literatur* (Bern and Munich, 1971), pp. 903–17. Most of the still-scattered work in the area is, of course, philological in the narrowest sense, but several recent discussions are particularly worth the nonspecialist's attention: Alan Cameron's *Claudian* (Oxford, 1970), passim; the enthusiastic appreciation of Nonnos by Jack Lindsay in *Leisure and Pleasure in Roman Egypt* (London, 1965), pp. 359–95; and a suggestive treatment of Paul the Silentiary—translation and commentary—by Ian Fletcher and D. S. Carne-Ross, "Ekphrasis: Lights in Santa Sophia," *Arion* 4 (1965): 563–81.

12 Text, as for John of Gaza below, from *Johannes von Gaza und Paulus Silentiarius*, ed. Paul Friedländer (Leipzig and Berlin, 1912).

13 In addition to Keydell's edition, the *Dionysiaca* is available in the Loeb edition of W. H. D. Rouse (London and Cambridge, Mass., 1940). For Nonnos's *Metabolē*, see the edition of Augustin Scheindler (Leipzig, 1881); or *Patrologia Graeca*, ed. J.-P. Migne (Paris, 1857–66), 43:749–920 (with a Latin translation by Daniel Heinsius). Collouthos may be found in the Loeb edition, *Oppian, Colluthus, Tryphiodorus*, ed. A. W. Mair (London and New York, 1928). Christodoros is widely available as Book 2 of the Palatine Anthology.

14 See Cameron, "Wandering Poets," *Historia* 14 (1965): 470–509.

15 Cameron, *Claudian*, pp. 11–12.

16 Kost, pp. 15–16.

17 Previously thought to be a follower of Nonnos; see Cameron, *Claudian*, pp. 18, 478–82.

18 The last inclusive edition of the Orphica is that of Eugen Abel (1885; reprint ed., Hildesheim, 1971); however, the *Argonautica* is available in the Budé series with a French translation: *Les Argonautiques d'Orphée*, ed. Georges Dottin (Paris, 1930).

Dionysios may be found in *Die griechischen Dichterfragmente der römischen Kaiserzeit*, ed. Ernst Heitsch (Göttingen, 1961–64), 1:60–77; the *Bassarica*, his poem on Dionysos, may be found with an English translation in Page, *Greek Literary Papyri*, pp. 536–41. For Claudian, see the edition of Theodor Birt (Berlin, 1892); the Loeb edition of Maurice Platnauer (London and New York, 1922), reprints Birt's text of the Latin poems but does not include the Greek Gigantomachy.

19 For a thorough survey of the genre in antiquity, see Friedländer, pp. 1–132; the genre's role in the epic tradition is explored briefly by George Kurman, "Ecphrasis in Epic Poetry," *CL* 26 (1974): 1–13.

20 A. K. Clarke, "Claudian's De Raptu Proserpinae," *Classical Association Proceedings* 27 (1930): 38.

21 Cameron, *Claudian*, p. 266n.; his reference is to Ernst Robert Curtius, *European Literature and the Latin Middle Ages*, trans. Willard Trask (1953; reprint ed., New York and Evanston, Ill., 1963), p. 474.

22 See Cameron, *Claudian*, pp. 279–84.

23 Triphiodoros, 560; *Dion.* 12.95, et al.; *Dion.* 10.125.

24 See my article, "Nonnos' Typhoon," *TSLL* 15 (1974): 851–56.

25 See Gelzer's edition, pp. 316–22; a book on the subject is promised.

26 The word for "word," curiously enough, does not appear in either *Hero and Leander* or the *Dionysiaca*, although it is, understandably, common in Nonnos's *Metabolē* of John. Mousaios does not even use the related verb *legō*.

27 Harry Levin, *The Overreacher* (Cambridge, Mass., 1952), p. 161.

28 See Ambroise Firmin-Didot, *Alde Manuce et l'hellénisme à Venise* (1875; reprint ed., Brussels, 1966), pp. 54–56; and Curt F. Bühler, "Aldus Manutius and his First Edition of the Greek Musaeus," in *Scritti sopra Aldo Manuzio*, ed. Roberto Ridolfi (Florence, 1955), pp. 3–7, 106–07. For a bibliography of Greek editions of Mousaios, see Kost, pp. 592–95 (including reprints, there are 34 by 1620). For a partial bibliography of translations and a good general account of commentary on the poem up to the eighteenth century, see Johann Albert Fabricius, *Bibliotheca Graeca*, 4th ed., revised by Gottlieb Christoph Harles (1790–1808; reprint ed., Hildesheim, 1966–67), 1:123–33.

29 The preface is reprinted in *Prefaces to the First Editions of the Greek and Roman Classics and of the Sacred Scriptures*, ed. Beriah Botfield (London, 1861), p. 182; there is a French translation in Firmin-Didot, pp. 55–56.

30 In a brief preface to Mousaios in the 1518 Aesop, sig. T1ᵛ.

31 Botfield, p. 564.

32 Isaac Casaubon ("Isaacus Hortibonus"), *Notae ad Diogenis Laertii libros* (Geneva, 1583), in a note on 1.3 of the Greek text. The commentary was incorporated into Estienne's edition in 1593 and widely reprinted in this form in the seventeenth century—e.g. (my own source), *Laertii Diogenis de uitis dogmatis et apophthegmatis eorum qui in philosophia claruerunt*; *libri X* (London, 1664; Wing D1515), sig. D4ᵛ.

33 See especially Kaspar von Barth, *Aduersariorum commentariorum libri LX* (Frankfurt, 1624), pp. 1006–09, 2230–31; and Joseph Juste Scaliger, *Epistolae omnes*, ed. Daniel Heinsius, 2d ed. (Frankfurt, 1628), pp. 487–88.

34 Julius Caesar Scaliger, *Poetices libri septem* (Lyons, 1561; facsimile reprint, Stuttgart, 1964), p. 5 (Bk. 1, chap. 2).

35 Ibid., p. 215 (Bk. 5, chap. 2); most of Scaliger's main discussion of Mousaios is on this page.

36 Specifically, he quotes: lines 8–9, 56, 94–95, 132, 135–40, 164–65, 183–84, 198–200, 224, 245–50, 255, 293–99, 314–18.

37 Immediately afterward Scaliger quotes lines 183–84, thus showing some attune-

ment to one of Mousaios's more important verbal obsessions—or at least that his
ear picks up the repetition.

38 Curtius, pp. 273–301.

39 J. J. Scaliger, p. 487.

40 J. C. Scaliger, p. 321 (Bk. 6, chap. 5).

41 Botfield, pp. 574–75.

42 One unconvincing proposal has been made for a Nonnian borrowing in *Romeo
and Juliet*: Albert S. Cook, "Notes on Shakespeare," *MLN* 21 (1906): 148–49.
The *Dionysiaca* was, however, read and admired by Poliziano, and does seem to
have influenced Italian literature of the later Renaissance; see Guglielmo Felice
Damiani, "Nuove fonti dell'Adone di Gio. Battista Marino," *GSLI* 32 (1898):
370–94.

43 For details, see Frederick S. Boas, *Christopher Marlowe* (Oxford, 1940), pp. 223–24.

44 Kost's apparatus does not take much notice of the Renaissance editions, and the
reader wishing to keep track of their text should use Arthur Ludwich's edition
(Bonn, 1912).

45 Generally assumed to be by the editor, Marcos Mousouros; see, however, Gelzer's
edition, p. 323 n., for evidence that it was actually done by the publisher.

46 See Bühler, p. 5, although he misinterprets the reason for the change: "The chief
reason—and, indeed, the only apparent one—which compelled Aldus to make
this alteration seems to have been a desire to improve the metre of the line."
Neither Latin line comes anywhere near scanning.

47 See the brief remarks of Carne-Ross, "The Means and the Moment," *Arion* 7
(1968): 549–57; there is a full study by Agostino Pertusi, *Leonzio Pilato fra Petrarca
e Boccaccio* (Venice and Rome, 1964).

48 Pound, *Literary Essays*, p. 264.

49 See Hugh Kenner, *The Pound Era* (Berkeley and Los Angeles, 1971), pp. 349–54.

50 Divo has recently turned up again, in a less flattering light but with further testimony to his influence; see Fred Schreiber, "The Etiology of a Misinterpretation,"
Classical Philology 70 (1975): 208–12. The little we know of Divo himself is
summarized there, p. 209.

51 Richard J. Schoeck, in a letter to Louis L. Martz, quoted in Martz's introduction
to *Hero and Leander . . . A Facsimile of the First Edition* (New York and Washington,
1972), p. 9 n.

52 E.g., Gottfried Heinrich Schaefer's revision of Johann Schrader's edition (Leipzig,
1825). In some instances changes made in the Latin are attributed and discussed.

53 Comparison of parallel texts suggests that Pape and Paolini had both read Delamare, though Paolini had not necessarily read Pape. The influence of the Aldine
translation is, of course, evident in all of them.

54 For general accounts of the poem, see Francesco Flamini, *Studi di storia letteraria
italiana e straniera* (Leghorn, 1895), pp. 395–401; and Fortunato Pintor, "Delle
liriche di Bernardo Tasso," *ASNSP* 14 (1900): 137–41.

55 The nymphs—who will be turning up again—may derive from Catullus 64.11–18
(Pintor, p. 139).

56 See William J. Kennedy, "Petrarchism in Short Narrative Poetry of the Renaissance," *CL* 26 (1974): 318–33. He does not mention Tasso, but the terms of his
discussion are obviously applicable.

57 Flamini, pp. 395–98; and Marcelino Menéndez Pelayo, *Antología de poetas
líricos castellanos*, ed. Enrique Sánchez Reyes (Madrid, 1945), 10:303–07. There
is some likelihood that Tasso and Boscán were personally acquainted.

58 See Otis H. Green, *The Literary Mind of Renaissance Spain* (Lexington, Ky., 1970),

pp. 133–40.

59   See Arnold G. Reichenberger, "Boscán and the Classics," *CL* 3 (1951): 103–12; and "Boscán and Ovid," *MLN* 65 (1950): 379–83.

60   Léonce Chabalier, *Héro et Léandre* (Paris, 1911), p. 7.

61   Ibid., p. 3.

62   *Polymēchanon* means "full of strategies," i.e. practical rhetoric; in Greek, the line picks up echoes from Hero's earlier refusal: "there is no way (*amēchanon estin*) to enter the bed of a virgin" (127). Leander is making a way, not just prettying things up ("plein de grand artifice"). The adjective is a particularly troublesome point for the Aldine translation and was constantly being changed. The Paris edition of 1538 has "artificiosum," and this may in fact be the text behind Marot's translation. Aldo's first edition has "excogitatum," the 1518 Aesop "percalidum," and later editions "solers."

63   George deF. Lord, *Homeric Renaissance* (New Haven, 1956), pp. 78–126.

64   The line scales down notably in the modernization of the 1875 edition: "Upon the rough back of the high sea leaps. . . . "

65   Millar Maclure, *George Chapman* (Toronto, 1966), pp. 213–14; see also Bush, *Mythology and the Renaissance Tradition*, pp. 210–11.

66   References (to poem number and line number) and text for Góngora from *Obras poéticas*, ed. R. Foulché-Delbosc (New York, 1921; reprint ed., 1970). Góngora's telling is split between two of his Romances, which form a continuous narrative but are never printed together: 75 ("Arrojòse el mancebito," 1589) gives the end of the story, and 228 ("Aunque entiendo poco Griego," 1610) the beginning.

67   Nashe tells the story as part of "The Praise of the Red Herring" in *Lenten Stuff* (1599); Jonson puts on the tale, conflated with that of Damon and Pythias, as a puppet show in *Bartholomew Fair* (1614). Both versions use tags from Marlowe. For the later tradition, see Bush, pp. 288–92.

68   "Ella entonces derramando / Dos mil perlas de ambas luces" (75.41–42).

69   Erich Segal, "Hero and Leander: Góngora and Marlowe," *CL* 15 (1963): 353. The best discussion of Marlowe's poem as comedy is that of Brian Morris, "Comic Method in Marlowe's *Hero and Leander*," in *Christopher Marlowe*, ed. Morris, pp. 115–31.

70   Pope may in fact have had Marlowe in mind; see John M. Eden, "Hero and Belinda," *N&Q* 202 (1957): 12–13.

71   Richard Neuse, "Atheism and Some Functions of Myth in Marlowe's *Hero and Leander*," *MLQ* 31 (1970): 430. See also S. Ann Collins, "Sundrie Shapes, Committing Headdie Ryots, Incest, Rapes," *Mosaic* 4, no. 1 (1970): 107–22; Martz's introduction to his edition of the poem, pp. 1–14; J. B. Steane, *Marlowe* (Cambridge, 1964), pp. 302–33; and Myron Turner, "Pastoral and Hermaphrodite: A Study in the Naturalism of Marlowe's *Hero and Leander*," *TSLL* 17 (1975): 397–414.

72   *Strife* and *strive* are particularly recurrent terms in the poem; cf. 1.12, 322, 334, 335, 364, 413; 2.159.

73   Gertrud Lazarus, *Technik und Stil von Hero and Leander* (Bonn, 1915), p. 32 n.

74   Baldwin, "Marlowe's Musaeus," *JEGP* 54 (1955): 481; G. P. Shannon, "Against Marot as a Source of Marlowe's *Hero and Leander*," *MLQ* 9 (1948): 387–88.

75   Paul Kocher, *Christopher Marlowe* (Chapel Hill, N.C., 1946), p. 295; the usage cited is in Gosson's *School of Abuse* (1579). For further discussion of the phrase, see William Keach, *Elizabethan Erotic Narratives* (New Brunswick, N.J., 1977), pp. 88–94.

76   Lewis Einstein, *The Italian Renaissance in England* (New York, 1907), p. 354.

77   Hallett Smith, *Elizabethan Poetry* (Cambridge, Mass., 1952), p. 78.

78   Both poets seem particularly interested in Ovid's account of Leander on the shore at Abydos: cf. *Her.* 18.24 ff. with Boscán, 2417 ff. (he goes on to imitate the apostrophe to Boreas) and Marlowe, 2.147–54.

79   Scattered quirks of vocabulary suggest this: "thirling" (1.108), "beldame" (1.353), "crooked Dolphin" (2.234), and the "tent" that Hero makes in bed (2.263) can all be paralleled in Turberville. The first three examples are in Maclure's notes; for the fourth, see Clifford Leech, "Venus and Her Nun," *SEL* 5 (1965): 252 n.

80   Bush, "Notes on Marlowe's *Hero and Leander*," *PMLA* 44 (1929): 760–61.

81   Baldwin, "Marlowe's Musaeus," pp. 478–80; I add Delamare and Pape to Baldwin's examples.

82   Ibid., pp. 480–81.

83   Reading, with the Aldine text, *helcos*, "wound," in line 95, rather than *callos*, "beauty."

84   Reading, with the Aldine text, *ēnemoentos*, "windy," in line 193, rather than *ēnemophōnos*, "wind-sounding."

85   Robert Constantin, *Lexicon Graecolatinum*, 2d ed. (Geneva, 1592). The evidence, unfortunately, is not as cogent as it might look, in view of Baldwin's very similar evidence, reported above, that Marlowe used Estienne. Neither example traces through both dictionaries with comparable neatness, and it is hard to imagine Marlowe using two in alternation. Perhaps more research is needed. Still, the use of any dictionary for a translation of *ochthē* or *ochthos* would produce something closer to Marlowe's topography than would use of the Aldine Latin.

86   Latin text and references for Apuleius are from *Metamorphoseon Libri XI*, ed. Rudolf Helm (Leipzig, 1931).

87   *The xi bookes of the golden asse, conteininge the Metamorphosie of Lucius Apuleius*, trans. William Adlington (London, 1566; *STC* 718). All of the quotations that follow are from Adlington's chap. 22—the story of Cupid and Psyche—which begins in Book 4 of Apuleius and continues into Book 6.

88   Rosemond Tuve, *Elizabethan and Metaphysical Imagery* (Chicago and London, 1947), p. 273; on *amplificatio* and *meraviglia*, see pp. 89–93.

89   Harold B. Segel, *The Baroque Poem* (New York, 1974), p. 29.

90   D. H. Lawrence, *Women in Love* (1920; reprint ed., New York, 1960), p. viii.

91   Turner, p. 404.

92   See John Mills, "The Courtship Ritual of Hero and Leander," *ELR* 2 (1972): 298–306.

93   Cf. Bradbrook, *Shakespeare and Elizabethan Poetry* (New York, 1952), p. 59; also Keach, pp. 115–16, Neuse, p. 439, and (more tentatively) Morris, p. 131.

94   Martz, p. 14; the interpretation has lately been put forward, apparently independently, by Raymond B. Waddington in his book on Chapman, *The Mind's Empire* (Baltimore and London, 1974), p. 155.

95   Paul W. Miller, "A Function of Myth in Marlowe's 'Hero and Leander,'" *SP* 50 (1953): 165–66.

96   Reading, with the Aldine text, *anephaine*, "appeared," in line 111, rather than the livelier *anetelle*, "sprang up."

97   Martz, p. 14.

CHAPTER 3: ROBERT HERRICK AND CLASSICAL LYRIC POETRY

For quotations from Herrick's poetry, I have used throughout *The Complete Poetry*, ed. J. Max Patrick, 2d ed. (New York, 1968). However, for reasons the text makes clear, the notes to L. C. Martin's edition (Oxford, 1956) have a particular relevance to my purposes; and since the two editions have incompatible systems of reference, I have used a double annotation. For a reference to Herrick, I give (1) the number of the poem in Patrick's edition; (2) the page number and order on the page of the poem in Martin's edition, according to Martin's own system (explained on p.vii); and (3) the line numbers, except when an entire poem is meant. The results are ungainly, to say the least, but I have found the system too useful to give up. (The problem is an old one; MacLeod's concordance uses a similar system.) Unexpanded allusions to "sources" may be presumed to be to Martin's notes; see also, however, the brief supplement by G. B. A. Fletcher, "Herrick and Latin Authors," *N&Q* 204 (1959): 231–32.

For classical authors, I have generally relied on the Oxford Classical Texts; in particular, Anacreon and Alcaios are cited as they appear in *Lyrica Graeca Selecta* (*LGS*), ed. Denys L. Page (Oxford, 1968). Quotations from the Anacreontea present special problems; there is nothing resembling a standard edition. The most accessible, and most recent, is the heavily emended Loeb text of J. M. Edmonds, paginated separately but bound with *Elegy and Iambus*, ed. Edmonds (London and New York, 1931), vol. 2. I have generally quoted, though, from the much more conservative text of Karl Preisendanz (Leipzig, 1912), with a few exceptions identified in my notes. The edition of Valentin Rose (Leipzig, 1868) is also useful for its fuller citation of the readings of Renaissance editions.

1   Kenner, ed., *Seventeenth Century Poetry* (New York, 1964), p. xxviii.
2   Robert H. Deming, *Ceremony and Art: Robert Herrick's Poetry* (The Hague and Paris, 1974), pp. 94–97.
3   Richard Cumberland, *Observer*, no. 74, in *The British Essayists*, ed. Alexander Chalmers (London, 1802–03), 42:205.
4   In addition to the references that follow, see John F. M. Dovaston, *Monthly Magazine* 39 (1815): 123–24; and Ernest Barker, *Spectator* 157 (1936): 890–91.
5   A. D. Fitton Brown, "Drink to me, Celia," *MLR* 54 (1959): 556.
6   Translated from the Greek text of the Loeb edition, *The Letters of Alciphron, Aelian and Philostratus*, ed. Allen Rogers Benner and Francis H. Fobes (London and Cambridge, Mass., 1949).
7   John Addington Symonds, "Ben Jonson's Song 'To Celia,'" *Academy* 26 (1884): 378.
8   These lines are, however, the site of the poem's one interpretive crux: see Marshall Van Deusen, "Criticism and Ben Jonson's 'To Celia,'" *EIC* 7 (1957): 95–103; and J. G. Nichols, *The Poetry of Ben Jonson* (London, 1969), pp. 163–64.
9   For, in fact, a documented case of one seventeenth-century reader trying to follow the game and missing Philostratos, see James A. Riddell, "Seventeenth-Century Identifications of Jonson's Sources in the Classics," *RenQ* 28 (1975): 204–18.
10 Maurice Castelain, *Ben Jonson* (Paris and London, 1907), p. 838; for an encounter with "Drinke to me, onely," see p. 840.
11 References (to volume and page number) and text for Ronsard are from *Les Oeuvres de Pierre de Ronsard: Texte de 1587*, ed. Isidore Silver (Chicago, London, and Paris, 1966–70). The line quoted here is the conclusion to *Sonnets pour Helene* 2.43 ("Quand vous serez bien vieille").
12 An anonymous Latin poem most readily available in editions of the *Appendix Vergiliana* but also, and more plausibly, attributed to Ausonius.
13 Evidence not noticed by Martin, however, for Herrick's use of Marlowe's trans-

lation of the *Amores* is presented below, pp. 225, 246.

14 Alfred Pollard, "Herrick Sources and Illustrations," *Modern Quarterly of Language and Literature* 1 (1898): 175.

15 For a similar example, cf. H-725/247/7–8 with Horace, *Carm.* 2.9.1–2; again, the italics signal that direct quotation is over.

16 For other such "mistranslations," see Floris Delattre, *Robert Herrick* (Paris, 1912), pp. 416–17.

17 Sidney, *An Apology for Poetry* (1595); Gregory Smith, ed., *Elizabethan Critical Essays*, 1:173. As Fletcher points out, Herrick's epitaph on Prudence Baldwin (H-782/262.1) derives with comparable inappropriateness from another sarcastic passage in Persius (1.38–40). William Oram reaches conclusions similar to mine in "Herrick's Use of Sacred Materials," in *Trust to Good Verses: Herrick Tercentenary Essays*, ed. J. Max Patrick and Roger B. Rollin (Pittsburgh, 1978).

18 See especially R. R. Bolgar, *The Classical Heritage and its Beneficiaries* (Cambridge, 1954), pp. 265–75.

19 Nathaniel Drake, *Literary Hours* (London, 1804), 3:45.

20 Lowell, *Among My Books* (Boston, 1870), p. 341. "Catullian" *sic* (a neo-Latin formation).

21 James A. S. McPeek, *Catullus in Strange and Distant Britain* (Cambridge, Mass., 1939), pp. 48–49. There is a three-page footnote on the subject in Delattre, pp. 408–10.

22 For a curiously close parallel to Herrick's dismemberment of the poem, see Jonson, *The Forest* 5 and 6 (8:102–03): the former begins with a loose translation of lines 1–6 of Catullus, while the latter contains the catalogue of kisses (with some additions suggested by Catullus 7). Similarly, Campion's famous poem, "My sweetest Lesbia," translates Catullus closely to the end of line 6, and then veers off.

23 On Martial, see Gosse, *Seventeenth Century Studies*, 4th ed. (London, 1913), pp. 152–53 (the original was in *Cornhill Magazine*, August 1875); and the replies of Alexander Grosart in his edition of Herrick (London, 1876), 1:ccxliii–lv; and Paul Nixon, "Herrick and Martial," *Classical Philology* 5 (1910): 189–202. (By the time it gets to Gosse, Drake's famous statement has been further shorn of "in some respects.") On Tibullus, see Pauline Aiken, *The Influence of the Latin Elegists on English Lyric Poetry, 1600–1650* (Orono, Maine, 1932), pp. 69 ff. On Horace, see Elizabeth Hazelton Haight, "Robert Herrick: The English Horace," *Classical Weekly* 4 (1911): 178–81, 186–89; M. J. Ruggles, "Horace and Herrick," *CJ* 31 (1936): 223–34; and (principally) Graydon W. Regenos, "The Influence of Horace on Robert Herrick," *PQ* 26 (1947): 268–84.

24 H-116/41.1, 10.63; H-131/47.1, 3.17; H-174/66.2, 8.69; H-344/138.3, 1.38; H-398/153.5 and H-1025/315.1, 11.66; H-419/158.4, 1.19; H-434/163.3, 8.35; H-463/173.4, 8.19 (Herrick expands one line into four, but it remains the same joke); H-577/207.2, 1.98; H-939/294.4, 4.22; H-975/303.3, 1.97. Also, two other poems of Herrick's—H-424/161.1 and H-1108/331.8—translate epigrams ascribed to Martial in the later Renaissance but now considered spurious. The Latin poems are not in the current Oxford text of Martial, and are now most accessible in the appendix to the Loeb edition (2:520 ff.), where they are nos. 2 and 4, respectively; Herrick would have known them as *Epigrammata* 4.78 and 7.100. For a thorough catalogue of Herrick's borrowings from Martial, see Nixon.

25 I give the count for Martial from the editions that Herrick would have used; the modern canon is 1,174.

26 The titles of Martial's poems have manuscript authority and were used in all

Renaissance editions. They are omitted from modern editions except for the last two Books, where internal references establish their genuineness. In Herrick, the concluding poems of the *Hesperides* and the *Noble Numbers*, as well as the quatrain introducing the errata, are untitled, probably because of their function as elements of the book's formal design.

27   Mention should be made of the Planudean Anthology, the other long classical book of short poems that Herrick would have known, and one generally more similar in content to Herrick's book than Martial's is. It was nevertheless usually labeled in the Renaissance as a collection of "epigrams." It differs from both Martial and Herrick in the clear thematic structure of its organization and the lack, understandably, of internal references to its own structure.

28   John L. Kimmey, in "Robert Herrick's Persona," *SP* 67 (1970): 221–36, and "Order and Form in Herrick's *Hesperides*," *JEGP* 70 (1971): 255–68, has argued for the interest, if not the readability, of Herrick's book as a formal structure. He detects certain symmetries and developments between the first and second halves, and traces something of an ongoing plot. Dorothy Matthis Huson, in her Ph.D. dissertation, "Robert Herrick's *Hesperides* Considered as an Organized Work" (Michigan State, 1972; *DAI* 34:275A–76A), describes a more rigorous seven-part structure, with the poems addressed to the king as dividers. That these efforts had to be made, and that Kimmey in particular has to demonstrate many of his arguments statistically, merely reinforces the point I am making here.

29   For Davies, see the facsimile of the first edition (ca. 1593–94) in *The Poems of Sir John Davies*, ed. Clare Howard (New York, 1941), p. 33. Jonson's "first book" is in some ways specifically an imitation of Book 1 of Martial: see Herford and Simpson, 2:350 ff.; and the recent remarks of Bruce R. Smith, "Ben Jonson's *Epigrammes*," *SEL* 14 (1974): 100–01.

30   Modern canon; the average for Renaissance editions is even closer, 98.9. This habit of Martial's is probably responsible for John Heywood's classification of his epigrams into "hundreds."

31   Pauline Kael, *Deeper into Movies* (Boston and Toronto, 1973), p. 184.

32   For a similar instance, see the kicker at the end of 11.8, a poem to which Herrick also goes for details in H-375 / 145.1.

33   *The Epigrams of Martial*, trans. James Michie (New York, 1973), p. 47.

34   See Heather Asals, "King Solomon in the Land of the *Hesperides*," *TSLL* 18 (1976): 362–80; and Kimmey, "Robert Herrick's Satirical Epigrams," *ES* 51 (1970): 312–23. The full story, of course, of even the English Renaissance epigram has yet to be written. The best treatments remain those of T. K. Whipple, *Martial and the English Epigram from Sir Thomas Wyatt to Ben Jonson* (Berkeley, 1925); and (unfinished) Hoyt Hopewell Hudson, *The Epigram in the English Renaissance* (Princeton, 1947). There is also a useful account of continental theory, particularly as regards the connections between the epigram and the sonnet, by Rosalie L. Colie in *Shakespeare's Living Art* (Princeton, 1974), pp. 80–96. She cites, p. 82, an especially interesting remark of Robortello's (1555) to the effect that the epigram encompasses all the other poetic genres in miniature.

35   Discussed in detail and passim by Earl Miner, *The Cavalier Mode from Jonson to Cotton* (Princeton, 1971).

36   F. R. Leavis, *Revaluations* (New York, 1947), p. 40; the comparison there is with Marvell.

37   References (to poem number and line number) and text for Suckling are from *The Non-dramatic Works*, ed. Thomas Clayton (Oxford, 1971).

38   *Anacreontis Teii odae ab Henrico Stephano luce et Latinitate nunc primùm donatae*

(Paris, 1554). For a fuller account of this important edition and its later history, see below, pp. 255–58.

39 Anacreontea 6 is ascribed to one "Julian" when it appears in the Planudean Anthology; in the Renaissance this was interpreted to be the sixth-century prefect of that name, of whom other poems survive. The ascription, however, has been disputed, e.g. by Edmonds, pp. 5 ff. Four and 8 also appear in the anthology, where they are attributed to Anacreon.

40 In his preface, in Greek, to the first edition; *Prefaces to the First Editions of the Greek and Roman Classics*, ed. Botfield, pp. 472–73.

41 Frag. 19 in *Iambi et Elegi Graeci*, ed. M. L. West (Oxford, 1971).

42 A bit more rigorously: the Anacreontic colon is classically defined ᴗᴗ–oo–-, where oo indicates anaclasis, free variation of x– and –x; the hemiambic is iambic dimeter catalectic, x–ᴗ–x–x, with certain further substitutions possible. For many of the Anacreontea, however, the details of the old rules are irrelevant.

43 For an intricate discussion of metrical matters, with the intent of dating the poems, see Edmonds, pp. 6–17. For another sample of the issues involved, as well as some interesting remarks on the collection's most famous poem, see Albrecht Dihle, "The Poem on the Cicada," *Harvard Studies in Classical Philology* 71 (1967): 107–13.

44 Botfield, p. 472.

45 Ibid., p. 471.

46 Miner, p. 107 n. As noted above, three of the Anacreontea are in the Planudean Anthology itself; for the connection between the Anacreontea and the Palatine Anthology, see below, p. 255.

47 J. C. Scaliger, *Poemata* (Heidelberg, 1574), sig. G5^r. The poem is from a fifty-page group of "Anacreontica"; the opening poem of the group, on the previous page, salutes Ronsard as "trepidus meus / Blandus, suauiloquus, dulcis Anacreon...." "Non elaboratum ad pedem" is Horace's description of Anacreon's poetry (*Epod.* 14.12).

48 See Paul Laumonier, *Ronsard: Poète lyrique*, 2d ed. (Paris, 1923), pp. 120 ff., 168–73, 591–617.

49 Charles A. Sainte-Beuve, *Tableau historique et critique de la poésie française et de théâtre française au XVIe siècle*, 2d ed. (Paris, 1869), p. 435. For further illustrations, see Achille Delboulle's anthology, *Anacréon et les poèmes anacréontiques* (1891; reprint ed., Geneva, 1970).

50 The preceding passage is of some interest for its description of what "Anacreon" can teach—essentially a network of lambent emotional decorum: "comme il faut souspirer, / Comme il faut esperer et se desesperer" (190). And so on at some length, with "comme il faut" as refrain. An affinity with Petrarchanism is made quite clear.

51 I read (with Estienne and many others) *gelōn*, "laughing," in line 3, rather than *legōn*, "speaking."

52 I read, with Barnes, *bryontas*, "luxuriant," in line 5, rather than *bremontas*, "raucous."

53 See Bruno Snell, *The Discovery of the Mind*, trans. Thomas G. Rosenmeyer (Oxford, 1953), pp. 47 ff.

54 Lewis, *English Literature in the Sixteenth Century*, p. 229.

55 There was, in fact, a curious literary controversy in classical times—the *oinopotai* vs. the *hydropotai*, the wine-drinkers vs. the water-drinkers—concerning the value of liquor as an aid to composition. For a convenient summary, see Steele Commager, *The Odes of Horace* (New Haven and London, 1962), pp. 28–29.

56 Delattre, p. 394; a catalogue follows, pp. 395–99. See also Michael Baumann, *Die Anakreonteen in englischen Übersetzungen* (Heidelberg, 1974), pp. 53–61.

57 H-81/26.3, 33; H-139/50.1, 35; H-170/65.1, 8; H-229/96.1, 6; H-519/191.4, 40; H-527/194.3, 51; H-852/277.1, 7 (with the conclusion reversed; on this see Baumann, p. 56 n.); H-996/309.1, 50; H-1017/313.1, 1. The versions of 7 and 35 are discussed in some detail and compared with other seventeenth-century versions by Charles Clay Doyle, "An Unhonored English Anacreon: John Birkenhead," *SP* 71 (1974): 192–205.

58 Delattre, pp. 405–06; for more on this matter, see below, p. 257.

59 H-540/197.1, H-993/308.1. The content of the latter, though, is not especially Anacreontic, and the adjective probably refers mainly to the extraordinarily short lines in which the poems are written; cf. Campion's proposal for a four-syllable English Anacreontic line in chapter 9 of his *Observations in the Art of English Poesy* (1602; see Gregory Smith, 2:349–50). Herrick's two poems are, however, definitely not like the Greek poems in rhythmic effect but are tightened by dense, emphatic rhyming and frequent shifts of cadence: the first alternates anapaestic and dactylic dimeters! But the "wit" of his verbal texture is consistently Herrick's least Anacreontic feature; almost nothing of what was said about "Anacreon's" metrical effects applies to him.

60 H-40/16.1, H-44/17.3, H-46/18.2, H-92/31.2, H-166/63.3, H-190/74.2, H-509/188.3, H-635/222.2, H-706/241.1, H-874/281.2, H-883/283.2, H-942/295.3, H-1120/333.4.

61 As Doyle, p. 196, points out, Herrick suppresses a dialogue in his version of Anacreontea 7.

62 Gosse, p. 126. The best essays in this line are Swinburne's introduction to Pollard's edition of Herrick (London, 1891) and George Saintsbury's introduction to his edition (London, 1893).

63 Grosart, 1:cxxiii.

64 "Peeping Tom," *TLS* 60 (1961): 898.

65 Obviously it makes more sense to take Marlowe's comma as, in effect, a period or semicolon, implying that something occurs during the caesura to make Corinna tired. Tucker Brooke, however, puts a colon there. Certainly Marlowe's rendering is open to misinterpretation, especially since there is nothing in the Latin about kissing. See Roma Gill, "Snakes Leape by Verse," in *Christopher Marlowe*, ed. Morris, p. 144.

66 *The Works of Thomas Campion*, ed. Walter R. Davis (Garden City, N.Y., 1967), p. 31. The situation described obviously intrigued Campion, who has two Latin versions of the same story (pp. 428–31, 505).

67 This last an epitaph for the poet Voconus, cited by Apuleius, *Apologia* 11. As an indication of how tightly defined the tradition was, note that each of these examples is an elegiac pentameter.

68 Paul R. Jenkins, "Rethinking What Moderation Means to Robert Herrick," *ELH* 39 (1972): 49–65 (esp. 58).

69 In the conversations with Drummond, Jonson, speaking of how "two accidents strange befell him," relates that "one other lay diverse tymes with a woman, who shew him all that he wished except the last act, which she would never agree unto" (1:140).

70 Suckling, "Against Fruition," two poems (40 and 41 in Clayton); Rochester, "The Platonic Lady." See Miner, pp. 238–39. Lovelace's "Love made in the first Age" seems to end, unexpectedly, with praise of masturbation as the preferred type of erotic activity.

71 See Clayton, pp. 181–85

72 N. E. Collinge, *The Structure of Horace's Odes* (London and New York, 1961), p. 111.

73 Herrick's frequent injunction to "take time" (H-149A / 56 / 120, H-691 / 238.3 / 1, H-806 / 267.3 / 1; perhaps also H-178 / 69 / 58) is, I suspect, a direct translation of "carpe diem," especially since the modern sense of "slow down" seems to be lacking—the context usually makes it quite clear that Herrick means "hurry up." Cf. Sidney: "Yong folkes, take time while you may" (*Astrophil and Stella*, fourth song 28). Also Shakespeare: "therefore take the present time" (*As You Like It* 5.3.30), from a song that also observes "How that a life was but a Flower" (28); and "hee meant to take the present time by the top" (*Much Ado* 1.2.14–15), i.e., do it immediately. But the modern nuance can figure as well: "Take time to pause" (*Midsummer Night's Dream* 1.1.83).

74 See Valerie Edden, "'The Best of Lyrick Poets,'" in *Horace*, ed. C. D. N. Costa (London and Boston, 1973), pp. 135–59.

75 I owe this observation to Chris Dahl.

76 R. G. M. Nisbet and Margaret Hubbard, *A Commentary on Horace: Odes Book I* (Oxford, 1970), p. 107.

77 Reported in a *Vita Horati*, attributed to Suetonius; see the Loeb edition of Suetonius, ed. J. C. Rolfe (London and New York, 1914), 2:488.

78 *Naps upon Parnassus* (London, 1658; Wing F1140), sig. A3ᵛ.

79 F. W. Moorman, *Robert Herrick* (London and New York, 1910), p. 217.

80 In addition to H-366/143.1, discussed above, and H-336/132.3, discussed below, see: H-106/34.3, *Carm.* 1.13.17 and 1.3.8; H-244/99.3, *Epod.* 5.45–46; H-415/157.3, *Carm.* 3.25.1–2; H-642/224.4, *Carm.* 4.7.1; H-771/259.1, *Epis.* 1.6.48; H-1066/ 323.2, *Serm.* 1.2.27 and 1.4.92.

81 H-6/7.1, *Ars* 417; H-95/32.1, *Ars* 359; H-459/173, *Carm.* 4.9.29–30; H-612/214.2, *Carm.* 1.1.36. There are also two two-line epigrams where Horace supplies the italicized conclusion: H-48 / 18.4, *Epis.* 2.2.176; H-607 / 213.3, *Epis.* 1.10.41.

82 The latter is from Catullus 68.147–48: "quare illud satis est, si nobis is datur unis / quem lapide illa dies candidiore notat." See John B. Emperor, *The Catullian Influence in English Lyric Poetry, Circa 1600–1650* (Columbia, Mo., 1928), p. 109; Martin cites only a weak parallel in Martial.

83 The most startling examples are at the beginnings of odes: 1.12 and Pindar, *Olympia* 2.1–2; 1.9 and *LGS* 157; 1.18 and *LGS* 159; 3.12 and *LGS* 108.

84 J. C. Scaliger, *Poetices libri septem*, p. 259 (Bk. 5, chap. 7); supplemented p. 345 (Bk. 6, chap. 7).

85 Giorgio Pasquali, *Orazio lirico* (1918; reprint ed., Florence, 1964), p. 9.

86 Eduard Fraenkel, *Horace* (Oxford, 1957), pp. 276 ff.

APPENDIX

1 S. F. W. Hoffmann, *Bibliographisches Lexicon der gesammten Literatur der Griechen* (1838; reprint ed., Amsterdam, 1961), 1:131 ff. Fabricius, *Bibliotheca Graeca*, 2: 91 ff., is less complete but has fuller incidental information.

2 David McPherson, "Ben Jonson's Library and Marginalia," *SP* 71, no. 5 (1974): 77.

3 Delattre, pp. 401–06; Baumann, pp. 55–56.

4 Not, however, an impossibly obscure source, since Jonson owned a copy of one of the later editions; McPherson, pp. 33–34.

BIBLIOGRAPHY

My only attempt to be thorough has been with the literature on Golding, for whom other bibliographical aids do not exist. Of Golding's own works I list only those available in modern editions or reprints; for a fuller account see Louis Golding (pp. 149–63), supplemented by Wortham (p. 339 n.) and Nelson. The various editions of Mousaios and Herrick are cited here mainly for the sake of the commentary in them.

GENERAL

Atkins, J. W. H. *English Literary Criticism: The Renascence.* 1947. Reprint. London: Methuen, and New York: Barnes and Noble, 1968.

Bolgar, R. R. *The Classical Heritage and its Beneficiaries.* Cambridge: Cambridge University Press, 1954.

Botfield, Beriah, ed. *Prefaces to the First Editions of the Greek and Roman Classics and of the Sacred Scriptures.* London: Bohn, 1861.

Brown, Huntington. "The Classical Tradition in English Literature: A Bibliography." *Harvard Studies and Notes in Philology and Literature* 18 (1935): 7–46.

Bush, Douglas. *Classical Influences in Renaissance Literature.* Martin Classical Lectures, vol. 13. Cambridge, Mass.: Harvard University Press, 1952.

———. *English Literature in the Earlier Seventeenth Century, 1600–1660.* Oxford History of English Literature, vol. 5. 2d ed. Oxford: Clarendon, 1962.

———. *Mythology and the Renaissance Tradition in English Poetry.* 1932. Reprint. New York: Pageant, 1957.

Curtius, Ernst Robert. *European Literature and the Latin Middle Ages.* Translated by Willard Trask. Bollingen Series, vol. 36. 1953. Reprint. New York and Evanston, Ill.: Harper and Row, 1963.

Fabricius, Johann Albert. *Bibliotheca Graeca: siue, Notitia Scriptorum Veterum Graecorum Quorumcumque Monumenta Integra aut Fragmenta Edita Exstant.* 4th ed., revised by Gottlieb Christoph Harles. 12 vols. 1790–1809. Reprint. Hildesheim: Olms, 1966–67.

———. *Bibliotheca Latina.* Revised by Johann August Ernst. 3 vols. Leipzig: Weidmann, 1773–74.

Highet, Gilbert. *The Classical Tradition: Greek and Roman Influences on Western Literature.* New York: Oxford University Press, 1949.

Hoffmann, S. F. W. *Bibliographisches Lexicon der gesammten Literatur der Griechen.* 3 vols. 1838. Reprint. Amsterdam: Hakkert, 1961.

Lewis, C. S. *English Literature in the Sixteenth Century, Excluding Drama.* Oxford History of English Literature, vol. 3. Oxford: Clarendon, 1954.

Pfeiffer, Rudolf. *History of Classical Scholarship from 1300 to 1850.* Oxford: Clarendon, 1976.

Sandys, John Edwin. *A History of Classical Scholarship.* 3 vols. Cambridge: Cambridge University Press, 1903–08.

Scaliger, Julius Caesar. *Poetices libri septem.* Lyons, 1561. Facsimile reprint. Stuttgart: Frommann, 1964.

Smith, G. Gregory, ed. *Elizabethan Critical Essays.* 2 vols. London: Oxford University Press, 1904.

Spingarn, J. E., ed. *Critical Essays of the Seventeenth Century.* 3 vols. 1908–09. Reprint. Bloomington and London: Indiana University Press, 1957.

Thomson, J. A. K. *The Classical Background of English Literature.* London: Allen and Unwin, 1948.

———. *Classical Influences on English Poetry.* London: Allen and Unwin, 1951.

———. *Classical Influences on English Prose.* London: Allen and Unwin, 1956.

GOLDING'S OVID

Alexander, Nigel, ed. *Elizabethan Narrative Verse.* Stratford-upon-Avon Library, vol. 3. Cambridge, Mass.: Harvard University Press, 1968.

Amos, Flora Ross. *Early Theories of Translation.* New York: Columbia University Press, 1920.

Baldwin, T. W. Review of the Nims edition of Golding's Ovid. *JEGP* 66 (1967): 124–27.

Behrens, Werner. *Lateinische Satzformen im Englischen: Latinismen in der Syntax der englischen Übersetzungen des Humanismus.* Universitas-Archiv: Anglistische Abteilung, vol. 3. Munster: Buschmann, 1937.

Binns, J. W., ed. *Ovid.* Greek and Latin Studies: Classical Literature and its Influence. London and Boston: Routledge and Kegan Paul, 1973.

Blake, Harriet Manning. "Golding's Ovid in Elizabethan Times." *JEGP* 14 (1915): 93–95.

Buell, Llewellyn M. "Arthur Golding and the Earthquake of 1580." *PQ* 24
    (1945): 227–32.

Chapman, George, trans. *Chapman's Homer: The Iliad, the Odyssey and the
    Lesser Homerica.* Edited by Allardyce Nicoll. Bollingen Series, vol. 41. 2d
    ed. 2 vols. Princeton: Princeton University Press, 1967.

Conley, C. H. *The First English Translators of the Classics.* 1927. Reprint.
    Port Washington, N.Y.: Kennikat, 1967.

Cooper, Clyde Barnes. *Some Elizabethan Opinions of the Poetry and Character
    of Ovid.* Menasha, Wis.: Collegiate Press, 1914.

Davis, Richard Beale. *George Sandys, Poet Adventurer: A Study in Anglo-
    American Culture in the Seventeenth Century.* London: Bodley Head, 1955.

Douglas, Gavin, trans. *Aeneid.* Edited by David F. C. Coldwell. Scottish
    Text Society, 3d ser., nos. 25 and 30. Edinburgh: Scottish Text Society,
    1957–64.

Fränkel, Hermann. *Ovid: A Poet Between Two Worlds.* Sather Classical
    Lectures, vol. 18. Berkeley and Los Angeles: University of California
    Press, 1945.

Galinsky, G. Karl. *Ovid's Metamorphoses: An Introduction to the Basic Aspects.*
    Oxford: Blackwell, 1975.

Golding, Arthur, trans. *The excellent and pleasant worke of Julius Solinus
    Polyhistor.* London, 1587; *STC* 22896. Facsimile reprint. Gainesville, Fla.:
    Scholars' Facsimiles and Reprints, 1955.

————. *The eyght bookes of Caius Julius Caesar conteyning his martiall exploytes
    in the realme of Gallia.* London, 1565; *STC* 4335. Facsimile reprint. The
    English Experience, vol. 36. Amsterdam: Theatrum Orbis Terrarum, and
    New York: Da Capo, 1968.

————. *The joyful and royal entertainment of the ryght high and mightie Prince,
    Frauncis the Frenche Kings only brother.* London, 1582; *STC* 11310. In *The
    Progresses and Public Processions of Queen Elizabeth*, edited by John Nichols.
    1823. Reprint. Research and Source Works Series, vol. 117. New York:
    Franklin, 1960. Vol. 2, pp. 354–85.

————. *Ovid's Metamorphoses: The Arthur Golding Translation.* Edited by
    John Frederick Nims. The Classics of Greek and Rome Series. New York
    and London: Macmillan, 1965.

————. *Shakespeare's Ovid: Being Arthur Golding's Translation of the Metamor-
    phoses.* Edited by W. H. D. Rouse. Centaur Classics. 1904. Reprint.
    London: Centaur Press, and Carbondale: Southern Illinois University
    Press, 1961. (Also reprint. New York: Norton, 1966.)

————. *A Tragedie of Abrahams Sacrifice, Written in French by Theodore Beza.*
    Edited by Malcolm W. Wallace. Toronto: University of Toronto Library,
    1906.

————. *The woorke of the excellent philosopher Lucius Annaeus Seneca concerning benefyting*. London, 1578; *STC* 22215. Facsimile reprint. The English Experience, vol. 694. Amsterdam: Theatrum Orbis Terrarum, and Norwood, N.J.: Walter J. Johnson, 1974.

Golding, Louis Thorn. *An Elizabethan Puritan: Arthur Golding, the Translator of Ovid's Metamorphoses and also of John Calvin's Sermons*. New York: Richard R. Smith, 1937.

Hale, David G. "The Source and Date of Golding's 'Fabletalke.'" *MP* 69 (1972): 326–27.

Harding, Davis P. *Milton and the Renaissance Ovid*. Illinois Studies in Language and Literature, vol. 30, no. 4. Urbana: University of Illinois Press, 1946.

Hatcher, O. L. "Aims and Methods of the Elizabethan Translators." *Englische Studien* 44 (1912): 174–92.

Jacobsen, Eric. *Translation, a Traditional Craft: An Introductory Sketch with a Study of Marlowe's Elegies*. Classica et Mediaevalia: Dissertationes, vol. 6. Copenhagen: Gyldendal, 1958.

Jiriczek, O. L., ed. *Specimens of Tudor Translations from the Classics, with a Glossary*. Germanische Bibliothek: Lesebücher, vol. 6. Heidelberg: Winter, 1923.

Johnson, W. R. "The Problem of the Counter-classical Sensibility and its Critics." *California Studies in Classical Antiquity* 3 (1970): 123 51.

Jones, Richard Foster. *The Triumph of the English Language: A Survey of Opinions Concerning the Vernacular from the Introduction of Printing to the Restoration*. Stanford: Stanford University Press, 1953.

Lanham, Richard A. *The Motives of Eloquence: Literary Rhetoric in the Renaissance*. New Haven and London: Yale University Press, 1976.

Lathrop, H. B. *Translations from the Classics into English from Caxton to Chapman, 1477–1620*. University of Wisconsin Studies in Language and Literature, vol. 35. Madison: University of Wisconsin, 1937.

Lowell, Robert. "The Muses Won't Help Twice." *Kenyon Review* 17 (1955): 317–24.

McIntyre, William Myron. "A Critical Study of Golding's Translation of Ovid's *Metamorphoses*." Ph.D. dissertation, University of California at Berkeley, 1965; *DA* 26 (1965): 1045–46.

Mason, H. A. *Humanism and Poetry in the Early Tudor Period*. London: Routledge and Kegan Paul, 1959.

Matthiessen, F. O. *Translation: An Elizabethan Art*. Cambridge, Mass.: Harvard University Press, 1931.

Miller, Edwin Haviland. *The Professional Writer in Elizabethan England: A Study of Nondramatic Literature*. Cambridge, Mass.: Harvard University Press, 1959.

Nelson, William. "A Morall Fabletalke." *CLC* 9, no. 1 (1959): 26–31.

Otis, Brooks. *Ovid as an Epic Poet*. 2d ed. Cambridge: Cambridge University

Press, 1970.

Ovid: Metamorphoses. Edited by Frank Justus Miller. Loeb Classical Library, vols. 42–43. London: Heinemann, and New York: Putnam, 1916.

Phaer, Thomas, trans. *The nyne fyrst bookes of the Eneidos of Virgil.* London, 1562; *STC* 24800.

Piper, William Bowman. *The Heroic Couplet.* Cleveland and London: Press of Case Western Reserve University, 1969.

Pound, Ezra. *The ABC of Reading.* 1934. Reprint. Norfolk, Conn.: New Directions, 1951.

————. *The Literary Essays of Ezra Pound.* Edited by T. S. Eliot. Norfolk, Conn.: New Directions, 1954.

Robinson, Forrest G. "A Note on the Sidney-Golding Translation of Philippe de Mornay's *De La Verité De La Religion Chrestienne.*" *HLB* 17 (1969): 98–102.

Rubel, Veré L. *Poetic Diction in the English Renaissance from Skelton through Spenser.* M.L.A. Revolving Fund Series, vol. 12. New York: M.L.A., and London: Oxford University Press, 1941.

Sandys, George, trans. *Ovid's Metamorphosis: Englished, Mythologized, and Represented in Figures by George Sandys.* Edited by Karl K. Hulley and Stanley T. Vandersall. Lincoln: University of Nebraska Press, 1970.

Sørensen, Knud. *Thomas Lodge's Translation of Seneca's De Beneficiis Compared with Arthur Golding's Version: A Textual Analysis with Special Reference to Latinisms.* Copenhagen: Gyldendal, 1960.

Stanyhurst, Richard, trans. *The First Four Books of the Aeneis of P. Virgilius Maro.* Edited by Edward Arber. The English Scholar's Library of Old and Modern Works, vol. 10. London: Arber, 1880.

————. *Richard Stanyhurst's Aeneis.* Edited by Dirk van der Haar. Amsterdam: H. J. Paris, 1933.

Steiner, Grundy. "Golding's Use of the Regius-Micyllus Commentary upon Ovid." *JEGP* 49 (1950): 317–23.

Surrey, Earl of, trans. *The Aeneid of Henry Howard Earl of Surrey.* Edited by Florence H. Ridley. University of California English Studies, vol. 26. Berkeley and Los Angeles: University of California Press, 1963.

Swan, M. W. S. "Concerning Benefyting." *More Books* 21 (1946): 123–28.

————. "A Study of Golding's Ovid." Ph.D. dissertation, Harvard University, 1942.

Taylor, A. B. "George Peele and Golding's *Metamorphoses.*" *N&Q* 214 (1969): 286–87.

————. "Thomas Peend and Arthur Golding." *N&Q* 214 (1969): 19–20.

Wallerstein, Ruth. "The Development of the Rhetoric and Metre of the Heroic Couplet, Especially in 1625–1645." *PMLA* 50 (1935): 166–209.

Webb, Henry J. "English Translations of Caesar's *Commentaries* in the

Sixteenth Century." *PQ* 28 (1949): 490–95.

Wilkinson, L. P. *Ovid Recalled*. Cambridge: Cambridge University Press, 1955.

Witz, Edmund. *Die englische Ovidübersetzungen des 16. Jahrhunderts*. Inaugural-Dissertation, University of Strassburg. Leipzig: Noske, 1915.

Wortham, James. "Arthur Golding and the Translation of Prose." *HLQ* 12 (1949): 339–67.

Golding and Shakespeare

Anders, H. R. D. *Shakespeare's Books: A Dissertation on Shakespeare's Reading and the Immediate Sources of his Works*. Schriften der deutschen Shakespeare-Gesellschaft, vol. 1. Berlin: Reimer, 1904.

Baldwin, T. W. "The Pedigree of Theseus' Pups. *Midsummer-Night's Dream*, IV, 1, 123–130." *SJH* (1968), pp. 109–20.

————. *William Shakspere's Small Latine and Lesse Greeke*. 2 vols. Urbana: University of Illinois Press, 1944.

Bullough, Geoffrey, ed. *Narrative and Dramatic Sources of Shakespeare*. 8 vols. London: Routledge and Kegan Paul, and New York: Columbia University Press, 1957–75.

Dickins, Bruce. "'Pythagoras concerning Wilde-Fowle.' (*Twelfth Night*, IV, ii, 52–8.)" *MLR* 20 (1925): 186.

Forrest, James F. "'Blocks' and 'Stones' in 'Julius Caesar.'" *N&Q* 218 (1973): 134–35.

Lee, Sidney. "Ovid and Shakespeare's Sonnets." *Quarterly Review* 210 (1909): 455–76.

Muir, Kenneth. "Pyramus and Thisbe: A Study in Shakespeare's Method." *SQ* 5 (1954): 141–53.

Rick, Leo. "Shakespeare und Ovid." *SJW* 55 (1919): 35–53.

Root, Robert Kilburn. *Classical Mythology in Shakespeare*. 1903. Reprint. New York: Gordian, 1965.

Spencer, Hazelton. "Shakespeare's Use of Golding in *Venus and Adonis*." *MLN* 44 (1929): 435–37.

Thomson, J. A. K. *Shakespeare and the Classics*. London: Allen and Unwin, 1952.

Trousdale, Marion, "Recurrence and Renaissance: Rhetorical Imitation in Ascham and Sturm." *ELR* 6 (1976): 156–79.

Velz, John W. *Shakespeare and the Classical Tradition: A Critical Guide to Commentary, 1660–1960*. Minneapolis: University of Minnesota Press, 1968.

Williams, W. H. "Shakespeare, 'King Lear,' IV, vi, 70–72." *MLR* 6 (1911): 88

Wilson, John Dover. "Shakespeare's 'Small Latin'—How Much?" *ShS* 10

(1957): 12–26.

Wilson, Robert F. "Golding's *Metamorphoses* and Shakespeare's Burlesque Method in *A Midsummer Night's Dream*." *ELN* 7 (1969): 18–25.

"THE DIVINE POEM OF MUSAEUS"

Baiardi, Giorgio Cerboni. *La lirica di Bernardo Tasso*. Pubblicazioni dell' Università di Urbino, Serie di Lettere e Filosofia, vol. 20. Urbino: Argalìa, 1966.

Baldi, Bernardino. *Versi e prose di Monsignor Bernardino Baldi da Urbino*. Venice, 1590.

———. *Versi e prose scelte di Bernardino Baldi*. Edited by Filippo Ugolini and Filippo-Luigi Polidori. Florence: Le Monnier, 1859.

Baldwin, T. W. "Marlowe's Musaeus." *JEGP* 54 (1955): 478–85.

Bo, Dominic. *Musaei Lexicon*. Hildesheim: Olms, 1966.

Boas, Frederick S. *Christopher Marlowe: A Biographical and Critical Study*. Oxford: Clarendon, 1940.

Boscán Almogáver, Juan. *Las obras de Boscan y algunas de la Vega repartidas en quarto libros*. Barcelona, 1543. Facsimile reprint. Colección Tesoro. San Sebastián: Biblioteca Nueva, 1936.

———. *Obras poéticas de Juan Boscán*. Vol. 1. Edited by Martin de Riquer, Antonio Comas, and Joaquín Molas. Biblioteca de Autores Barceloneses. Barcelona: Facultad de Filosofía y Letras, 1957.

Bradbrook, M. C. "'Hero and Leander.'" *Scrutiny* 2 (1933): 59–64.

———. *Shakespeare and Elizabethan Poetry: A Study of his Earlier Work in Relation to the Poetry of the Time*. New York: Oxford University Press, 1952.

Braden, Gordon. "Nonnos' Typhoon: *Dionysiaca*, Books I and II." *TSLL* 15 (1974): 851–79.

Bühler, Curt F. "Aldus Manutius and his First Edition of the Greek Musaeus." In *Scritti sopra Aldo Manuzio*, edited by Roberto Ridolfi. Florence: Olschki, 1955. Pp. 3–7, 106–07.

Bush, Douglas. "The Influence of Marlowe's *Hero and Leander* on Early Mythological Poems." *MLN* 42 (1927): 211–17.

———. "Musaeus in English Verse." *MLN* 43 (1928): 101–04.

———. "Notes on Marlowe's *Hero and Leander*." *PMLA* 44 (1929): 760–64.

Cameron, Alan. *Claudian: Poetry and Propaganda at the Court of Honorius*. Oxford: Clarendon, 1970.

———. "Wandering Poets: A Literary Movement in Byzantine Egypt." *Historia* 14 (1965): 470–509.

Cantelupe, Eugene B. "*Hero and Leander*, Marlowe's Tragicomedy of Love." *CE* 24 (1963): 295–98.

Chabalier, Léonce. *Héro et Léandre: Poème de Christopher Marlowe et George Chapman et sa fortune en Angleterre*. Paris: Imprimerie Polyglotte Hugonis, 1911.

Chapman, George, trans. *The divine poem of Musaeus. First of all bookes*. London, 1616; *STC* 18304.

Claudian. Edited by Maurice Platnauer. Loeb Classical Library, vols. 135–36. London: Heinemann, and New York: Putnam, 1922.

————. *Claudii Claudiani Carmina*. Edited by Theodor Birt. Monumenta Germaniae Historica: Auctorum Antiquissimorum, vol. 10. Berlin: Weidmann, 1892.

Collins, S. Ann. "Sundrie Shapes, Committing Headdie Ryots, Incest, Rapes: Functions of Myth in Determining Narrative and Tone in Marlowe's *Hero and Leander*." *Mosaic* 4, no. 1 (1970): 107–22.

Crawford, Charles. *The Marlowe Concordance*. 1911–32. Reprint. 2 vols. Vaduz: Kraus, 1963.

Cubeta, Paul M. "Marlowe's Poet in *Hero and Leander*." *CE* 26 (1965): 500–05.

Donno, Elizabeth Story, ed. *Elizabethan Minor Epics*. New York: Columbia University Press, and London: Routledge and Kegan Paul, 1963.

Eden, John M. "Hero and Belinda." *N&Q* 202 (1957): 12–13.

Ellis-Fermor, Una M. *Christopher Marlowe*. London: Methuen, 1927.

Firmin-Didot, Ambroise. *Alde Manuce et l'hellénisme à Venise*. 1875. Reprint. Brussels: Culture et Civilisation, 1966.

Flamini, Francesco. *Studi di storia letteraria italiana et straniera*. Leghorn: Giusti, 1895.

Fletcher, Ian, and Carne-Ross, D. S. "Ekphrasis: Lights in Santa Sophia, from Paul the Silentiary." *Arion* 4 (1965): 563–81.

Fraser, Russell A. "The Art of *Hero and Leander*." *JEGP* 57 (1958): 743–54.

Gelzer, Thomas. "Bemerkungen zu Sprache und Text des Epikers Musaios." *MH* 24 (1967): 129–48, and 25 (1968): 11–47.

Góngora y Argote, Luis. *Obras poéticas*. Edited by R. Foulché-Delbosc. Bibliotheca Hispanica. 3 vols. New York: Hispanic Society of America, 1921.

Gordon, D. J. "Chapman's 'Hero and Leander.'" *EM* 5 (1954): 41–94.

Green, Otis H. *The Literary Mind of Medieval and Renaissance Spain*. Lexington: University Press of Kentucky, 1970.

————. *Spain and the Western Tradition: The Castilian Mind in Literature from El Cid to Calderón*. 4 vols. Madison, Milwaukee, and London: University of Wisconsin Press, 1963–66.

Heitsch, Ernst, ed. *Die griechischen Dichterfragmente der römischen Kaiserzeit*. Abhandlungen der Akademie der Wissenschaften in Göttingen, philologisch-historische Klasse, 3d ser., vols. 49 and 58. Göttingen: Vandenhoeck and Ruprecht, 1961–64.

Ippolito, Gennaro d'. *Studi nonniani: L'epillio nelle Dionisiache.* Istituto di Filologia Greca, vol. 3. Palermo: Presso l'Accademia, 1964.

Jellinek, Max Hermann. *Die Sage von Hero und Leander in der Dichtung.* Berlin: Spener and Peters, 1890.

Johannes von Gaza und Paulus Silentiarius: Kunstbeschreibungen justinianischer Zeit. Edited by Paul Friedländer. Sammlung wissenschaftlicher Kommentare zu griechischen und römischen Schriftstellern. Leipzig and Berlin: Teubner, 1912.

Johnson, Robert C. *Christopher Marlowe, 1946–1965.* Elizabethan Bibliographies Supplements, vol. 6. London: Nether Press, 1967.

Keach, William. *Elizabethan Erotic Narratives: Irony and Pathos in the Ovidian Poetry of Shakespeare, Marlowe, and Their Contemporaries.* New Brunswick, N.J.: Rutgers University Press, 1977.

Kocher, Paul. *Christopher Marlowe: A Study of his Thought, Learning, and Character.* Chapel Hill: University of North Carolina Press, 1946.

Kostič, Veselin. "Marlowe's *Hero and Leander* and Chapman's Continuation." In *Renaissance and Modern Essays Presented to Vivian de Sola Pinto,* edited by G. R. Hibbard. London: Routledge and Kegan Paul, 1966. Pp. 25–34.

Lazarus, Gertrud. *Technik und Stil von Hero and Leander: Begun by Christopher Marlowe and finished by George Chapman.* Inaugural-Dissertation, University of Bonn. Bonn: Rhenania, 1915.

Leech, Clifford. "Venus and Her Nun: Portraits of Women in Love by Shakespeare and Marlowe." *SEL* 5 (1965): 247–68.

Lesky, Albin. *Geschichte der griechischen Literatur.* 3d ed. Bern and Munich: Francke, 1971.

———. *A History of Greek Literature.* Translated by James Willis and Cornelis de Heer. New York: Crowell, 1966.

Levin, Harry. *The Overreacher: A Study of Christopher Marlowe.* Cambridge, Mass.: Harvard University Press, 1952.

Lewis, C. S. "Hero and Leander." *PBA* 28 (1952): 23–37.

Lindsay, Jack. *Leisure and Pleasure in Roman Egypt.* London: Muller, 1965.

Lord, George deF. *Homeric Renaissance: The Odyssey of George Chapman.* Yale Studies in English, vol. 131. New Haven: Yale University Press, 1956.

Maclure, Millar. *George Chapman: A Critical Study.* Toronto: University of Toronto Press, 1966.

Marlowe, Christopher. *The Complete Works of Christopher Marlowe.* Edited by Fredson Bowers. 2 vols. Cambridge: Cambridge University Press, 1973.

———. *Hero and Leander by Christopher Marlowe: A Facsimile of the First Edition, London 1598.* Edited by Louis L. Martz. New York: Johnson Reprint, and Washington: Folger Shakespeare Library, 1972.

————. *Marlowe's Poems.* Edited by L. C. Martin. The Works and Life of Christopher Marlowe, vol. 4. London: Methuen, 1931.

————. *The Poems.* Edited by Millar Maclure. The Revels Plays. London: Methuen, 1968.

Marot, Clément. *Les Oeuvres de Clément Marot.* Edited by Georges Guiffrey. 5 vols. Paris: Claye, Quantin, and Schemit, 1876–1931.

Menéndez Pelayo, Marcelino. *Antología de poetas líricos castellanos.* Edited by Enrique Sánchez Reyes. 10 vols. Edición Nacional de las Obras Completas de Menéndez Pelayo, vols. 17–26. Madrid: Santander, 1945.

Miller, Paul W. "A Function of Myth in Marlowe's 'Hero and Leander.'" *SP* 50 (1953): 158–67.

————. "The Problem of Justice in Marlowe's 'Hero and Leander.'" *N&Q* 202 (1957): 163–64.

Mills, John. "The Courtship Ritual of Hero and Leander." *ELR* 2 (1972): 298–306.

Morris, Brian, ed. *Christopher Marlowe.* Mermaid Critical Commentaries. London: Benn, 1968.

Mousaios. Färber, Hans, ed. *Hero und Leander.* Tusculum-Bücherei. Munich: Heimeran, 1961.

————. Gelzer, Thomas, ed. *Musaeus: Hero and Leander.* Translated by Cedric Whitman. Bound with *Callimachus: Aetia, Iambi, Lyric Poems, Hecale, Minor Epic and Elegiac Poems, and Other Fragments,* edited by C. A. Trypanis. Loeb Classical Library, vol. 421. London: Heinemann, and Cambridge, Mass.: Havard University Press, 1975.

————. Kost, Karlheinz, ed. *Hero und Leander.* Bonn: Grundmann, 1971.

————. Ludwich, Arthur, ed. *Hero und Leandros, mit ausgewählten Varianten und Scholen.* Bonn: Marcus and Weber, 1912.

————. Malcovati, Enrica, ed. *Ero e Leandro.* Classici Greci e Latini. Milan: Istituto Editoriale Italiano, 1947.

————. Orsini, Pierre, ed. *Héro et Léandre.* L'Association Guillaume Budé. Paris: Les Belles Lettres, 1968.

————. Schrader, Johann, ed. *Musaei Grammatici de Herone et Leandro Carmen.* 2d ed., revised by Gottfried Heinrich Schaefer. Leipzig: Hartmann, 1825.

Moya del Baño, Francisco. *El tema de Hero y Leandro en la literatura española.* Murcia: Publicaciones de la Universidad de Murcia, 1966.

Neuse, Richard. "Atheism and Some Functions of Myth in Marlowe's *Hero and Leander.*" *MLQ* 31 (1970): 424–39.

Nonnos: Dionysiaca. Edited by W. H. D. Rouse. Loeb Classical Library, vols. 344, 354, and 356. London: Heinemann, and Cambridge, Mass.: Harvard University Press, 1940.

————. *Nonni Panopolitani Dionysiaca.* Edited by Rudolf Keydell. 2 vols. Berlin: Weidmann, 1959.

————. *Nonni Panopolitani Paraphrasis S. Euangelii Ioannei.* Edited by Augustin
     Scheindler. Bibliotheca Scriptorum Graecorum et Romanorum Teub-
     neriana. Leipzig: Teubner, 1881.
Norwood, Francis. "Hero and Leander." *Phoenix* 4 (1950): 9–20.
Oppian, Colluthus, Tryphiodorus. Edited by A. W. Mair. Loeb Classical
     Library, vol. 219. London: Heinemann, and New York: Putnam, 1928.
"Orpheus." *Les Argonautiques d'Orphée.* Edited by Georges Dottin. L'Asso-
     ciation Guillaume Budé. Paris: Les Belles Lettres, 1930.
————. *Orphica.* Edited by Eugen Abel. 1885. Reprint. Hildesheim: Ger-
     stenberg, 1971.
Page, Denys L., ed. *Greek Literary Papyri: Poetry.* Loeb Classical Library,
     vol. 360. 2d ed. London: Heinemann, and Cambridge, Mass.: Harvard
     University Press, 1942.
Peek, Werner. *Lexikon zu den Dionysiaka des Nonnos.* Alpha-Omega: Lexika,
     Indizes, Konkordanzen zur klassischen Philologie, vol. 3. 4 vols. Hildes-
     heim: Olms, 1968–75.
Pintor, Fortunato. "Delle liriche di Bernardo Tasso." *ASNSP*, vol. 14 (1900).
Poirier, Michel. *Christopher Marlowe.* London: Chatto and Windus, 1951.
Reichenberger, Arnold G. "Boscán and Ovid." *MLN* 65 (1950): 379–83.
————. "Boscán and the Classics." *CL* 3 (1951): 97–118.
Segal, Erich. "Hero and Leander: Góngora and Marlowe." *CL* 15 (1963):
     338–56.
Shannon, G. P. "Against Marot as a Source of Marlowe's *Hero and Leander*."
     MLQ 9 (1948): 387–88.
Smith, Hallett. *Elizabethan Poetry: A Study in Conventions, Meaning, and
     Expression.* Cambridge, Mass.: Harvard University Press, 1952.
Steane, J. B. *Marlowe: A Critical Study.* Cambridge: Cambridge University
     Press, 1964.
Symonds, John Addington. *Studies of the Greek Poets.* 3d ed. 2 vols. London:
     Adam and Charles Black, 1893.
Tannenbaum, Samuel A. *Christopher Marlowe (A Concise Bibliography).*
     Elizabethan Bibliographies, vol. 1. New York: Scholars' Facsimiles and
     Reprints, 1937.
Tannenbaum, Samuel A., and Tannenbaum, Dorothy R. *Supplement to a
     Bibliography of Christopher Marlowe.* New York: Tannenbaum, 1947.
Tasso, Bernardo. *Rime di M. Bernardo Tasso.* Edited by Pierantonio Serassi.
     2 vols. Bergamo: Lancellotto, 1749.
————. *I tre libri de gli amori di M. Bernardo Tasso.* Venice, 1555.
Turner, Myron. "Pastoral and Hermaphrodite: A Study in the Naturalism
     of Marlowe's *Hero and Leander*." *TSLL* 17 (1975): 397–414.
Tuve, Rosemond. *Elizabethan and Metaphysical Imagery: Renaissance Poetic
     and Twentieth-Century Critics.* Chicago and London: University of Chicago

Press, 1947.

Waddington, Raymond B. *The Mind's Empire: Myth and Form in George Chapman's Narrative Poems.* Baltimore and London: Johns Hopkins University Press, 1974.

Walsh, William P. "Sexual Discovery and Renaissance Morality in Marlowe's 'Hero and Leander.'" *SEL* 12 (1972): 33–54.

Wifstrand, Albert. *Von Kallimachos zu Nonnos: Metrisch-stilistische Untersuchungen zur späteren griechischen Epik und zu verwandten Gedichtgattungen.* Publications of the New Society of Letters at Lund, vol. 16. Lund: Ohlssons, 1933.

Williams, Martin T. "The Temptations in Marlowe's *Hero and Leander.*" *MLQ* 16 (1955): 226–31.

Williamson, Edward. *Bernardo Tasso.* Rome: Edizioni di Storia e Letteratura, 1951.

Zocca, Louis R. *Elizabethan Narrative Poetry.* New Brunswick, N. J.: Rutgers University Press, 1950.

ROBERT HERRICK AND CLASSICAL LYRIC POETRY

Aiken, Pauline. *The Influence of the Latin Elegists on English Lyric Poetry, 1600–1650: With Particular Reference to the Works of Robert Herrick.* University of Maine Studies, 2d ser., vol. 22. Orono: University of Maine Press, 1932.

"Anacreon." Delboulle, Achille, ed. *Anacréon et les poèmes anacréontiques: Texte grec avec les traductions et imitations des poètes du XVIᵉ siècle.* 1891. Reprint. Geneva: Slatkine, 1970.

———. Edmonds, J. M., ed. *The Anacreontea.* Bound with *Elegy and Iambus,* vol. 2, edited by Edmonds. Loeb Classical Library, vol. 259. London: Heinemann, and New York: Putnam, 1931.

———. Preisendanz, Karl, ed. *Carmina Anacreontea.* Bibliotheca Scriptorum Graecorum et Romanorum Teubneriana. Leipzig: Teubner, 1912.

———. Rose, Valentin, ed. *Anacreontis Teii quae Vocantur* Symposiaca Hēmiambia. Bibliotheca Scriptorum Graecorum et Romanorum Teubneriana. Leipzig: Teubner, 1868.

Armstrong, David, ed. Horace Issue. *Arion* 9, nos. 2–3 (1970).

Asals, Heather. "King Solomon in the Land of the *Hesperides.*" *TSLL* 18 (1976): 362–80.

Barker, Ernest. "Drink to Me Only." *Spectator* 157 (1936): 890–91.

Baumann, Michael. *Die Anakreonteen in englischen Übersetzungen: Ein Beitrag zur Rezeptionsgeschichte der anakreontischen Sammlung.* Studien zum Fortwirken der Antike, vol. 7. Heidelberg: Winter, 1974.

Beaurline, L. A. "The Selective Principle in Jonson's Shorter Poems."

  Criticism 8 (1966): 64–74.

Berman, Ronald. "Herrick's Secular Poetry." *ES* 52 (1971): 20–30.

Briggs, Katherine M. *The Anatomy of Puck: An Examination of Fairy Beliefs among Shakespeare's Contemporaries and Successors.* London: Routledge and Kegan Paul, 1959.

Brooks, Cleanth. *The Well Wrought Urn: Studies in the Structure of Poetry.* New York: Harcourt Brace, 1947.

Capwell, Richard L. "Herrick and the Aesthetic Principle of Variety and Contrast." *SAQ* 71 (1972): 488–95.

Carew, Thomas. *The Poems of Thomas Carew, with his Masque Coelum Britannicum.* Edited by Rhodes Dunlap. Oxford: Clarendon, 1949.

Castelain, Maurice. *Ben Jonson: L'Homme et l'oeuvre.* Paris and London: Hachette, 1907.

Catullus. *C. Valerii Catulli Carmina.* Edited by R. A. B. Mynors. Oxford Classical Texts. Oxford: Clarendon, 1958.

Chambers, A. B. "Herrick and the Trans-shifting of Time." *SP* 72 (1975): 85–114.

Chute, Marchette. *Two Gentle Men: The Lives of George Herbert and Robert Herrick.* New York: Dutton, 1959.

Colie, Rosalie L. *Shakespeare's Living Art.* Princeton: Princeton University Press, 1974.

Collinge, N. E. *The Structure of Horace's Odes.* London and New York: Oxford University Press, 1961.

Commager, Steele. *The Odes of Horace: A Critical Study.* New Haven and London: Yale University Press, 1962.

Costa, C. D. N., ed. *Horace.* Greek and Latin Studies: Classical Literature and its Influence. London and Boston: Routledge and Kegan Paul, 1973.

Cumberland, Richard. *Observer*, no. 74. In *The British Essayists*, edited by Alexander Chalmers. London, 1802–03. Vol. 42, pp. 205–13.

Delattre, Floris. *Robert Herrick: Contribution à l'étude de la poésie lyrique en Angleterre au dix-septième siècle.* Paris: Alcan, 1912.

Deming, Robert H. *Ceremony and Art: Robert Herrick's Poetry.* De Proprietatibus Litterarum, Series Practica, vol. 64. The Hague and Paris: Mouton, 1974.

DeNeef, A. Leigh. *"This Poetick Liturgie": Robert Herrick's Ceremonial Mode.* Durham, N.C.: Duke University Press, 1974.

Dihle, Albrecht. "The Poem on the Cicada." *Harvard Studies in Classical Philology* 71 (1967): 107–13.

Dovaston, John F. M. *Monthly Magazine* 39 (1815): 123–24.

Doyle, Charles Clay. "An Unhonored English Anacreon: John Birkenhead." *SP* 71 (1974): 192–205.

Drake, Nathaniel. *Literary Hours: or, Sketches, Critical, Narrative, and Poetical.*

3 vols. London: Cadell and Davies, 1804. Vol. 3, pp. 25–88.

Emperor, John Bernard. *The Catullian Influence in English Lyric Poetry, Circa 1600–1650*. University of Missouri Studies, vol. 3, no. 3. Columbia: University of Missouri, 1928.

Fitton Brown, A.D. "Drink to me, Celia." *MLR* 54 (1959): 554–57.

Fletcher, G. B. A. "Herrick and Latin Authors." *N&Q* 204 (1959): 231–32.

Fraenkel, Eduard. *Horace*. Oxford: Clarendon, 1957.

Gertzman, Jay A. "Robert Herrick's Recreative Pastoral." *Genre* 7 (1974): 183–95.

Gilbert, Allan H. "Robert Herrick on Death." *MLQ* 5 (1944): 61–67.

Gosse, Edmund. *Seventeenth Century Studies: A Contribution to the History of English Poetry*. 4th ed. London: Heinemann, 1913.

Guffey, George Robert. *Robert Herrick, 1949–1965; Ben Jonson, 1947–1965; Thomas Randolph, 1949–1965*. Elizabethan Bibliographies Supplements, vol. 3. London: Nether Press, 1968.

Hageman, Elizabeth H. "Recent Studies in Herrick." *ELR* 3 (1973): 462–71.

Haight, Elizabeth Hazelton. "Robert Herrick: The English Horace." *Classical Weekly* 4 (1911): 178–81 and 186–89.

Herrick, Robert. Grosart, Alexander B., ed. *The Complete Poems of Robert Herrick*. 3 vols. London: Chatto and Windus, 1876.

———. Hazlitt, W. Carew, ed. *Hesperides: The Poems and Other Remains Now First Collected*. 2 vols. London: John Russell Smith, 1869.

———. Martin, L. C., ed. *The Poetical Works of Robert Herrick*. Oxford: Clarendon, 1956.

———. Meadows, Peter, ed. *Delighted Earth: A Selection by Peter Meadows from Herrick's "Hesperides."* London: Fanfrolico Press, 1927.

———. Moorman, F. W., ed. *The Poetical Works of Robert Herrick*. Oxford: Clarendon, 1915.

———. Nott, John, ed. *Select Poems from the Hesperides, or Works Both Human and Divine, of Robert Herrick, Esq.* Bristol: J. M. Gutch, 1810.

———. Patrick, J. Max, ed. *The Complete Poetry of Robert Herrick*. 2d ed. The Norton Seventeenth-Century Series. New York: Norton, 1968.

———. Pollard, Alfred, ed. *The Hesperides and Noble Numbers*. Introduction by A. C. Swinburne. 2 vols. London: Lawrence and Bullen, and New York: Scribner's, 1891.

———. Saintsbury, George, ed. *The Poetical Works of Robert Herrick*. 2 vols. London: George Bell, 1893.

———. Singer, S. W., ed. *Hesperides: or, The Works Both Humane and Divine of Robert Herrick Esq.* 2 vols. London: Pickering, 1846.

Horace. *Q. Horati Flacci Opera*. Edited by Edward C. Wickham. 2d ed., revised by H. W. Garrod. Oxford Classical Texts. Oxford: Clarendon, 1912.

Hudson, Hoyt Hopewell. *The Epigram in the English Renaissance*. Princeton: Princeton University Press, 1947.

Huson, Dorothy Matthis. "Robert Herrick's *Hesperides* Considered as an Organized Work." Ph.D. dissertation, Michigan State University, 1972; *DAI* 34 (1972): 275A–76A.

Jenkins, Paul R. "Rethinking What Moderation Means to Robert Herrick." *ELH* 39 (1972): 49–65.

Jiriczek, O. L. "Der elisabethanische Horaz." *SJW* 47 (1911): 42–68.

Jonson, Ben. *Ben Jonson*. Edited by C. H. Herford and Percy and Evelyn Simpson. 11 vols. Oxford: Clarendon, 1925–52.

Kimmey, John L. "Order and Form in Herrick's *Hesperides*." *JEGP* 70 (1971): 255–68.

———. "Robert Herrick's Persona." *SP* 67 (1970): 221–36.

———. "Robert Herrick's Satirical Epigrams." *ES* 51 (1970): 312–23.

Laumonier, Paul. *Ronsard: Poète Lyrique*. 2d ed. Paris: Hachette, 1923.

Leavis, F. R. *Revaluations: Tradition and Development in English Poetry*. New York: George W. Stewart, 1947.

Lee, M. Owen. *Word, Sound, and Image in the Odes of Horace*. Ann Arbor: University of Michigan Press, 1969.

Lovelace, Richard. *The Poems of Richard Lovelace*. Edited by C. H. Wilkinson. Oxford: Clarendon, 1930.

McEuen, Kathryn Anderson. *Classical Influence upon the Tribe of Ben*. 1939. Reprint. New York: Octagon, 1968.

MacLeod, Malcolm. *A Concordance to the Poems of Robert Herrick*. New York: Oxford University Press, 1936.

McPeek, James A. S. *Catullus in Strange and Distant Britain*. Harvard Studies in Comparative Literature, vol. 15. Cambridge, Mass.: Harvard University Press, 1939.

McPherson, David. "Ben Jonson's Library and Marginalia." *SP* 71, no. 5 (1974).

Martial: Epigrams. Edited Walter C. A. Ker. Loeb Classical Library, vols. 94–95. London: Heinemann, and New York: Putnam, 1919.

———. *M. Val. Martialis Epigrammata*. Edited by W. M. Lindsay. Oxford Classical Texts. 2d ed. Oxford: Clarendon, 1929.

Marvell, Andrew. *The Poems and Letters of Andrew Marvell*. Edited by H. M. Margoliouth. 3d ed., revised by Pierre Legouis and E. E. Duncan-Jones. 2 vols. Oxford: Clarendon, 1971.

Miner, Earl. *The Cavalier Mode from Jonson to Cotton*. Princeton: Princeton University Press, 1971.

Moorman, F. W. *Robert Herrick: A Biographical and Critical Study*. London and New York: John Lane, 1910.

Musgrove, Sydney. *The Universe of Robert Herrick*. 1950. Reprint. Folcroft,

Pa.: Folcroft Library, 1971.

Nichols, J. G. *The Poetry of Ben Jonson*. London: Routledge and Kegan Paul, 1969.

Nisbet, R. G. M., and Hubbard, Margaret. *A Commentary on Horace: Odes Book I*. Oxford: Clarendon, 1970.

Nixon, Paul. "Herrick and Martial." *Classical Philology* 5 (1910): 189–202.

Nolhac, Pierre de. *Ronsard et l'humanisme*. Bibliothèque de l'Ecole des Hautes Etudes, Section des Sciences Historiques et Philologiques, vol. 227. Paris: Champion, 1921.

Ovid. *P. Ouidi Nasonis Amores, Medicamina Faciei Femineae, Ars Amatoria, Remedia Amoris*. Edited by E. J. Kenney. Oxford Classical Texts. Oxford: Clarendon, 1961.

Page, Denys L., ed. *Lyrica Graeca Selecta*. Oxford Classical Texts. Oxford: Clarendon, 1968.

Pasquali, Giorgio. *Orazio lirico: Studi*. 1918. Reprint. Florence: Le Monnier, 1964.

Patrick, J. Max, and Rollin, Roger B., eds. *Trust to Good Verses: Herrick Tercentenary Essays*. Pittsburgh: University of Pittsburgh Press, 1978.

"Peeping Tom." *TLS* 60 (1961): 898.

Pollard, Alfred. "Herrick Sources and Illustrations." *Modern Quarterly of Language and Literature* 1 (1898): 175–84.

Press, John. *Robert Herrick*. Writers and their Work, vol. 132. London: Longmans, Green, 1961.

Rea, J. "Persephone in 'Corinna's Going A-Maying.'" *CE* 26 (1965): 544–46.

Reckford, Kenneth J. *Horace*. Twayne's World Authors Series, vol. 73. New York: Twayne, 1969.

Reed, Edward B. "Herrick's Indebtedness to Ben Jonson." *MLN* 17 (1902): 478–83.

Reed, Mark L. "Herrick Among the Maypoles: Dean Prior and the *Hesperides*." *SEL* 5 (1965): 133–50.

Regenos, Graydon W. "The Influence of Horace on Robert Herrick." *PQ* 26 (1947): 268–84.

Richmond, H. M. *The School of Love: The Evolution of the Stuart Love Lyric*. Princeton: Princeton University Press, 1964.

Riddell, James A. "Seventeenth-Century Identifications of Jonson's Sources in the Classics." *RenQ* 28 (1975): 204–18.

Røstvig, Maren-Sophie. *The Happy Man: Studies in the Metamorphosis of a Classical Ideal, 1600–1700*. Oslo Studies in English, vol. 2. 2d ed. Oslo: Norwegian Universities Press, 1962.

Rollin, Roger B. *Robert Herrick*. Twayne's English Authors Series, vol. 34. New York: Twayne, 1966.

Ronsard, Pierre de. *Les Oeuvres de Pierre de Ronsard: Texte de 1587*. Edited by Isidore Silver. 8 vols. Chicago and London: University of Chicago Press, and Paris: Didier, 1966–70.

Ruggles, M. J. "Horace and Herrick." *CJ* 31 (1936): 223–34.

Sainte-Beuve, Charles A. *Tableau historique et critique de la poésie française et de théâtre française au XVIᵉ siècle.* 2d ed. Paris: Charpentier, 1869.

Schleiner, Louise. "Herrick's Songs and the Character of *Hesperides*." *ELR* 6 (1976): 77–91.

Scott, George Walton. *Robert Herrick, 1591–1674.* London: Sidgwick and Jackson, 1974.

Smith, Bruce R. "Ben Jonson's *Epigrammes:* Portrait-Gallery, Theater, Commonwealth." *SEL* 14 (1974): 91–109.

Smith, G. C. Moore. "Herrick's 'Hesperides.'" *MLR* 9 (1914): 373–74.

Stanley, Thomas. *The Poems and Translations of Thomas Stanley.* Edited by Galbraith Miller Crump. Oxford: Clarendon, 1962.

Staudt, Victor P. "Horace and Herrick on *Carpe Diem*." *Classical Bulletin* 33 (1957): 55–56.

Suckling, John. *The Works of Sir John Suckling: The Non-dramatic Works.* Edited by Thomas Clayton. Oxford: Clarendon, 1971.

Summers, Joseph H. *The Heirs of Donne and Jonson.* New York: Oxford University Press, 1970.

Swardson, H. R. *Poetry and the Fountain of Light: Observations on the Conflict Between Christian and Classical Traditions in Seventeenth-Century Poetry.* Columbia: University of Missouri Press, 1962.

Symonds, John Addington. "Ben Jonson's Song 'To Celia.'" *Academy* 26 (1884): 377–78.

Tannenbaum, Samuel A., and Tannenbaum, Dorothy R. *Robert Herrick (A Concise Bibliography).* Elizabethan Bibliographies, vol. 40. New York: Tannenbaum, 1949.

Van Deusen, Marshall. "Criticism and Ben Jonson's 'To Celia.'" *EIC* 7 (1957): 95–103.

Wentersdorf, Karl P. "Herrick's Floral Imagery." *SN* 36 (1964): 69–81.

Whipple, T. K. *Martial and the English Epigram from Sir Thomas Wyatt to Ben Jonson.* University of California Publications in Modern Philology, vol. 10, no. 4. Berkeley: University of California Press, 1925.

Whitaker, Thomas R. "Herrick and the Fruits of the Garden." *ELH* 22 (1955): 16–33.

Wilkinson, L. P. *Horace and his Lyric Poetry.* Cambridge: Cambridge University Press, 1952.

Woodward, Daniel H. "Herrick's Oberon Poems." *JEGP* 64 (1965): 270–84.

INDEX OF PRINCIPAL
AUTHORS AND WORKS

Anacreontea

1: 206, 210, 213–14, 256–58
2: 198, 237, 239
6: 210, 256, 257
8: 201, 215, 258
9: 197–98, 237
11: 200
13: 209–10
14: 212, 219
16: 212
18: 256
20: 240, 256, 257
23: 198, 239
26: 209
29: 202
30: 210
32: 201
37: 210–11, 219, 225
38: 202
39: 197
40: 198–99, 200, 215, 216
41: 208, 256
43: 200, 207
44: 207–08
50: 198, 216
53: 237
58: 256
60: 205, 256

Golding, *Metamorphosis*

Epistle: 8, 12, 14
Preface: 8

I.1–4: 38, 52
I.11–13: 30
I.19: 23
I.38–40: 33
I.42: 30
I.85: 31
I.117–20: 35, 162
I.134: 23
I.136: 5
I.151: 17
I.191: 13
I.198: 13
I.355: 27
II.1–43: 39–47, 49
II.33–39: 4–5, 7, 46
II.74–75: 29
II.455–58: 36
II.962–63: 14–15
II.984: 12
II.1063: 4, 7, 47
III.46–47: 31
III.270: 5
III.439–40: 28
III.443–46: 49
III.521–22: 14
III.521: 35
III.563: 24
III.641–42: 34
III.742: 18
IV.4: 12
IV.35: 20
IV.47–48: 12, 52
IV.70: 23

Golding, *Metamorphosis (continued)*
IV.74–82: 50
IV.147–49: 53
IV.347–51: 26
IV.459: 17
V.139–44: 24
V.256–57: 33
V.400–01: 15
V.417: 5
VI.7–8: 13
VI.98–100: 32
VI.128: 30
VI.156–57: 21, 161
VI.159–60: 31
VI.748–53: 20
VII.265–66: 6
VII.272: 6
VII.303: 16
VII.349: 36
VIII.806: 5
VIII.889: 12
VIII.908: 12
VIII.933: 18
VIII.995: 17
VIII.1040–44: 27
IX.625: 24
X.598–99: 13
X.605: 13
X.634: 27
X.690: 13
X.741: 13
XI.204: 13
XI.687: 4
XII.271–72: 23
XII.478: 5
XIII.945–46: 29
XV.127: 17
XV.133–41: 24–25
XV.142–44: 26, 32
XV.159–61: 25, 33
XV.292: 16
XV.801: 15

Herrick, *Hesperides*

Errata: 184
H-1/5.1: 228, 234
H-5/6.3: 182
H-6/7.1: 175, 182
H-14/9.1: 175
H-19/10.4: 221

H-31/13.4: 230
H-35/14.3: 175
H-39/15.3: 219
H-41/16.2: 158, 222
H-43/17.2: 221–22
H-47/18.3: 155
H-56/20.3: 224
H-62/21.6: 248
H-66/22.4: 165
H-74/24.2: 178, 229–30
H-88/30.1: 156
H-105/34.2: 224
H-106/34.3: 174, 234
H-111/39.3: 235
H-116/41.1: 192
H-121/42.3: 257
H-128/45.1: 164, 217, 235
H-131/47.1: 192
H-132/47.2: 165
H-144/51.3: 166
H-149A/53.2: 223
H-170/65.1: 214, 258
H-174/66.2: 193
H-178/67.3: 175, 176, 179
H-181/70.1: 218, 248
H-186/73.1: 178
H-191/74.3: 160
H-197/77.2: 164, 217
H-201/80.2: 174, 244–45, 252–53
H-205/83.1: 159
H-208/84.1: 171, 174
H-211/85.1: 244
H-223/90.3: 188
H-229/96.1: 257
H-231/96.3: 176
H-235/97.3: 228
H-238/98.2: 172, 174
H-256/103.3: 178
H-271/109.4: 258
H-283/112.3: 157–58, 160
H-289/117.4: 228
H-304/122.3: 236
H-322/128.2: 154–55
H-325/129.2: 163
H-327/129.4: 175
H-329/130.2: 217
H-334/132.1: 252
H-336/132.3: 175, 228, 248–52
H-349/139.3: 154, 155, 159, 163, 189, 194, 223

H-366/143.1: 244
H-375/145.1: 187
H-377/146.1: 174
H-414/157.2: 157
H-415/157.3: 219–20
H-419/158.4: 189
H-431/162.5: 258
H-443/165.1: 155–56, 157
H-459/172.3: 173
H-475/178.2: 160–61
H-488/182.2: 173
H-497/185.4: 186
H-519/191.4: 215
H-525/194.1: 195
H-544/198.1: 235
H-546/199.2: 227
H-554/200.4: 244
H-562/203.2: 194
H-569/204.4: 164, 165, 228
H-575/205.5: 178, 214
H-604/212.7: 244
H-613/214.3: 164
H-615/215.1: 247
H-618/216.2: 160
H-633/220.3: 157, 228
H-636/223.1: 192, 194
H-668/232.4: 190
H-674/234.4: 164
H-713/242.1: 180
H-727/247.2: 230–31
H-728/247.3: 190
H-779/261.2: 175
H-782/262.1: 159
H-816/269.3: 190
H-817/269.4: 186
H-838/274.2: 175
H-863/278.6: 155
H-927/292.6: 176
H-939/294.4: 218, 223
H-983/305.3: 183
H-988/307.1: 236
H-996/309.1: 216
H-1017/313.1: 213–14, 218, 221, 228, 257
H-1019/313.3: 183
H-1028/315.4: 175
H-1068/323.4: 218
H-1092/329.1: 182
H-1126/334.4: 184
H-1129/335.2: 182

H-1130/335.3: 184, 226
S-4/410.1: 220

Horace, *Carmina*

1.1: 241, 242
1.4: 235
1.6: 239
1.7: 236
1.9: 232
1.11: 233–34, 254
1.14: 250
1.17: 237
1.22: 250
1.27: 236
1.28: 249
1.32: 238, 241
1.37: 245–46, 252–53
1.38: 232
2.7: 237
2.11: 232
2.12: 239
2.14: 243, 248–50, 252
2.16: 250
2.17: 174
3.3: 247–48
3.4: 241, 242, 253
3.8: 236
3.9: 218, 248
3.19: 237, 238
3.27: 234
3.30: 242, 244, 246
4.2: 240, 242–43
4.3: 241
4.6: 242
4.7: 250
4.9: 239
4.11: 242
4.12: 237

Marlowe, *Hero and Leander*

1.1–4: 125, 149
1.5: 127
1.7–8: 141
1.25–26: 152
1.31–34: 140–41
1.45: 124, 127–28
1.51–53: 126, 127, 149
1.53–54: 128
1.63–65: 120

Marlowe, *Hero and Leander (continued)*
1.83: 128
1.87–96: 128
1.103–04: 120, 129
1.107–12: 129–30
1.113–17: 122
1.117–23: 140
1.122–27: 120–21
1.131–34: 149
1.149–50: 123
1.158–66: 152–53
1.174–76: 130
1.183–91: 122, 123, 130–31, 146, 151–52
1.192–93: 149
1.223: 141
1.295–99: 120
1.311–13: 143
1.319–20: 124, 132
1.332: 132
1.333–34: 143
1.338: 132
1.339–40: 152
1.343–56: 123, 133, 146
1.357–59: 135, 148
1.364: 143
1.385: 125
1.410–11: 136
1.415–24: 142
1.457: 137
1.463: 145
2.39–42: 142
2.61–64: 121
2.65–67: 123
2.72: 135
2.87–90: 122
2.112: 126
2.113: 145
2.126–28: 143
2.136–39: 145
2.147: 147
2.150–53: 147
2.153–54: 135, 146
2.156: 124
2.160–64: 124, 146
2.191–93: 141
2.235–38: 121, 147
2.243–46: 121, 141
2.269–72: 141
2.279–82: 149

2.289–93: 123, 135, 136, 143
2.293–96: 144
2.297–300: 123
2.303–04: 150
2.317–24: 150
2.327–34: 122, 150, 151

Martial, *Epigrammata*

1.2: 182
1.4: 227
1.19: 190
1.86: 185–86
1.103: 174
1.118: 183
2.8: 184
2.36: 189
3.1: 183
3.9: 184
3.17: 192
4.22: 218, 223
4.32: 186
4.59: 186
4.89: 183
5.15: 183
5.16: 184–85
5.37: 187–88
6.1: 183
6.15: 186
7.89: 172
8.3: 183
8.29: 181
8.69: 193
9.69: 191, 194
10.1: 181, 182
10.63: 192
11.18: 188, 195
12.4: 181

Mousaios, *Hero and Leander*

lychnos: 59–63, 79–81, 88, 90–93, 108, 112–13, 114–16, 119, 135, 148
1–17: 58–63, 88
1: 68, 87
4: 116
5: 90–93
6–7: 87, 88, 108, 116
11: 87
13: 90
15: 102
16–17: 94, 125

17: 76
19–23: 67, 87–88, 94–95, 102, 107, 111, 127
26–27: 95, 128, 145
29: 91
30: 110
31: 124
33: 136
36–37: 66
42–45: 80, 128–29
48: 117
49: 129
51–54: 128–29
55–59: 65, 69, 83, 101, 112, 129, 130
67–68: 129, 136
71–72: 115–16, 129
74–83: 81
78: 76
84: 109–10
94–95: 130
101–06: 78, 116, 131
109–16: 109, 131, 146, 151
113: 87, 90, 91, 106, 117, 122, 131
118: 67, 76, 87, 106, 111, 116, 146
119: 110
123: 111
124: 133
125: 67, 110
126: 133
128–32: 78, 89, 92, 132
133–34: 66, 95, 101, 105–08
135–40: 84, 98, 107
141: 124, 132
160: 78
164–65: 64, 78, 83, 98
174: 111
175: 67, 132
181: 67
182–84: 78–79
187–93: 108, 116, 133–34, 145, 146
194–95: 113
199–200: 135
202: 112
207: 117
212: 88
214: 69
216–18: 88, 115
220: 108
224: 83
228: 79

231: 117–18
232–37: 93–94
232: 87, 91, 93, 106, 117
233: 110
234–41: 79, 88, 91–92
234: 65, 86, 95, 106, 108
237: 57, 68, 87
238: 96
242: 79
245–50: 64, 135, 147
255: 56, 83
267: 77, 85–86, 97, 108, 112, 118, 147–48
274–81: 79–80, 135
285: 76
286: 117
293–95: 83
307: 145
313: 76, 85, 118
314–18: 83
314: 66
315: 77
323: 145
324–25: 67
335: 150
336: 76, 85
338: 63, 102
340: 111

Ovid, *Metamorphoses*

i.1–4: 38, 52
i.11–12: 30
i.36–37: 33
i.117–18: 23
i.134: 17
i.167: 13
i.171–72: 13
i.175–76: 13
i.304: 27
ii.1–32: 40–47, 49, 138
ii.27: 4, 46
ii.30: 5, 46
ii.56: 29
ii.772: 14
ii.850–51: 4, 7
iii.224: 5
iii.353: 28
iii.356–58: 49
iii.417: 14

Ovid, *Metamorphoses* (*continued*)
iii.509–10: 34
iii.585: 18
iv.4: 12
iv.38–39: 12, 52
iv.59–64: 50
iv.121–24: 53
iv.272: 52
iv.285–87: 26
iv.370: 17
v.315–16: 15
v.327–28: 5
vi.5: 13
vi.80–82: 31
vi.103ff.: 138
vi.125: 21
vi.278: 175
vi.587–91: 20
vii.197–98: 6
vii.204: 6
vii.230–31: 16
vii.268: 36
viii.620: 52

viii.630: 5
viii.707: 12
viii.724: 12
viii.746: 18
viii.801: 17
viii.838–41: 27
x.300: 13
x.307: 14
x.314–15: 13
x.319: 14
x.470: 14
x.524: 13
x.520–21: 13
x.547–48: 27
x.591: 13
x.630: 12
xi.181: 13
xii.242–43: 23
xiii.802–03: 29
xv.116: 17
xv.266: 16
xv.359: 52
xv.716: 15

GENERAL INDEX

Achilles Tatios, 71
Adlington, William, 138–40
Aesop, 12, 90, 134
Aiken, Pauline, 180
Alcaios, 203, 256; and Horace, 235, 238–41, 252–53
Aldo Manuzio: edition of Mousaios, 81, 85–86; Latin translation, 86–90; and other Latin translations, 91–92; and Tasso, 96; and Marot, 109; and Chapman, 114, 116, 117, 118, 134; and Marlowe, 124, 126, 127, 130, 133–34
Alfred, King, 17
Anacreon: in Renaissance editions, 196, 203, 256–57; and Anacreontea, 199–201, 205–07, 211, 240; and Horace, 235, 236, 237, 239, 241
Anacreontea ("Anacreon"): Renaissance publication, 196–97, 202–03, 255–58; and Greek literature, 197–203; and French literature, 203–05; as tradition, 205–09; psychology, 209–13; imitated by Herrick, 213–17; similarities with Herrick, 217–32 passim; and Horace, 235–40
Anders, H. R. D., 5
André, Elie, 256–57
Anthology, Palatine, 60, 255, 258
Anthology, Planudean, 203, 256, 258
Apuleius, 71, 85, 226; and Marlowe, 138–40
Archilochos, 201
Aristophanes, 22, 59, 60

Aristotle, 81
Athenaios, 258
Aucassin et Nicolette, 119
Augustus, Emperor, 240, 242

Baldi, Bernardino: translation of Mousaios, 93, 105–08; and Marot, 109, 111, 112; and Chapman, 114, 117
Baldwin, T. W., 3, 5–6, 126–27
Bastard, Thomas, 193
Batrachomyomachia, 59
Benjamin, Walter, 52, 54
Bentley, Richard, 167
Blundeville, Thomas, 1
Boccaccio, Giovanni, 88
Bold, Henry, 231
Boscán Almogáver, Juan: *Historia de Leandro y Hero,* 55, 86, 100–05; and Marot, 112; and Góngora, 119; and Marlowe, 124–25, 127
Bulleyn, William, 19
Burghley, William, Lord, 8, 11
Bush, Douglas, 9, 57–58

Callimachos, 67, 74, 240
Calvin, John, 8, 9, 10, 12, 14
Cambises, 23
Camden, William, 8
Cameron, Alan, 71, 74
Campion, Thomas, 225–26
Casaubon, Isaac, 82, 257–58
Castelain, Maurice, 171
Castiglione, Baldassare, 103

Catullus, 171, 234, 243; and Herrick, 177–80, 226–27, 250
Cavalcanti, Guido, 99–100
Cavell, Stanley, 173
Caxton, William, 18
Chabalier, Léonce, 111–12
Chapman, George: translation of Homer, 2, 88, 116; and Golding, 22–23, 25
—*Hero and Leander:* continuation of Marlowe, 56, 101, 114, 119, 126, 153
—translation of Mousaios, 55, 82, 86, 90, 93, 114–19; and Marlowe, 126, 134, 135, 146–47
Chaucer, Geoffrey, 52, 144
Christodoros, 70
Clarke, A. K., 74
Claudian: and the school of Nonnos, 71, 72, 73–74; in the Renaissance, 84, 85
Clement, John, 255
Collinge, N. E., 233
Collouthos: and the school of Nonnos, 70, 72, 76; and Marlowe, 85, 137
Constantin, Robert, 134
Cooper, Thomas, 4, 17, 126
Cotton, Robert, 8
Coverdale, Miles, 17
Cumberland, Richard, 167
Curtius, Ernst Robert, 74, 84

Daniel, Samuel, 220
Dante, 2, 99
Davies, Sir John, 182–83
Delamare, Guillaume (de Mara): translation of Mousaios, 90–92, 107; and Marlowe, 126, 127
Delattre, Floris, 214, 216
Diogenes Laertios, 82
Dionysios (epic poet), 71, 74, 77
Divo, Andrea, 88
Douglas, Gavin, 18
Drake, Nathaniel, 177
Drant, Thomas, 12
duBartas, Salluste, 84

Edmonds, J. M., 209
Eliot, T. S., 179, 194
Elyot, Thomas, 4
Empedocles, 137
Erasmus, Desiderius, 17

Estienne, Henri (Stephanus): edition of Mousaios, 81, 85–86, 147, 203; *Thesaurus,* 126; edition of Anacreontea, 196–97, 202–05, 216, 253, 255–58
Euripides, 59, 198

Falkenburg, Gerhard, 85
Fitton Brown, A. D., 167
Fraenkel, Eduard, 253
Fraunce, Abraham, 37, 55, 124–25
Froben, Johannes, 81

Gascoigne, George, 176
Gelzer, Thomas, 77
Golding, Arthur: life and contacts, 7–8; and Earl of Oxford, 7–8, 10–11; Puritanism, 8–16 passim; later life, 11–12
—*Metamorphosis:* reception, 1–3; and Shakespeare, 2, 3–7, 26, 31, 35–38, 47–48; moralization, 8, 12–15; and humanist scholarship, 15; diction, 15–22; meter, 22–28 and passim; and Sandys, 28–31, 45–46, 49–53; tone, 31–35 and passim; invocation, 38; story of Phaethon, 39–48; storytelling, 48–55; and Herrick, 161–62
Góngora y Argote, Luis, 119, 120
Gosse, Edmund, 180, 220
Gower, John, 53
Gracián, Barsilaso, 84
Grosart, Alexander B., 180, 220

Hadrian, Emperor, 227
Hazlitt, W. Carew, 177
Heliodoros, 37
Hephaistion, 200
Herbert, George, 155, 161
Herford, C. H., 166
Herrick's *Hesperides,* 154–61; and flowers, 34; as lyric oeuvre, 161–63 and passim; and classical gods, 163–66; and classical quotations, 171–77; and Catullus, 177–80; formal structures compared with Martial, 180–84; humor compared with Martial, 186, 187, 188–96; imitation of Anacreontea, 213–17; similarities with Anacreontea, 217–32 passim; sexuality, 221–26; chastity, 226–32;

similarities with Horace, 234–36, 244–45, 252–54; imitation of Horace, 245–52; and editions of Anacreontea, 257–58

Hesiod, 57, 60, 170

Homer, 52, 81, 253; in Renaissance translation, 2, 22–23, 25, 88, 116; and Mousaios, 58–67 passim, 76, 82, 85, 127; and school of Nonnos, 71–75; and Anacreontea, 198, 239; and Horace, 236, 239

Horace: translated by Drant, 12; imitated by Herrick, 174, 175, 180, 196, 218, 245–52; similarities with Herrick, 232–35, 244–45, 252–55; and Anacreontea, 235–40; and lyric tradition, 239–45, 252–53

Hubbard, Margaret, 236

Jenkins, Paul R., 229

John of Gaza, 70, 73

Johnson, W. R., 54

Jonson, Ben: and Golding, 6; and Marlowe, 119; and Herrick, 158, 162, 166, 174, 229–31; use of classical materials, 164, 166–71; and Martial, 182–83, 187; and editions of Anacreontea, 257

Justinus, 10

Kael, Pauline, 185

Kayser, C. L., 168

Kenner, Hugh, 164

Kost, Karlheinz, 68, 69

Lascaris, Janus, 85–86, 147

Lawrence, D. H., 144

Leavis, F. R., 194

Leicester, Robert Dudley, Earl of, 8, 12, 14

Levin, Harry, 81

Lewis, C. S., 213; on Golding, 17, 20, 25, 48, 49

Lord, George deF., 116

Lowell, James Russell, 177

Lowell, Robert, 3, 51, 52

Lubin, Eilhard, 257

Lucan, 58

Maclure, Millar, 118, 138

McPeek, James A. S., 178

Marlowe, Christopher: and Golding, 39–40, 41; and Herrick, 225, 246

—Hero and Leander, 101, 105, 114; comparison (general) with Mousaios, 55–58, 122–24, 145–53; imitation (specific) of Mousaios, 63, 125–36; and school of Nonnos, 84, 85, 136–41; as parody, 119–21; as baroque, 141–44

Marot, Clément: translation of Mousaios, 93, 108–14; and Baldi, 107; and Chapman, 116, 117, 118; and Marlowe, 123, 124

Martial: imitated by Herrick (misc.), 172–73, 174, 186, 187, 218, 223, 227, 246; formal structures compared with Herrick, 180–84, 243; aesthetic, 184–92; humor compared with Herrick, 188–96

Martin, L. C.: edition of Marlowe, 126, 138; edition of Herrick, 173, 175, 216

Martz, Louis L., 149, 153

Marvell, Andrew, 179

Melancthon, Philip, 257

Michie, James, 189

Milton, John, 2, 16, 170

Mimnermos, 240

Molsheyn, Jacob (Micyllus), 15

Montaigne, Michel de, 171

Moorman, F. W., 246

More, Thomas, 255

Mornay, Philippe de, 8, 16

Mousaios' Hero and Leander, 196, 203; and Marlowe, 55–58, 122–36, 145–53; style, general, 57–58, 63–68; style, opening paragraph, 58–63; and school of Nonnos, 68–77; as allegory, 77–81; and Renaissance criticism, 82–85; Aldine edition, 85–90; Latin metrical translations, 90–92; and Sachs, 93–94; and Tasso, 94–100; and Boscán, 100–05; and Baldi, 105–08; and Marot, 108–14; and Chapman, 114–19

Mulcaster, Richard, 37

Naps upon Parnassus, 244

Narcissus, The Fable of Ovid treting of (anonymous translation), 34, 48–49

Nashe, Thomas, 14, 119

Neuse, Richard, 121–22
Nims, John Frederick, 2–3, 8, 27, 29
Nisbet, R. G. M., 236
Nonnos of Panopolis, school of, 68–75, 100, 119, 208; and Mousaios, 75–77, 78; in Renaissance, 81–85; and Marlowe, 136–40

Orpheus, 81; poems attributed to, 56, 71
Orsini, Fulvio, 257
Ovid, 57, 82, 171; and Mousaios, 56, 81; and Marlowe, 58, 125, 134, 138, 225, 246; and Boscán, 103, 125; and Herrick, 174, 176, 225, 227, 246
—Metamorphoses, 7, 13–14, 38; rhetoric, 28–30; story of Phaethon, 39–48; storytelling, 51–54. See also Golding, Arthur, Metamorphosis
Owen, William, 19
Oxford, Edward de Vere, Earl of, 7–8, 10–11

Paolini, Fabio (Paulinus): translation of Mousaios, 91–92; and Baldi, 107; and Marlowe, 126, 127
Pape, André de (Papius): on Mousaios, 86; translation of Mousaios, 90–92; and Baldi, 107; and Marlowe, 126, 127
Pareus, Daniel, 82
Parker, Matthew, 8
Pasquali, Giorgio, 253
Patrick, J. Max, 155
Paul the Silentiary, 70
Peend, Thomas, 1
Persius, 175–76, 250
Petowe, Henry, 150
Petrarch, Francesco, 88, 209, 213; Petrarchanism, 64, 100, 103, 120, 208–09, 212, 220
Petronius, poem attributed to, 229–31
Phaer, Thomas: translation of Vergil, 14, 19–20, 22, 24
Philostratos, 167–70
Pilato, Leonzio, 88
Pindar, 158; and Anacreontea, 203–05, 240, 257; and Ronsard, 204–05, 244; and Horace, 239, 240, 253
Pliny the Younger, 226

Pollard, Alfred, 173
Pope, Alexander, 15, 28, 120, 187, 192
Pound, Ezra, 2–3, 88, 175
Preisendanz, Karl, 255
Procopios of Gaza, 71
Propertius, 239–40
Puttenham, George, 19–20

Quintus of Smyrna, 66, 71

Regio, Raffaele, 15
Ronsard, Pierre de, 171, 204–05, 243–44
Rosis Nascentibus, De, 171

Sachs, Hans: "Die unglückhafft lieb Leandri mit fraw Ehron," 93–94, 117
Sainte-Beuve, Charles A., 204
Sandys, George: translation of Ovid, 1, 18; rhetoric, 28–31; story of Phaethon, 45, 46; storytelling, 49–53
Sappho, 163, 164, 239; and Anacreontea, 202, 203, 209, 240, 256
Saumaise, Claude de (Salmasius), 255
Scaliger, Joseph Juste, 84
Scaliger, Julius Caesar, 82–84, 203, 204, 253
Scapula, Johann, 126
Schoeck, Richard J., 89, 92
Segal, Erich, 120
Segel, Harold B., 143
Seneca, 85, 174
Servius, 58
Shakespeare, William, 34, 53, 56, 117, 208, 213; and Golding, 2, 3–8, 12, 26, 31, 35–38, 47–48
Sidney, Philip, 8, 176
Simonides, 239, 257
Simpson, Percy, 166
Singer, S. W., 177
Skelton, John, 20
Sophocles, 57, 64, 197
Sørensen, Knud, 17
Spalletti, Giuseppe, 255, 256, 257
Spenser, Edmund, 170, 226; and Golding, 8, 17, 21–22; and Marlowe, 138, 140; and Herrick, 171
Sponde, Jean de (Spondanus), 88
Stanley, Thomas, 214

Stanyhurst, Richard: translation of Vergil, 14, 17, 19
Statius, 58
Stephanus. *See* Estienne, Henri
Stesichoros, 239
Stow, John, 8
Suckling, John, 195, 222, 231
Surrey, Henry Howard, Earl of: translation of Vergil, 18–19
Swan, M. W. S., 27
Symonds, John Addington, 169

Tasso, Bernardo: *Favola di Leandro et d'Hero,* 94–100; and Boscán, 100–05; and Baldi, 105–08; and Marot, 108–14; and Marlowe, 124, 126, 127
Tasso, Torquato, 171
Tibullus, 180, 246
Triphiodoros, 71–73, 81, 85

Turberville, George, 17, 125, 134
Turner, Myron, 146
Tuve, Rosemond, 140

Vatel, Jean, 86, 90, 91
Vere. *See* Oxford, Edward de Vere, Earl of
Vergil, 52, 53, 58, 170, 253; in Tudor translation, 14, 18–19; and Boscán, 103–04

Waller, Edmund, 172, 187, 231
Watkins, B. J., 166
Watson, Thomas, 85
Webbe, William, 2, 3
Wilkinson, L. P., 53
Wilson, John Dover, 3
Wortham, James, 3, 12

Zocca, Louis R., 3